BEGINNING FLUTTER®

BEGINNING

Flutter®

BEGINNING

Flutter®

A HANDS ON GUIDE TO APP DEVELOPMENT

Marco L. Napoli

wrox™

A Wiley Brand

Beginning Flutter®: A Hands On Guide To App Development

Published by
John Wiley & Sons, Inc.
10475 Crosspoint Boulevard
Indianapolis, IN 46256
www.wiley.com

ISBN: 978-1-119-55082-2
ISBN: 978-1-119-55087-7 (ebk)
ISBN: 978-1-119-55085-3 (ebk)

Manufactured in the United States of America

Library of Congress Control Number: 2019940772

C10013751_090919

*To God; my wife Carla; my children, Michael, Timothy,
and Joseph; and you, the reader.*

ABOUT THE AUTHOR

Marco L. Napoli is the CEO of Pixolini, Inc., and an experienced mobile, web, and desktop app developer. He has a strong proven record in developing visually elegant and simple-to-use systems. He wrote his first native iOS app in 2008. His work and published apps can be seen at www.pixolini.com.

He has loved computers from an early age. His dad noticed and bought him a PC, and he has been developing software since. He attended the University of Miami for an architecture degree, but he had already started his own business, and after four years he decided architecture was not for him. He developed systems for a diverse mix of industries including banking, healthcare, real estate, education, trucking, entertainment, and horizontal markets. Later, a leading banking software company acquired his MLN Enterprises, Inc., company. The main products were mortgage banking, processing, and marketing software.

Next, he started consulting and later created IdeaBlocks, Inc., with the purpose of software development consulting. He developed for a client that sold hospitality software for mobile, desktop, and web platforms. The main product focus was on hotel sales, catering, webspace, guest service, and maintenance software. The products synced via cloud servers using Microsoft SQL Server with encryption applied to sensitive data. His client's customers included Hyatt Place and Summerfield, Hilton Hotel, Holiday Inn, Hampton Inn, Marriott, Best Western, Radisson Hotel, Sheraton Hotels, Howard Johnson, Embassy Suites, and many more. Once his contract was done, he closed IdeaBlocks.

Today, his focus is running Pixolini. He develops mobile, desktop, and web apps for iOS, Mac, Android, Windows, and the Web. He also teaches a course at Udemy using a web app that he developed for analyzing real estate investment calculations. He has developed and published more than 10 apps in each respective store.

He was interviewed by Hillel Coren for the "It's All Widgets Flutter Podcast" on November 27, 2018, and the episode can be found at https://itsallwidgets.com/podcast/episodes/1/marco-napoli.

"I cannot code without espresso, cappuccino, or coffee, and I love martial arts."

Marco is married to Carla, and they have three amazing children.

ABOUT THE TECHNICAL EDITOR

Zeeshan Chawdhary is an avid technologist, with 14 years of experience in the industry. Having started his career with mobile development with J2ME, he soon ventured into web development, creating robust and scalable web applications. As a chief technology officer, he has led teams to build web and mobile apps for companies such as Nokia, Motorola, Mercedes, GM, American Airlines, and Marriott. He is currently director of development on an international team, serving clients with technologies like Magento, WordPress, WooCommerce, Laravel, NodeJS, Google Puppeteer, ExpressJS, ReactJS, and .NET. He has also authored books on iOS, Windows Phone, and iBooks.

Zeeshan is based in Mumbai, India. He can be reached at imzeeshanc@gmail.com or on Twitter @imzeeshan, and he maintains a Medium publication at https://medium.com/@imzeeshan.

ACKNOWLEDGMENTS

I want to thank the talented team at Wiley, including all of the editors, managers, and many people behind the scenes who helped to get this book published. My thanks to Devon Lewis for recognizing early on that Flutter is having a major impact on the industry, to Candace Cunningham for her project editing skills and her insights, to Zeeshan Chawdhary for his technical input and suggestions, to Barath Kumar Rajasekaran and his team for getting the production of the book ready, and to Pete Gaughan for always being available.

A special thanks to the Flutter team at Google, especially Tim Sneath, Ray Rischpater, and Filip Hráček, for their kindness and invaluable feedback.

A thank-you to my wife and children who have patiently listened and given feedback for the projects created in this book.

CONTENTS

PART II: INTERMEDIATE FLUTTER: FLESHING OUT AN APP

INTRODUCTION

Flutter was unveiled at the 2015 Dart Developer Summit under the name Sky. Eric Seidel (engineer director for Flutter at Google) opened his talk by saying that he was there to speak about Sky, which was an experimental project presented as "Dart on mobile." He had built and published a demo on the Android Play Store, and he started the demo by stating that there was no Java drawing this application, meaning it was native. The first feature Eric showed was a square spinning. Driving the device at 60 Hertz was Dart, which was the first goal for the system: to be fast and responsive. (He wanted to go much faster [i.e., 120 Hertz], but he was restricted by the capability of the device he was using.) Eric went on to show multitouch, fast scrolling, and other features. Sky provided the best mobile experience (for users and developers); the developers took lessons from working on the Web, and they thought they could do better. The user interface (UI) and the business logic were both written in Dart. The goal was to be platform-agnostic.

Fast-forward to 2019, and Flutter now is powering Google's smart display platform including the Google Home Hub and is the first step toward supporting desktop apps with Chrome OS. The result is that Flutter supports desktop apps running on Mac, Windows, and Linux. Flutter is described as a portable UI framework for all screens like mobile, web, desktop, and embedded devices from a single codebase.

This book teaches you how to develop mobile applications for iOS and Android from a single codebase by using the Flutter framework and Dart as the programming language. As Flutter is expanding beyond mobile, you can take the knowledge that you learn in this book and apply it to other platforms. You don't need to have previous programming experience; the book starts with the basics and progresses to developing production-ready applications.

I wrote this book in a simple, down-to-earth style to teach you each concept. You can follow the "Try It Out" practice-style exercises to implement what you learn and create feature-focused applications.

Each chapter builds upon the previous ones and adds new concepts to advance your knowledge for building fast, beautiful, animated, and functional apps. By the end of this book, you'll be able to take the knowledge and techniques you have learned and apply them to develop your own applications. In the last four chapters of the book, you'll create a journal app with the ability to save data locally and a second journal app that adds mood tracking with state management, authentication, and multidevice data cloud syncing capabilities including offline sync, which is a must for today's mobile applications. I have made every effort to teach you the techniques using a friendly and commonsense approach so you can learn the basics all the way to advanced concepts needed for the workplace.

From the first time I saw Google presenting Flutter, it has captured my attention. What especially attracted me to Flutter was the widgets concept. You take widgets and nest (*composition*) them together to create the UI needed, and best of all, you can easily create your own custom widgets. The other major item that attracted me to Flutter was the ability to develop for iOS and Android from a single codebase; this is something I had been needing for a long time and never found a great solution until Flutter. Flutter is declarative; it's a modern reactive framework where widgets handle what the UI should look like according to their current state.

My passion for developing with Flutter and Dart keeps growing, and I decided to write this book to share my experiences and expertise with others. I firmly believe the book teaches everyone from beginners to knowledgeable developers, giving them the tools and knowledge to build and advance as a multiplatform developer. This book is full of tips, insights, what-if scenarios, diagrams, screenshots, sample code, and exercises. All of the project source code is available for download on this book's web page at www.wiley.com/go/beginningflutter.

WHO THIS BOOK IS FOR

This book is for everyone who wants to learn how to program mobile, multiplatform applications by using Flutter and Dart. It is for absolute beginners who want to learn to develop modern, fast native performance, and reactive mobile applications for iOS and Android. However, it also takes you from absolute beginner to learning the advanced concepts required to develop production-ready applications. It's also for people who are familiar with programming who want to learn the Flutter framework and the Dart language.

This book is written with the assumption of having no prior programming, Flutter, or Dart experience. If you have programmed in other languages or are familiar with Flutter and Dart, you'll simply get a deeper understanding of each concept and technique.

WHAT THIS BOOK COVERS

The early chapters introduce and cover the architecture of the Flutter framework, the Dart language, and steps for creating a new project. You'll use that knowledge to create new projects for each exercise in the book. Each chapter is written to advance your knowledge by focusing on new concepts. The chapters are also written to be reference material to refresh your knowledge of each concept.

Starting in Chapter 2, as you learn each concept and technique, you'll follow the "Try It Out" practice-style exercises and create new application projects to put into practice what you've learned. As you move forward, each chapter is designed to teach you more advanced topics. The last four chapters focus on creating two production-ready applications by applying previously learned materials and implementing new advanced concepts. You can also find these exercises as part of the code downloads on this book's page at www.wiley.com/go/beginningflutter.

HOW THIS BOOK IS STRUCTURED

This book is divided into 16 chapters. Although each chapter builds upon the previous concepts, they are also self-contained and written for you to be able to jump to a particular interest to learn or refresh that topic.

Part I: The Foundations of Flutter Programming

In the first part of the book, you'll get to know the core aspects of Flutter so you have a solid foundation to build on.

Chapter 1: Introducing Flutter and Getting Started—You'll learn how the Flutter framework works behind the scenes and about the benefits of the Dart language. You'll see how `Widget`, `Element`, and `RenderObject` are related, and you'll get an understanding of how they form the widget tree, element tree, and render tree. You'll get an introduction to `StatelessWidget` and `StatefulWidget` and their lifecycle events. You'll learn that Flutter is declarative, meaning Flutter builds the UI to reflect the state of the app. You'll learn how to install the Flutter framework, Dart, editor, and plugins on macOS, Windows, or Linux.

Chapter 2: Creating a Hello World App—You'll learn how to create your first Flutter project to get familiarized with the process. By writing this minimal example, you'll learn the basic structure of an application, how to run the app on the iOS simulator and the Android emulator, and how to make changes to the code. At this point, do not worry about understanding the code yet; I'll walk you through it step-by-step in later chapters.

Chapter 3: Learning Dart Basics—Dart is the foundation of learning to develop Flutter applications, and in this chapter you'll understand Dart's basic structure. You'll learn how to comment your code, how the `main()` function starts the app, how to declare variables, and how to use the `List` to store an array of values. You'll learn about the operator symbols and how to use them to perform arithmetic, equality, logical, conditional, and cascade notation. You'll learn how to use external packages and classes and how to use the `import` statement. You'll learn how to implement asynchronous programming by using a `Future` object. You'll learn how to create classes to group code logic and use variables to hold data and how to define functions to execute logic.

Chapter 4: Creating a Starter Project Template—You'll learn the steps to create a new project that you'll use and replicate to create all of the exercises in this book. You'll learn how to organize files and folders in your project. You'll create the most commonly used names to group your widgets, classes, and files by the type of action needed. You'll learn how to structure widgets and import external packages and libraries.

Chapter 5: Understanding the Widget Tree—The widget tree is the result of *composing* (nesting) widgets to create simple and complex layouts. As you start nesting widgets, the code can become harder to follow, so good practice is to try to keep the widget tree as shallow as possible. You'll get an introduction to the widgets that you'll use in this chapter. You'll get an understanding of the effects of a deep widget tree, and you'll learn how to refactor it into a shallow widget tree, resulting in more manageable code. You'll learn three ways to create a shallow widget tree by refactoring with a constant, with a method, and with a widget class. You'll learn the benefits and cons of each technique.

Part II: Intermediate Flutter: Fleshing Out an App

In Part II of the book, you'll get your hands dirty, stepping through how to add functionality that creates great user experiences.

Chapter 6: Using Common Widgets—You'll learn how to use the most common widgets, which are the base building blocks for creating beautiful UI and user experience (UX). You'll learn how to load images from the application's asset bundle and over the Web via a uniform resource locator (URL). You'll learn how to use the included Material Components icons and how to apply decorators to enhance the look and feel of widgets or use them as input guides to entry fields. You'll learn how to use the `Form` widget to validate text field entry widgets as a group. You'll learn different ways to detect orientation to lay out widgets accordingly depending on whether the device is in portrait or landscape mode.

Chapter 7: Adding Animation to an App—You'll learn how to add animation to an app to convey action. When animation is used appropriately, it improves the UX, but too many or unnecessary animations can make the UX worse. You'll learn how to create `Tween` animations. You'll learn how to use the built-in animations by using the `AnimatedContainer`, `AnimatedCrossFade`, and `AnimatedOpacity` widgets. You'll learn how to create custom animations by using the `AnimationController` and `AnimatedBuilder` classes. You'll learn how to create staggered animations by using multiple `Animation` classes. You'll learn how to use the `CurvedAnimation` class for nonlinear effects.

Chapter 8: Creating an App's Navigation—You'll learn that good navigation creates a great UX, making it easy to access information. You'll learn that adding animation while navigating to another page can also improve the UX as long as it conveys an action, rather than being a distraction. You'll learn how to use the `Navigator` widget to manage a stack of routes to move between pages. You'll learn how to use the `Hero` widget to convey a navigation animation to move and size a widget from one page to another. You'll learn different ways to add navigation by using the `BottomNavigationBar`, `BottomAppBar`, `TabBar`, `TabBarView`, and `Drawer` widgets. You'll also learn how to use the `ListView` widget together with the `Drawer` widget to create a list of navigational menu items.

Chapter 9: Creating Scrolling Lists and Effects—You'll learn how to use different widgets to create a scrolling list to help users view and select information. You'll learn how to use the `Card` widget to group information used in conjunction with the scrolling list widgets. You'll learn how to use the `ListView` widget to build a linear list of scrollable widgets. You'll learn how to use the `GridView` to display tiles of scrollable widgets in a grid format. You'll learn how to use the `Stack` widget to overlap, position, and align its children widgets in conjunction with a scrolling list. You'll learn how to implement the `CustomScrollView` to create custom scrolling effects like parallax animation by using sliver widgets like `SliverSafeArea`, `SliverAppBar`, `SliverList`, `SliverGrid`, and more.

Chapter 10: Building Layouts—You'll learn how to nest widgets to build professional layouts. This concept is a major part of creating beautiful layouts, and it's known as *composition*. Basic and complex layouts are mostly based on vertical or horizontal widgets or a combination of both. This chapter's goal is to create a journal entry page displaying details like a header image, title, diary detail, weather, (journal location) address, tags, and footer images. To lay out the page, you'll use widgets such as `SingleChildScrollView`, `SafeArea`, `Padding`, `Column`, `Row`, `Image`, `Divider`, `Text`, `Icon`, `SizedBox`, `Wrap`, `Chip`, and `CircleAvatar`.

Chapter 11: Applying Interactivity—You'll learn how to add interactivity to an app by using gestures. In mobile applications, gestures are the heart of listening to user interaction, and making use of gestures can result in an app with a great UX. However, overusing gestures without adding value by conveying an action can create a poor UX. You'll learn how to use the GestureDetector gestures such as the tap, double tap, long press, pan, vertical drag, horizontal drag, and scale. You'll learn how to use the Draggable widget to drag over the DragTarget widget to create a drag-and-drop effect to change the widget color. You'll learn how to implement the InkWell and InkResponse widgets that respond to touch and visually show a splash animation. You'll learn how to implement the Dismissible widget that is dismissed by dragging. You'll learn how to use the Transform widget and the Matrix4 class to scale and move widgets.

Chapter 12: Writing Platform-Native Code—In some cases, you need to access specific iOS or Android API functionality, and you'll learn how to use platform channels to send and receive messages between the Flutter app and the host platform. You'll learn how to use the Method-Channel to send messages from the Flutter app (client side) and the FlutterMethodChannel on iOS and MethodChannel on Android to receive calls (host side) and send back results.

Part III: Creating Production-Ready Apps

For the final four chapters of the book, you'll move into more advanced territory and prepare to release your sample apps to production.

Chapter 13: Saving Data with Local Persistence—You'll learn how to build a journal app. You'll learn how to persist data over app launches by using the JSON file format and saving the file to the local iOS and Android filesystem. JavaScript Object Notation (JSON) is a common open-standard and language-independent file data format with the benefits of being human-readable text. You'll learn how to create database classes to write, read, and serialize JSON files. You'll learn how to format a list and sort it by date.

In a mobile application, it's important not to block the UI while processing, and you'll learn how to use the Future class and the FutureBuilder widget. You'll learn how to present a date-selection calendar, validate user entry data, and move focus between entry fields.

You'll also learn how to delete records using the Dismissible widget by dragging or flinging on an entry. To sort entries by date, you'll learn how to use the List().sort method and the Comparator function. To navigate between pages, you'll use the Navigator widget, and you'll learn how to use the CircularProgressIndicator widget to show that an action is running.

Chapter 14: Adding the Firebase and Firestore Backend —Spanning this chapter, Chapter 15, and Chapter 16, you'll use techniques that you have learned in previous chapters along with new concepts and tie them together to create a production-level mood journaling app. In a production-level app, how would you combine what you learned, improve performance by redrawing only the widgets with data changes, pass state between pages and up the widget tree, handle the user authentication credentials, sync data between devices and the cloud, and create classes that handle platform-independent logic between mobile and web apps? These are the reasons why these last three chapters will teach you how to apply the previous techniques you learned along with new important ones to develop a production-level mobile app.

In these last three chapters, you'll learn how to implement app-wide and local-state management and maximize platform code sharing by implementing the Business Logic Component (BLoC) pattern.

You'll learn how to use authentication and persist data to a cloud database by using Google's Firebase backend server infrastructure, Firebase Authentication, and Cloud Firestore. You'll learn that Cloud Firestore is a NoSQL document database to store, query, and sync data with offline support for mobile and web apps. You'll be able to synchronize data between multiple devices. You'll learn how to set up and build serverless applications.

Chapter 15: Adding State Management to the Firestore Client App—You'll continue to edit the mood journaling app created in Chapter 14. You'll learn how to create app-wide and local-state management that uses the InheritedWidget class as a provider to manage and pass State between widgets and pages.

You'll learn how to use the BLoC pattern to create BLoC classes, for example, managing access to the Firebase Authentication and Cloud Firestore database service classes. You'll learn how to use the InheritedWidget class to pass a reference between the BLoC and pages. You'll learn how to use the reactive approach by using StreamBuilder, StreamController, and Stream to populate and refresh data.

You'll learn how to create service classes to manage the Firebase Authentication API and the Cloud Firestore database API. You'll create and take advantage of an abstract class to manage user credentials. You'll learn how to create a data model class to handle the mapping of the Cloud Firestore QuerySnapshot to individual records. You'll learn how to create a class to manage a list of mood icons, description, and icon rotation position according to the selected mood. You'll use the intl package and learn how to create a date formatting class.

Chapter 16: Adding BLoCs to Firestore Client App Pages—You'll continue to edit the mood journaling app created in Chapter 14 with the additions from Chapter 15.

You'll learn how to apply the BLoC, service, provider, model, and utility classes to the UI widget pages. The benefit of using the BLoC pattern allows for separation of the UI widgets from the business logic. You'll learn how to use dependency injection to inject service classes into the BLoC classes. By using dependency injection, the BLoCs remain platform-agnostic. This concept is extremely important since the Flutter framework is expanding beyond mobile and onto web, desktop, and embedded devices.

You'll learn how to apply app-wide authentication state management by implementing classes that apply the BLoC pattern. You'll learn how to create a login page that implements the BLoC pattern class to validate emails, passwords, and user credentials. You'll learn how to pass state between pages and the widget tree by implementing provider classes (InheritedWidget). You'll learn how to modify the home page to implement and create BLoC pattern classes to handle login credentials validation, create a journal entries list, and add and delete individual entries. You'll learn how to create the journal edit page that implements the BLoC pattern classes to add, modify, and save existing entries.

WHAT YOU NEED TO USE THIS BOOK

You'll need to install the Flutter framework and Dart to create the example projects. This book uses Android Studio as its primary development tool, and all projects compile for iOS and Android. For compiling iOS applications, you'll need a Mac computer with Xcode installed. You can also use other editors like Microsoft Visual Studio Code or IntelliJ IDEA. For the last major project, you'll need to create a free Google Firebase account to take advantage of cloud authentication and data syncing, including offline support.

The source code for the samples is available for download from `www.wiley.com/go/beginningflutter`.

CONVENTIONS

To help you get the most from the text and keep track of what's happening, we've used a number of conventions throughout the book.

TRY IT OUT You should work through all the *Try It Out* exercises in the book.

1. These exercises consist of a set of numbered steps.
2. Follow the steps with your copy of the database.

HOW IT WORKS

At the end of each *Try It Out,* the code you've typed will be explained in detail.

As for styles in the text:

➤ We *italicize* new terms and important words when we introduce them.

➤ We show keyboard strokes like this: Ctrl+A.

➤ We show filenames, URLs, and code within the text like so:

`persistence.properties`

We present code in two different ways:

```
We use a monofont type with no highlighting for most code examples.
We use bold to emphasize code that is particularly important in the present
   context or to show changes from a previous code snippet.
```

ERRATA

We make every effort to ensure that there are no errors in the text or in the code. However, no one is perfect, and mistakes do occur. If you find an error in one of our books, like a spelling mistake or faulty piece of code, we would be very grateful for your feedback. By sending in errata, you may save another reader hours of frustration, and at the same time, you will be helping us provide even higher-quality information.

To find the errata page for this book, go to this the book's page at www.wiley.com/go/beginning-flutter and click the Errata link. On this page, you can view all errata that have been submitted for this book and posted by Wrox editors.

If you don't spot "your" error on the Book Errata page, please email our customer service team at wileysupport@wiley.com with the subject line "Possible Book Errata Submission." We'll check the information and, if appropriate, post a message to the book's errata page and fix the problem in subsequent editions of the book.

PART I
The Foundations of Flutter Programming

1

Introducing Flutter and Getting Started

WHAT YOU WILL LEARN IN THIS CHAPTER

➤   What the Flutter framework is

➤   What Flutter's benefits are

➤   How Flutter and Dart work together

➤   What a Flutter `Widget` is

➤   What an `Element` is

➤   What a `RenderObject` is

➤   What type of Flutter widgets are available

➤   What the stateless and stateful `Widget` lifecycle is

➤   How the widget tree and element tree work together

➤   How to install the Flutter SDK

➤   How to install Xcode on macOS and Android Studio on macOS, Windows, and Linux

➤   How to configure an editor

➤   How to install the Flutter and Dart plugins

In this chapter, you'll learn how the Flutter framework works behind the scenes. Flutter uses widgets to create the user interface (UI), and Dart is the language used to develop the applications. Once you understand how Flutter handles and implements widgets, it will help you in architecting your apps.

You'll learn how to install the Flutter SDK on macOS, Windows, and Linux. You'll configure Android Studio to install the Flutter plugin to run, debug, and use hot reload. You'll install the Dart plugin for code analysis, code validation, and code completion.

INTRODUCING FLUTTER

Flutter is Google's portable UI framework for building modern, native, and reactive applications for iOS and Android. Google is also working on Flutter desktop embedding and Flutter for the Web (Hummingbird) and embedded devices (Raspberry Pi, home, automotive, and more). Flutter is an open-source project hosted on GitHub with contributions from Google and the community. Flutter uses Dart, a modern object-oriented language that compiles to native ARM code and production-ready JavaScript code. Flutter uses the Skia 2D rendering engine that works with different types of hardware and software platforms and is also used by Google Chrome, Chrome OS, Android, Mozilla Firefox, Firefox OS, and others. Skia is sponsored and managed by Google and is available for any-one to use under the BSD Free Software License. Skia uses a CPU-based path render and also supports the OpenGL ES2-accelerated backend.

Dart is the language that you'll use to develop your Flutter applications, and you'll learn more about it in Chapter 3, "Learning Dart Basics." Dart is ahead-of-time (AOT) compiled to native code, making your Flutter application fast. Dart is also just-in-time (JIT) compiled, making it fast to display your code changes such as via Flutter's stateful hot reload feature.

Flutter uses Dart to create your user interface, removing the need to use separate languages like Markup or visual designers. Flutter is declarative; in other words, Flutter builds the UI to reflect the state of the app. When the state (data) changes, the UI is redrawn, and Flutter constructs a new instance of the widget. In the "Understanding the Widget Tree and the Element Tree" section of this chapter, you'll learn how widgets are configured and mounted (rendered) creating the widget tree and element tree, but under the hood, the render tree (a third tree) uses the `RenderObject`, which com-putes and implements the basic layout and paint protocols. (You won't need to interact directly with the render tree or the `RenderObject`, and I won't discuss them further in this book.)

Flutter is fast, and the rendering runs at 60 frames per second (fps) and 120fps for capable devices. The higher the fps, the smoother the animations and transitions.

Applications made in Flutter are built from a single codebase, are compiled to native ARM code, use the graphics processing unit (GPU), and can access specific iOS and Android APIs (like GPS location, image library) by communicating via platform channels. You'll learn more about platform channels in Chapter 12, "Writing Platform-Native Code."

Flutter provides the developer with tools to create beautiful and professional-looking applications and with the ability to customize any aspect of the application. You'll be able to add smooth anima-tions, gesture detection, and splash feedback behavior to the UI. Flutter applications result in native performance for both iOS and Android platforms. During development, Flutter uses hot reload to refresh the running application in milliseconds when you change the source code to add new features or modify existing ones. Using hot reload is a great way to see the changes you make to your code on the simulator or device while keeping the application's state, the data values, on the screen.

Defining Widgets and Elements

The Flutter UI is implemented by using widgets from a modern reactive framework. Flutter uses its own rendering engine to draw widgets. In Chapter 5, "Understanding the Widget Tree," you'll get an introduction to widgets, and in Chapter 6, "Using Common Widgets," you'll learn how to implement widgets.

You might be asking, what is a widget? Widgets can be compared to LEGO blocks; by adding blocks together, you create an object, and by adding different kinds of blocks, you can alter the look and behavior of the object. Widgets are the building blocks of a Flutter app, and each widget is an immutable declaration of the user interface. In other words, widgets are configurations (instructions) for different parts of the UI. Placing the widgets together creates the widget tree. For example, say an architect draws a blueprint of a house; all of the objects like walls, windows, and doors in the house are the widgets, and all of them work together to create the house or, in this case, the application.

Since widgets are the configuration pieces of the UI and together they create the widget tree, how does Flutter use these configurations? Flutter uses the widget as the configuration to build each element, which means the element is the widget that is mounted (rendered) on the screen. The elements that are mounted on the screen create the element tree. You'll learn more about the widget tree and element tree in the next section, "Understanding the Widget Tree and the Element Tree." You'll also learn to manipulate the widget tree in detail in Chapter 5.

Here's a brief look at the wide array of widgets at your disposal:

➤ Widgets with structuring elements such as a list, grid, text, and button

➤ Widgets with input elements such as a form, form fields, and keyboard listeners

➤ Widgets with styling elements such as font type, size, weight, color, border, and shadow

➤ Widgets to lay out the UI such as row, column, stack, centering, and padding

➤ Widgets with interactive elements that respond to touch, gestures, dragging, and dismissible

➤ Widgets with animation and motion elements such as hero animation, animated container, animated crossfade, fade transition, rotation, scale, size, slide, and opacity

➤ Widgets with elements like assets, images, and icons

➤ Widgets that can be nested together to create the UI needed

➤ Custom widgets you can create yourself

UNDERSTANDING WIDGET LIFECYCLE EVENTS

In programming, you have different lifecycle events that usually happen in a linear mode, one after another as each stage is completed. In this section, you'll learn the widget lifecycle events and their purpose.

To build the UI, you use two main types of widgets, StatelessWidget and StatefulWidget. A stateless widget is used when the values (state) do not change, and the stateful widget is used when values (state) change. In Chapter 2, "Creating a Hello World App," you'll learn in detail when to use a `StatelessWidget` or a `StatefulWidget`. Each stateless or stateful widget has a `build` method with a `BuildContext` that handles the location of the widget in the widget tree. The `BuildContext` objects are actually `Element` objects, an instantiation of the `Widget` at a location in the tree.

The StatelessWidget Lifecycle

A `StatelessWidget` is built based on its own configuration and does not change dynamically. For example, the screen displays an image with a description and will not change. The stateless widget is declared with one class, and you'll learn about classes in Chapter 3. The `build` (the UI portions) method of the stateless widget can be called from three different scenarios. It can be called the first time the widget is created, when the widget's parent changes, and when an `InheritedWidget` has changed. In Chapter 15, "Adding State Management to the Firestore Client App," you'll learn how to implement the `InheritedWidget`.

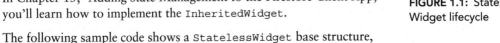

FIGURE 1.1: Stateless-Widget lifecycle

The following sample code shows a `StatelessWidget` base structure, and Figure 1.1 displays the widget's lifecycle.

```
class JournalList extends StatelessWidget {
  @override
  Widget build(BuildContext context) {
    return Container();
  }
}
```

The StatefulWidget Lifecycle

A `StatefulWidget` is built based on its own configuration but can change dynamically. For example, the screen displays an icon with a description, but values can change based on the user's interaction, like choosing a different icon or description. This type of widget has a mutable state that can change over time. The stateful widget is declared with two classes, the `StatefulWidget` class and the `State` class. The `StatefulWidget` class is rebuilt when the widget's configuration changes, but the `State` class can persist (remain), enhancing performance. For example, when the state changes, the widget is rebuilt. If the `StatefulWidget` is removed from the tree and then inserted back into the tree sometime in the future, a new `State` object is created. Note that under certain circumstances and restrictions, you can use a `GlobalKey` (unique key across entire app) to reuse (not re-create) the `State` object; however, global keys are expensive, and unless they're needed, you might want to consider not using them. You call the `setState()` method to notify the framework that this object has changes, and the widget's `build` method is called (scheduled). You would set the new state values inside the `setState()` method. In Chapter 2, you'll learn how to call the `setState()` method.

The following example shows a `StatefulWidget` base structure, and Figure 1.2 displays the widget's lifecycle. You have two classes, the `JournalEdit StatefulWidget` class and the `_JournalEditState` class.

```
class JournalEdit extends StatefulWidget {
  @override
  _ JournalEditState createState() => _ JournalEditState();
```

```
    }

class _JournalEditState extends State<JournalEdit> {
  @override
  Widget build(BuildContext context) {
    return Container();
  }
}
```

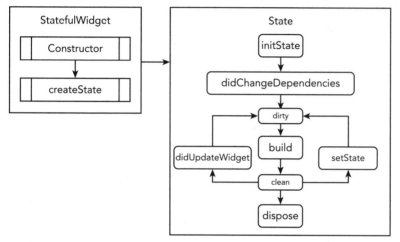

FIGURE 1.2: StatefulWidget lifecycle

You can override different portions of the StatefulWidget to customize and manipulate data at different points of the widget lifecycle. Table 1.1 shows some of the stateful widget main overrides, and the majority of the time you'll use the initState(), didChangeDependencies(), and dispose() methods. You'll use the build() method all of the time to build your UI.

TABLE 1.1: StatefulWidget lifecycle

METHOD	DESCRIPTION	SAMPLE CODE
initState()	Called once when this object is inserted into the tree.	```@override void initState() { super.initState(); print('initState'); }```
dispose()	Called when this object is removed from the tree permanently.	```@override void dispose() { print('dispose'); super.dispose(); }```

continues

TABLE 1.1 (*continued*)

METHOD	DESCRIPTION	SAMPLE CODE
`didChangeDependencies()`	Called when this `State` object changes.	```@override void didChangeDependencies() { super.didChangeDependencies(); print('didChangeDependencies'); }```
`didUpdateWidget-(Contacts oldWidget)`	Called when the widget configuration changes.	```@override void didUpdateWidget(Contacts oldWidget) { super.didUpdateWidget(oldWidget); print('didUpdateWidget: $oldWidget'); }```
`deactivate()`	Called when this object is removed from the tree.	```@override void deactivate() { print('deactivate'); super.deactivate(); }```
`build(BuildContext context)`	Can be called multiple times to build the UI, and the `BuildContext` handles the location of this widget in the widget tree.	```@override Widget build(BuildContext context) { print('build'); return Container(); }```
`setState()`	Notifies the framework that the state of this object has changed to schedule calling the `build` for this `State` object.	```setState(() { name = _newValue; });```

UNDERSTANDING THE WIDGET TREE AND THE ELEMENT TREE

In the previous section, you learned that widgets contain the instructions to create the UI, and when you compose (nest) widgets together, they create the widget tree. The Flutter framework uses the widgets as the configurations for each element that is mounted (rendered) on the screen. The mounted elements displayed on the screen create the element tree. You now have two trees, the widget tree that has the widget configurations and the element tree that represents the rendered widgets on the screen (Figure 1.3).

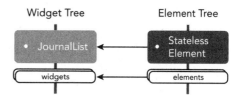

FIGURE 1.3: Widget tree and element tree

When the application starts, the `main()` function calls the `runApp()` method, usually taking a `StatelessWidget` as the argument, and is mounted as the root element for the application. The Flutter framework processes through all of the widgets, and each corresponding element is mounted.

The following is sample code that starts a Flutter application, and the `runApp()` method inflates the `MyApp StatelessWidget`, meaning the main application itself is a widget. As you can see, just about everything in Flutter is a widget.

```
void main() => runApp(MyApp());

class MyApp extends StatelessWidget {
  @override
  Widget build(BuildContext context) {
    return MaterialApp(
      title: 'Flutter App',
      theme: ThemeData(
        primarySwatch: Colors.blue,
      ),
      home: MyHomePage(title: 'Home'),
    );
  }
}
```

Elements have a reference to the widget and are responsible for comparing the widget differences. If a widget is responsible for building child widgets, then elements are created for each child widget. When you see the use of `BuildContext` objects, they are the `Element` objects. To discourage direct manipulation of the `Element` objects, the `BuildContext` interface is used instead. The Flutter framework uses `BuildContext` objects to discourage you from manipulating the `Element` objects. In other words, you'll be using widgets to create your UI layouts, but it's good to know how the Flutter framework is architected and how it works behind the scenes.

As noted earlier, there is a third tree called the *render tree* that is a low-level layout and painting system that inherits from the `RenderObject`. The `RenderObject` computes and implements the basic layout and paint protocols. You won't need to interact directly with the render tree, however, and will be using the widgets.

Stateless Widget and Element Trees

A stateless widget has the configuration to create a stateless element. Each stateless widget has a corresponding stateless element. The Flutter framework calls the `createElement` method (create an instance), and the stateless element is created and mounted to the element tree. In other words, the Flutter framework makes a request from the widget to create an element and then mounts (adds) the element to the element tree. Each element contains a reference back to the widget. The element calls the widget's `build` method to check for children widgets, and each child widget (like an Icon or Text) creates its own element and is mounted to the element tree. This process results in two trees: the widget tree and the element tree.

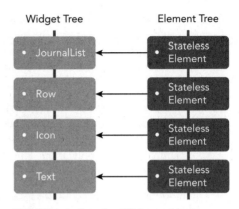

FIGURE 1.4: StatelessWidget widget tree and element tree

Figure 1.4 shows the `JournalList StatelessWidget` that has Row, Icon, and Text widgets representing the widget tree. The Flutter framework asks each widget to create the element, and each element has a reference back to the widget. This process happens for each widget down the widget tree and creates the element tree. The widget contains the instructions to build the element mounted on the screen. Note that you the developer create the widgets, and the Flutter framework handles mounting the elements, creating the element tree.

```
// Simplified sample code
class JournalList extends StatelessWidget {
  @override
  Widget build(BuildContext context) {
    return Row(
      children: <Widget>[
        Icon(),
        Text(),
      ],
    );
  }
}
```

Stateful Widget and Element Trees

A stateful widget has the configuration to create a stateful element. Each stateful widget has a corresponding stateful element. The Flutter framework calls the `createElement` method to create the stateful element, and the stateful element is mounted to the element tree. Since this is a stateful widget, the stateful element requests that the widget create a state object by calling the `Stateful-Widget` class's `createState` method.

The stateful element now has a reference to the state object and the widget at the given location in the element tree. The stateful element calls the state object widget's `build` method to check for child widgets, and each child widget creates its own element and is mounted to the element tree. This process results in two trees: the widget tree and the element tree. Note that if a child widget displaying the state (journal note) is a stateless widget like the Text widget, then the element created for this widget is a stateless element. The state object maintains a reference to the widget (StatefulWidget class) and also handles the construction for the Text widget with the latest value. Figure 1.5 shows the widget tree, the element tree, and the state object. Note that the stateful element has a reference to the stateful widget and the state object.

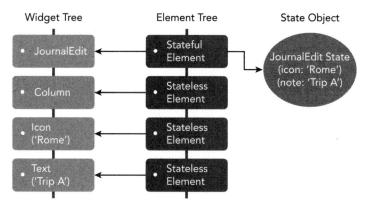

FIGURE 1.5: StatefulWidget widget tree, the element tree, and the state object

To update the UI with new data, you call the setState() method that you learned about in the "The StatefulWidget Lifecycle" section. To set new data (properties/variables) values, call the setState() method to update the state object, and the state object marks the element as dirty (has changed) and causes the UI to be updated (scheduled). The stateful element calls the state object's build method to rebuild the children widgets. A new widget is created with the new state value, and the old widget is removed.

For example, you have a StatefulWidget JournalEntry class, and in the State object class you call the setState() method to change the Text widget description from 'Trip A' to 'Trip B' by setting the note variable value to 'Trip B'. The state object note variable is updated to the 'Trip B' value, the state object marks the element as dirty, and the build method rebuilds the UI children widgets. The new Text widget is created with the new 'Trip B' value, and the old Text widget with the 'Trip A' value is removed (Figure 1.6).

```
// Simplified sample code
class JournalEdit extends StatefulWidget {
  @override
  _JournalEditState createState() => _JournalEditState();
}

class _JournalEditState extends State<JournalEdit> {
  String note = 'Trip A';

  void _onPressed() {
    setState(() {
      note = 'Trip B';
    });
  }
```

```
@override
Widget build(BuildContext context) {
  return Column(
    children: <Widget>[
      Icon(),
      Text('$note'),
      FlatButton(
        onPressed: _onPressed,
      ),
    ],
  );
}
}
```

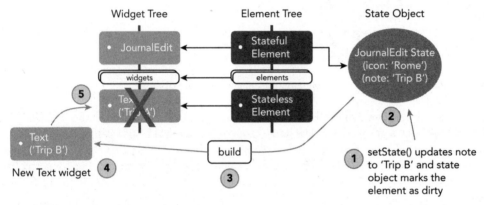

FIGURE 1.6: Updating the state process

Since both the old and new widgets are both Text widgets, the existing element updates its reference to the new widget, and the element stays in the element tree. The Text widget is a stateless widget, and the corresponding element is a stateless element; although the Text widget has been replaced, the state is maintained (persists). State objects have a long life span and remain attached to the element tree as long as the new widget is the same type as the old widget.

Let's continue with the previous example; the old Text widget with the 'Trip A' value is removed and replaced by the new Text widget with the 'Trip B' value. Since both the old and new widgets are of the same type of Text widgets, the element stays on the element tree with the updated reference to the new Text 'Trip B' widget (Figure 1.7).

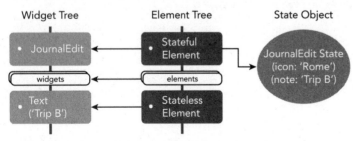

FIGURE 1.7: Updated state for the widget tree and element tree

INSTALLING THE FLUTTER SDK

Installing the Flutter SDK requires downloading the current version, which is 1.5.4 at the time of writing (your version might be higher), of the SDK from the Flutter website. This chapter includes sections for installing on macOS, Windows, and Linux. (Note that targeting and compiling for the iOS platform requires a Mac computer and Xcode, Apple's development environment). Do not get discouraged by the number of steps; you'll do this the first time you install only.

You'll be using the Terminal window to run installation and configuration commands.

Installing on macOS

Before starting the installation, you need to make sure your Mac supports the minimum hardware and software requirements.

System Requirements

➤ macOS (64-bit)

➤ 700 MB of disk space (does not include disk space for the integrated development environment and other tools)

➤ The following command-line tools:

> ➤ Bash
>
> ➤ mkdir
>
> ➤ rm
>
> ➤ git
>
> ➤ curl
>
> ➤ unzip
>
> ➤ which

Get the Flutter SDK

The latest installation details are available online on the Flutter website at `https://flutter.dev/docs/get-started/install/macos/`. Execute steps 2 and following from your Mac's Terminal window.

1. Download the following installation file to get the latest release, v1.7.8 (your version might be higher), of the Flutter SDK:

`https://storage.googleapis.com/flutter_infra/releases/stable/macos/flutter_macos_v1.7.8+hotfix.4-stable.zip`.

2. Extract the file in the desired location by using the Terminal window.

```
cd ~/development
unzip ~/Downloads/flutter_macos_v1.7.8+hotfix.4-stable.zip
```

3. Add the Flutter tool to your path (pwd means present working directory; in your case, it will be the development folder).

    ```
    export PATH="$PATH:`pwd`/flutter/bin"
    ```

4. Update the path permanently.

    a. Get the path that you used in step 3. For example, replace MacUserName with your path to the development folder.

    ```
    /Users/MacUserName/development/flutter/bin
    ```

    b. Open or create $HOME/.bash_profile. Your file path or filename might be different on your computer.

    c. Edit .bash_profile (will open a command-line editor).

    d. Type **nano .bash_profile**.

    e. Type **export PATH=/Users/MacUserName/development/flutter/bin:$PATH**.

    f. Save by pressing ^X (Control+X), confirm by pressing Y (Yes), and press Enter to accept the filename.

    g. Close the Terminal window.

    h. Reopen the Terminal window and type **echo $PATH** to verify that the path has been added. Then type **flutter** to make sure the path is working. If the command is not recognized, something went wrong with the PATH. Check to make sure you have the correct username for your computer in the path.

Check for Dependencies

Run the following command from the Terminal window to check for dependencies that need to be installed to finish the setup:

```
flutter doctor
```

View the report and check for other software that may be needed.

iOS Setup: Install Xcode

A Mac with Xcode 10.0 or newer is required.

1. Open App Store and install Xcode.

2. Configure the Xcode command-line tools by running **sudo xcode-select --switch / Applications/Xcode.app/Contents/Developer** from the Terminal window.

3. Confirm that the Xcode license agreement is signed by **running sudo xcodebuild -license** from the terminal.

Android Setup: Install Android Studio

Full installation details are available at https://flutter.dev/docs/get-started/install/macos#android-setup. Flutter requires a full installation of Android Studio for the Android platform dependencies. Keep in mind that Flutter apps can be written in different editors such as Visual Code or IntelliJ IDEA.

1. Download and install Android Studio from `https://developer.android.com/studio/`.

2. Start Android Studio and follow the Setup Wizard, which installs all of the Android SDKs required by Flutter. If it asks you to import previous settings, you can click Yes to use the current settings or No to start with the default settings.

Set Up the Android Emulator

You can view details on how to create and manage virtual devices at `https://developer.android.com/studio/run/managing-avds`.

1. Enable VM acceleration on your machine. Directions are available at `https://developer.android.com/studio/run/emulator-acceleration`.

2. If this is your first time installing Android Studio, to access the AVD Manager, you need to create a new project. Launch Android Studio, click Start A New Android Studio Project, and give it any name and accept the defaults. Once the project is created, continue with these steps.

Currently, Android Studio requires an open Android project before you can access the Android submenu.

3. From Android Studio, select Tools ⇨ Android ⇨ AVD Manager ⇨ Create Virtual Device.

4. Select a device of your choice and click Next.

5. Select an x86 or x86_64 image for the Android version to emulate.

6. If available, make sure you select Hardware – GLES 2.0 to enable hardware acceleration. This hardware acceleration will make the Android emulator run faster.

7. Click the Finish button.

8. To check that the emulator image has been installed correctly, select Tools ⇨ AVD Manager and then click the Run button (play icon).

Installing on Windows

Before starting the installation, you need to make sure your Windows supports the minimum hardware and software requirements.

System Requirements

➤ Windows 7 SP1 or later (64-bit)

➤ 400 MB of disk space (does not include disk space for an integrated development environment and other tools)

➤ The following command-line tools:

  ➤ PowerShell 5.0 or newer

  ➤ Git for Windows (`Git` from the Windows Command Prompt)

Get the Flutter SDK

The latest installation details are available at `https://flutter.dev/docs/get-started/install/windows/`.

1. Download the following installation file to get the latest release, v1.7.8 at the time of writing (your version might be higher), of the Flutter SDK:

   `https://storage.googleapis.com/flutter_infra/releases/stable/windows/flutter_windows_v1.7.8+hotfix.4-stable.zip`.

2. Extract the file in the desired location.

   Replace `WindowsUserName` with your own Windows username. Do not install Flutter in directories that require elevated privileges like `C:\Program Files\`. I used the following folder location:

   `C:\Users\WindowsUserName\flutter`

3. Look in `C:\Users\WindowsUserName\flutter` and double-click the `flutter_console.bat` file.

4. Update the path permanently (the following is for Windows 10):

   a. Open Control Panel and drill down to Desktop App ⇨ User Accounts ⇨ User Accounts ⇨ Change My Environment Variables.

   b. Under User Variables for `WindowsUserName`, select the `Path` variable and click the Edit button. If the `Path` variable is missing, skip to the next substep, c.

      i. In the Edit environment variable, click the New button.

      ii. Type the path `C:\Users\WindowsUserName\flutter\bin`.

      iii. Click the OK button and then close the Environment Variables screen.

   c. Under User Variables for `WindowsUserName`, if the `Path` variable is missing, then click the New button instead and type `Path` for the Variable name and `C:\Users\WindowsUserName\flutter\bin` for the Variable value.

5. Reboot Windows to apply the changes.

Check for Dependencies

Run the following command from the Windows command prompt to check for dependencies that need to be installed to finish the setup:

```
flutter doctor
```

View the report and check for other software that may need to be installed.

Install Android Studio

Full installation details are available at `https://flutter.dev/docs/get-started/install/windows#android-setup`. Flutter requires a full installation of Android Studio for the Android platform dependencies. Keep in mind that Flutter apps can be written in different editors like Visual Code or IntelliJ IDEA.

1. Download and install Android Studio from `https://developer.android.com/studio/`.

2. Start Android Studio and follow the Setup Wizard, which installs all of the Android SDKs required by Flutter. If it asks you to import previous settings, you can click Yes to use the current settings or No to start with the default settings.

Set Up the Android Emulator

You can view details on how to create and manage virtual devices at `https://developer.android.com/studio/run/managing-avds`.

1. Enable VM acceleration on your machine. Directions are available at `https://developer.android.com/studio/run/emulator-acceleration`.

2. If this is your first time installing Android Studio, to access the AVD Manager, you need to create a new project. Launch Android Studio and click Start A New Android Studio project and give it any name and accept the defaults. Once the project is created, continue with these steps.

   Currently, Android Studio requires an open Android project before you can access the Android submenu.

3. From Android Studio, select Tools ➪ Android ➪ AVD Manager ➪ Create Virtual Device.

4. Select a device of your choice and click Next.

5. Select an x86 or x86_64 image for the Android version to emulate.

6. If available, make sure you select Hardware – GLES 2.0 to enable hardware acceleration. This hardware acceleration will make the Android emulator run faster.

7. Click the Finish button.

8. To check that the emulator image has been installed correctly, select Tools ➪ AVD Manager and then click the Run button (play icon).

Installing on Linux

Before starting the installation, you need to make sure your Linux supports the minimum hardware and software requirements.

System Requirements

➤ Linux (64-bit)

➤ 600 MB of disk space (does not include disk space for an integrated development environment and other tools)

➤ The following command-line tools:

  ➤ Bash

  ➤ curl

  ➤ git 2.x

> ➤ `mkdir`

> ➤ `rm`

> ➤ `unzip`

> ➤ `which`

> ➤ `xz-utils`

➤ The libGLU.so.1 shared library provided by mesa packages (e.g., libglu1-mesa on Ubuntu/Debian)

Get the Flutter SDK

The latest installation details are available at `https://flutter.dev/docs/get-started/install/linux/`.

1. Download the following installation file to get the latest release, which is v1.7.8 at the time of writing (your version might be higher), of the Flutter SDK:

   `https://storage.googleapis.com/flutter_infra/releases/stable/linux/flutter_linux_v1.7.8+hotfix.4-stable.tar.xz`.

2. Extract the file in the desired location by using the Terminal window:

   ```
   cd ~/development
   tar xf ~/Downloads/flutter_linux_v1.7.8+hotfix.4-stable.tar.xz
   ```

3. Add the Flutter tool to your path (`pwd` means present working directory; in your case, it will be the `development` folder).

   ```
   export PATH="$PATH:`pwd`/flutter/bin"
   ```

4. Update the path permanently.

   a. Get the path that you used in step 3. For example, replace `PathToDev` with your path to the development folder.

   `/PathToDev/development/flutter/bin`

   b. Open or create `$HOME/.bash_profile`. Your file path or filename might be different on your computer.

   c. Edit `.bash_profile` (will open a command-line editor).

   d. Add the following line and make sure you replace the `PathToDev` with your path: **`export PATH="$PATH :/PathToDev/development/flutter/bin"`** .

   e. Run **`source $HOME/.bash_profile`** to refresh the current window.

   f. In the Terminal window, type **`echo $PATH`** to verify that the path is added. Then type **`flutter`** to make sure the path is working. If the command is not recognized, something went wrong with the PATH. Check to make sure you have the correct path.

Check for Dependencies

Run the following command from the Terminal window to check for dependencies that need to be installed to finish the setup:

```
flutter doctor
```

View the report and check for other software that may be needed.

Install Android Studio

Full installation details are available at `https://flutter.dev/docs/get-started/install/linux#android-setup`. Flutter requires a full installation of Android Studio for the Android platform dependencies. Keep in mind that Flutter apps can be written in different editors like Visual Code or IntelliJ IDEA.

1. Download and install Android Studio from `https://developer.android.com/studio/`.

2. Start Android Studio and follow the Setup Wizard, which installs all of the Android SDKs required by Flutter. If it asks you to import previous settings, you can click Yes to use current settings or No to start with default settings.

Set Up the Android Emulator

You can view details on how to create and manage virtual devices at `https://developer.android.com/studio/run/managing-avds`.

1. Enable VM acceleration on your machine. Directions are available at `https://developer.android.com/studio/run/emulator-acceleration`.

2. If this is your first time installing Android Studio, to access the AVD Manager, you need to create a new project. Launch Android Studio, click Start A New Android Studio Project, and give it any name and accept the defaults. Once the project is created, continue with these steps.

Currently, Android Studio requires an open Android project before you can access the Android submenu.

3. From Android Studio, select Tools ➪ Android ➪ AVD Manager ➪ Create Virtual Device.

4. Select a device of your choice and click Next.

5. Select an x86 or x86_64 image for the Android version to emulate.

6. If available, make sure you select Hardware – GLES 2.0 to enable hardware acceleration. This hardware acceleration will make the Android emulator run faster.

7. Click the Finish button.

8. To check that the emulator image has been installed correctly, select Tools ➪ AVD Manager and then click the Run button (play icon).

CONFIGURING THE ANDROID STUDIO EDITOR

The editor you'll be using is Android Studio. Android Studio is the official integrated development environment for Google's Android operating system and is specifically designed for Android development. It's also a great development environment for developing apps with Flutter. Before starting to build an app, the editor needs the Flutter and Dart plugins installed to make it easier to write code. (Other editors that support these plugins are IntelliJ or Visual Studio Code.) The editor plugins give code completion, syntax highlighting, run and debug support, and more. Using a plain-text editor to write your code without any plugins would also work, but without the use of plugin features is not recommended.

Instructions for setting up different code editors are available at `https://flutter.dev/docs/ get-started/editor/`. To support Flutter development, install the following plugins:

➤ Flutter plugin for developer workflows such as running, debugging, and hot reload

➤ Dart plugin for code analysis such as instant code validation and code completion

Follow these steps to install the Flutter and Dart plugins:

1. Start Android Studio.
2. Click Preferences ➪ Plugins (on macOS) or File ➪ Settings ➪ Plugins (on Windows and Linux).
3. Click Browse Repositories, select the Flutter plug-in, and click the Install button.
4. Click Yes when prompted to install the Dart plugin.
5. Click Restart when prompted.

SUMMARY

In this chapter, you learned how the Flutter framework architecture works behind the scenes. You learned that Flutter is a great portable UI framework to build mobile applications for iOS and Android. Flutter also plans on supporting development for desktop, web, and embedded devices. You learned that Flutter applications are built from a single codebase that uses widgets to create the UI and that you develop with the Dart language. You learned that Flutter uses the Skia 2D rendering engine that works with different types of hardware and software.

You learned that the Dart language is AOT compiled to native code, resulting in fast performance for your applications. You learned that Dart is JIT compiled, making it fast to display code changes with Flutter's stateful hot reload.

You learned that widgets are the building blocks for composing the UI, and each widget is an immutable declaration of the UI. Widgets are the configuration to create elements. Elements are the widgets made concrete, meaning mounted and painted on the screen. You learned that the `RenderObject` implements the basic layout and paint protocols.

You learned about the lifecycle events for the stateless and stateful widgets. You learned that the stateless widget is declared by a single class that extends (inherits) from the `StatelessWidget` class. You learned that the stateful widget is declared with two classes, the `StatefulWidget` class and the `State` class.

You learned that Flutter is declarative and the UI rebuilds itself when the state changes. You learned that widgets are the building blocks of a Flutter app and that widgets are the configurations for the UI.

You learned that nesting (*composition*) widgets results in creating the widget tree. The Flutter framework uses the widget as the configuration to build each element, resulting in creating the element tree. The element is the widget that is mounted (rendered) on the screen. The previous process results in creating the render tree that is a low-level layout and painting system. You'll be using widgets and will not need to interact directly with the render tree. You learned that stateless widgets have the configuration to create stateless elements. You learned that stateful widgets have the configuration to create stateful elements and the stateful element requests from the widget to create a state object.

You learned how to install the Flutter SDK, Xcode for compiling for iOS, and Android Studio for compiling for Android devices. When Android Studio is installed on a Mac, it handles compiling for both iOS (via Xcode) and Android devices. You learned how to install the Flutter and Dart plugins to help developer workflows such as code completion, syntax highlighting, run, debug, hot reload, and code analysis.

In the next chapter, you'll learn how to create your first app and use hot reload to view changes immediately. You'll also learn how to use themes to style the app, when to use stateless or stateful widgets, and how to use external packages to add features such as GPS and charts quickly.

▶ WHAT YOU LEARNED IN THIS CHAPTER

TOPIC	KEY CONCEPTS
Flutter	Flutter is a portable UI framework to build modern, native, and reactive mobile applications for iOS and Android from a single codebase. Flutter has also expanded development for desktop, web, and embedded devices.
Skia	Flutter uses the Skia 2D rendering engine that works with different hardware and software platforms.
Dart	Dart is the language used to develop Flutter applications. Dart is ahead-of-time (AOT) compiled to native code for fast performance. Dart is just-in-time (JIT) compiled to quickly display code changes via Flutter's stateful hot reload.
Declarative user interface (UI)	Flutter is declarative and builds the UI to reflect the state of the app. When the state changes, the UI is redrawn. Flutter uses Dart to create the UI.
`Widget`	Widgets are the building blocks of a Flutter app, and each widget is an immutable declaration of the user interface (UI). Widgets are the configuration to create an element.
`Element`	Elements are widgets that are mounted (rendered) on the screen. Elements are created by the widget's configuration.
`RenderObject`	The `RenderObject` is an object in the render tree that computes and implements the basic layout and paint protocols.
Widgets lifecycle events	Each stateless or stateful widget has a build method with a `BuildContext` that handles the location of the widget in the widget tree. The `BuildContext` objects are `Element` objects, meaning an instantiation of the `Widget` at a location in the tree.
`StatelessWidget`	The `StatelessWidget` is built based on its own configuration and does not change dynamically. The stateless widget is declared with one class.
`StatefulWidget`	The `StatefulWidget` is built based on its own configuration but can change dynamically. The stateful widget is declared with two classes, the `StatefulWidget` class and the `State` class.
Widget tree	The widget tree is created when you compose (nest) widgets; this is known as *composition*. Three trees are created: the widget tree, the element tree, and the render tree.
Element tree	The element tree represents each element mounted (rendered) on the screen.

TOPIC	KEY CONCEPTS
Render tree	The render tree is a low-level layout and painting system that inherits from the `RenderObject`. The `RenderObject` implements the basic layout and paint protocols. You'll be using widgets and will not need to interact directly with the render tree.
Flutter SDK and Dart	The mobile software development kit has expanded to desktop, web, and embedded devices.
Xcode and Android Studio	Development tools to build iOS and Android Mobile applications.
Flutter plugin	This plugin helps with developer workflows such as running, debugging, and hot reload.
Dart plugin	This plugin helps with code analysis such as instance code validation and code completion.

2

Creating a Hello World App

WHAT YOU WILL LEARN IN THIS CHAPTER

➤ How to create a new Flutter mobile app

➤ How to refresh the running app with hot reload

➤ How to style the app with themes

➤ When to use a stateless or stateful widget

➤ How to add external packages

A great way to learn a new development language is to write a basic app. In programming, Hello World is the most basic program to write. It simply displays the words *Hello World* on the screen. In this chapter, you'll learn the main steps of how to develop this basic program as a Flutter app. Do not worry about understanding the code yet; I'll walk you through it step-by-step later in this book.

Writing this minimal example helps you learn the basic structure of a Flutter app, how to run the app on the iOS simulator and the Android emulator, and how to make changes to the code.

SETTING UP THE PROJECT

The initial project setup for each app is the same. I'm using Android Studio to create the sample apps in this book, but you can choose a different editor such as IntelliJ or Visual Studio Code. An overview of the process in Android Studio is as follows: you create a new Flutter project, select the Flutter application as the project type (template), and enter the project name. The Flutter software development kit (SDK) then creates the project for you, including creating a project directory with the same name as the project name. Within the project directory, the `lib` folder contains the `main.dart` file with the source code (in other words, `project_name/lib/main.dart`). You'll also have an `android` folder for the Android app, the `ios` folder for the iOS app, and a `test` folder for unit testing.

In this chapter, the `lib` folder and the `main.dart` file are your primary focus. In Chapter 4, "Creating a Starter Project Template," you will learn how to create a Flutter starter project and how to structure code into separate files.

By default, the Flutter app uses Material Components widgets based on Material Design. Material Design is a system of best-practice guidelines for user interface design. The components in a Flutter project include visual, behavioral, and motion widgets. Flutter projects also include unit testing for widgets, which are files that contain individual code to test whether the logic performs as designed.

Flutter applications are built with the Dart programming language, and you will learn the basics of Dart in Chapter 3, "Learning Dart Basics."

TRY IT OUT   Creating a New App

In this exercise, you will be creating a new Flutter app named `ch2_my_counter`. The app name is the same as the project name. This app uses the minimal default Flutter project template and includes a floating action button (the + button) that appears at the bottom right of the device screen. Every time this button is tapped, a counter increases by one.

The current Flutter template creates the basic app that has a counter and a + button (the floating action button). In future Flutter releases, there might be other template options available. Why did the Flutter team decide to use a counter as the template? It's clever because it shows how to take data, manipulate it, and maintain state (the counter value) with *hot reload*.

1. Start Android Studio.

2. If you have a project open, click the menu bar and select File ➪ New ➪ New Flutter Project. If no project is open, click Start A New Flutter Project.

3. Select Flutter Application.

4. The customary naming convention is to separate words with an underscore, so enter the project name **ch2_my_counter** and click Next. Note that the Flutter SDK path is the installation folder you have chosen in Chapter 1. You can optionally change the project location and description.

5. Enter your company name in the Company Domain field, and format it like `domainname.com`. Use any unique name if you do not have a company name.

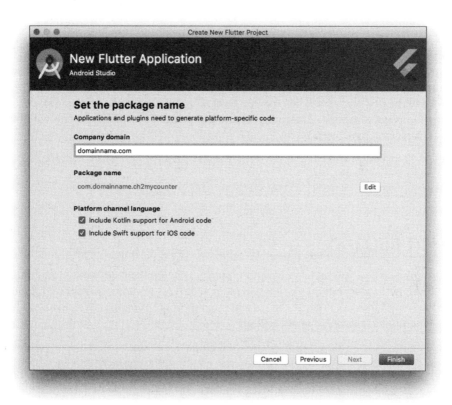

6. On the same screen as step 5 for the Platform Channel Language, select both the options for Kotlin and Swift.

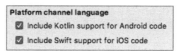

These choices will ensure that you are using the latest programming languages for both Android (Kotlin) and iOS (Swift). Using the platform channel—a way for communicating between the app's Dart code and platform-specific code—allows you to use Android and iOS platform-specific application programming interfaces (APIs) by writing code in each native language, such as writing native code in Kotlin (Android) and Swift (iOS) to handle playing audio while the app is in background mode. You will take a closer look at platform channels, Kotlin, and Swift in Chapter 12, "Writing Platform-Native Code."

7. Click the Finish button.

How It Works

A Flutter project is created with the folder name ch2_my_counter, the same as the project name. It uses the standard Flutter project template, which shows how to update a counter by tapping the + button. By default, Android's Material Design components are used. In a Flutter project, these include visual, behavioral, and motion widgets. For each project you create, there is a directory called lib, and the main.dart file will be first executed when the app runs. The main.dart file contains Dart code with the main() function that starts the app. The goal of creating this app is to familiarize you with how a Flutter application is created and structured.

Chapter 3 covers Dart basics, and Chapter 4 covers the main.dart file in more detail, particularly how you structure and separate code logic.

USING HOT RELOAD

Flutter's hot reload helps you see code and user interface changes immediately while retaining state to an app running the Dart virtual machine. In other words, every time you make code changes, you don't need to reload the app, because the current page shows the changes immediately. This is an incredible time-saving feature for any developer.

In Flutter, the State class stores mutable (changeable) data. For example, the app starts with the counter value set to zero, but each time you tap the + button, the counter value increases by one. When the + button is tapped three times, the counter value shows a value of three. The counter value is mutable, so it can change over time. By using hot reload, you can make code logic changes, and the app's counter state (value) does not reset to zero but instead retains the current value of three.

TRY IT OUT   Running the App

To see how hot reload works, you'll start the emulator/simulator, make changes to the page title, save them, and see the changes happen immediately.

From Chapter 1, the iOS simulator was automatically created when you installed Xcode, and you manually created the Android emulator. The iOS simulator is available only if running Android Studio on a Mac computer because it requires Apple's Xcode to be installed. It's assumed that you have both the iOS simulator and Android emulator installed. If not, use the Android emulator.

1.   From Android Studio, click the Flutter device selection button on the right of the toolbar. A drop-down list shows the available iOS simulator and Android emulator.

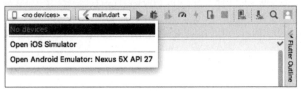

2.   Select either the iOS simulator or the Android emulator.

3.   Click the Run icon in the toolbar.

Run   Reload

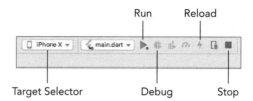

Target Selector   Debug   Stop

4. You should see the `ch2_my_counter` app in the simulator. Follow step 2 to run the app on both the iOS simulator (if available) and the Android emulator. Running the app on both iOS and Android, it is apparent that it looks the same but inherits the traits from each mobile operating system. Note in the iOS simulator that the app title is centered, but in the Android emulator, the title is on the left.

5. Click the + floating action button on the bottom right, and you will see the counter increase each time you click it.

6. In the `main.dart` file, change `MyHomePage(title: 'Flutter Demo Home Page')` to `MyHomePage(title: 'Hello World')` and save by pressing ⌘ (in Windows ⊞). Immediately you will see that the app bar title changes and the state of the counter remains the same, without resetting to zero. This instant change is called *hot reload*, and you'll use it often to improve your productivity.

How It Works

Hot reload is an incredible time-saving feature to view the results of source code changes immediately while keeping the current state. While the Dart virtual machine is running, hot reload injects the updated source code, and the Flutter framework rebuilds the widget tree. (The widget tree will be covered in detail in Chapter 5, "Understanding the Widget Tree.")

USING THEMES TO STYLE YOUR APP

The theme widgets are a great way to style and define global colors and font styles for your app. There are two ways to use theme widgets—to style the look and feel globally or to style just a portion of the app. For instance, you can use themes to style the color brightness (light text on a dark background or vice versa); the primary and accent colors; the canvas color; and the color of app bars, cards, dividers, selected and unselected options, buttons, hints, errors, text, icons, and so on. The beauty of Flutter is that most items are widgets, and just about everything is customizable. In fact, customizing the `ThemeData` class allows you to change the color and typography of widgets. (You'll learn more about widgets in detail in Chapter 5, "Understanding the Widget Tree," and Chapter 6, "Using Common Widgets.")

Using a Global App Theme

Let's take the new `ch2_my_counter` app and modify the primary color. The current color is blue, so let's change it to light green. Add a new line below the `primarySwatch` and add code to change the background color (`canvasColor`) to `lightGreen`.

```
primarySwatch: Colors.blue,
// Change it to
primarySwatch: Colors.lightGreen,
canvasColor: Colors.lightGreen.shade100,
```

Save by pressing ⌘ (in Windows 🪟). Hot reload is invoked, so the app bar and the canvas are now both a light shade of green.

To show a little Flutter awesomeness, add a `platform` property of `TargetPlatform.iOS` after the `canvasColor` property, and run the app from the Android emulator. Suddenly, the iOS traits are running on Android. The app bar's title is not left aligned but changed to the center, which is the customary iOS style (Figure 2.1).

```
primarySwatch: Colors.blue,
// Change it to
primarySwatch: Colors.lightGreen,
canvasColor: Colors.lightGreen.shade100,
platform: TargetPlatform.iOS
```

This can be done in reverse by using `TargetPlatform`. Specifically, to show Android traits on iOS, change the `platform` property to `TargetPlatform.android` and run the app from the iOS simulator. The app bar's title is not center aligned but has changed to be left aligned, which is the customary Android style (Figure 2.2). Once navigation with multiple pages is implemented, this will be even more apparent. In iOS when navigating to a new page, you usually slide the next page from the right side of the screen towards the left. In Android when navigating to a new page, you usually slide the next page from bottom to top. `TargetPlatform` has three choices: Android, Fuchsia (the operating system under development from Google), and iOS.

```
primarySwatch: Colors.blue,
// Change it to
primarySwatch: Colors.lightGreen,
canvasColor: Colors.lightGreen.shade100,
platform: TargetPlatform.android
```

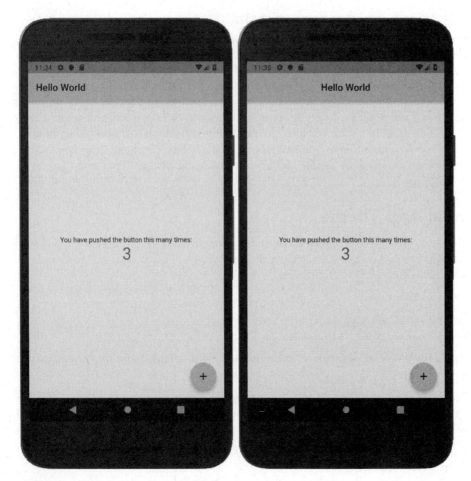

FIGURE 2.1: iOS traits running in Android

Here's another example of using a global app theme: if you have a red debug banner on the upper right of the emulator, you can turn it off with the following code. Google intended to let developers know that the app performance is not in release mode. Flutter builds a debug version of the app, and performance is slower. Using release (device only) mode, it creates an app with speed optimization. Add the debugShowCheckedModeBanner property and set the value to false, and the red debug banner is removed. Turning off the red debug banner is for aesthetic purposes only; you are still running a debug version of the app.

```
return new MaterialApp(
  debugShowCheckedModeBanner: false,
  title: 'My Counter',
  theme: new ThemeData(
    ...
```

FIGURE 2.2: Android traits running in iOS

Using a Theme for Part of an App

To override the app-wide theme, you can wrap widgets in a `Theme` widget. This method will completely override the app `ThemeData` instance without inheriting any styles.

In the previous section, you changed `primarySwatch` and `canvasColor` to `lightGreen`, which affected all widgets in the app. What if you want only one widget on a page to have a different color scheme and the rest of the widgets to use the default global app theme? You override the default theme with a `Theme` widget that uses the `data` property to customize `ThemeData` (such as `card-Color`, `primaryColor`, and `canvasColor`), and the child widget uses the `data` property to customize the colors.

```
body: Center(
  child: Theme(
    // Unique theme with ThemeData - Overwrite
```

```
      data: ThemeData(
        cardColor: Colors.deepOrange,
      ),
      child: Card(
        child: Text('Unique ThemeData'),
      ),
    ),
  ),
```

I recommend extending the app parent theme, changing only the properties needed and inheriting the rest. Use the copyWith method to create a copy of the app parent theme and replace only the properties that you need to change. Breaking it down, Theme.of(context).copyWith() extends the parent Theme, and you can override the properties needed inside copyWith(cardColor: Colors.deepOrange).

```
body: Center(
  child: Theme(
    // copyWith Theme - Inherit (Extended)
    data: Theme.of(context).copyWith(cardColor: Colors.deepOrange),
    child: Card(
      child: Text('copyWith Theme'),
    ),
  ),
),
```

The following sample code shows how to change the default Card color to deepOrange with Theme overwritten (ThemeData()) and extended (Theme.of().copyWith()) to produce the same result. The two Theme widgets are wrapped inside a Column widget to align them vertically. At this point, do not worry about the Column widget, as it's covered in Chapter 6.

```
body: Column(
  children: <Widget>[
    Theme(
      // Unique theme with ThemeData - Overwrite
      data: ThemeData(
        cardColor: Colors.deepOrange,
      ),
      child: Card(
        child: Text('Unique ThemeData'),
      ),
    ),
    Theme(
      // copyWith Theme - Inherit (Extended)
      data: Theme.of(context).copyWith(cardColor: Colors.deepOrange),
      child: Card(
        child: Text('copyWith Theme'),
      ),
    ),
  ],
),
```

UNDERSTANDING STATELESS AND STATEFUL WIDGETS

Flutter widgets are the building blocks for designing the user interface (UI). Widgets are built using a modern react-style framework. The UI is created by nesting widgets together into a *widget tree*.

Flutter's react-style framework means it observes when the state of a widget changes and then compares it to the previous state to determine the least number of changes to make. Flutter manages the relationship between the state and the UI and rebuilds only those widgets when the state changes.

In this section, you'll compare stateless and stateful widgets and learn how to implement each class and most importantly which one to use depending on the requirement. In later chapters, you'll create apps for each scenario. The appropriate class is extended (making it a subclass) by using the keyword extends followed by either StatelessWidget or StatefulWidget.

StatelessWidget is used when data does not change, and it relies on the initial information. It's a widget without state, and the values are final. Some examples are Text, Button, Icon, and Image.

```
class Instructions extends StatelessWidget {
  @override
  Widget build(BuildContext context) {
    return Text('When using a StatelessWidget...');
  }
}
```

StatefulWidget is used when data changes. It's a widget with state that might change over time, requiring two classes. For changes to propagate to the UI, making a call to the setState() method is necessary.

➤ StatefulWidget class—This creates an instance of the State class.

➤ State class—This is for data that can be read synchronously when the widget is built and might change over time.

➤ setState()—From within the State class, you make a call to the setState() method to refresh changed data, telling the framework that the widget should redraw because the state has changed. For all the variables that need changes, modify the values in setState(() { _myValue += 50.0;}). Any variable values modified outside the setState() method will not refresh the UI. Therefore, it is best to place calculations that do not need state changes outside the setState() method.

Consider the example of a page that shows your maximum bid on a product. Every time the Increase Bid button is tapped, your bid increases by $50. You begin by creating a MaximumBid class that extends the StatefulWidget class. Create a _MaximumBidState class that extends the state of the MaximumBid class.

In the _MaximumBidState class, you declare a variable named _maxBid. The _increaseMyMaxBid() method calls the setState() method, which increments the _maxBid value by $50. The UI consists of a `Text` widget that shows the `'My Maximum Bid: $_maxBid'` value and a `FlatButton` with an `onPressed` property that calls the `_increaseMyMaxBid()` method. The `_increaseMyMaxBid()` method executes the `setState()` method, which adds $50 to the `_maxBid` variable, and the `Text` widget amount is redrawn.

```
class MaximumBid extends StatefulWidget {
  @override
  _MaximumBidState createState() => _MaximumBidState();
}

class _MaximumBidState extends State<MaximumBid> {
  double _maxBid = 0.0;

  void _increaseMyMaxBid() {
    setState(() {
      // Add $50 to my current bid
      _maxBid += 50.0;
    });
  }

  @override
  Widget build(BuildContext context) {
    return Column(
      children: <Widget>[
        Text('My Maximum Bid: $_maxBid'),
        FlatButton.icon(
            onPressed: () => _increaseMyMaxBid(),
            icon: Icon(Icons.add_circle),
            label: Text('Increse Bid'),
        ),
      ],
    );
  }
}
```

USING EXTERNAL PACKAGES

Sometimes it's not worth building a widget from scratch. Flutter supports third-party packages for the Flutter and Dart ecosystems. Packages contain the source code logic and are easily shared. There are two types of packages, Dart and plugin.

➤ Dart packages are written in Dart and may contain Flutter-specific dependencies.

➤ Plugin packages are written in Dart (with the Dart code exposing the API) but are combined with platform-specific code implementations for Android (Java or Kotlin) and/or iOS (Objective-C or Swift). Most plugin packages aim to support both Android and iOS.

Let's say you are looking to add functionality to your app such as showing some charts, accessing a device's GPS locations, playing background audio, or accessing a database like Firebase. There are packages for all that.

Searching for Packages

In the app, say you need to store the user preferences on both iOS and Android and want to find a package to do that for you.

1. Start your web browser and navigate to `https://pub.dartlang.org/flutter`. Packages are published at this location often by other developers and Google.

2. Click the Search Flutter Packages search bar. Enter **shared preferences**, and the results will be sorted by relevance.

3. Click the link for the `shared_preferences` package. (The direct link is `https://pub.dart-lang.org/packages/shared_preferences`.)

4. Details on how to install and use the `shared_preferences` package are available at this location. The Flutter team authors this particular package. Click the Installing tab for detailed instructions. Each package has instructions on how to install and use it. Most of the packages' installation is similar, but they differ on how to use and implement the code. The instructions are located on the home page of each package.

TRY IT OUT Installing Packages

You've learned how to find third-party packages. Next you'll learn how to implement the `shared_pref-erences` external package in your app.

1. Open the `ch2_my_counter` app with Android Studio.

2. Open the `pubspec.yaml` file by double-clicking.

3. In the `dependencies:` section, add `shared_preferences: ^0.5.1+1`. (Your version might be higher.)

4. Save the file, and the package will install. If you do not see the process automatically run, you can manually invoke it by entering `flutter packages get` in your Terminal window in Android Studio. Once finished, the message will say `Process finished with exit code 0`.

5. Import the package in the `main.dart` file after the `material.dart` import line, located at the top of the file. Save the changes.

```
import 'package:flutter/material.dart';
import 'package:shared_preferences/shared_preferences.dart';
```

How It Works

By adding the `shared_preference` dependencies in the `pubspec.yaml` file, the dependencies are downloaded to the local project. Use the `import` statement to make the `shared_preference` package available.

Using Packages

Each package has its unique way of being implemented. It's always good to read the documentation. For the `shared_preferences` package, you need to add a few lines to implement it. Please remember the main point here is not how to use this package but how to add external packages to your app in general.

TRY IT OUT Implementing and Initializing a Package

In the `_MyHomePageState` class, add a function called `_updateSharedPreferences()`.

```
class _MyHomePageState extends State<MyHomePage> {
  // ...
  void _updateSharedPreferences() async {
    SharedPreferences prefs = await SharedPreferences.getInstance();
    int counter = (prefs.getInt('counter') ?? 0) + 1;
```

```
        print('Pressed $counter times.');
        await prefs.setInt('counter', counter);
      }
      // ...
    }
```

How It Works

This package saves users' preferences in both iOS and Android with a few lines of Dart code, which is extremely powerful. There's no need to write native code for iOS or Android. This is the power of using packages, but be careful of overdoing it because you are relying on the authors of the packages to keep them up-to-date.

SUMMARY

In this chapter, you learned how to create your first app and use hot reload to view changes instantaneously. You also saw how to use themes to style apps, when to use stateless and stateful widgets, and how to add external packages to save yourself from reinventing the wheel. You now have a general understanding of the main ideas behind Flutter app development. Do not worry about understanding the actual code yet. You'll learn all about it throughout the book.

In the next chapter, you'll learn the basics of the Dart language that is used to create Flutter apps.

▶ WHAT YOU LEARNED IN THIS CHAPTER

TOPIC	KEY CONCEPTS
Creating a Flutter app	You can now code a basic app and lay out widgets.
Using hot reload	Hot reload shows code changes immediately in a running app while maintaining state.
Applying a theme	Themes set the style and colors throughout an app.
Using external packages	External packages search for and install third-party packages to add functionalities such as GPS, charting, and more.

3

Learning Dart Basics

WHAT YOU WILL LEARN IN THIS CHAPTER

➤ Why you use Dart

➤ How to comment code

➤ How to use the top-level `main()` function

➤ How to reference variables such as numbers, strings, Booleans, lists, maps, and runes

➤ How common flow statements (such as `if`, `for`, `while`, and the ternary operator), loops, and `switch` and `case` work

➤ How functions are used to group reusable logic

➤ How to use the `import` statement for external packages, libraries or classes

➤ How to create classes

➤ How to use asynchronous programming to avoid blocking the user interface

Dart is the foundation of learning to develop Flutter projects. In this chapter, you'll start understanding Dart's basic structure. In future chapters, you'll create apps that implement these concepts. All the sample code is in the `ch3_dart_basics` folder. (In the sample code, don't worry about how it's laid out; just take a look so you can see how Dart code is written. Tap the floating action button located on the bottom right to see log results.)

WHY USE DART?

Before you can start developing Flutter apps, you need to understand the programming language used, namely, Dart. Google created Dart and uses it internally with some of its big products such as Google AdWords. Made available publicly in 2011, Dart is used to build mobile, web, and server applications. Dart is productive, fast, portable, approachable, and most of all reactive.

Dart is an object-oriented programming (OOP) language, has a class-based style, and uses a C-style syntax. If you are familiar with the C#, C++, Swift, Kotlin, and Java/JavaScript languages, you will be able to start developing in Dart quickly. But don't worry—even if you are not familiar with these other languages, Dart is a straightforward language to learn, and you can get started relatively quickly.

What are some of the benefits of using Dart?

➤ Dart is *ahead-of-time* (AOT) compiled to native code, making your Flutter app fast. In other words, there's no intermediary to interpret one language to another, and there are no bridges. AOT compilation is used when compiling your app for release mode (such as to the Apple App Store and Google Play).

➤ Dart also is *just-in-time* (JIT) compiled, making it fast to display your code changes such as via Flutter's stateful hot reload feature. JIT compilation is used when debugging your app by running it in the simulator/emulator.

➤ Since Flutter uses Dart, all the sample user interface (UI) code in this book is written in Dart, removing the need to use separate languages (markup, visual designer) to create the UI.

➤ Flutter rendering runs at 60 frames per second (fps) and 120fps (for capable devices of 120Hz). The more fps, the smoother the app.

COMMENTING CODE

In any app, comments help the readability of the code, as long as they're not overdone. Comments can be used to describe the logic and dependencies of the app.

There are three types of comments: single-line, multiline, and documentation comments. Single-line comments are commonly used to add a short description. Multiline comments are best suited for long descriptions that span multiple lines. Documentation comments are used to fully document a piece of code logic, usually giving detailed explanations and sample code in the comments.

Single-line comments begin with //, and the Dart compiler ignores everything to the end of the line.

```
// Retrieve from the database the list filtered by company
_listOrders.get(...
```

Multiline comments begin with /* and end with */. The Dart compiler ignores everything between the slashes.

```
/*
 * Allow users to filter by multiple options
 _listOrders.get(filterBy: _userFilter...
*/
```

Documentation comments begin with ///, and the Dart compiler ignores everything to the end of the line unless enclosed in brackets. Using brackets, you can refer to classes, methods, fields, top-level variables, functions, and parameters. In the following example, the generated documentation, `[FilterBy]`, becomes a link to the API documentation for the class. You can use the SDK's documentation generation tool (dartdoc) to parse Dart code and generate HTML documentation.

```
/// Multiple filter options
///
/// Different [FilterBy]
enum FilterBy {
    COMPANY,
    CITY,
    STATE
}
```

RUNNING THE MAIN() ENTRY POINT

Every app must have a top-level `main()` function, which is the entry point to the app. The `main()` function is where the app execution starts and returns a `void` with an optional `List<String>` parameter for arguments. Each function can return a value, and for the `main()` function the data return type is a `void` (empty, contains nothing), meaning that it does not return a value.

In the following code, you see three different ways to use the `main()` function, but in all the example projects in this book, you will be using the first example—the arrow syntax `void main() =>` `runApp(MyApp());`. All three ways to call the `main()` function are acceptable, but I prefer using the arrow syntax since it keeps the code on one line for better readability. However, the main reason to use the arrow syntax is that in all the example projects there is no need to call multiple statements. The arrow syntax `=> runApp(MyApp())` is the same as `{ runApp(MyApp()); }`.

```
// arrow syntax
void main() => runApp(MyApp());

// or
void main() {
    runApp(MyApp());
}

// or with a List of Strings parameters
void main(List<Strings> filters) {
    print('filters: $filters');
}
```

REFERENCING VARIABLES

In the previous section, you learned that `main()` is the top-level entry to an app, and before you start writing code, it's important to learn about Dart variables. Variables store *references* to a value. Some of the built-in variable types are numbers, strings, Booleans, lists, maps, and runes. You can use `var` to declare (you will learn declaring variables in the next section) a variable without specifying the type. Dart infers the type of variable automatically. Although there is nothing wrong with using `var`, as a personal preference, I usually stay away from using it unless I need to do so. Declaring the variable type makes for better code readability, and it's easier to know which type of value is expected. Instead of using `var`, use the variable type expected: `double`, `String`, and so on. (The variable types are covered in the "Declaring Variables" section.)

An uninitialized variable has a value of `null`. When declaring a variable without giving it an initial value, it's called *uninitialized*. For example, a variable of type `String` is declared like `String bookTitle`; and is uninitialized because the `bookTitle` value equals `null` (no value). However, if you declare it with an initial value of `String bookTitle = 'Beginning Flutter'`, the `bookTitle` value equals `'Beginning Flutter'`.

Use `final` or `const` when the variable is not intended to change the initial value. Use `const` for variables that need to be *compile-time constants*, meaning the value is known at compile time.

DECLARING VARIABLES

Now you know that variables store references to a value. Next, you'll learn different options for declaring variables.

In Dart, all variables are declared public (available to all) by default, but by starting the variable name with an underscore (_), you can declare it as private. By declaring a variable private, you are saying it cannot be accessed from outside classes/functions; in other words, it can be used only from within the declaration class/function. (You will learn about classes and functions in the "Functions" and "Classes" sections later in this chapter.) Note some built-in Dart variable types are lowercase like `double` and some uppercase like `String`.

What if the value of a variable doesn't need to change? Begin the declaration of the variable with `final` or `const`. Use `final` when the value is assigned at runtime (can be changed by the user). Use `const` when the value is known at compile time (in code) and will not change at runtime.

```
// Declared without specifying the type - Infers type
var filter = 'company';

// Declared by type
String filter = 'company';

// Uninitialized variable has an initial value of null
String filter;

// Value will not change
final filter = 'company';

// or
final String filter = 'company';

// or
const String filter = 'company';

// or
const String filter = 'company' + filterOption;
```

```
// Public variable (variable name starts without underscore)
String userName = 'Sandy';

// Private variable (variable name starts with underscore)
String _userID = 'XW904';
```

Numbers

Declaring variables as numbers restricts the values to numbers only. Dart allows numbers to be `int` (integer) or `double`. Use the `int` declaration if your numbers do not require decimal point precision, like 10 or 40. Use the `double` declaration if your numbers require decimal point precision, like 50.25 or 135.7521. Both `int` and `double` allow for positive and negative numbers, and you can enter extremely large numbers and decimal precision since they both use 64-bit (computer memory) values.

```
// Integer
int counter = 0;
double price = 0.0;
price = 125.00;
```

Strings

Declaring variables as `string` allows values to be entered as a sequence of text characters. To add a single line of characters, you can use single or double quotes like `'car'` or `"car"`. To add multiline characters, use triple quotes, like `'''car'''`. Strings can be concatenated (combined) by using the plus (+) operator or by using adjacent single or double quotes.

```
// Strings
String defaultMenu = 'main';

// String concatenation
String combinedName = 'main' + ' ' + 'function';
String combinedNameNoPlusSign = 'main' ' ' 'function';

// String multi-line
String multilineAddress = '''
  123 Any Street
  City, State, Zip
''';
```

Booleans

Declaring variables as `bool` (Boolean) allows a value of `true` or `false` to be entered.

```
// Booleans
bool isDone = false;
isDone = true;
```

Lists

Declaring variables as `List` (comparable to arrays) allows multiple values to be entered; a `List` is an ordered group of objects. In programming, an array is an iterable (accessed sequentially) collection of objects, with each element accessible by the index position or a key. To access elements, the `List` uses zero-based indexing, where the first element index is at 0, and the last element is at the List length (number of rows) minus 1 (since the first index is 0, not 1).

A List can be of fixed length or growable, depending on your needs. By default, a List is created as growable by using List() or []. To create a fixed-length List, you add the number of rows required by using this format: List(25). The following example uses string interpolation for the print statement: print('filter: $filter'). The $ sign before the variable converts the expression value to a string.

```
// List Growable
List contacts = List();

// or
List contacts = [];
List contacts = ['Linda', 'John', 'Mary'];

// List fixed-length
List contact = List(25);

// Lists - In Dart List is an array
List listOfFilters = ['company', 'city', 'state'];
listOfFilters.forEach((filter) {
    print('filter: $filter');
});
// Result from print statement
// filter: company
// filter: city
// filter: state
```

Maps

Maps are invaluable in associating a List of values by a Key and a Value. Mapping allows recalling values by their Key ID. The Key and Value can be any type of object, such as String, Number, and so on. Keep in mind that the Key needs to be unique since the Value is retrieved by the Key.

```
// Maps - An object that associates keys and values.
// Key: Value - 'KeyValue': 'Value'
Map mapOfFilters = {'id1': 'company', 'id2': 'city', 'id3': 'state'};

// Change the value of third item with Key of id3
mapOfFilters['id3'] = 'my filter';

print('Get filter with id3: ${mapOfFilters['id3']}');
// Result from print statement
// Get filter with id3: my filter
```

Runes

In Dart, declaring variables as Runes are the UTF-32 code points of a String. Emojis, anyone?

Unicode defines a numeric value for each letter, digit, and symbol. Dart uses the sequence of UTF-16 code units to represent a 32-bit Unicode value from a string require a special syntax (\uXXXX). A Unicode code point is \uXXXX, where XXXX is a four-digit hexadecimal value. Runes return the integer value of the Unicode; then you use `String.fromCharCodes()` to allocate a new `String` for the specified `charCode`.

```
// Emoji smiling angel Unicode is u+1f607
// Remove the Plus sign and replace with curly brackets
Runes myEmoji = Runes('\u{1f607}');
print(myEmoji);
// Result from print statement
// (128519)

print(String.fromCharCodes(myEmoji));
// Result from print statement
// 😇
```

USING OPERATORS

An operator is a symbol used to perform arithmetic, equality, relational, type test, assignment, logical, conditional, and cascade notation. Tables 3.1 through 3.7 go over some of the common operators. For the sample code, I use the values directly to simplify the examples instead of using variables.

TABLE 3.1: Arithmetic operators

OPERATOR	DESCRIPTION	SAMPLE CODE
+	Add	`7 + 3 = 10`
-	Subtract	`7 - 3 = 4`
*	Multiply	`7 * 3 = 21`
/	Divide	`7 / 3 = 2.33`

TABLE 3.2: Equality and relational operators

OPERATOR	DESCRIPTION	SAMPLE CODE
==	Equal	`7 == 3 = false`
!=	Not equal	`7 != 3 = true`
>	Greater than	`7 > 3 = true`
<	Less than	`7 < 3 = false`
>=	Greater than or equal to	`7 >= 3 = true` `4 >= 4 true`
<=	Less than or equal to	`7<= 3 = false` `4 <= 4 = true`

TABLE 3.3: Type test operators

OPERATOR	DESCRIPTION	SAMPLE CODE
as	Typecast like import library prefixes.	import 'travelpoints .dart' as travel;
is	If the object contains the specified type, it evaluates to true.	if (points is Places) = true
is!	If the object contains the specified type, it evaluates to false (not usually used).	if (points is! Places) = false

TABLE 3.4: Assignment operators

OPERATOR	DESCRIPTION	SAMPLE CODE
=	Assigns value	7 = 3 = 3
??=	Assigns value only if variable being assigned to has a value of null	Null ??= 3 = 3 7 ??= 3 = 7
+=	Adds to current value	7 += 3 = 10
-=	Subtracts from current value	7 -= 3 = 4
*=	Multiplies from current value	7 *= 3 = 21
/=	Divides from current value	7 /= 3 = 2.33

TABLE 3.5: Logical operators

OPERATOR	DESCRIPTION	SAMPLE CODE
!	! is a logical 'not'. Returns the opposite value of the variable/expression.	if (!(7 > 3)) = false
&&	&& is a logical 'and'. Returns true if the values of the variable/expression are all true.	if ((7 > 3) && (3 < 7)) = true if ((7 > 3) && (3 > 7)) = false
!!	!! is a logical 'or'. Returns true if at least one value of the variable/expression is true.	if ((7 > 3) || (3 > 7)) = true if ((7 < 3) || (3 > 7)) = false

TABLE 3.6: Conditional expressions

OPERATOR	DESCRIPTION	SAMPLE CODE

condition
? value1 :
value2
	If the condition evaluates to `true`, it returns `value1`. If the condition evaluates to `false`, it returns `value2`. The value can also be obtained by calling methods.	`(7 > 3) ? true :`
		`false = true`
		`(7 < 3) ? true :`
		`false = false`

TABLE 3.7: Cascade notation (..)

OPERATOR	DESCRIPTION	SAMPLE CODE

`..`	The cascade notation is represented by double dots (..) and allows you to make a sequence of operations on the same object.	`Matrix4.identity()`
		`..scale(1.0, 1.0)`
		`..translate(30,`
		`30);`

USING FLOW STATEMENTS

To control the logic flow of the Dart code, take a look at the following flow statements:

➤ `if` and `else` are the most common flow statements; they decide which code to run by comparing multiple scenarios.

➤ The ternary operator is similar to the `if` and `else` statements but used when only two choices are needed.

➤ `for` loops allow iterating a `List` of values.

➤ `while` and `do-while` are a common pair. Use the `while` loop to evaluate the condition before running the loop, and use `do-while` to evaluate the condition after the loop.

➤ `while` and `break` are useful if you need to stop evaluating the condition in the loop.

➤ `continue` is for when you need to stop the current loop and start the next loop iteration.

➤ `switch` and `case` are alternatives to the `if` and `else` statements, but they require a default clause.

if and else

The `if` statement compares an expression, and if `true`, it executes the code logic. The expression is wrapped by open and close parentheses followed by the code logic wrapped in braces. The `if` statement also supports multiple optional `else` statements, which are used to evaluate multiple scenarios. There are two types of `else` statements: `else if` and `else`. You can use multiple `else if` statements, but you can have only one `else` statement, usually used as a catchall scenario.

In the following example, the `if` statement is checking whether the store is open or closed and whether items are out of stock or nothing matched. `isClosed`, `isOpen`, and `isOutOfStock` are `bool` variables. The first `if` statement checks whether the `isClosed` variable is `true`, and if yes, it prints to the log `'Store is closed'`. How does it know you are checking for `true` or `false` without the equality operator? When checking for `bool` values, the `if` statement checks by default if the variable is `true`; this is the equivalent of `isClosed == true`. To check whether a variable is `false`, you can use the not equal (`!=`) operator like `isClosed != true` or the equality (`==`) operator like `isClosed == false`. The `else if` statement (`isOpen`) checks whether the `isOpen` variable equals `true`, and it's the same for the `else if (isOutOfStock)` variable. The last `else` statement does not have a condition; it's a catchall scenario if none of the other conditions is met.

```
// If and else
if (isClosed) {
    print('Store is closed');
}
else if (isOpen) {
    print('Store is open');
}
else if (isOutOfStock) {
    print('Item is out of stock');
}
else {
    print('Nothing matched');;
}
```

ternary operator

The ternary operator takes three arguments, and it's usually used when only two actions are needed. The ternary operator checks the first argument for comparison, the second is the action if the argument is `true`, and the third is the action if the argument is `false` (see Table 3.8).

TABLE 3.8: ternary operator

COMPARISON		TRUE		FALSE
isClosed	?	askToOpen()	:	askToClose()

This will look familiar to you from the "Operators" section's conditional expressions because it's used often to make code flow decisions.

```
// Shorter way of if and else statement
isClosed ? askToOpen() : askToClose();
```

for Loops

The standard `for` loop allows you to iterate a `List` of values. Values are obtained by restricting the number of loops by a defined length. An example is to loop through the top three values, which means you specify the number of times to execute the loop. Using a `List` of values also allows you to use the `for-in` type of `Iteration`. The `Iteration` class needs to be of type `Iterable` (a collection of values), and the List class conforms to this type. Unlike the standard for loop, the for-in loop iterates through every object in the List, exposing each object's properties values.

Let's take a look at two examples showing how to use the standard for loop and the for-in loops. In the first example, you'll use the standard for loop and iterate through a List of String values with the listOfFilters variable. The standard for loop takes three parameters.

➤ The first parameter initializes the variable i as an int variable counting each loop executed. Since the List uses zero-based indexing, the i variable is initialized with 0 and not 1.

➤ The second parameter controls how many times to loop through the List by comparing the current number of loops (i) to the total number of loops (listOfFilters.length) to execute. Since the List uses zero-based indexing, the i variable value has to be less than the number of rows in the List.

➤ The third parameter increases the number of loops executed by increasing the i variable with each loop. Inside the loop, the print statement is used to show each value from the listOfFilters List.

```
// Standard for loop
List listOfFilters = ['company', 'city', 'state'];
for (int i = 0; i < listOfFilters.length; i++) {
   print('listOfFilters: ${listOfFilters[i]}');
}
// Result from print statement
// listOfFilters: company
// listOfFilters: city
// listOfFilters: state
```

In the following example, you'll use the for-in loop and iterate through a List of int values with the listOfNumbers variable. The for-in loop takes one parameter that exposes the object (listOf-Numbers) properties. You declare the int number variable to access the properties of the listOfNum-bers List. Inside the loop, the print statement is used to show each value from listOfNumbers by using the number variable value.

```
// or for-in loop
List listOfNumbers = [10, 20, 30];
for (int number in listOfNumbers) {
   print('number: $number');
}
// Result from print statement
// number: 10
// number: 20
// number: 30
```

while and do-while

Both the while and do-while loops evaluate a condition and continue to loop as long as the condition returns a value of true. The while loop evaluates the condition before the loop is executed. The do-while loop evaluates the condition after the loop is executed at least once. Let's look at two examples that show how to use the while and do-while loops.

In both examples, the askToOpen() method is called in the loop, executing logic that sets the isClosed variable as a bool value of true or false. Use the while loop if you already have enough information to evaluate the condition (isClosed) before the loop is executed. Use the do-while if you need to execute the loop first before you have enough information to evaluate the condition (isClosed).

In the first example, you'll use the while loop and iterate as long as the isClosed variable returns a value of true. In this case, the loop continues to execute as long as the isClosed variable is true and continues to loop. Once the isClosed variable returns false, the while stops from executing the next loop.

```
// While - evaluates the condition before the loop
while (isClosed){
    askToOpen();
}
```

In the second example, you'll use the do-while loop and iterate as long as the isClosed variable returns a value of true, like the first example. The loop is first executed at least once; then the condition is evaluated, and as long as it returns true, it continues to loop. Once the isClosed variable returns false, do-while stops from executing the next loop.

```
// Do While - evaluates the condition after the loop
do {
    askToOpen();
} while (isClosed);
```

while and break

Using the break statement allows you to stop looping by evaluating a condition inside the while loop.

In this example, the askToOpen() method is called inside the loop by the if statement, executing logic that returns a bool value of true or false. As long as the value returned is false, the loop continues as normal by calling the checkForNewOrder() method. But once askToOpen() returns a value of true, the break statement is executed, stopping the loop. The checkForNewOrder() method is not called, and the entire while statement stops from running again.

```
// Break - to stop loop
while (isClosed) {
    if (askToOpen()) break;
    checkForNewOrder();
}
```

continue

By using the continue statement, you can stop at the current loop location and skip to the start of the next loop iteration.

In this example, the for statement loops through a List of numbers from 10 to 80. Inside the loop, the if statement checks whether the number is less than 30 and greater than 50, and if the condition is met, the continue statement stops the current loop and starts the next iteration. Using the print statement, you see that only the numbers 30, 40, and 50 are printed to the log.

```
// Continue - skip to the next loop iteration
List listOfNumbers = [10, 20, 30, 40, 50, 60, 70, 80];
for (int number in listOfNumbers) {
   if (number < 30 || number > 50) {
      continue;
   }
   print('number: $number'); // Will print number 30, 40, 50
}
```

switch and case

The `switch` statement compares integer, string, or compile-time constants using `==` (equality). The `switch` statement is an alternative to the `if` and `else` statements. The `switch` statement evaluates an expression and uses the `case` clause to match a condition and executes code inside the matching case. Each `case` clause ends by placing a `break` statement as the last line. It's not commonly used, but if you have an empty (no code) `case` clause, the `break` statement is not needed since Dart allows it to fall through. If you need a catchall scenario, you can use the `default` clause to execute code that is not matched by any of the `case` clauses, placed after all the `case` clauses. The `default` clause does not require a `break` statement. Make sure that the last `case` is a `default` clause that executes logic if no previous `case` clause has a match.

In our example, we have the `String coffee` variable initialized to the `'espresso'` value. The `switch` statement uses the `coffee` variable expression where each `case` clause needs to match the `coffee` variable value. When the `case` clause matches the correct value, the code associated with the clause is executed. If none of the `case` clauses matches the `coffee` variable value, the `default` clause is selected and executes the associated code.

```
// switch and case
String coffee = 'espresso';
switch (coffee) {
   case 'flavored':
      orderFlavored();
      break;
   case 'dark-roast':
      orderDarkRoast();
      break;
   case 'espresso':
      orderEspresso();
      break;
   default:
      orderNotAvailable();
}
```

USING FUNCTIONS

Functions are used to group reusable logic. A function can optionally take parameters and return values. I love this feature. Because Dart is an object-oriented language, functions can be assigned to variables or passed as arguments to other functions. If the function executes a single expression, you can use the arrow (`=>`) syntax. All functions return a value by default, and if no return statement is specified, Dart automatically appends to the function body the `return null` statement, which is implicitly added for you.

Since all functions return a value, you start each function by specifying the return type expected. When calling a function and a return value is not needed, then start the function with the `void` type, meaning nothing. Using the `void` type is not required, but it's recommended for readability. But when the function is expected to return a value, start the function with the type of data being passed back (`bool`, `int`, `String`, `List`. . .) and use the `return` statement to pass a value.

The following examples show different ways to create/call functions and return different types of values. The first example shows that the app's `main()` is a function with `void` as the `return` type.

```
// Functions - Our main() is a function
void main() => runApp(new MyApp());
```

The second example has a `void` as the `return` type, but the function takes an `int` as a parameter, and when the code is executed, the `print` statement shows the value to the log terminal. Since the function is expecting a parameter, you call it by passing the value like `orderEspresso(3)`.

```
// Function - pass value
void orderEspresso(int howManyCups) {
    print('Cups #: $howManyCups');
}
orderEspresso(3);
// Result from print statement
// Cups #: 3
```

The third example builds upon the second example of receiving a parameter and returns a `bool` value as a `return` type. Just after the function, a `bool` `isOrderDone` variable is initialized by calling the function and passing a value of three; then the `print` statement shows the `bool` value sent back by the function.

```
// Function - pass value and return value
bool orderEspresso(int howManyCups) {
    print('Cups #: $howManyCups');
    return true;
}
bool isOrderDone = orderEspresso(3);
print('Order Done: $isOrderDone');
// Result from print statement
// Cups #: 3
// Order Done: true
```

The fourth example builds upon the third example by making the function parameter optional by wrapping the `[int howManyCups]` variable inside square brackets.

```
// Function - pass optional value and return value
// Optional value is enclosed in square brackets []
bool orderEspresso1([int howManyCups]) {
    print('Cups #: $howManyCups');
    bool ordered = false;
        if (howManyCups != null) {
            ordered = true;
        }
    return ordered;
```

```
    }
    bool isOrderDone1 = orderEspresso1();
    print('Order Done1: $isOrderDone1');
    // Result from print statement
    // Cups #: null
    // Order Done: false
```

IMPORT PACKAGES

To use an external package, library or an external class, use the `import` statement. Separating code logic into different class files allows you to separate and group code into manageable objects. The `import` statement allows access to external packages and classes. It requires only one argument, which specifies the uniform resource identifier (URI) of the class/library. If the library is created by a package manager, then you specify the `package:` scheme before the URI. If importing a class, you specify the location and class name or the `package:` directive.

```
// Import the material package
import 'package:flutter/material.dart';

// Import external class
import 'charts.dart';

// Import external class in a different folder
import 'services/charts_api.dart';

// Import external class with package: directive
import 'package:project_name/services/charts_api.dart';
```

USING CLASSES

All classes descend from `Object`, the base class for all Dart objects. A class has members (variables and methods) and uses a constructor to create an object. If a constructor is not declared, a default constructor will be provided automatically. The default constructor provided for you has no arguments.

What is a constructor, and why is it needed? A constructor has the same name as the class, with optional parameters. The parameters serve as getters of values when initializing a class for the first time. Dart uses syntactic sugar to make it easy to access values by using the `this` keyword, referring to the current state in the class.

```
// Getter
this.type = type;

// Syntactic Sugar
this.type;
```

A basic class with a constructor would have this simple layout:

```
class Fruit {
    String type;

    // Constructor - Same name as class
    Fruit(this.type);
}
```

The previous example uses a constructor with syntactic sugar, `Fruit(this.type)`, and the constructor is called in this manner: `Fruit = Fruit('apple');`. To use named parameters, enclose the parameter in curly brackets, `Fruit({this.type})`, and call the constructor in this manner: `Fruit = Fruit(type: 'Apple');`. Imagine passing three or four parameters; I prefer to use named parameters to keep the code readable. Each parameter is optional unless you specify with `@required` that it is a required parameter.

```
// Required parameter
Fruit({@required this.type});

// Constructor - With optional parameter name at init
Fruit({this.type});
```

In addition to marking a parameter `@required`, you can add the `assert` statement to show an error if a value is missing. The `assert` statement throws an error during development (debug) mode and has no effect in production code (release).

```
// Constructor - Required parameter plus assert
class Fruit {
  String type;

  Fruit({@required this.type}) : assert(type != null);
}

// Call the Fruit class
Fruit fruit = Fruit(type: 'Apple');
print('fruit.type: ${fruit.type}');
```

In a class, methods are functions that provide logic for an object. Methods can return a value or `void` (no return value, empty).

```
// Method in the class
calculateFruitCalories() {
    // Logic to calculate calories
}
```

Let's look at one example of a class without a constructor and two examples of a class with a constructor and a named constructor.

First let's look at creating a class that does not define a constructor and declares two variables to hold the barista's `name` and `experience`. Since the example does not declare a constructor, a default constructor without any arguments is provided for you. What does this mean? Inside the class, it's the same as if you had typed `BaristaNoConstructor();`, which is a default constructor without arguments. You create an instance of the class by declaring a `BaristaNoConstructor baristaNoConstructor` variable initialized with `BaristaNoConstructor()`, which is the default constructor provided for you. By taking the `baristaNoConstructor` variable, you can use the dot operator like `baristaNoConstructor.experience` and give it a value of 10.

```
// Declare Classes

// Class Default No Arguments Constructor
class BaristaNoConstructor {
    String name;
    int experience;
}
```

```
// Class Default No Arguments Constructor
BaristaNoConstructor baristaNoConstructor = BaristaNoConstructor();
baristaNoConstructor.experience = 10;
print('baristaNoConstructor.experience: ${baristaNoConstructor.experience}');
// baristaNoConstructor.experience: 10
```

Next let's look at creating a class that defines a constructor with named parameters that hold the barista name and experience. This example shows how to add a method whatIsTheExperience() that returns the class's experience variable value. You create an instance of the class by declaring a BaristaWithConstructor barista variable initialized with the BaristaWithConstructor(name: 'Sandy', experience: 10) constructor. The benefits are immediately obvious when creating a class with a constructor. You can initialize each class's variables by passing the values via the constructor. You can still use the dot operator to modify any of the variables, such as barista.experience.

```
// Class Named Constructor
class BaristaWithConstructor {
    String name;
    int experience;

    // Constructor - Named parameters by using { }
    BaristaWithConstructor({this.name, this.experience});

    // Method - return value
    int whatIsTheExperience() {
        return experience;
    }
}


// Class Named Constructor and return value
BaristaWithConstructor barista = BaristaWithConstructor(name: 'Sandy', experience: 10);
int experienceByProperty = barista.experience;
int experienceByFunction = barista.whatIsTheExperience();
print('experienceByProperty: $experienceByProperty');
print('experienceByFunction: $experienceByFunction');
// experienceByProperty: 10
// experienceByFunction: 10
```

Named constructors allow you to implement multiple constructors for a class and provide clear intentions of initialized data.

Now let's look at creating a class that defines a named constructor that holds the barista name and experience. In this example, you'll build upon the previous example and add a second constructor—to be precise, a named constructor. You declare it by using the class name, the dot operator, and the name of the constructor, like BaristaNamedConstructor.baristaDetails(name: 'Sandy', experience: 10), giving you a named constructor using named parameters. You can still use the dot operator to modify any of the variables, such as barista.experience.

```
// Class with additional named constructor
class BaristaNamedConstructor {
    String name;
    int experience;
```

```
    // Constructor - Named parameters { }
    BaristaNamedConstructor({this.name, this.experience});

    // Named constructor - baristaDetails - With named parameters
    BaristaNamedConstructor.baristaDetails({this.name, this.experience});
}

BaristaNamedConstructor barista = BaristaNamedConstructor.baristaDetails(name:
'Sandy', experience: 10);
print('barista.name: ${barista.name} - barista.experience: ${barista.experience}');
// barista.name: Sandy - barista.experience: 10
```

Class Inheritance

In programming, inheritance allows objects to share traits. To inherit from other classes, use the `extends` keyword. Use the `super` keyword to refer to the superclass (the parent class). Constructors are not inherited in the subclass.

In this example, you'll take the previous `BaristaNamedConstructor` class and use inheritance to create a new class that inherits the parent class traits. Declare a new class with the name `BaristaInheritance` using the `extends` keyword and the name of the class you are extending, which here is `BaristaNamedConstructor`. The inherited class constructor looks just a little bit different than the previous declarations; at the end of the constructor, you add a colon (`:`) and `super()`, referring to the superclass. When the `BaristaInheritance` class is initialized, it inherits the parent class traits, meaning it can access variables and methods (class functions) from `BaristaNamedConstructor`.

```
// Class inheritance
class BaristaInheritance extends BaristaNamedConstructor {
  int yearsOnTheJob;

  BaristaInheritance({this.yearsOnTheJob}) : super();
}

// Init Inherited Class
BaristaInheritance baristaInheritance = BaristaInheritance(yearsOnTheJob: 7);
// Assign Parent Class variable
baristaInheritance.name = 'Sandy';
print('baristaInheritance.yearsOnTheJob: ${baristaInheritance.yearsOnTheJob}');
print('baristaInheritance.name: ${baristaInheritance.name}');
```

Class Mixins

Mixins are used to add features to a class and allow you to reuse the class code in different classes. In other words the mixins allow you to access class code between unrelated classes. To use a mixin, you add the `with` keyword followed by one or more mixin names. Place the `with` keyword right after the class name declaration. The class that implements a mixin does not declare a constructor. Usually the mixin class is a collection of methods. In Chapter 7, "Adding Animation to an App," you'll create two animation apps that use mixins. For example, using `AnimationController` relies on `TickerProviderStateMixin`.

In the following example, the mixin class `BaristaMixinNoConstructor` has a method called `findBaristaFromLocation(String location)` that returns a `String`. This method calls the `locateBarista()` service and returns the barista name in a specified location. Usually, you would have multiple methods in the class that perform different code logic.

The class `BaristaWithMixin` uses the `BaristaMixinNoConstructor` mixin class via the `with` keyword. Classes that use a mixin can declare constructors. In this class, you have the method `retrieveBaristaNameFromLocation()` that calls the mixin class method `findBaristaFromLocation(this.location)` to retrieve the barista name from a location. Notice that you call `findBaristaFromLocation(this.location)` without specifying the class it belongs to.

```
// Mixin Class declared without a constructor
class BaristaMixinNoConstructor {

  String findBaristaFromLocation(String location) {
    // Call service to find barista
    String baristaName = BaristaLocator().locateBarista(location);
    return baristaName;
  }
}

// Class using a mixin
class BaristaWithMixin with BaristaMixinNoConstructor {
  String location;

  // Constructor
  BaristaWithMixin({this.location});

  // The power of mixin we have full access to BaristaNamedConstructor
  String retrieveBaristaNameFromLocation() {
    return findBaristaFromLocation(this.location);
  }
}

// Mixin
BaristaWithMixin baristaWithMixin = BaristaWithMixin();
String name = baristaWithMixin.findBaristaFromLocation('Huston');
print('baristaWithMixin name: $name');
// baristaWithMixin name: Sandy
```

IMPLEMENTING ASYNCHRONOUS PROGRAMMING

In a mobile application, you will use a lot of asynchronous, or *async*, programming. Async functions perform time-consuming operations without waiting for the operation to complete. In Dart, to not block the UI, you use functions that return `Future` or `Stream` objects.

A `Future` object represents a value that will be available at some point in the future. For example, calling a web service to retrieve values might be fast or take a long time, and you do not want to stop the user from using the app while the process is running. By using a `Future` object, as the function retrieves values, it returns control to the UI, and the user continues to use the app. Once the values are retrieved, it will update the UI with the new data. In Chapter 13, "Local Persistence: Saving Data," you'll look at how to use `Stream` objects, which allow data to be added or returned in the future. To accomplish this, Dart uses `StreamController` and `Stream`.

The `async` and `await` keywords are used in conjunction. Mark the function as `async` and place the `await` keyword before the function that will return data in the future. Note that functions marked `async` must have a return type assignable to `Future`.

In this example, the `totalCookiesCount()` function implements a `Future` object that returns an int value. To implement a `Future` object, you start the function with `Future<int>` (int or any valid data type), the function name, and the `async` keyword. The code inside the function that returns a future value is marked with the `await` keyword. The `lookupTotalCookiesCountDatabase()` method represents a call to a web server to retrieve data and is preceded by the `await` keyword. The `await` keyword allows the request to be made, and instead of waiting for the data to come back, it continues executing the next block of code. Once the data is retrieved, the code continues to finish the function and returns the value.

```
// Async and await Function with Future - return value of integer
Future<int> totalCookiesCount() async {
    int cookiesCount = await lookupTotalCookiesCountDatabase(); // Returns 33
    return cookiesCount;
}

// Async method to call web server
Future<int> lookupTotalCookiesCountDatabase() async {
  // In a real world app we call the web server to retrieve live data
  return 33;
}

// User pressed button
totalCookiesCount()
    .then((count) {
      print('cookiesCount: ${count}');
    });
print('This will print before cookiesCount');
// This will print before cookiesCount
// cookiesCount: 33
```

SUMMARY

This chapter covered the basics of the Dart language. You learned how to comment your code for better readability and how to use the `main()` function that starts the app. You learned how to declare variables to reference different kinds of values such as numbers, strings, Booleans, lists, and more. You used the `List` to store an array of filters and learned how to iterate through each value. You looked at operator symbols commonly used to perform arithmetic, equality, logical, conditional, and cascade notation. The cascade notation is a powerful operator to make multiple sequence calls on the same object such as scaling and translating (positioning) an object.

To use external packages, libraries and classes, you used the `import` statement. You looked at an example of how to use asynchronous programming with a `Future` object. The example called a simulated web server to look up a total cookie count in the background while the user continued to use the app without interruptions.

Finally, you learned how to use classes to group code logic that used variables to hold data such as a barista name and experience. Classes also define functions that execute code logic such as looking up the barista experience.

In the next chapter, you'll create a starter app. This starter app is the basic template used to start every new project.

▶ WHAT YOU LEARNED IN THIS CHAPTER

TOPIC	KEY CONCEPTS
Commenting the code	There are single-line, multiline, and documentation comments.
Accessing `main()`	`main()` is the top-level function.
Using variables	You can store values such as numbers, strings, Booleans, lists, maps, and runes.
Using operators	An operator is a symbol used to perform arithmetic, equality, relational, type test, assignment, logical, conditional, and cascade notation.
Using flow statements	Flow statements include `if` and `else`, the ternary operator, `for` loops, `while` and `do-while`, `while` and `break`, `continue`, and `switch` and `case`.
Using functions	Functions are used to group reusable logic.
Importing packages	You can use the `import` statement to import external packages, libraries or classes.
Using classes	You can create classes to separate code logic.
Implementing asynchronous programming	You can use asynchronous programming so as to not block the user interface.

Creating a Starter Project Template

WHAT YOU WILL LEARN IN THIS CHAPTER

➤ How to create folders in the project, grouping them by file types

➤ How to separate and structure widgets into different files

In this chapter, you will learn how to create a Flutter starter project and how to structure the widgets. (I'll cover widgets in depth in the next three chapters.) In future chapters, every time you start a new example, I'll refer to this chapter, which contains the steps to create a new starter project. Like when building a home, the foundation is the most critical factor, and the same is true when creating new apps.

CREATING AND ORGANIZING FOLDERS AND FILES

All the example apps created in this book start with the same steps in this chapter for creating a starter project, so I'll refer to this process often. To keep the project code organized, you'll create different folders and files to group similar logic together and to structure the widgets.

TRY IT OUT Creating the Folder Structure

Create a new Flutter project by following the steps in Chapter 2, "Creating a Hello World App."

1. In step 4 of the "Creating a New App" section, enter **ch4_starter_exercise** for the project name and click Next. This app is the sample exercise to structure future projects. Note that the Flutter SDK path is the installation folder you have chosen in Chapter 1. You can optionally change the project location and description.

It's time to create the folder structure to keep you organized. This structure is my personal preference, and depending on the project complexity, you might require more or fewer folders. At the
very least, for every new project, create the pages folder. It contains all the new pages created for
the app, keeping them separate for maintainability.

2. Click the Terminal button at the bottom of the Android Studio window.

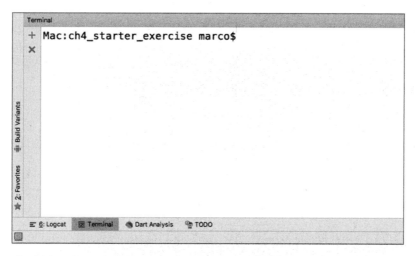

3. To create the folder structures, execute the `mkdir -p folder/subfolder` command. This `mkdir` command creates a folder, and the -p parameter creates a folder and subfolder in one run. The last parameter you pass is the `folder/subfolder` structure.

4. Run each `mkdir` command in the Terminal window to create each folder structure. For example, run the `mkdir -p assets/images` command to create the `assets/images` folders. Repeat the `mkdir` command for each folder structure listed here. For your convenience, I've listed the commands for both Mac and Windows.

```
// From Terminal enter below commands
Mac:starter_exercise marco$ mkdir -p assets/images
Mac:starter_exercise marco$ mkdir -p lib/pages
Mac:starter_exercise marco$ mkdir -p lib/models
Mac:starter_exercise marco$ mkdir -p lib/utils
Mac:starter_exercise marco$ mkdir -p lib/widgets
Mac:starter_exercise marco$ mkdir -p lib/services

// From Windows Command Prompt enter below commands
F:\Pixolini\Flutter\starter_exercise>mkdir assets\images
F:\Pixolini\Flutter\starter_exercise>mkdir lib\pages
F:\Pixolini\Flutter\starter_exercise>mkdir lib\models
F:\Pixolini\Flutter\starter_exercise>mkdir lib\utils
F:\Pixolini\Flutter\starter_exercise>mkdir lib\widgets
F:\Pixolini\Flutter\starter_exercise>mkdir lib\services
```

Take a look at the new folder structures. Not every project will use all of them, but it's a great way to stay organized. The `assets` and `lib` folders are located at the root folder of the project. The `assets` folder contains items such as images, data files, and fonts, and the `lib` folder contains all the source code logic, including the UI.

➤ `assets/images`: The `assets` folder holds subfolders such as images, fonts, and configuration files.

➤ `lib/pages`: The `pages` folder holds user interface (UI) files such as logins, lists of items, charts, and settings.

➤ `lib/models`: The `models` folder holds classes for your data such as customer information and inventory items.

➤ `lib/utils`: The `utils` folder holds helper classes such as date calculations and data conversion.

➤ `lib/widgets`: The `widgets` folder holds different Dart files separating widgets to reuse through the app.

➤ `lib/services`: The `services` folder holds classes that help to retrieve data from services over the Internet. A great example is when using Google Cloud Firestore, Cloud Storage, Realtime Database, Authentication, or Cloud Functions. You can retrieve data from social media accounts, database servers, and so on. In Chapters 14, 15, and 16, you will learn how to use state management to authenticate users, retrieve and sync database records from the cloud by using Cloud Firestore.

How It Works

Using either the Mac Terminal or the Windows command prompt, run the `mkdir` command with the folder name parameter. The `mkdir` command creates the folder structure at the location specified.

STRUCTURING WIDGETS

Before you start developing an app, it's important to create your structure; like when building a house, the foundation is created first. (In Chapter 5, "Understanding the Widget Tree," you'll explore widgets in more detail.) Structuring widgets in an organized manner improves the code's readability and maintainability. When creating a new Flutter project, the software development kit (SDK) does not automatically create the separate home.dart file, which contains the main presentation page when the app starts. Therefore, to have code separation, you must manually create the pages folder and the home.dart file inside it. The main.dart file contains the main() function that starts the app and calls the Home widget in the home.dart file.

TRY IT OUT Creating the Dart Files and Widgets

A great way to learn how Flutter works is to start from a blank slate. Delete all the contents of the main.dart file. The main.dart file has three main sections.

➤ The import package/file

➤ The main() function

➤ A class that extends a StatelessWidget widget and returns the app as a widget (like I said before, just about everything is a widget)

Note for the import package that you'll be using Google's Material Design. All the examples in the book import and use Material Design. In Chapter 2, you learned that Material Design is a system of best-practice guidelines for user interface design. The Material Design components in a Flutter project are *visual*, *behavioral*, and *motion* widgets. Cupertino can also be used to adhere to Apple's iOS design language that supports iOS-style widgets. You can use both standards in different parts of your app. Right off the bat, Flutter is smart enough to show the native actions in both operating systems without you having to worry about it.

For example, by importing the cupertino.dart library, you can mix some of the Cupertino widgets with Material Design. The date and time picker work differently in Android and iOS, and you can specify in the code which widget to show depending on the operating system. However, you'll need to choose up front either Material Design or Cupertino for the entire look and feel of the app. Why? Well, the base of your app needs to be either a MaterialApp widget or a CupertinoApp widget because this determines the availability of widgets. In step 3 of this exercise, you'll learn how to use the MaterialApp widget.

Let's start by adding the code to the main.dart file and saving it.

1. Import the package/file. The default import is the material.dart library to allow the use of Material Design. (To use the Cupertino iOS-style widgets, you import the cupertino.dart library instead of material.dart. For the apps in this book, I'll use Material Design.) Then import the home.dart page located in the pages folder.

```
import 'package:flutter/material.dart';
import 'package:ch4_starter_exercise/pages/home.dart';
```

2. After the two `import` statements, leave a blank line and enter the `main()` function listed next. The `main()` function is the entry point to the app and calls the `MyApp` class.

    ```
    void main() => runApp(MyApp());
    ```

3. Type the `MyApp` class that extends `StatelessWidget`.

    The `MyApp` class returns a `MaterialApp` widget declaring `title`, `theme`, and `home` properties. There are many other `MaterialApp` properties available. Notice that the `home` property calls the `Home()` class, which is created later in the `home.dart` file.

    ```
    class MyApp extends StatelessWidget {
      // This widget is the root of your application.
      @override
      Widget build(BuildContext context) {
        return MaterialApp(
          debugShowCheckedModeBanner: false,
          title: 'Starter Template',
          theme: ThemeData(
            primarySwatch: Colors.blue,
          ),
          home: Home(),
        );
      }
    }
    ```

    Android Studio shows a red squiggly line under the `import` statement `pages/home.dart` as well as the `Home()` method, which has this error: The method "Home" isn't defined for the class `'MyApp'`. By hovering your mouse over `pages/home.dart` and `Home()`, you can read each error.

    ```
    main.dart ×
    1    import 'package:flutter/material.dart';
    2    import 'package:ch4_starter_exercise/pages/home.dart';
    3
    4    void main() => runApp(MyApp());
    5
    6    class MyApp extends StatelessWidget {
    7      // This widget is the root of your application.
    8      @override
    9      Widget build(BuildContext context) {
    10       return MaterialApp(
    11         debugShowCheckedModeBanner: false,
    12         title: 'Starter Template',
    13         theme: ThemeData(
    14           primarySwatch: Colors.blue,
    15         ), // ThemeData
    16         home: Home(),
    17    ┌──────────────────────────────────────────────────┐
    18    │ The method 'Home' isn't defined for the class 'MyApp'. │
    19  } └──────────────────────────────────────────────────┘
    20
    21
    22
    ```

This is normal since you have not created the `home.dart` file containing the home page. This name can be anything you like, but it's always good to have a descriptive name for each page.

4. Create a new Dart file in the `pages` folder. Right-click the `pages` folder, select New ⇨ Dart File, enter **home.dart**, and click the OK button to save.

5. Like in step 1, import the `material.dart` package/file. As a reminder, I'll be using Material Design for all the example apps.

```
import 'package:flutter/material.dart';
```

6. Start typing **st** and—wow—the autocompletion help opens. As you type the abbreviation for a `StatefulWidget` class, the Android Studio Live Templates automatically fills in the Flutter widget's basic structure. Select the `stful` abbreviation.

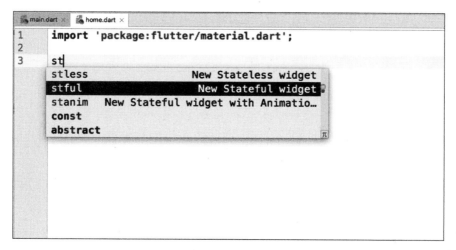

7. Now all you need to do is to give the `StatefulWidget` class its name: `Home`. Since it's a class, the naming convention is to start the word with an uppercase letter.

```
// home.dart
import 'package:flutter/material.dart';

class Home extends StatefulWidget {
  @override
  _HomeState createState() => _HomeState();
}

class _HomeState extends State<Home> {
  @override
  Widget build(BuildContext context) {
    return Container();
  }
}
```

You're using `StatefulWidget` for the `Home` class because in a real-world application most likely a state would be kept for data. An example of when you would need a state is a `PopupMenuItem` widget on the `AppBar` widget showing a selected date used by multiple pages. If the `Home` class does not need to keep state, then use `StatelessWidget`.

```
class Home extends StatelessWidget {
  @override
  Widget build(BuildContext context) {
    return Container();
  }
}
```

8.   Replace the `Container()` widget with a `Scaffold` widget. The `Scaffold` widget implements the basic Material Design visual layout, allowing the simple addition of `AppBar`, `BottomAppBar`, `FloatingActionButton`, `Drawer`, `SnackBar`, `BottomSheet`, and more. (If this were a `CupertinoApp`, you could use either `CupertinoPageScaffold` or `CupertinoTabScaffold`.)

```
class _HomeState extends State<Home> {
  @override
  Widget build(BuildContext context) {
    return Scaffold(
      appBar: AppBar(
        title: Text('Home'),
      ),
      body: Container(),
    );
  }
}
```

The following is the full source code for both the `main.dart` and `home.dart` files:

```
// main.dart
import 'package:flutter/material.dart';
import 'package:ch4_starter_exercise/pages/home.dart';

void main() => runApp(MyApp());

class MyApp extends StatelessWidget {
  // This widget is the root of your application.
  @override
  Widget build(BuildContext context) {
    return MaterialApp(
      debugShowCheckedModeBanner: false,
      title: 'Starter Template',
      theme: ThemeData(
        primarySwatch: Colors.blue,
      ),
      home: Home(),
    );
  }
}

// home.dart
import 'package:flutter/material.dart';

class Home extends StatefulWidget {
  @override
```

```
    _HomeState createState() => _HomeState();
}

class _HomeState extends State<Home> {
  @override
  Widget build(BuildContext context) {
    return Scaffold(
      appBar: AppBar(
        title: Text('Home'),
      ),
      body: Container(),
    );
  }
}
```

Go ahead and run the project and see how your app is looking.

Notice that I added the following to Scaffold and AppBar: Container (this can be a TabController, PageController, and so on) and FloatingActionButton.

How It Works

To keep your code readable and maintainable, you structure appropriate widgets in their own classes and Dart files. You structure your starting projects with the `main.dart` file containing the `main()` function that starts the app. The `main()` function calls the `Home` widget in the `home.dart` file. The `Home` widget is the main presentation page shown when the app starts. For example, the `Home` widget might contain a `TabBar` or `BottomNavigationBar` widget.

SUMMARY

In this chapter, you learned how to create the starter project you'll use for all future apps in this book. You created folders with the `mkdir` command and named them accordingly to group the logic. You also created two Dart files: `main.dart` for the `main()` function that starts the app and `home.dart` to contain the code for the `Home` widget.

In the next chapter, we analyze the widget tree. Flutter works by nesting widgets together, and we find out quickly that readability and maintainability takes a hit quickly. We take a look at an example of how to flatten the widget tree.

▶ **WHAT YOU LEARNED IN THIS CHAPTER**

TOPIC	KEY CONCEPTS
`mkdir`	This is the command to create folders by name.
`main.dart`	The `main()` function starts the app and returns either a `MaterialApp` (Android) or `CupertinoApp` (iOS).
`home.dart`	This contains widgets that show the first page's layout, or home page.

5

Understanding the Widget Tree

WHAT YOU WILL LEARN IN THIS CHAPTER

➤ The fundamentals of widgets

➤ How to use a full widget tree

➤ How to use a shallow widget tree

The `widget tree` is how you create your UI; you position widgets within each other to build simple and complex layouts. Since just about everything in the Flutter framework is a widget, and as you start nesting them, the code can become harder to follow. A good practice is to try to keep the widget tree as shallow as possible. To understand the full effects of a deep tree, you'll look at a `full widget tree` and then refactor it into a `shallow widget tree`, making the code more manageable. You'll learn three ways to create a shallow widget tree by refactoring: with a constant, with a method, and with a widget class.

INTRODUCTION TO WIDGETS

Before analyzing the widget tree, let's look at the short list of widgets that you will use for this chapter's example apps. At this point, do not worry about understanding the functionality for each widget; just focus on what happens when you nest widgets and how you can separate them into smaller sections. In Chapter 6, "Using Common Widgets," you'll take a deeper look at using the most common widgets by functionality.

As I mentioned in Chapter 4, "Creating a Starter Project Template," this book uses Material Design for all the examples. The following are the widgets (usable only with Material Design) that you'll use to create the full and shallow widget tree projects for this chapter:

➤ `Scaffold`—Implements the Material Design visual layout, allowing the use of Flutter's Material Components widgets

➤ `AppBar`—Implements the toolbar at the top of the screen

➤ `CircleAvatar`—Usually used to show a rounded user profile photo, but you can use it for any image

➤ `Divider`—Draws a horizontal line with padding above and below

If the app you are creating is using Cupertino, you can use the following widgets instead. Note that with Cupertino you can use two different scaffolds, a page scaffold or a tab scaffold.

➤ `CupertinoPageScaffold`—Implements the iOS visual layout for a page. It works with `CupertinoNavigationBar` to provide the use of Flutter's Cupertino iOS-style widgets.

➤ `CupertinoTabScaffold`—Implements the iOS visual layout. This is used to navigate multiple pages, with the tabs at the bottom of the screen allowing you to use Flutter's Cupertino iOS-style widgets.

➤ `CupertinoNavigationBar`—Implements the iOS visual layout toolbar at the top of the screen.

Table 5.1 summarizes a short list of the different widgets to use based on platform.

TABLE 5.1: Material Design vs. Cupertino Widgets

MATERIAL DESIGN	CUPERTINO
Scaffold	CupertinoPageScaffold CupertinoTabScaffold
AppBar	CupertinoNavigationBar
CircleAvatar	n/a
Divider	n/a

The following widgets can be used with both Material Design and Cupertino:

➤ `SingleChildScrollview`—This adds vertical or horizontal scrolling ability to a single child widget.

➤ `Padding`—This adds left, top, right, and bottom padding.

➤ `Column`—This displays a vertical list of child widgets.

➤ `Row`—This displays a horizontal list of child widgets.

➤ `Container`—This widget can be used as an empty placeholder (invisible) or can specify height, width, color, transform (rotate, move, skew), and many more properties.

➤ `Expanded`—This expands and fills the available space for the child widget that belongs to a `Column` or `Row` widget.

➤ `Text`—The `Text` widget is a great way to display labels on the screen. It can be configured to be a single line or multiple lines. An optional `style` argument can be applied to change the color, font, size, and many other properties.

➤ `Stack`—What a powerful widget! `Stack` lets you stack widgets on top of each other and use a `Positioned` (optional) widget to align each child of the `Stack` for the layout needed. A great example is a shopping cart icon with a small red circle on the upper right to show the number of items to purchase.

➤ `Positioned`—The `Positioned` widget works with the Stack widget to control child positioning and size. A `Positioned` widget allows you to set the height and width. You can also specify the position location distance from the top, bottom, left, and right sides of the `Stack` widget.

You've learned about each widget that you will implement for the rest of this chapter. You'll now create a full widget tree, and then you'll learn how to refactor it to a shallow widget tree.

BUILDING THE FULL WIDGET TREE

To show how a widget tree can start to expand quickly, you'll use a combination of `Column`, `Row`, `Container`, `CircleAvatar`, `Divider`, `Padding`, and `Text` widgets. You'll take a closer look at these widgets in Chapter 6. The code that you'll write is a simple example, and you can immediately see how the widget tree can grow quickly (Figure 5.1).

FIGURE 5.1: Full widget tree view

Creating the Full Widget Tree

Create a new Flutter project called `ch5_widget_tree`. You can follow the instructions from Chapter 4. For this project, you need to create the `pages` folder only. You can view the full widget tree at the end of the steps.

1. Open the `home.dart` file.

2. Add to the `Scaffold` `body` property a `SafeArea` widget with the `child` property set to a `SingleChildScrollview`. Add a `Padding` widget as a `child` of the `SingleChildScrollView`. Set the `padding` property to `EdgeInsets.all(16.0)`.

```
body: SafeArea(
  child: SingleChildScrollView(
    child: Padding(
      padding: EdgeInsets.all(16.0),
    ),
  ),
),
```

3. Add to the `Padding` `child` property a `Column` widget with the `children` property set to a `Row`.

```
body: SafeArea(
  child: SingleChildScrollView(
    child: Padding(
      padding: EdgeInsets.all(16.0),
      child: Column(
        children: <Widget>[
          Row(
            children: <Widget>[
            ],
          ),
        ],
      ),
    ),
  ),
),
```

4. Add to the `Row` children widgets in this order: `Container`, `Padding`, `Expanded`, `Padding`, `Container`, and `Padding`. You are not done adding widgets; in the next step, you'll add a `Row` widget with multiple nested widgets.

```
Row(
  children: <Widget>[
    Container(
      color: Colors.yellow,
      height: 40.0,
      width: 40.0,
    ),
    Padding(padding: EdgeInsets.all(16.0),),
    Expanded(
      child: Container(
        color: Colors.amber,
        height: 40.0,
```

```
          width: 40.0,
        ),
      ),
      Padding(padding: EdgeInsets.all(16.0),),
      Container(
        color: Colors.brown,
        height: 40.0,
        width: 40.0,
      ),
    ],
  ),
```

5. Add a `Padding` widget to create a space before the next `Row` widget.

```
Padding(padding: EdgeInsets.all(16.0),),
```

6. Add a `Row` widget with the `children` property set to a `Column`. Add to the `Column` children a `Container`, `Padding`, `Container`, `Padding`, `Container`, `Divider`, `Row`, `Divider` and `Text`. You are still not done adding widgets, and in the next step, you'll add another `Row` widget with multiple nested widgets.

```
Row(
  children: <Widget>[
    Column(
      crossAxisAlignment: CrossAxisAlignment.start,
      mainAxisSize: MainAxisSize.max,
      children: <Widget>[
        Container(
          color: Colors.yellow,
          height: 60.0,
          width: 60.0,
        ),
        Padding(padding: EdgeInsets.all(16.0),),
        Container(
          color: Colors.amber,
          height: 40.0,
          width: 40.0,
        ),
        Padding(padding: EdgeInsets.all(16.0),),
        Container(
          color: Colors.brown,
          height: 20.0,
          width: 20.0,
        ),
        Divider(),
        Row(
          children: <Widget>[
            // Next step we'll add more widgets
          ],
        ),
        Divider(),
        Text('End of the Line'),
      ],
    ),
  ],
),
```

7. Modify the last `Row` widget (from step 6) and set the `children` property to a `CircleAvatar` with a `child` as a `Stack`. Add to the `Stack` `children` property three `Container` widgets.

```
Row(
  children: <Widget>[
    CircleAvatar(
      backgroundColor: Colors.lightGreen,
      radius: 100.0,
      child: Stack(
        children: <Widget>[
          Container(
            height: 100.0,
            width: 100.0,
            color: Colors.yellow,
          ),
          Container(
            height: 60.0,
            width: 60.0,
            color: Colors.amber,
          ),
          Container(
            height: 40.0,
            width: 40.0,
            color: Colors.brown,
          ),
        ],
      ),
    ),
  ],
),
```

8. After the `Stack` widget (from step 7), add a `Divider` widget and then a `Text` widget with a string of `'End of the Line'`.

```
Divider(),
Text('End of the Line'),
```

You've added a lot of nested widgets to build a complex layout. The full code is shown next. In a real-world app, this is common. Immediately you'll start to see how the widget tree can grow, making the code unreadable and unmanageable. To keep the example focused on how quickly the widget tree can grow, here you used basic widgets. In a production-level app, you would have even more widgets such as text fields to allow the user to enter text.

```
import 'package:flutter/material.dart';

class Home extends StatefulWidget {
  @override
  _HomeState createState() => _HomeState();
}

class _HomeState extends State<Home> {
  @override
  Widget build(BuildContext context) {
```

```
return Scaffold(
  appBar: AppBar(
    title: Text('Widget Tree'),
  ),
  body: SafeArea(
    child: SingleChildScrollView(
      child: Padding(
        padding: EdgeInsets.all(16.0),
        child: Column(
          children: <Widget>[
            Row(
              children: <Widget>[
                Container(
                  color: Colors.yellow,
                  height: 40.0,
                  width: 40.0,
                ),
                Padding(padding: EdgeInsets.all(16.0),),
                Expanded(
                  child: Container(
                    color: Colors.amber,
                    height: 40.0,
                    width: 40.0,
                  ),
                ),
                Padding(padding: EdgeInsets.all(16.0),),
                Container(
                  color: Colors.brown,
                  height: 40.0,
                  width: 40.0,
                ),
              ],
            ),
            Padding(padding: EdgeInsets.all(16.0),),
            Row(
              children: <Widget>[
                Column(
                  crossAxisAlignment: CrossAxisAlignment.start,
                  mainAxisSize: MainAxisSize.max,
                  children: <Widget>[
                    Container(
                      color: Colors.yellow,
                      height: 60.0,
                      width: 60.0,
                    ),
                    Padding(padding: EdgeInsets.all(16.0),),
                    Container(
                      color: Colors.amber,
                      height: 40.0,
                      width: 40.0,
                    ),
```

```
                    Padding(padding: EdgeInsets.all(16.0),),
                    Container(
                      color: Colors.brown,
                      height: 20.0,
                      width: 20.0,
                    ),
                    Divider(),
                    Row(
                      children: <Widget>[
                        CircleAvatar(
                          backgroundColor: Colors.lightGreen,
                          radius: 100.0,
                          child: Stack(
                            children: <Widget>[
                              Container(
                                height: 100.0,
                                width: 100.0,
                                color: Colors.yellow,
                              ),
                              Container(
                                height: 60.0,
                                width: 60.0,
                                color: Colors.amber,
                              ),
                              Container(
                                height: 40.0,
                                width: 40.0,
                                color: Colors.brown,
                              ),
                            ],
                          ),
                        ),
                      ],
                    ),
                    Divider(),
                    Text('End of the Line'),
                  ],
                ),
              ],
            ),
          ],
        ),
      ),
    ),
  );
}
}
```

The following image shows the page layout resulting from the widget tree.

How It Works

To create a page layout, you nest widgets to create a custom UI. The result of adding widgets together is called the *widget tree*. As the number of widgets increases, the widget tree starts to expand quickly and makes the code hard to read and manage.

BUILDING A SHALLOW WIDGET TREE

To make the example code more readable and maintainable, you'll refactor major sections of the code into separate entities. You have multiple refactor options, and the most common techniques are constants, methods, and widget classes.

Refactoring with a Constant

Refactoring with a constant initializes the widget to a `final` variable. This approach allows you to separate widgets into sections, making for better code readability. When widgets are initialized with a constant, they rely on the `BuildContext` object of the parent widget.

What does this mean? Every time the parent widget is redrawn, all the constants will also redraw their widgets, so you can't do any performance optimization. In the next section, you'll take a detailed look at refactoring with a method instead of a constant. The benefits of making the widget tree shallower are similar with both techniques.

The following sample code shows how to use a constant to initialize the `container` variable as `final` with the `Container` widget. You insert the `container` variable in the widget tree where needed.

```
final container = Container(
  color: Colors.yellow,
  height: 40.0,
  width: 40.0,
);
```

Refactoring with a Method

Refactoring with a method returns the widget by calling the method name. The method can return a value by a general widget (`Widget`) or a specific widget (`Container`, `Row`, and others).

The widgets initialized by a method rely on the `BuildContext` object of the parent widget. There could be unwanted side effects if these kinds of methods are nested and call other nested methods/functions. Since each situation is different, do not assume that using methods is not a good choice. This approach allows you to separate widgets into sections, making for better code readability. However, like when refactoring with a constant, every time the parent widget is redrawn, all the methods will also redraw their widgets. That means the widget tree is not optimizable for performance.

The following sample code shows how to use a method to return a `Container` widget. This first method returns the `Container` widget as a general `Widget`, and the second method returns the `Container` widget as a `Container` widget. Both approaches are acceptable. You insert the `_buildContainer()` method name in the widget tree where needed.

```
// Return by general Widget Name
Widget _buildContainer() {
  return Container(
    color: Colors.yellow,
    height: 40.0,
    width: 40.0,
  );
}

// Or Return by specific Widget like Container in this case
Container _buildContainer() {
  return Container(
    color: Colors.yellow,
    height: 40.0,
```

```
    width: 40.0,
  );
}
```

Let's look at an example that refactors by using methods. This approach improves code readability by separating the main parts of the widget tree into separate methods. The same approach could be taken by refactoring with a constant.

What is the benefit of using the method approach? The benefit is pure and simple code readability, but you lose the benefits of Flutter's subtree rebuilding: performance.

TRY IT OUT | Refactoring with a Method to Create a Shallow Widget Tree

To refactor the widgets, use the `method` pattern to flatten the widget tree.

1. Open the `home.dart` file.

2. Place the cursor on the first `Row` widget and right-click.

3. Select Refactor ⇨ Extract ⇨ Method and click Method.

```
     main.dart    home.dart
 1    import 'package:flutter/material.dart';
 2
 3    class Home extends StatefulWidget {
 4      @override
 5      _HomeState createState() => _HomeState();
 6    }
 7
 8    class _HomeState extends State<Home> {
 9      @override
10      Widget build(BuildContext context) {
11        return Scaffold(
12          appBar: AppBar(
13            title: Text('Widget Tree'),
14          ), // AppBar
15          body: SafeArea(
16            child: Padding(
17              padding: EdgeInsets.all(16.0),
18              child: Column(
19                children: <Widget>[
20                  Row(
21                          Copy Reference          ⌥⇧⌘C
22                          Paste                      ⌘V
23                          Paste from History...     ⇧⌘V
24                          Paste Simple           ⌥⇧⌘V
25                          Column Selection Mode    ⇧⌘8
26                          Find Usages                ⌥F7
27                          Find Sample Code           ⌥F8   sets.all(16.0),),.
28                          Refactor              ▶   Rename...              ⇧F6
29
30                          Folding               ▶   Move...                 F6
31                          Analyze               ▶   Copy...                 F5
32                          Reformat Code with dartfmt   Safe Delete...       ⌘⌦
33                          Go To                 ▶   Extract          ▶   Variable...   ⌥⌘V
34                          Generate...          ⌘N   Inline...       ⌥⌘N   Constant...   ⌥⌘C
35                                                                              Method...    ⌥⌘M
36                          Local History         ▶   Migrate...                Flutter Widget...
37                          Compare with Clipboard    Remove Unused Resources...   Type Parameter...
38                          File Encoding             Migrate App To AppCompat...
39                          Create Gist...            Add RTL Support Where Possible...
40                  ), // Container
41                ], // <Widget>[]
42              ), // Row
43              Padding(padding: EdgeInsets.all(16.0),),
44              Row(
45                children: <Widget>[
46                  Column(
47                    crossAxisAlignment: CrossAxisAlignment.start,
48                    mainAxisSize: MainAxisSize.max,
```

4. In the Extract Method dialog, enter _buildHorizontalRow for the method name. Notice the underscore before *build*; this lets Dart know that it is a private method. Notice that the entire Row widget and the children are highlighted to make it easy to view the affected code.

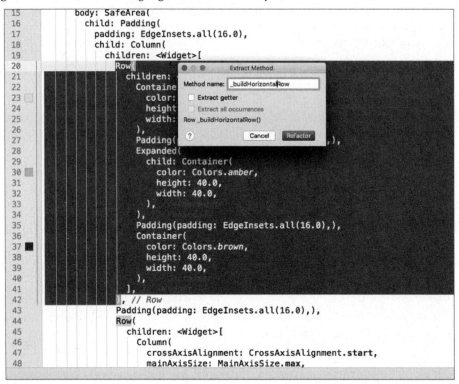

5. The Row widget is replaced with the _buildHorizontalRow() method. Scroll to the bottom of the code, and the method and widgets are nicely refactored.

```
Row _buildHorizontalRow() {
  return Row(
    children: <Widget>[
      Container(
        color: Colors.yellow,
        height: 40.0,
        width: 40.0,
      ),
      Padding(padding: EdgeInsets.all(16.0),),
      Expanded(
        child: Container(
          color: Colors.amber,
          height: 40.0,
          width: 40.0,
        ),
      ),
      Padding(padding: EdgeInsets.all(16.0),),
      Container(
        color: Colors.brown,
```

```
          height: 40.0,
          width: 40.0,
        ),
    ],
  );
}
```

6. Continue and refactor the other Rows and the Row and Stack widgets.

The full source code for home.dart is shown next. Notice how the widget tree is flattened, making it easier to read. Deciding on how shallow to make the widget tree depends on each circumstance and your personal preference. For example, say you are working on your code and you start noticing that you are doing a lot of scrolling vertically or horizontally to make changes. This is a good indication that you can refactor portions of the code into separate sections.

```
// home.dart
import 'package:flutter/material.dart';

class Home extends StatefulWidget {
  @override
  _HomeState createState() => _HomeState();
}

class _HomeState extends State<Home> {
  @override
  Widget build(BuildContext context) {
    return Scaffold(
      appBar: AppBar(
        title: Text('Widget Tree'),
      ),
      body: SafeArea(
        child: SingleChildScrollView(
          child: Padding(
            padding: EdgeInsets.all(16.0),
            child: Column(
              children: <Widget>[
                _buildHorizontalRow(),
                Padding(padding: EdgeInsets.all(16.0),),
                _buildRowAndColumn(),
              ],
            ),
          ),
        ),
      ),
    );
  }

  Row _buildHorizontalRow() {
    return Row(
      children: <Widget>[
        Container(
          color: Colors.yellow,
          height: 40.0,
          width: 40.0,
        ),
```

```
          Padding(padding: EdgeInsets.all(16.0),),
          Expanded(
            child: Container(
              color: Colors.amber,
              height: 40.0,
              width: 40.0,
            ),
          ),
          Padding(padding: EdgeInsets.all(16.0),),
          Container(
            color: Colors.brown,
            height: 40.0,
            width: 40.0,
          ),
        ],
      );
}

Row _buildRowAndColumn() {
  return Row(
    children: <Widget>[
      Column(
        crossAxisAlignment: CrossAxisAlignment.start,
        mainAxisSize: MainAxisSize.max,
        children: <Widget>[
          Container(
            color: Colors.yellow,
            height: 60.0,
            width: 60.0,
          ),
          Padding(padding: EdgeInsets.all(16.0),),
          Container(
            color: Colors.amber,
            height: 40.0,
            width: 40.0,
          ),
          Padding(padding: EdgeInsets.all(16.0),),
          Container(
            color: Colors.brown,
            height: 20.0,
            width: 20.0,
          ),
          Divider(),
          _buildRowAndStack(),
          Divider(),
          Text('End of the Line'),
        ],
      ),
    ],
  );
}

Row _buildRowAndStack() {
  return Row(
    children: <Widget>[
```

```
                CircleAvatar(
                  backgroundColor: Colors.lightGreen,
                  radius: 100.0,
                  child: Stack(
                    children: <Widget>[
                      Container(
                        height: 100.0,
                        width: 100.0,
                        color: Colors.yellow,
                      ),
                      Container(
                        height: 60.0,
                        width: 60.0,
                        color: Colors.amber,
                      ),
                      Container(
                        height: 40.0,
                        width: 40.0,
                        color: Colors.brown,
                      ),
                    ],
                  ),
                ),
              ],
            );
          }

        }
```

How It Works

Creating a shallow widget tree means each widget is separated into its own method by functionality. Keep in mind that how you separate widgets will be different depending on the functionality needed. Separating widgets by method improves code readability, but you lose the performance benefits of Flutter's subtree rebuilding. All the widgets in the method rely on the parent's BuildContext, meaning every time the parent is redrawn, the method is also redrawn.

In this example, you created the _buildHorizontalRow() method to build the horizontal Row widget with child widgets. The _buildRowAndColumn() method is an excellent example of flattening it even more by calling the _buildRowAndStack() method for one of the Column children widgets. Separating _buildRowAndStack() is done to keep the widget tree flat because the _buildRownAndStack() method builds a widget with multiple children widgets.

Refactoring with a Widget Class

Refactoring with a widget class allows you to create the widget by subclassing the StatelessWidget class. You can create reusable widgets within the current or separate Dart file and initiate them anywhere in the application. Notice that the constructor starts with a const keyword, which allows you to cache and reuse the widget. When calling the constructor to initiate the widget, use the const keyword. By calling with the `const` keyword, the widget does not rebuild when other widgets change their state in the tree. If you omit the `const` keyword, the widget will be called every time the parent widget redraws.

The widget class relies on its own `BuildContext`, not the parent like the constant and method approaches. `BuildContext` is responsible for handling the location of a widget in the widget tree. In Chapter 7, "Adding Animation to an App," you'll build an example that refactors and separates widgets with multiple `StatefulWidgets` instead of the `StatelessWidget` class.

What does this mean? Every time the parent widget is redrawn, all the widget classes will not redraw. They are built only once, which is great for performance optimization.

The following sample code shows how to use a widget class to return a `Container` widget. You insert the `const ContainerLeft()` widget in the widget tree where needed. Note the use of the `const` keyword to take advantage of caching.

```
class ContainerLeft extends StatelessWidget {
  const ContainerLeft({
    Key key,
  }) : super(key: key);

  @override
  Widget build(BuildContext context) {
    return Container(
      color: Colors.yellow,
      height: 40.0,
      width: 40.0,
    );
  }
}

// Call to initialize the widget and note the const keyword
const ContainerLeft(),
```

Let's look at an example that refactors by using widget classes (a Flutter widget). This approach improves code readability and performance by separating the main parts of the widget tree into separate widget classes.

What is the benefit of using the widget classes? It's pure and simple performance during screen updates. When calling a widget class, you need to use the `const` declaration; otherwise, it will be rebuilt every time, without caching. An example of refactoring with a widget class is when you have a UI layout where only specific widgets change state and others stay the same.

TRY IT OUT   Refactoring with a Widget Class to Create a Shallow Widget Tree

To refactor the widgets, use the widget class pattern to flatten the widget tree.

Create a new Flutter project called `ch5_widget_tree_performance`. You can follow the instructions from Chapter 4. For this project, you need to create the `pages` folder only. To keep this example simple, you'll create the widget classes in the home.dart file, but in Chapter 7 you'll learn how to separate them into separate files.

1. Open the home.dart file. Copy the original full widget tree in home.dart (from the "Building the Full Widget Tree" section of this chapter) to this project's home.dart file.

2. Place the cursor on the first Row widget and right-click.

3. Select Refactor ⇨ Extract ⇨ Flutter Widget.

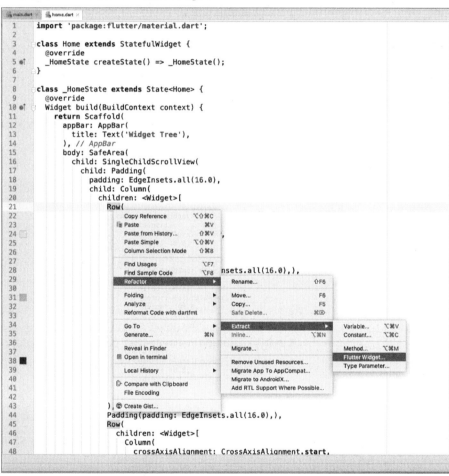

4. In the Extract Widget dialog, enter **RowWidget** for the widget name.

```
15        body: SafeArea(
16          child: Padding(
17            padding: EdgeInsets.all(16.0),
18            child: Column(
19              children: <Widget>[
20                Row(
21                  children: <Widget>[
22                    Contain ● ● ●        Extract Widget
23                      color  Widget name: RowWidget
24                      heigh
25                      width   ?        Cancel   Refactor
26                  ), // Container
27                  Padding(padding: EdgeInsets.all(16.0),),
28                  Expanded(
29                    child: Container(
30                      color: Colors.amber,
31                      height: 40.0,
32                      width: 40.0,
33                    ), // Container
34                  ), // Expanded
35                  Padding(padding: EdgeInsets.all(16.0),),
36                  Container(
37                    color: Colors.brown,
38                    height: 40.0,
39                    width: 40.0,
40                  ), // Container
41                ], // <Widget>[]
42              ), // Row
43              Padding(
44                padding: EdgeInsets.all(16.0),
45              ), // Padding
46              Row(
47                children: <Widget>[
48                  Column(
```

5. The Row widget is replaced with the RowWidget() widget class. Since the Row widget will not change state, add the const keyword before calling the RowWidget() class. Scroll to the bottom of the code, and the widgets are nicely refactored into the RowWidget (StatelessWidget) class.

```
class RowWidget extends StatelessWidget {
  const RowWidget({
    Key key,
  }) : super(key: key);

  @override
  Widget build(BuildContext context) {
    print('RowWidget');

    return Row(
      children: <Widget>[
        Container(
          color: Colors.yellow,
          height: 40.0,
          width: 40.0,
        ),
        Padding(
          padding: EdgeInsets.all(16.0),
        ),
```

```
              Expanded(
                child: Container(
                  color: Colors.amber,
                  height: 40.0,
                  width: 40.0,
                ),
              ),
              Padding(
                padding: EdgeInsets.all(16.0),
              ),
              Container(
                color: Colors.brown,
                height: 40.0,
                width: 40.0,
              ),
            ],
          );
        }
      }
```

6. Continue and refactor the other Rows (RowAndColumnWidget class) and the Row and Stack (RowAndStackWidget class) widgets.

The full source code for home.dart is listed next. Notice how the widget tree is flattened, making it easier to read. Deciding on how shallow to make the widget tree depends on each circumstance and your personal preference.

```
// home.dart
import 'package:flutter/material.dart';

class Home extends StatefulWidget {
  @override
  _HomeState createState() => _HomeState();
}

class _HomeState extends State<Home> {
  @override
  Widget build(BuildContext context) {
    return Scaffold(
      appBar: AppBar(
        title: Text('Widget Tree'),
      ),
      body: SafeArea(
        child: SingleChildScrollView(
          child: Padding(
            padding: EdgeInsets.all(16.0),
            child: Column(
              children: <Widget>[
                const RowWidget(),
                Padding(
                  padding: EdgeInsets.all(16.0),
                ),
                const RowAndColumnWidget(),
              ],
            ),
          ),
```

```
            ),
          ),
        ),
      );
    }
}

class RowWidget extends StatelessWidget {
  const RowWidget({
    Key key,
  }) : super(key: key);

  @override
  Widget build(BuildContext context) {
    return Row(
      children: <Widget>[
        Container(
          color: Colors.yellow,
          height: 40.0,
          width: 40.0,
        ),
        Padding(
          padding: EdgeInsets.all(16.0),
        ),
        Expanded(
          child: Container(
            color: Colors.amber,
            height: 40.0,
            width: 40.0,
          ),
        ),
        Padding(
          padding: EdgeInsets.all(16.0),
        ),
        Container(
          color: Colors.brown,
          height: 40.0,
          width: 40.0,
        ),
      ],
    );
  }
}

class RowAndColumnWidget extends StatelessWidget {
  const RowAndColumnWidget({
    Key key,
  }) : super(key: key);

  @override
  Widget build(BuildContext context) {
    return Row(
      children: <Widget>[
        Column(
          crossAxisAlignment: CrossAxisAlignment.start,
```

```
            mainAxisSize: MainAxisSize.max,
            children: <Widget>[
              Container(
                color: Colors.yellow,
                height: 60.0,
                width: 60.0,
              ),
              Padding(
                padding: EdgeInsets.all(16.0),
              ),
              Container(
                color: Colors.amber,
                height: 40.0,
                width: 40.0,
              ),
              Padding(
                padding: EdgeInsets.all(16.0),
              ),
              Container(
                color: Colors.brown,
                height: 20.0,
                width: 20.0,
              ),
              Divider(),
              const RowAndStackWidget(),
              Divider(),
              Text('End of the Line. Date: ${DateTime.now()}'),
            ],
          ),
        ],
      );
    }
}

class RowAndStackWidget extends StatelessWidget {
  const RowAndStackWidget({
    Key key,
  }) : super(key: key);

  @override
  Widget build(BuildContext context) {
    return Row(
      children: <Widget>[
        CircleAvatar(
          backgroundColor: Colors.lightGreen,
          radius: 100.0,
          child: Stack(
            children: <Widget>[
              Container(
                height: 100.0,
                width: 100.0,
                color: Colors.yellow,
              ),
              Container(
                height: 60.0,
```

```
            width: 60.0,
            color: Colors.amber,
          ),
          Container(
            height: 40.0,
            width: 40.0,
            color: Colors.brown,
          ),
        ],
      ),
    ),
  ],
);
}
}
```

How It Works

Creating a shallow widget tree means each widget is separated into its own widget class by functionality. Keep in mind that how you separate widgets will be different depending on the functionality needed.

In this example, you created the RowWidget() widget class to build the horizontal Row widget with children widgets. The RowAndColumnWidget() widget class is an excellent example of flattening it even more by calling the RowAndStackWidget() widget class for one of the Column children widgets. Separating by adding the additional RowAndStackWidget() is done to keep the widget tree flat because the RowAndStackWidget() class builds a widget with multiple children.

In the project source code, I added for your convenience a button that increases a counter value, and each widget class uses a print statement to show each time each is called when the state for the counter changes.

The following is the log file showing every time a widget is called. When the button is tapped, the CounterTextWidget widget is redrawn to show the new counter value, but notice that the RowWidget, RowAndColumnWidget, and RowAndStackWidget widgets are called only once and do not redraw when the state changes. By using the widget class technique, only the widgets that need redrawing are called, improving the overall performance.

```
// App first loaded
flutter: RowWidget
flutter: RowAndColumnWidget
flutter: RowAndStackWidget
flutter: CounterTextWidget 0

// Increase value button is called and notice the row widgets are not redrawn
flutter: CounterTextWidget 1
flutter: CounterTextWidget 2
flutter: CounterTextWidget 3
```

SUMMARY

In this chapter, you learned that the widget tree is the result of nested widgets. As the number of widgets increases, the widget tree expands quickly and lessens code readability and manageability. I call this the *full* widget tree. To improve code readability and manageability, you can separate widgets into their own widget class, creating a shallower widget tree. In each app, you should strive to keep the widget tree shallow.

By refactoring with a widget class, you can take advantage of Flutter's subtree rebuilding, which improves performance.

In the next chapter, you'll look at using basic widgets. You'll learn how to implement different types of buttons, images, icons, decorators, forms with text field validation and orientation.

► WHAT YOU LEARNED IN THIS CHAPTER

TOPIC	KEY CONCEPTS
Nesting widgets	You learned about the available widgets for Material Design and Cupertino and how to nest widgets to compose the UI layout.
	The basic widgets we covered for Material Design were `Scaffold`, `AppBar`, `CircleAvatar`, `Divider`, `SingleChildScrollView`, `Padding`, `Column`, `Row`, `Container`, `Expanded`, `Text`, `Stack`, and `Positioned`.
	The basic widgets we covered for Cupertino were `CupertinoPageScaffold`, `CupertinoTabScaffold`, and `CupertinoNavigationBar`.
Creating a full widget tree	A full widget tree is the result of nesting widgets to create the page UI. The more widgets added, the harder the code is to read and manage.
Creating a shallow widget tree	A shallow widget tree is the result of separating widgets into manageable sections to accomplish each task. The widgets can be separated by a constant variable, method, or widget class. The goal is to keep the widget tree shallow to improve code readability and manageability.
	To improve performance, you can refactor by using the widget class that takes advantage of Flutter's subtree rebuilding.

PART II
Intermediate Flutter: Fleshing Out an App

Using Common Widgets

WHAT YOU WILL LEARN IN THIS CHAPTER

➤ How to use basic widgets such as `Scaffold`, `AppBar`, `SafeArea`, `Container`, `Text`, `RichText`, `Column`, and `Row`, as well as different types of buttons

➤ How to nest the Column and Row widgets together to create different UI layouts

➤ Ways to include images, icons, and decorators

➤ How to use text field widgets to retrieve, validate, and manipulate data

➤ How to check your app's orientation

In this chapter, you'll learn how to use the most common widgets. I call them our base building blocks for creating beautiful UIs and UXs. You'll learn how to load images locally or over the Web via a uniform resource locator (URL), use the included rich Material Components icons, and apply decorators to enhance the look and feel of widgets or use them as input guides to entry fields. You'll also explore how to take advantage of the `Form` widget to validate text field entry widgets as a group, not just individually. Additionally, to account for the variety of device sizes, you'll see how using the `MediaQuery` or `OrientationBuilder` widget is a great way to detect orientation—because using the device orientation and layout widgets accordingly based on portrait or landscape is extremely important. For example, if the device is in portrait mode, you can show a row of three images, but when the device is turned to landscape mode, you can show a row of five images since the width is a larger area than in portrait mode.

USING BASIC WIDGETS

When building a mobile app, you'll usually implement certain widgets for the base structure. Being familiar with them is necessary.

Scaffold As you learned in Chapter 4, "Creating a Starter Project Template," the Scaffold widget implements the basic Material Design visual layout, allowing you to easily add various widgets such as AppBar, BottomAppBar, FloatingActionButton, Drawer, SnackBar, BottomSheet, and more.

AppBar The AppBar widget usually contains the standard title, toolbar, leading, and actions properties (along with buttons), as well as many customization options.

   title The title property is typically implemented with a Text widget. You can customize it with other widgets such as a DropdownButton widget.

   leading The leading property is displayed before the title property. Usually this is an IconButton or BackButton.

   actions The actions property is displayed to the right of the title property. It's a list of widgets aligned to the upper right of an AppBar widget usually with an IconButton or PopupMenuButton.

   flexibleSpace The flexibleSpace property is stacked behind the Toolbar or TabBar widget. The height is usually the same as the AppBar widget's height. A background image is commonly applied to the flexibleSpace property, but any widget, such as an Icon, could be used.

SafeArea The SafeArea widget is necessary for today's devices such as the iPhone X or Android devices with a notch (a partial cut-out obscuring the screen usually located on the top portion of the device). The SafeArea widget automatically adds sufficient padding to the child widget to avoid intrusions by the operating system. You can optionally pass a minimum amount of padding or a Boolean value to not enforce padding on the top, bottom, left, or right.

Container The Container widget is a commonly used widget that allows customization of its child widget. You can easily add properties such as color, width, height, padding, margin, border, constraint, alignment, transform (such as rotating or sizing the widget), and many others. The child property is optional, and the Container widget can be used as an empty placeholder (invisible) to add space between widgets.

Text The Text widget is used to display a string of characters. The Text constructor takes the arguments string, style, maxLines, overflow, textAlign, and others. A *constructor* is how the arguments are passed to initialize and customize the Text widget.

RichText The RichText widget is a great way to display text using multiple styles. The RichText widget takes TextSpans as children to style different parts of the strings.

Column A Column widget displays its children vertically. It takes a children property containing an array of List<Widget>, meaning you can add multiple widgets. The children align vertically without taking up the full height of the screen. Each child widget can be embedded in an Expanded widget to fill the available space. CrossAxisAlignment, MainAxisAlignment, and MainAxisSize can be used to align and size how much space is occupied on the main axis.

Row A Row widget displays its children horizontally. It takes a children property containing an array of List<Widget>. The same properties that the Column contains are applied to the Row widget with the exception that the alignment is horizontal, not vertical.

Buttons There are a variety of buttons to choose from for different situations such as RaisedButton, FloatingActionButton, FlatButton, IconButton, PopupMenuButton, and ButtonBar.

TRY IT OUT Adding AppBar Widgets

Create a new Flutter project and name it ch6_basics; you can follow the instructions in Chapter 4. For this project, you need to create only the pages folder. The goal of this app is to provide a look at how to use the basic widgets, not necessarily to design the best-looking UI. In Chapter 10, "Building Layouts," you'll focus on building complex and beautiful layouts.

1. Open the main.dart file. Change the primarySwatch property from blue to lightGreen.

```
primarySwatch: Colors.lightGreen,
```

2. Open the home.dart file. Start by customizing the AppBar widget properties.

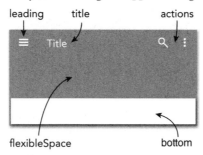

3. Add to the AppBar a leading IconButton. If you override the leading property, it is usually an IconButton or BackButton.

```
leading: IconButton(
  icon: Icon(Icons.menu),
  onPressed: () { },
),
```

4. The title property is usually a Text widget, but it can be customized with other widgets such as a DropdownButton. By following the instructions from Chapter 4, you have already added the Text widget to the title property; if not, add the Text widget with a value of 'Home'.

```
title: Text('Home'),
```

5. The actions property takes a list of widgets; add two IconButton widgets.

```
actions: <Widget>[
  IconButton(
    icon: Icon(Icons.search),
    onPressed: () {},
  ),
  IconButton(
    icon: Icon(Icons.more_vert),
    onPressed: () {},
  ),
],
```

6. Because you are using an Icon for the flexibleSpace property, let's add a SafeArea and an Icon as a child.

```
flexibleSpace: SafeArea(
  child: Icon(
```

```
        Icons.photo_camera,
        size: 75.0,
        color: Colors.white70,
      ),
    ),
```

No SafeArea

With SafeArea

7. Add a `PreferredSize` for the `bottom` property with a `Container` for a child.

```
bottom: PreferredSize(
  child: Container(
    color: Colors.lightGreen.shade100,
    height: 75.0,
    width: double.infinity,
    child: Center(
        child: Text('Bottom'),
    ),
  ),
  preferredSize: Size.fromHeight(75.0),
),
```

How It Works

You learned how to customize the `AppBar` widget by using widgets to set the `title`, `toolbar`, `leading`, and `actions` properties. All the properties that you learned about in this example are related to customizing the `AppBar`.

In Chapter 9, "Creating Scrolling Lists and Effects" you'll learn to use the `SliverAppBar` widget, which is an `AppBar` embedded in a `sliver` using a `CustomScrollView`, making any app come to life with pinpoint customizations such as parallax animation. I absolutely love using `slivers` because they add an extra layer of customization.

In the next section, you'll learn how to customize the `Scaffold` body property by nesting widgets to build the page content.

SafeArea

The `SafeArea` widget is a must for today's devices such as the iPhone X or Android devices with a notch (a partial cut-out obscuring the screen usually located on the top portion of the device). The `SafeArea` widget automatically adds sufficient padding to the child widget to avoid intrusions by the operating system. You can optionally pass minimum padding or a Boolean value to not enforce padding on the top, bottom, left, or right.

TRY IT OUT Adding a SafeArea to the Body

Continue modifying the `home.dart` file.

Add a `Padding` widget to the `body` property with a `SafeArea` as a `child`. Because this example packs in different uses of widgets, add a `SingleChildScrollView` as a `child` of the `SafeArea`. The `SingleChildScrollView` allows the user to scroll and view hidden widgets; otherwise, the user sees a yellow and black bar conveying that the widgets are overflowing.

```
body: Padding(
  padding: EdgeInsets.all(16.0),
```

```
    child: SafeArea(
      child: SingleChildScrollView(
        child: Column(
          children: <Widget>[

          ],
        ),
      ),
    ),
  ),
```

Sample Wrap Widget Tip

There is a great way to wrap a current widget as a child of another widget. Place your cursor on top of the current widget to wrap and then press Option+Enter on your keyboard. The Dart/quick assist pops up. Choose the Wrap with new widget option.

Do not add the following steps to your project; this is a tip on how to quickly wrap a widget with another.

1. Place the cursor on the widget to wrap.
2. Press Option+Enter (Alt+Enter in Windows). The Dart/quick assist pops up.

3. Select a Wrap with new widget option such as `body: widget(child: Container())`,.
4. Rename the widget to `SafeArea` and notice that `child:` is automatically the `Container()` widget. Make sure you add a comma after the `Container()` widget, as shown here. Placing a comma after every property ensures correct Flutter formatting over multiple lines.

```
    body: SafeArea(child: Container(),),
```

How It Works

Adding the `SafeArea` widget automatically adjusts padding for devices that have a notch. Any `SafeArea` child widgets are constrained to the correct padding.

Container

The `Container` widget has an optional `child` widget property and can be used as a decorated widget with a custom border, color, constraint, alignment, transform (such as rotating the widget), and more. This widget can be utilized as an empty placeholder (invisible), and if a child is omitted, it sizes to the full available screen size.

TRY IT OUT Adding a Container

Continue modifying the `home.dart` file. Since you want to keep your code readable and manageable, you'll create widget classes to build each `body` widget section of the `Column` list of widgets.

1. Add to the body property a `Padding` widget with the `child` property set to a `SafeArea` widget. Add to the `SafeArea` child a `SingleChildScrollView`. Add to the `SingleChildScrollView` child a `Column`. For the `Column` children, add the call to the `ContainerWithBoxDecorationWidget()` widget class, which you will create next. Make sure the widget class uses the `const` keyword to take advantage of caching (performance).

```
body: Padding(
  padding: EdgeInsets.all(16.0),
  child: SafeArea(
    child: SingleChildScrollView(
      child: Column(
        children: <Widget>[
          const ContainerWithBoxDecorationWidget(),
        ],
      ),
    ),
  ),
),
```

2. Create the `ContainerWithBoxDecorationWidget()` widget class after `class Home extends StatelessWidget {...}`. The widget class will return a `Widget`. Note that when you refactor by creating widget classes, they are of type `StatelessWidget` unless you specify to use a `StatefulWidget`.

```
class ContainerWithBoxDecorationWidget extends StatelessWidget {
  const ContainerWithBoxDecorationWidget({
    Key key,
  }) : super(key: key);

  @override
  Widget build(BuildContext context) {
    return Column(
      children: <Widget>[
        Container(),
      ],
    );
  }
}
```

3. Start adding properties to the `Container` by adding a height of 175.0 pixels. Note the comma after the number, which separates properties and helps to keep the Dart code formatted. Go to the next line to add the `decoration` property, which accepts a `BoxDecoration` class. The `BoxDecoration` class provides different ways to draw a box, and in this case, you are adding a `BorderRadius` class to the `bottomLeft` and `bottomRight` of the `Container`.

```
Container(
  height: 100.0,
  decoration: BoxDecoration(),
),
```

4. Using the named constructor `BorderRadius.only()` allows you to control the sides to draw round corners. I purposely made the `bottomLeft` radius much bigger than the `bottomRight` to show the custom shapes you can create.

    ```
    BoxDecoration(
      borderRadius: BorderRadius.only(
        bottomLeft: Radius.circular(100.0),
        bottomRight: Radius.circular(10.0),
      ),
    ),
    ```

The `BoxDecoration` also supports a `gradient` property. You are using a `LinearGradient`, but you could also have used a `RadialGradient`. The `LinearGradient` displays the gradient colors linearly, and the `RadialGradient` displays the gradient colors in a circular manner. The `begin` and `end` properties allow you to choose the start and end positions for the gradient by using the `AlignmentGeometry` class. `AlignmentGeometry` is a base class for `Alignment` that allows direction-aware resolution. You have many directions to choose from such as `Alignment.bottomLeft`, `Alignment.centerRight`, and more.

```
begin: Alignment.topCenter,
end: Alignment.bottomCenter,
```

The `colors` property requires a `List` of `Color` types, `List<Color>`. The list of `Colors` is entered within square brackets separated by commas.

```
colors: [
  Colors.white,
  Colors.lightGreen.shade500,
],
```

Here's the full gradient property source code:

```
gradient: LinearGradient(
  begin: Alignment.topCenter,
  end: Alignment.bottomCenter,
  colors: [
    Colors.white,
    Colors.lightGreen.shade500,
  ],
),
```

5. The `boxShadow` property is a great way to customize a shadow, and it takes a list of `BoxShadows`, called `List<BoxShadow>`. For the `BoxShadow`, set the `color`, `blurRadius`, and `offset` properties.

    ```
    boxShadow: [
      BoxShadow(
        color: Colors.white,
        blurRadius: 10.0,
        offset: Offset(0.0, 10.0),
      )
    ],
    ```

The last part of the `Container` is to add a child `Text` widget wrapped by a `Center` widget. The `Center` widget allows you to center the `child` widget on the screen.

```
child: Center(
  child: Text('Container'),
),
```

6. Add a Center widget as a child of the Container, and add to the Center widget child a Text widget with the string Container. (In the next section, I'll go over the Text widget in detail.)

```
child: Center(
  child: Text('Container'),
),
```

Here's the full ContainerWithBoxDecorationWidget() widget class source code:

```
class ContainerWithBoxDecorationWidget extends StatelessWidget {
  const ContainerWithBoxDecorationWidget({
    Key key,
  }) : super(key: key);

  @override
  Widget build(BuildContext context) {
    return Column(
      children: <Widget>[
        Container(
          height: 100.0,
          decoration: BoxDecoration(
            borderRadius: BorderRadius.only(
              bottomLeft: Radius.circular(100.0),
              bottomRight: Radius.circular(10.0),
            ),
            gradient: LinearGradient(
              begin: Alignment.topCenter,
              end: Alignment.bottomCenter,
              colors: [
                Colors.white,
                Colors.lightGreen.shade500,
              ],
            ),
            boxShadow: [
              BoxShadow(
                color: Colors.grey,
                blurRadius: 10.0,
                offset: Offset(0.0, 10.0),
              ),
            ],
          ),
          child: Center(
            child: RichText(
              text: Text('Container'),                ),
          ),
        ),
      ],
    );
  }
}
```

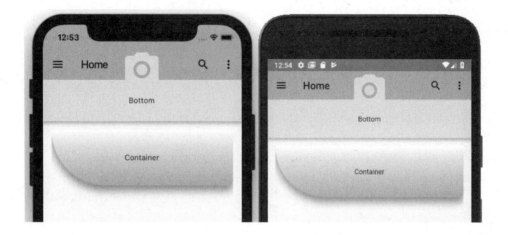

How It Works

Containers can be powerful widgets full of customization. By using decorators, gradients, and shadows, you can create beautiful UIs. I like to think of containers as enhancing an app in the same way a great-looking frame adds to a painting.

Text

You've already used the `Text` widget in the preceding examples; it's an easy widget to use but also customizable. The `Text` constructor takes the arguments `string`, `style`, `maxLines`, `overflow`, `text-Align`, and others.

```
Text(
  'Flutter World for Mobile',
  style: TextStyle(
    fontSize: 24.0,
    color: Colors.deepPurple,
    decoration: TextDecoration.underline,
    decorationColor: Colors.deepPurpleAccent,
    decorationStyle: TextDecorationStyle.dotted,
    fontStyle: FontStyle.italic,
    fontWeight: FontWeight.bold,
  ),
  maxLines: 4,
  overflow: TextOverflow.ellipsis,
  textAlign: TextAlign.justify,
),
```

RichText

The `RichText` widget is a great way to display text using multiple styles. The `RichText` widget takes `TextSpan` as children to style different parts of the strings (Figure 6.1).

> *Flutter World for Mobile*

FIGURE 6.1: RichText with TextSpan

TRY IT OUT Replacing Text with a RichText Child Container

Instead of using the previous Container Text widget to show a plain-text property, you can use a RichText widget to enhance and emphasize the words in your string. You can change each word's color and styles.

1. Find the Container child Text widget and delete Text('Container').

    ```
    child: Center(
      child: Text('Container'),
    ),
    ```

2. Replace the Container child's Text widget with a RichText widget. The RichText text property is a TextSpan object (class) that is customized by using a TextStyle for the style property. The TextSpace has a children list of TextSpan where you place different TextSpan objects to format different portions of the entire RichText.

    By using the RichText widget and combining different TextSpan objects, you create rich-text formatting like with a word processor.

    ```
    child: Center(
      child: RichText(
        text: TextSpan(
          text: 'Flutter World',
          style: TextStyle(
            fontSize: 24.0,
            color: Colors.deepPurple,
            decoration: TextDecoration.underline,
            decorationColor: Colors.deepPurpleAccent,
            decorationStyle: TextDecorationStyle.dotted,
            fontStyle: FontStyle.italic,
            fontWeight: FontWeight.normal,
          ),
          children: <TextSpan>[
            TextSpan(
              text: ' for',
            ),
            TextSpan(
              text: ' Mobile',
              style: TextStyle(
                  color: Colors.deepOrange,
                  fontStyle: FontStyle.normal,
                  fontWeight: FontWeight.bold),
            ),
          ],
        ),
      ),
    ),
    ```

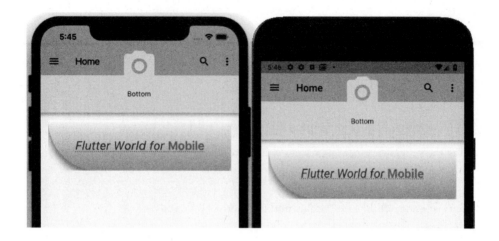

How It Works

`RichText` is a powerful widget when combined with the `TextSpan` object (class). There are two main parts to styling, the default `text` property and the `children` list of `TextSpan`. The `text` property using a `TextSpan` sets the default styling for the `RichText`. The `children` list of `TextSpan` allows you to use multiple `TextSpan` objects to format different strings.

Column

A `Column` widget (Figures 6.2 and 6.3) displays its children vertically. It takes a `children` property containing an array of `List<Widget>`. The children align vertically without taking up the full height of the screen. Each child widget can be embedded in an `Expanded` widget to fill available space. You can use `CrossAxisAlignment`, `MainAxisAlignment`, and `MainAxisSize` to align and size how much space is occupied on the main axis.

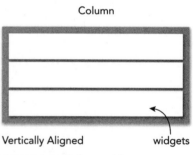

Column

Vertically Aligned   widgets

FIGURE 6.2: Column widget

```
Column(
  crossAxisAlignment: CrossAxisAlignment.center,
  mainAxisAlignment: MainAxisAlignment.spaceEvenly,
  mainAxisSize: MainAxisSize.max,
  children: <Widget>[
    Text('Column 1'),
    Divider(),
    Text('Column 2'),
    Divider(),
    Text('Column 3'),
  ],
),
```

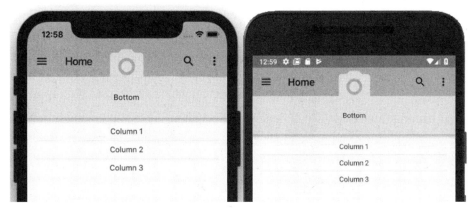

FIGURE 6.3: Column widget rendered in app

Row

A Row widget (Figures 6.4 and 6.5) displays its children horizontally. It takes a `children` property containing an array of
List<Widget>. The same properties that the Column contains
are applied to the Row widget with the exception that the
alignment is horizontal, not vertical.

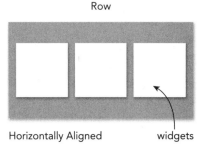

FIGURE 6.4: Row widget

```
Row(
  crossAxisAlignment: CrossAxisAlignment.start,
  mainAxisAlignment: MainAxisAlignment.
spaceEvenly,
  mainAxisSize: MainAxisSize.max,
  children: <Widget>[
    Row(
      children: <Widget>[
        Text('Row 1'),
        Padding(padding: EdgeInsets.all(16.0),),
        Text('Row 2'),
        Padding(padding: EdgeInsets.all(16.0),),
        Text('Row 3'),
      ],
    ),
  ],
),
```

Column and Row Nesting

A great way to create unique layouts is to combine Column and Row widgets for individual needs.
Imagine having a journal page with Text in a Column with a nested Row containing a list of images
(Figures 6.6 and 6.7).

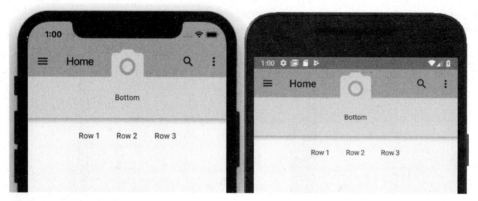

FIGURE 6.5: Row widget rendered in app

Add a Row widget inside the Column widget. Use mainAxis-Alignment: MainAxisAlignment.spaceEvenly and add three Text widgets.

Column with Row

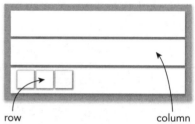

row   column

FIGURE 6.6: Column and Row nesting

```
Column(
  crossAxisAlignment: CrossAxisAlignment.start,
  mainAxisAlignment: MainAxisAlignment.
spaceEvenly,
  mainAxisSize: MainAxisSize.max,
  children: <Widget>[
    Text('Columns and Row Nesting 1',),
    Text('Columns and Row Nesting 2',),
    Text('Columns and Row Nesting 3',),
    Padding(padding: EdgeInsets.all(16.0),),
    Row(
      mainAxisAlignment: MainAxisAlignment.spaceEvenly,
      children: <Widget>[
        Text('Row Nesting 1'),
        Text('Row Nesting 2'),
        Text('Row Nesting 3'),
      ],
    ),
  ],
),
```

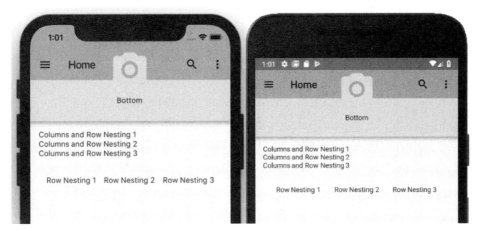

FIGURE 6.7: Column and Row widgets rendered in app

TRY IT OUT Adding Column, Row, and Nesting the Row and Column together as Widget Classes

You'll add three widget classes to the body property section of the Column list of widgets. Between each widget class, you'll add a simple Divider() widget to draw separation lines between sections.

1. Add the widget class names ColumnWidget(), RowWidget(), and ColumnAndRowNestingWidget() to the Column children widget list. The Column widget is located in the body property. Add a Divider() widget between each widget class name. Make sure each widget class uses the const keyword.

```
body: Padding(
  padding: EdgeInsets.all(16.0),
  child: SafeArea(
    child: SingleChildScrollView(
      child: Column(
        children: <Widget>[
          const ContainerWithBoxDecorationWidget(),
          Divider(),
          const ColumnWidget(),
          Divider(),
          const RowWidget(),
          Divider(),
          const ColumnAndRowNestingWidget(),
        ],
      ),
    ),
  ),
),
```

2. Create the `ColumnWidget()` widget class after the `ContainerWithBoxDecorationWidget()` widget class.

```
class ColumnWidget extends StatelessWidget {
  const ColumnWidget({
    Key key,
  }) : super(key: key);

  @override
  Widget build(BuildContext context) {
    return Column(
      crossAxisAlignment: CrossAxisAlignment.center,
      mainAxisAlignment: MainAxisAlignment.spaceEvenly,
      mainAxisSize: MainAxisSize.max,
      children: <Widget>[
        Text('Column 1'),
        Divider(),
        Text('Column 2'),
        Divider(),
        Text('Column 3'),
      ],
    );
  }
}
```

3. Create the `RowWidget()` widget class after the `ColumnWidget()` widget class.

```
class RowWidget extends StatelessWidget {
  const RowWidget({
    Key key,
  }) : super(key: key);

  @override
  Widget build(BuildContext context) {
    return Row(
      crossAxisAlignment: CrossAxisAlignment.start,
      mainAxisAlignment: MainAxisAlignment.spaceEvenly,
      mainAxisSize: MainAxisSize.max,
      children: <Widget>[
        Row(
          children: <Widget>[
            Text('Row 1'),
            Padding(padding: EdgeInsets.all(16.0),),
            Text('Row 2'),
            Padding(padding: EdgeInsets.all(16.0),),
            Text('Row 3'),
          ],
        ),
      ],
    );
  }
}
```

4. Create the `ColumnAndRowNestingWidget()` widget class after the `RowWidget()` widget class.

```
class ColumnAndRowNestingWidget extends StatelessWidget {
  const ColumnAndRowNestingWidget({
    Key key,
  }) : super(key: key);

  @override
  Widget build(BuildContext context) {
    return Column(
      crossAxisAlignment: CrossAxisAlignment.start,
      mainAxisAlignment: MainAxisAlignment.spaceEvenly,
      mainAxisSize: MainAxisSize.max,
      children: <Widget>[
        Text('Columns and Row Nesting 1',),
        Text('Columns and Row Nesting 2',),
        Text('Columns and Row Nesting 3',),
        Padding(padding: EdgeInsets.all(16.0),),
        Row(
          mainAxisAlignment: MainAxisAlignment.spaceEvenly,
          children: <Widget>[
            Text('Row Nesting 1'),
            Text('Row Nesting 2'),
            Text('Row Nesting 3'),
          ],
        ),
      ],
    );
  }
}
```

How It Works

`Column` and `Row` are handy widgets to lay out either vertically or horizontally. Nesting the `Column` and `Row` widgets creates flexible layouts needed for each circumstance. Nesting widgets is at the heart of designing Flutter UI layouts.

Buttons

There are a variety of buttons to choose from, depending on the situation, such as `FloatingAction-Button`, `FlatButton`, `IconButton`, `RaisedButton`, `PopupMenuButton`, and `ButtonBar`.

FloatingActionButton

The `FloatingActionButton` widget is usually placed on the bottom right or center of the main screen in the `Scaffold floatingActionButton` property. Use the `FloatingActionButtonLocation` widget to either dock (notch) or float above the navigation bar. To dock a button to the navigation bar, use the `BottomAppBar` widget. By default, it's a circular button but can be customized to a stadium shape by using the named constructor `FloatingActionButton.extended`. In the example code, I commented out the stadium shape button for you to test.

```
floatingActionButtonLocation: FloatingActionButtonLocation.endDocked,
floatingActionButton: FloatingActionButton(
  onPressed: () {},
  child: Icon(Icons.play_arrow),
  backgroundColor: Colors.lightGreen.shade100,
),
// or
// This creates a Stadium Shape FloatingActionButton
// floatingActionButton: FloatingActionButton.extended(
//   onPressed: () {},
//   icon: Icon(Icons.play_arrow),
//   label: Text('Play'),
// ),
bottomNavigationBar: BottomAppBar(
  hasNotch: true,
  color: Colors.lightGreen.shade100,
  child: Row(
    mainAxisAlignment: MainAxisAlignment.spaceEvenly,
    children: <Widget>[
      Icon(Icons.pause),
      Icon(Icons.stop),
      Icon(Icons.access_time),
      Padding(
        padding: EdgeInsets.all(32.0),
      ),
    ],
  ),
),
```

Figure 6.8 shows the `FloatingActionButton` widget on the bottom right of the screen with the notch enabled.

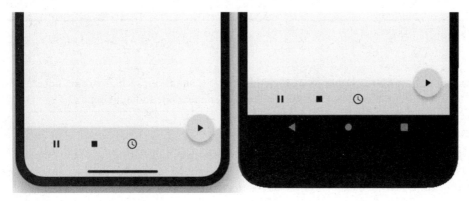

FIGURE 6.8: FloatingActionButton with notch

FlatButton

The `FlatButton` widget is the most minimalist button used; it displays a text label without any borders or elevation (shadow). Since the text label is a widget, you could use an `Icon` widget instead or another widget to customize the button. `color`, `highlightColor`, `splashColor`, `textColor`, and other properties can be customized.

```
// Default - left button
FlatButton(
  onPressed: () {},
  child: Text('Flag'),
),

// Customize - right button
FlatButton(
  onPressed: () {},
  child: Icon(Icons.flag),
  color: Colors.lightGreen,
  textColor: Colors.white,
),
```

Figure 6.9 shows the default `FlatButton` widget on the left and the customized `FlatButton` widget on the right.

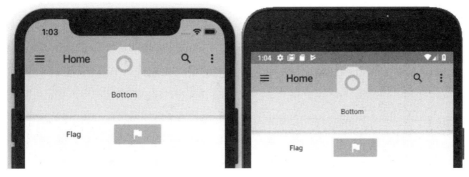

FIGURE 6.9: FlatButton

RaisedButton

The `RaisedButton` widget adds a dimension, and the elevation (shadow) increases when the user presses the button.

```
// Default - left button
RaisedButton(
  onPressed: () {},
  child: Text('Save'),
),
```

```
// Customize - right button
RaisedButton(
  onPressed: () {},
  child: Icon(Icons.save),
  color: Colors.lightGreen,
),
```

Figure 6.10 shows the default `RaisedButton` widget on the left and the customized `RaisedButton` widget on the right.

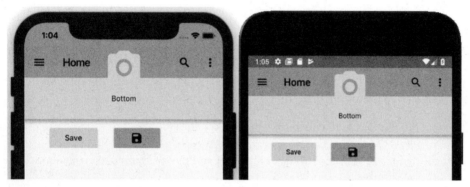

FIGURE 6.10: RaisedButton

IconButton

The `IconButton` widget uses an `Icon` widget on a Material Component widget that reacts to touches by filling with color (ink). The combination creates a nice tap effect, giving the user feedback that an action has started.

```
// Default - left button
IconButton(
  onPressed: () {},
  icon: Icon(Icons.flight),
),

// Customize - right button
IconButton(
  onPressed: () {},
  icon: Icon(Icons.flight),
  iconSize: 42.0,
  color: Colors.white,
  tooltip: 'Flight',
),
```

Figure 6.11 shows the default `IconButton` widget on the left and the customized `IconButton` widget on the right.

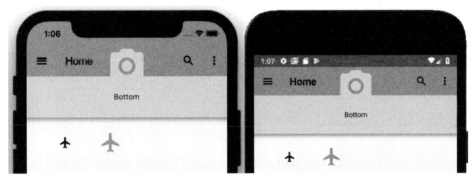

FIGURE 6.11: IconButton

PopupMenuButton

The `PopupMenuButton` widget displays a list of menu items. When a menu item is pressed, the value passes to the `onSelected` property. A common use of this widget is placing it on the top right of the `AppBar` widget for the user to select different menu options. Another example is to place the `Popup-MenuButton` widget in the middle of the `AppBar` widget showing a list of search filters.

TRY IT OUT   Creating the PopupMenuButton and the Items' Class and List

Before you add the `PopupMenuButton` widgets, let's create the `Class` and `List` necessary to build the items to be displayed. Usually, the `TodoMenuItem` (model) class would be created in a separate Dart file, but to keep the example focused, you'll add it to the `home.dart` file. In the final three chapters of this book, you'll separate classes into their own files.

1. Create a `TodoMenuItem` class. When you create this class, make sure it's not inside another class. Create the class and list at the end of the file after the last closing curly bracket, }. The `TodoMenuItem` class contains a `title` and an `icon`.

    ```
    class TodoMenuItem {
      final String title;
      final Icon icon;

      TodoMenuItem({this.title, this.icon});
    }
    ```

2. Create a `List` of `TodoMenuItem`. This `List<TodoMenuItem>` will be called `foodMenuList` and will contain a `List` (array) of `TodoMenuItems`.

    ```
    // Create a List of Menu Item for PopupMenuButton
    List<TodoMenuItem> foodMenuList = [
      TodoMenuItem(title: 'Fast Food', icon: Icon(Icons.fastfood)),
      TodoMenuItem(title: 'Remind Me', icon: Icon(Icons.add_alarm)),
      TodoMenuItem(title: 'Flight', icon: Icon(Icons.flight)),
      TodoMenuItem(title: 'Music', icon: Icon(Icons.audiotrack)),
    ];
    ```

3. Create a `PopupMenuButton`. You will use an `itemBuilder` to build the `List` of `TodoMenuItems`. If you do not set an icon for the `PopupMenuButton`, a default menu icon is used by default. The `onSelected` will retrieve the item selected on the list. Use the `itemBuilder` to build a list of `foodMenuList` and map to `TodoMenuItem`. A `PopupMenuItem` is returned for each item in the `foodMenuList`. For the `PopupMenuItem` child, you use a `Row` widget to show the `Icon` and `Text` widgets together.

```
PopupMenuButton<TodoMenuItem>(
  icon: Icon(Icons.view_list),
  onSelected: ((valueSelected) {
    print('valueSelected: ${valueSelected.title}');
  }),
  itemBuilder: (BuildContext context) {
    return foodMenuList.map((TodoMenuItem todoMenuItem) {
      return PopupMenuItem<TodoMenuItem>(
        value: todoMenuItem,
        child: Row(
          children: <Widget>[
            Icon(todoMenuItem.icon.icon),
            Padding(padding: EdgeInsets.all(8.0),),
            Text(todoMenuItem.title),
          ],
        ),
      );
    }).toList();
  },
),
```

4. Modify the `AppBar` `bottom` property by adding the widget class name: `PopupMenuButtonWidget()`.

```
bottom: PopupMenuButtonWidget(),
```

5. Create the `PopupMenuButtonWidget()` widget class after the `ColumnAndRowNestingWidget()` widget class. Since the `bottom` property is expecting a `PreferredSizeWidget`, you use the keyword `implements PreferredSizeWidget` in the class declaration. The class extends the `StatelessWidget` and implements the `PreferredSizeWidget`.

After the widget build, implement the `@override` `preferredSize` getter; this is a required step because the purpose of `PreferredSizeWidget` is to provide the size for the widget; in this example, you'll set the `height` property. Without this step, we'd have no size specified.

```
@override
// implement preferredSize
Size get preferredSize => Size.fromHeight(75.0);
```

The following is the entire `PopupMenuButtonWidget` widget class. Note that the `Container` widget's height property uses the `preferredSize.height` property that you set in the `PreferredSize-Widget` getter.

```
class PopupMenuButtonWidget extends StatelessWidget implements PreferredSizeWidget {
  const PopupMenuButtonWidget({
    Key key,
  }) : super(key: key);

  @override
  Widget build(BuildContext context) {
    return Container(
      color: Colors.lightGreen.shade100,
      height: preferredSize.height,
      width: double.infinity,
      child: Center(
        child: PopupMenuButton<TodoMenuItem>(
          icon: Icon(Icons.view_list),
          onSelected: ((valueSelected) {
            print('valueSelected: ${valueSelected.title}');
          }),
          itemBuilder: (BuildContext context) {
            return foodMenuList.map((TodoMenuItem todoMenuItem) {
              return PopupMenuItem<TodoMenuItem>(
                value: todoMenuItem,
                child: Row(
                  children: <Widget>[
                    Icon(todoMenuItem.icon.icon),
                    Padding(
                      padding: EdgeInsets.all(8.0),
                    ),
                    Text(todoMenuItem.title),
                  ],
                ),
              );
            }).toList();
          },
        ),
      ),
    );
  }

  @override
  // implement preferredSize
  Size get preferredSize => Size.fromHeight(75.0);
}
```

How It Works

The `PopupMenuButton` widget is a great widget to display a `List` of items such as menu choices. For the list of items, you created a `TodoMenuItem` `Class` to hold a `title` and `icon`. You created the foodMenuList, which is a List of each TodoMenuItem. In this case, the List items are hard-coded, but in a real-world app, the values can be read from a web service. In Chapters 14, 15 and 16, you'll implement Cloud Firestore to access data from a web server.

ButtonBar

The ButtonBar widget (Figure 6.12) aligns buttons horizontally. In this example, the ButtonBar widget is a child of a Container widget to give it a background color.

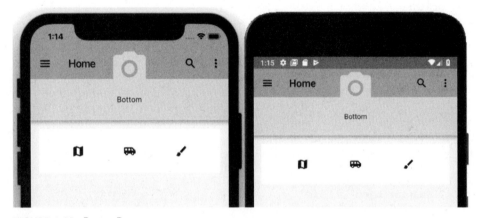

FIGURE 6.12: ButtonBar

```
Container(
  color: Colors.white70,
  child: ButtonBar(
    alignment: MainAxisAlignment.spaceEvenly,
    children: <Widget>[
      IconButton(
        icon: Icon(Icons.map),
        onPressed: () {},
      ),
      IconButton(
        icon: Icon(Icons.airport_shuttle),
        onPressed: () {},
      ),
      IconButton(
        icon: Icon(Icons.brush),
        onPressed: () {},
      ),
    ],
  ),
),
```

TRY IT OUT   Adding Buttons as Widget Classes

You've looked at the `FloatingActionButton`, `FlatButton`, `RaisedButton`, `IconButton`, `PopupMenu-Button`, and `ButtonBar` widgets. Here you'll create two widget classes to organize the buttons' layout.

1. Add the widget class names `ButtonsWidget()` and `ButtonBarWidget()` to the `Column` children widget list. The `Column` is located in the `body` property. Add a `Divider()` widget between each widget class name. Make sure each widget class uses the `const` keyword.

```
body: Padding(
  padding: EdgeInsets.all(16.0),
  child: SafeArea(
    child: SingleChildScrollView(
      child: Column(
        children: <Widget>[
          const ContainerWithBoxDecorationWidget(),
          Divider(),
          const ColumnWidget(),
          Divider(),
          const RowWidget(),
          Divider(),
          const ColumnAndRowNestingWidget(),
          Divider(),
          const ButtonsWidget(),
          Divider(),
          const ButtonBarWidget(),
        ],
      ),
    ),
  ),
),
```

2. Create the `ButtonsWidget()` widget class after the `ColumnAndRowNestingWidget()` widget class. The class returns a `Column` with three `Row` widgets for the `children` list of `Widget`. Each `Row` children list of `Widget` contains different buttons such as the `FlatButton`, `RaisedButton`, and `IconButton` buttons.

```
class ButtonsWidget extends StatelessWidget {
  const ButtonsWidget({
    Key key,
  }) : super(key: key);

  @override
  Widget build(BuildContext context) {
    return Column(
      children: <Widget>[
        Row(
          children: <Widget>[
            Padding(padding: EdgeInsets.all(16.0)),
            FlatButton(
              onPressed: () {},
```

```
            child: Text('Flag'),
          ),
        Padding(padding: EdgeInsets.all(16.0)),
        FlatButton(
          onPressed: () {},
          child: Icon(Icons.flag),
          color: Colors.lightGreen,
          textColor: Colors.white,
        ),
    ],
  ),
  Divider(),
  Row(
    children: <Widget>[
      Padding(padding: EdgeInsets.all(16.0)),
      RaisedButton(
        onPressed: () {},
        child: Text('Save'),
      ),
      Padding(padding: EdgeInsets.all(16.0)),
      RaisedButton(
        onPressed: () {},
        child: Icon(Icons.save),
        color: Colors.lightGreen,
      ),
    ],
  ),
  Divider(),
  Row(
    children: <Widget>[
      Padding(padding: EdgeInsets.all(16.0)),
      IconButton(
        icon: Icon(Icons.flight),
        onPressed: () {},
      ),
      Padding(padding: EdgeInsets.all(16.0)),
      IconButton(
        icon: Icon(Icons.flight),
        iconSize: 42.0,
        color: Colors.lightGreen,
        tooltip: 'Flight',
        onPressed: () {},
      ),
    ],
  ),
```

```
          Divider(),
        ],
      );
    }
  }
```

3.   Create the `ButtonBarWidget()` widget class after the `ButtonsWidget()` widget class. The class
returns a `Container` with a `ButtonBar` as a child. The `ButtonBar` children list of `Widget`
contains three `IconButton` widgets.

```
class ButtonBarWidget extends StatelessWidget {
  const ButtonBarWidget({
    Key key,
  }) : super(key: key);

  @override
  Widget build(BuildContext context) {
    return Container(
      color: Colors.white70,
      child: ButtonBar(
        alignment: MainAxisAlignment.spaceEvenly,
        children: <Widget>[
          IconButton(
            icon: Icon(Icons.map),
            onPressed: () {},
          ),
          IconButton(
            icon: Icon(Icons.airport_shuttle),
            onPressed: () {},
          ),
          IconButton(
            icon: Icon(Icons.brush),
            highlightColor: Colors.purple,
            onPressed: () {},
          ),
        ],
      ),
    );
  }
}
```

How It Works

The `FloatingActionButton`, `FlatButton`, `RaisedButton`, `IconButton`, `PopupMenuButton`, and
`ButtonBar` widgets are configurable by setting the properties `icon`, `iconSize`, `tooltip`, `color`,
`text`, and more.

USING IMAGES AND ICONS

Images can make an app look tremendous or ugly depending on the quality of the artwork. Images, icons, and other resources are commonly embedded in an app.

AssetBundle

The AssetBundle class provides access to custom resources such as images, fonts, audio, data files, and more. Before a Flutter app can use a resource, you must declare it in the pubspec.yaml file.

```
// pubspec.yaml file to edit
# To add assets to your application, add an assets section, like this:
```

```
assets:
 —assets/images/logo.png
 —assets/images/work.png
 —assets/data/seed.json
```

Instead of declaring each asset, which can get very long, you can declare all the assets in each directory. Make sure you end the directory name with a forward slash, /. Throughout the book, I'll use this approach when adding assets to the projects.

```
// pubspec.yaml file to edit
# To add assets to your application, add an assets section, like this:
assets:
 —assets/images/
 —assets/data/
```

Image

The `Image` widget displays an image from a local or URL (web) source. To load an `Image` widget, there are a few different constructors to use.

➤ `Image()`—Retrieves image from an `ImageProvider` class

➤ `Image.asset()`—Retrieves image from an `AssetBundle` class using a key

➤ `Image.file()`—Retrieves image from a `File` class

➤ `Image.memory()`—Retrieves image from a `Uint8List` class

➤ `Image.network()`—Retrieves image from a `URL` path

Press Ctrl+Spacebar to invoke the code completion for the available options (Figure 6.13).

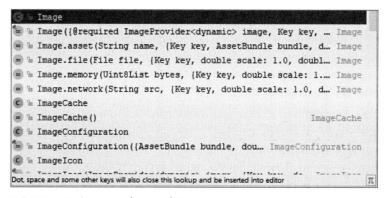

FIGURE 6.13: Image code completion

As a side note, the `Image` widget also supports animated GIFs.

The following sample uses the default `Image` constructor to initialize the `image` and `fit` arguments. The `image` argument is set by using the `AssetImage()` constructor with the default bundle location of the `logo.png` file. You can use the `fit` argument to size the `Image` widget with the `BoxFit` options, such as `contain`, `cover`, `fill`, `fitHeight`, `fitWidth`, or `none` (Figure 6.14).

```
// Image - on the left side
Image(
  image: AssetImage("assets/images/logo.png"),
  fit: BoxFit.cover,
),

// Image from a URL - on the right side
Image.network(
  'https://flutter.io/images/catalog-widget-placeholder.png',
),
```

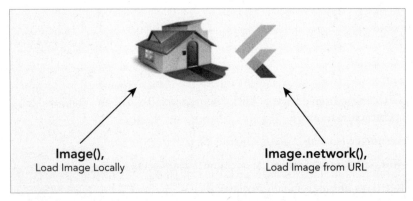

Image(),
Load Image Locally

Image.network(),
Load Image from URL

FIGURE 6.14: Images loaded locally and from network (web)

If you add color to the image, it colorizes the image portion and leaves any transparencies alone, giving a silhouette look (Figure 6.15).

```
// Image
Image(
  image: AssetImage("assets/images/logo.png"),
  color: Colors.deepOrange,
  fit: BoxFit.cover,
),
```

FIGURE 6.15: Silhouette-style image

Icon

The Icon widget is drawn with a glyph from a font described in IconData. Flutter's icons.dart file has the full list of icons available from the font MaterialIcons. A great way to add custom icons is to add to the AssetBundle fonts containing glyphs. Once example is Font Awesome, which has a high-quality list of icons and a Flutter package. Of course, there are many other high-quality icons available from other sources.

The Icon widget allows you to change the Icon widget's color, size, and other properties (Figure 6.16).

```
Icon(
  Icons.brush,
  color: Colors.lightBlue,
  size: 48.0,
),
```

FIGURE 6.16: Icons with custom sizes

TRY IT OUT Creating the Images Project; Adding Assets; and Loading Images, Icons, and Decorators

Create a new Flutter project and name it ch6_images; you can follow the instructions in Chapter 4. For this project, you need to create only the pages and assets/images folders. Create the Home class as a StatelessWidget. The goal of this app is to provide a look at how to use the Image and Icon widgets.

In this example, you'll customize the width property of the two Image widgets according to the device screen size. To obtain the device screen size, you can use the MediaQuery.of() method.

1. Open the pubspec.yaml file to add resources. In the assets section, add the assets/images/ folder declaration. I like to create an assets folder at the root of the project and add subfolders for each type of resource, as shown in Chapter 4.

   ```
   # To add assets to your application, add an assets section, such as this:
   assets:
    - assets/images/
   ```

   Add the folder assets and subfolder images at the project's root and then copy the logo.png file to the images folder. Click the Save button, and depending on the editor you are using, it automatically runs flutter packages get. Once finished, it shows this message: Process finished with exit code 0. If it does not automatically run the command for you, open the Terminal window (located at the bottom of your editor) and type **flutter packages get**.

2. Open the home.dart file and modify the body property. Add a SafeArea widget to the body property with a SingleChildScrollView as a child of the SafeArea widget. Add Padding as a child of SingleChildScrollView and then add a Column as a child of the Padding.

   ```
   body: SafeArea(
     child: SingleChildScrollView(
       child: Padding(
         padding: EdgeInsets.all(16.0),
         child: Column(
           children: <Widget>[
           ],
         ),
       ),
     ),
   ),
   ```

3. Add the widget class name `ImagesAndIconWidget()` to the `Column` children widget list. The `Column` is located in the `body` property.

```
body: SafeArea(
  child: SingleChildScrollView(
    child: Padding(
      padding: EdgeInsets.all(16.0),
      child: Column(
        children: <Widget>[
          const ImagesAndIconWidget(),
        ],
      ),
    ),
  ),
),
```

4. Add the `ImagesAndIconWidget()` widget class after `class Home extends StatelessWidget` `{...}`. In the widget class, a local image is loaded by the `AssetImage` class. Using the `Image.network` constructor an image is loaded by a URL string. The `Image` widget's `width` property uses the `MediaQuery.of(context).size.width / 3` to calculate the `width` value as one-third of the device width.

```
class ImagesAndIconWidget extends StatelessWidget {
  const ImagesAndIconWidget({
    Key key,
  }) : super(key: key);

  @override
  Widget build(BuildContext context) {
    return Row(
      mainAxisAlignment: MainAxisAlignment.spaceEvenly,
      children: <Widget>[
        Image(
          image: AssetImage("assets/images/logo.png"),
          //color: Colors.orange,
          fit: BoxFit.cover,
          width: MediaQuery.of(context).size.width / 3,
        ),
        Image.network(
          'https://flutter.io/images/catalog-widget-placeholder.png',
          width: MediaQuery.of(context).size.width / 3,
        ),
        Icon(
          Icons.brush,
          color: Colors.lightBlue,
          size: 48.0,
        ),
      ],
    );
  }
}
```

How It Works

By declaring your assets in the `pubspec.yaml` file, they are accessible by the `AssetImage` class from an `AssetBundle`. The `Image` widget through the `image` property loads a local image with the `AssetBundle` class. To load an image over a network (such as the Web), you use the `Image.network` constructor by passing a URL string. The `Icon` widget uses the `MaterialIcons` font library, which draws a glyph from the font described in the `IconData` class.

USING DECORATORS

Decorators help to convey a message depending on the user's action or customize the look and feel of a widget. There are different types of decorators for each task.

➤   `Decoration`—The base class to define other decorations.

➤   `BoxDecoration`—Provides many ways to draw a box with `border`, `body`, and `boxShadow`.

➤   `InputDecoration`—Used in `TextField` and `TextFormField` to customize the border, label, icon, and styles. This is a great way to give the user feedback on data entry, specifying a hint, an error, an alert icon, and more.

A `BoxDecoration` class (Figure 6.17) is a great way to customize a `Container` widget to create shapes by setting the `borderRadius`, `color`, `gradient`, and `boxShadow` properties.

```
// BoxDecoration
Container(
  height: 100.0,
  width: 100.0,
  decoration: BoxDecoration(
    borderRadius: BorderRadius.all(Radius.
circular(20.0)),
    color: Colors.orange,
    boxShadow: [
      BoxShadow(
        color: Colors.grey,
        blurRadius: 10.0,
        offset: Offset(0.0, 10.0),
      )
    ],
  ),
),
```

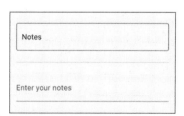

FIGURE 6.17: BoxDecoration applied to a Container

The `InputDecoration` class (Figure 6.18) is used with a `TextField` or `TextFormField` to specify labels, borders, icons, hints, errors, and styles. This is helpful in communicating with the user as they enter data. For the `border` property shown here, I am implementing two ways to customize it, with `UnderlineInputBorder` and with `OutlineInputBorder`:

FIGURE 6.18: InputDecoration with OutlineInputBorder and default border

```
// TextField
TextField(
```

```
      keyboardType: TextInputType.text,
      style: TextStyle(
        color: Colors.grey.shade800,
        fontSize: 16.0,
      ),
      decoration: InputDecoration(
        labelText: "Notes",
        labelStyle: TextStyle(color: Colors.purple),
        //border: UnderlineInputBorder(),
        border: OutlineInputBorder(),

      ),
    ),

    // TextFormField
    TextFormField(
      decoration: InputDecoration(
        labelText: 'Enter your notes',
      ),
    ),
```

TRY IT OUT **Continuing the Images Project by Adding Decorators**

Still editing the `home.dart` file, you'll add the `BoxDecoratorWidget()` and `InputDecoratorsWidget()` widget classes.

1. Add the widget class names `BoxDecoratorWidget()` and `InputDecoratorsWidget()` after the `ImagesAndIconWidget()` widget class. Add a `Divider()` widget between each widget class name.

    ```
    body: SafeArea(
      child: SingleChildScrollView(
        child: Padding(
          padding: EdgeInsets.all(16.0),
          child: Column(
            children: <Widget>[
              const ImagesAndIconWidget(),
              Divider(),
              const BoxDecoratorWidget(),
              Divider(),
              const InputDecoratorsWidget(),
            ],
          ),
        ),
      ),
    ),
    ```

2. Add the `BoxDecoratorWidget()` widget class after the `ImagesAndIconWidget()` widget class. The widget class returns a `Padding` widget with the `Container` widget as a child. The `Container` `decoration` property uses the `BoxDecoration` class. Using the `BoxDecoration` `borderRadius`, `color`, and `boxShadow` properties, you create a rounded button shape such as the one in Figure 6.17.

    ```
    class BoxDecoratorWidget extends StatelessWidget {
      const BoxDecoratorWidget({
    ```

```
      Key key,
    }) : super(key: key);

    @override
    Widget build(BuildContext context) {
      return Padding(
        padding: EdgeInsets.all(16.0),
        child: Container(
          height: 100.0,
          width: 100.0,
          decoration: BoxDecoration(
            borderRadius: BorderRadius.all(Radius.circular(20.0)),
            color: Colors.orange,
            boxShadow: [
              BoxShadow(
                color: Colors.grey,
                blurRadius: 10.0,
                offset: Offset(0.0, 10.0),
              )
            ],
          ),
        ),
      );
    }
  }
```

3. Add the `InputDecoratorsWidget()` widget class after the `BoxDecoratorWidget()` widget class. You take a `TextField` and use `TextStyle` to change the `color` and `fontSize` properties. The `InputDecoration` class is used to set the `labelText`, `labelStyle`, `border`, and `enabledBorder` values to customize the border properties. I am using the `OutlineInputBorder` here, but you could also use the `UnderlineInputBorder` class instead. I left `border` `UnderlineInputBorder` and `enabledBorder` `OutlineInputBorder()` commented out, allowing you to test both classes.

The following code adds two `TextField` widgets customized by two different decorations. The first `TextField` customizes different `InputDecoration` properties to show a purple notes label with the `OutlineInputBorder()`. The second `TextField` widget uses the decoration without customizing the border property.

```
    class InputDecoratorsWidget extends StatelessWidget {
      const InputDecoratorsWidget({
        Key key,
      }) : super(key: key);

      @override
      Widget build(BuildContext context) {
        return Column(
          children: <Widget>[
            TextField(
              keyboardType: TextInputType.text,
              style: TextStyle(
                color: Colors.grey.shade800,
                fontSize: 16.0,
              ),
              decoration: InputDecoration(
```

```
              labelText: "Notes",
              labelStyle: TextStyle(color: Colors.purple),
              //border: UnderlineInputBorder(),
              //enabledBorder: OutlineInputBorder(borderSide: BorderSide(color.
Colors.purple)),
              border: OutlineInputBorder(),
            ),
          ),
          Divider(
            color: Colors.lightGreen,
            height: 50.0,
          ),
          TextFormField(
            decoration: InputDecoration(labelText: 'Enter your notes'),
          ),
        ],
      );
    }
  }
```

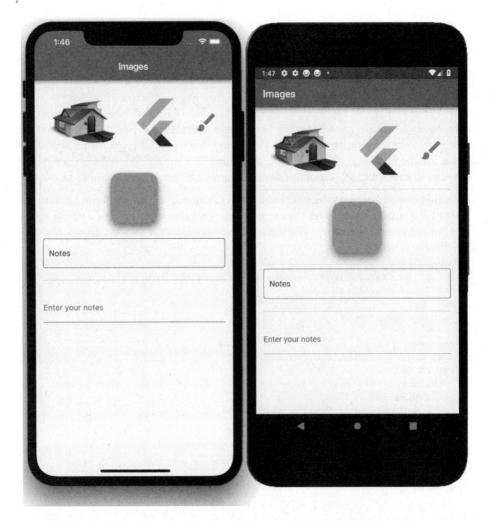

How It Works

Decorators are invaluable to enhance the look and feel of widgets. The `BoxDecoration` provides many ways to draw a box with `border`, `body`, and `boxShadow`. The `InputDecoration` is used in either a `Text-Field` or `TextFormField`. Not only does it allow the customization of the `border`, `label`, `icon`, and `styles`, but it also gives users feedback on data entry with hints, errors, icons, and more.

USING THE FORM WIDGET TO VALIDATE TEXT FIELDS

There are different ways to use text field widgets to retrieve, validate, and manipulate data. The `Form` widget is optional, but the benefits of using a `Form` widget are to validate each text field as a group. You can group `TextFormField` widgets to manually or automatically validate them. The `TextForm-Field` widget wraps a `TextField` widget to provide validation when enclosed in a `Form` widget.

If all text fields pass the `FormState validate` method, then it returns `true`. If any text fields contain errors, it displays the appropriate error message for each text field, and the `FormState validate` method returns `false`. This process gives you the ability to use `FormState` to check for any validation errors instead of checking each text field for errors and not allowing the posting of invalid data.

The `Form` widget needs a unique key to identify it and is created by using `GlobalKey`. This `GlobalKey` value is unique across the entire app.

In the next example, you'll create a form with two `TextFormFields` (Figure 6.19) to enter an item and quantity to order. You'll create an `Order` class to hold the item and quantity and fill the order once the validation passes.

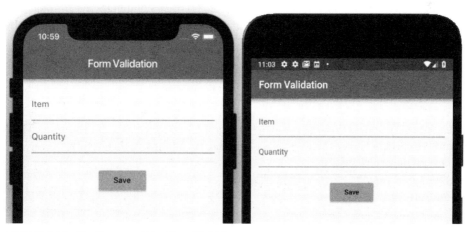

FIGURE 6.19: The Form and TextFormField layout

TRY IT OUT Creating the Form Validation App

Create a new Flutter project and name it `ch6_form_validation`. You can follow the instructions in Chapter 4. For this project, you need to create only the `pages` folder. The goal of this app is to show how to validate data entry values.

1. Open the `home.dart` file and add to the body a `SafeArea` widget with `Column` as a `child`. In the `Column` children, add the `Form()` widget, which you modify in step 7.

    ```
    body: SafeArea(
      child: Column(
        children: <Widget>[
          Form(),
        ],
      ),
    ),
    ```

2. Create the `Order` class after `class _HomeState extends State<Home> {...}`. The `Order` class will hold `item` as a `String` value and `quantity` as an `int` value.

    ```
    class _HomeState extends State<Home> {
      //...
    }

    class Order {
      String item;
      int quantity;
    }
    ```

3. After the `class _HomeState extends State<Home>` declaration and before `@override`, add the variables `_formStateKey` for the `GlobalKey` value and `_order` to initiate the `Order` class.

    Create the unique key for the form by using `GlobalKey<FormState>` and mark it `final` since it will not change.

    ```
    class _HomeState extends State<Home> {
      final GlobalKey<FormState> _formStateKey = GlobalKey<FormState>();

      // Order to Save
      Order _order = Order();
    ```

4. Create the `_validateItemRequired(String value)` method that accepts a `String` value. Use the ternary operator to check whether the value is set to `isEmpty`, and if yes, then return `'Item Required'`. Otherwise, return `null`.

    ```
    String _validateItemRequired(String value) {
      return value.isEmpty ? 'Item Required' : null;
    }
    ```

5. Create the `_validateItemCount(String value)` method that accepts a `String` value. Use the ternary operator to convert `String` to `int`. Then check whether `int` is greater than zero; if it's not, return `'At least one Item is Required'`.

    ```
    String _validateItemCount(String value) {
      // Check if value is not null and convert to integer
    ```

```
      int _valueAsInteger = value.isEmpty ? 0 : int.tryParse(value);
      return _valueAsInteger == 0 ? 'At least one Item is Required' : null;
   }
```

6. Create the _submitOrder() method called by the FlatButton widget to check whether all TextFormField fields pass validation and call Form save() to gather values from all TextFormFields to the Order class.

```
void _submitOrder() {
  if(_formStateKey.currentState.validate()) {
    _formStateKey.currentState.save();
    print('Order Item: ${order.item}');
    print('Order Quantity: ${order.quantity}');
  }
}
```

7. Add to the Form() widget a private key variable called _formStateKey, set autovalidate to true, add Padding for the child property, and add Column as a child of Padding.

Setting autovalidate to true allows the Form() widget to check validation for all fields as the user enters information and to display an appropriate message. If autovalidate is set to false, no validation happens until the _formStateKey.currentState.validate() method is manually called.

```
Form(
  key: _formStateKey,
  autovalidate: true,
  child: Padding(
    padding: EdgeInsets.all(16.0),
    child: Column(
      children: <Widget>[

      ],
    ),
  ),
),
```

8. Add two TextFormField widgets to the Column children list of Widget. The first TextFormField is an item description, and the second TextFormField is a quantity of items to order.

9. Add an InputDecoration class with hintText and labelText for each TextFormField.

```
hintText: 'Espresso',
labelText: 'Item',
```

10. Add a call for the validator and onSaved methods. The validator method is called to validate characters as they are entered, and the onSaved method is called by the Form save() method to gather values from each TextFormField.

For the validator, pass the value entered in the TextFormField widget by naming the variable value inside parentheses and use the fat arrow syntax (=>) to call the method _validateItemRequired(value). The fat arrow syntax is shorthand for { return mycustomexpression; }.

```
validator: (value) => _validateItemRequired(value),
```

Note that in step 2 you created an `Order` class to hold the item and quantity values to be collected by the `onSaved` methods. When the `Form save()` method is called, all of the `TextField-Form onSaved` methods are called, and values are collected in the `Order` class such as `order.item = value`.

```
onSaved: (value) => order.item = value,
```

The following code shows both `TextFormFields`:

```
TextFormField(
  decoration: InputDecoration(
    hintText: 'Espresso',
    labelText: 'Item',
  ),
  validator: (value) => _validateItemRequired(value),
  onSaved: (value) => order.item = value,
),
TextFormField(
  decoration:  InputDecoration(
    hintText: '3',
    labelText: 'Quantity',
  ),
  validator: (value) => _validateItemCount(value),
  onSaved: (value) => order.quantity = int.tryParse(value),
),
```

Notice that you use `int.tryParse()` to convert the quantity value from `String` to `int`.

11. Add a `Divider` and a `RaisedButton` after the last `TextFormField`. For the `onPressed`, call the `_submitOrder()` method created in step 6.

```
Divider(height: 32.0,),
RaisedButton(
  child: Text('Save'),
  color: Colors.lightGreen,
  onPressed: () => _submitOrder(),
),
```

How It Works

When retrieving data from input fields, the Form widget is an incredible helper, and you used the GlobalKey class to assign a unique key to identify it. Use the Form widget to group TextFormField widgets to manually or automatically validate them. The FormState validate method validates data, and if it passes, it returns true. If the FormState validate method fails, it returns false, and each text field displays the appropriate error message. Each TextFormField validator property has a method to check for the appropriate value. Each TextFormField onSaved property passes the currently entered value to the Order class. In a real-world app, you would take the Order class values and save them to a database locally or on a web server. In Chapters 14, 15 and 16, you'll learn how to implement Cloud Firestore to access data from a web server.

CHECKING ORIENTATION

Under certain scenarios, knowing the device orientation helps in laying out the appropriate UI. There are two ways to figure out orientation, MediaQuery.of(context).orientation and OrientationBuilder.

A huge note on OrientationBuilder: it returns the amount of space available to the parent to figure out orientation. This means it does not guarantee the actual device orientation. I prefer using MediaQuery to obtain the actual device orientation because of its accuracy.

TRY IT OUT **Creating the Orientation App**

Create a new Flutter project and name it ch6_orientation. You can follow the instructions in Chapter 4. For this project, you only need to create the pages folder.

In this example, the UI layout will change depending on orientation. When the device is in portrait mode, it will show one Icon, and when in landscape mode, it will show two Icons. You'll take a look at a Container widget that will grow in size and change color, and you'll use a GridView widget to show two or four columns. Lastly, I added the OrientationBuilder widget to show that when the OrientationBuilder is not a parent widget, the correct orientation is not calculated correctly. But if you place the OrientationBuilder as a parent, it works correctly; note that using SafeArea does not affect the outcome. The following image shows the final project.

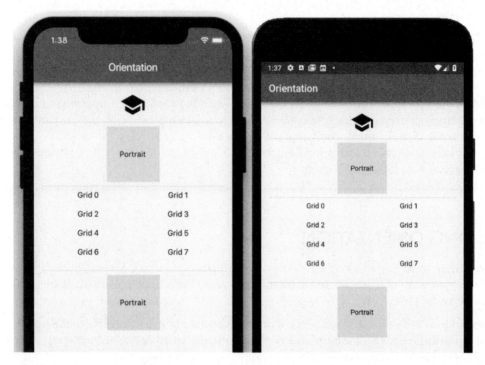

1. Open the `home.dart` file and add to the body a `SafeArea` with `SingleChildScrollView` as a child. Add `Padding` as a child of the `SingleChildScrollView`. Add a `Column` as a `child` of the `Padding`. In the `Column` `children` property, add the widget class called `OrientationLayoutIconsWidget()`, which you will create next. Make sure you add the `const` keyword before the widget class name to take advantage of caching to improve performance.

```
body: SafeArea(
  child: SingleChildScrollView(
    child: Padding(
      padding: EdgeInsets.all(16.0),
      child: Column(
        children: <Widget>[
          const OrientationLayoutIconsWidget(),
        ],
      ),
    ),
  ),
),
```

2. Add the `OrientationLayoutIconsWidget()` widget class after `class Home extends StatelessWidget {...}`. The first variable to initialize is the current orientation by calling `MediaQuery.of()` after `Widget build(BuildContext context)`.

```
class OrientationLayoutIconsWidget extends StatelessWidget {
  const OrientationLayoutIconsWidget({
    Key key,
  }) : super(key: key);
```

```
      @override
      Widget build(BuildContext context) {
        Orientation _orientation = MediaQuery.of(context).orientation;
        return Container();
      }
    }
```

3. Based on the current `Orientation`, you return a different layout of `Icon` widgets. Use a ternary operator to check whether `Orientation` is `portrait`, and if so, return a single `Row` icon. If `Orientation` is `landscape`, return a `Row` of two `Icon` widgets. Replace the current `return Container()` with the following code:

```
    return _orientation == Orientation.portrait
        ? Row(
          mainAxisAlignment: MainAxisAlignment.center,
          children: <Widget>[
            Icon(
              Icons.school,
              size: 48.0,
            ),
          ],
        )
        : Row(
          mainAxisAlignment: MainAxisAlignment.center,
          children: <Widget>[
            Icon(
              Icons.school,
              size: 48.0,
            ),
            Icon(
              Icons.brush,
              size: 48.0,
            ),
          ],
        );
```

4. Putting all of the code together, you get the following:

```
    class OrientationLayoutIconsWidget extends StatelessWidget {
      const OrientationLayoutIconsWidget({
        Key key,
      }) : super(key: key);

      @override
      Widget build(BuildContext context) {
        Orientation _orientation = MediaQuery.of(context).orientation;
        return _orientation == Orientation.portrait
            ? Row(
          mainAxisAlignment: MainAxisAlignment.center,
          children: <Widget>[
            Icon(
              Icons.school,
              size: 48.0,
            ),
          ],
```

```
      )
          : Row(
        mainAxisAlignment: MainAxisAlignment.center,
        children: <Widget>[
          Icon(
            Icons.school,
            size: 48.0,
          ),
          Icon(
            Icons.brush,
            size: 48.0,
          ),
        ],
      );
    }
  }
```

5. After `OrientationLayoutIconsWidget()`, add a `Divider` widget and the `OrientationLayoutWidget()` widget class to create.

The steps are similar to the earlier ones, but instead of using rows and icons, you are using containers: obtain the `Orientation` mode and for portrait return a yellow `Container` widget with a width of 100.0 pixels. When the device is rotated, the landscape returns a green `Container` widget with a width of 200.0 pixels.

```
class OrientationLayoutWidget extends StatelessWidget {
  const OrientationLayoutWidget({
    Key key,
  }) : super(key: key);

  @override
  Widget build(BuildContext context) {
    Orientation _orientation = MediaQuery.of(context).orientation;

    return _orientation == Orientation.portrait
        ? Container(
      alignment: Alignment.center,
```

```
                color: Colors.yellow,
                height: 100.0,
                width: 100.0,
                child: Text('Portrait'),
            )
                : Container(
                alignment: Alignment.center,
                color: Colors.lightGreen,
                height: 100.0,
                width: 200.0,
                child: Text('Landscape'),
            );
        }
    }
```

6. After `OrientationLayoutWidget()`, add a `Divider` widget and the `GridViewWidget()` widget class that you will create.

Although you will take a closer look at the `GridView` widget in Chapter 9, it is appropriate to use it now since it's the closest to a real-world example. In portrait mode, the `GridView` widget shows two columns, and in landscape mode, it shows four columns.

There are a few items to note here. Since the `GridView` widget is inside a `Column` widget, set the `GridView.count` constructor shrinkWrap argument to `true` or it will break the constraints. I also set the `physics` argument to `NeverScrollableScrollPhysics()` or the `GridView` will scroll its children from within. Remember, you have all these widgets inside a `SingleChildScrollView`.

```
class GridViewWidget extends StatelessWidget {
    const GridViewWidget({
        Key key,
    }) : super(key: key);

    @override
    Widget build(BuildContext context) {
        Orientation _orientation = MediaQuery.of(context).orientation;

        return GridView.count(
            shrinkWrap: true,
            physics: NeverScrollableScrollPhysics(),
            crossAxisCount: _orientation == Orientation.portrait ? 2 : 4,
            childAspectRatio: 5.0,
            children: List.generate(8, (int index) {
                return Text("Grid $index", textAlign: TextAlign.center,);
            }),
        );
    }
}
```

7. After `GridViewWidget()`, add a `Divider` widget and the `OrientationBuilderWidget()` widget class that you will create.

As mentioned previously, I use `MediaQuery.of()` to obtain orientation because it's more accurate, but it's good to know how to use `OrientationBuilder`.

OrientationBuilder requires a `builder` property to be passed and cannot be `null`. The `builder` property takes two parameters: `BuildContext` and `Orientation`.

```
builder: (BuildContext context, Orientation orientation) {}
```

The steps and result are the same as with `_buildOrientationLayout()`. Use the ternary operator to check for the orientation, and for portrait, and return a yellow `Container` widget with a width of 100.0 pixels. When the device is rotated, the landscape returns a green `Container` widget with a width of 200.0 pixels.

Note that `OrientationBuilder` runs the risk of not detecting the orientation mode correctly because it is a `child` widget and relies on the parent screen size instead of the device orientation. Because of this, I recommend using `MediaQuery.of()` instead.

```
// OrientationBuilder as a child does not give correct Orientation. i.e Child
of Column...
// OrientationBuilder as a parent gives correct Orientation
class OrientationBuilderWidget extends StatelessWidget {
  const OrientationBuilderWidget({
    Key key,
  }) : super(key: key);

  @override
  Widget build(BuildContext context) {
    return OrientationBuilder(
      builder: (BuildContext context, Orientation orientation) {
        return orientation == Orientation.portrait
            ? Container(
          alignment: Alignment.center,
          color: Colors.yellow,
          height: 100.0,
          width: 100.0,
          child: Text('Portrait'),
        )
            : Container(
          alignment: Alignment.center,
          color: Colors.lightGreen,
          height: 100.0,
          width: 200.0,
          child: Text('Landscape'),
        );
      },
    );
  }
}
```

How It Works

You can detect device orientation by calling MediaQuery.of(context).orientation, which returns either a portrait or landscape value. There is also OrientationBuilder, which returns the amount of space available to the parent to figure out the orientation. I recommend using MediaQuery to retrieve the correct device orientation.

SUMMARY

In this chapter, you learned about the most commonly used (basic) widgets. These basic widgets are the building blocks to designing mobile apps. You also explored different types of buttons to choose depending on the situation. You learned how to add assets to your app via AssetBundle by listing items in the pubspec.yaml file. You used the Image widget to load images from the local device or a web server through a URL string. You saw how the Icon widget gives you the ability to load icons by using the MaterialIcons font library.

To modify the appearance of widgets, you learned how to use BoxDecoration. To improve giving users feedback on data entry, you implemented InputDecoration. Validating multiple text field data entries can be cumbersome, but you can use the Form widget to manually or automatically validate them. Lastly, using MediaQuery to find out the current device orientation is extremely powerful in any mobile app to lay out widgets depending on the orientation.

In the next chapter, you'll learn how to use animations. You'll start by using widgets such as AnimatedContainer, AnimatedCrossFade, and AnimatedOpacity and finish with the powerful AnimationController for custom animation.

▶ **WHAT YOU LEARNED IN THIS CHAPTER**

TOPIC	KEY CONCEPTS
Using basic widgets	You learned to use `Scaffold`, `SafeArea`, `AppBar`, `Container`, `Text`, `RichText`, `Column`, `Row`, `Column` and `Row` Nesting, Buttons, `FloatingActionButton`, `FlatButton`, `RaisedButton`, `IconButton`, `PopupMenuButton`, and `ButtonBar`.
Using images	You learned to use `AssetBundle`, `Image`, and `Icon`.
Using decorators	You learned to use `Decoration`, `BoxDecoration`, and `InputDecoration`.
Using forms for text field validation	You learned to use the `Form` widget to validate each `TextFormField` as a group.
Detecting orientation	You learned to use `MediaQuery.of(context).orientation` and `OrientationBuilder` to detect device orientation.

7

Adding Animation to an App

WHAT YOU WILL LEARN IN THIS CHAPTER

➤ How to use `AnimatedContainer` to gradually change values over time

➤ How to use `AnimatedCrossFade` to cross-fade between two children widgets

➤ How to use `AnimatedOpacity` to show or hide widget visibility by animated fading over time

➤ How to use the `AnimationController` to create custom animations

➤ How to use the `AnimationController` to control staggered animations

In this chapter, you'll learn how to add animation to an app to convey action, which can improve the user experience (UX) if appropriately used. Too many animations without conveying the appropriate action can make the UX worse. Flutter has two types of animation: physics-based and Tween. This chapter will focus on Tween animations.

Physics-based animation is used to mimic real-world behavior. For example, when an object is dropped and hits the ground, it will bounce and continue to move forward, but with each bounce, it continues to slow down with smaller rebounds and eventually stop. As the object gets closer to the ground with each bounce, the velocity increases, but the height of the bounce decreases.

Tween is short for "in-between," meaning that the animation has beginning and ending points, a timeline, and a curve that specifies the timing and speed of the transition. The beauty is that the framework automatically calculates the transition from the beginning to end point.

USING ANIMATEDCONTAINER

Let's start with a simple animation by using the `AnimatedContainer` widget. This is a `Container` widget that gradually changes values over a period of time. The `AnimatedContainer` constructor has arguments called `duration`, `curve`, `color`, `height`, `width`, `child`, `decoration`, `transform`, and many others.

TRY IT OUT   Creating the AnimatedContainer App

In this project, you'll animate the width of a `Container` widget by tapping it. For example, you could use this type of animation to animate a horizontal bar chart.

1. Create a new Flutter project and name it `ch7_animations`. You can follow the instructions in Chapter 4, "Creating a Starter Project Template." For this project, you need to create only the `pages` and `widgets` folders.

2. Create a new Dart file in the `widgets` folder. Right-click the `widgets` folder, select New ⇨ Dart File, enter **animated_container.dart**, and click the OK button to save.

3. Import the `material.dart` library, add a new line, and then start typing **st**. The autocompletion help opens. Select the `stful` abbreviation and give it a name of `AnimatedContainerWidget`.

4. After the class `_AnimatedContainerWidgetState extends State<AnimatedContainerWidget>` and before `@override`, add the variables `_height` and `_width` and the `_increaseWidth()` method.

The `_height` and `_width` variables are of type `double`.

```
double _height = 100.0;
```

The `_increaseWidth()` method calls the `setState()` method to notify the framework that the `_width` value has changed and schedules a build for the state of this object to redraw the subtree. If you do not call `setState()`, the `_width` value still changes, but the `AnimatedContainer` widget will not redraw with the new value.

```
class _AnimatedContainerWidgetState extends State<AnimatedContainerWidget> {
  double _height = 100.0;
  double _width = 100.0;

  _increaseWidth() {
    setState(() {
      _width = _width >= 320.0 ? 100.0 : _width += 50.0;
    });
  }

  @override
  Widget build(BuildContext context) {
```

When the page loads, the `_height` and `_width` variables are initiated with values of 100.0 pixels. When the `FlatButton` is tapped, the `onPressed` property calls the `_increaseWidth()` method.

Here you'll use 320.0 pixels as the maximum allowed width, but this could have been the device width instead. With each tap event, you increase the current width by 50.0 pixels starting from 100.0 pixels. As the width increases, once it goes above 320.0 pixels, you reset the size to 100.0 pixels. To calculate AnimatedContainer's new _width, use the ternary operator. If the _width is greater than or equal to 320.0 pixels, then set _width to the original 100.0 pixels. This will animate AnimatedContainer back to the original size. Otherwise, take the current _width value and add 50.0 pixels. Note that the plus and equal signs (+=) are used to take the current value and add to it.

Notice that the height and width values are private variables, _height and _width, since you are leading them with the underscore symbol.

The FlatButton child is the label that shows the message "Tap to Grow Width." I am using \n to continue the text on the next line and using the $ sign to pass the _width value.

Once the FlatButton is pressed, you add a call to the method _increaseWidth() in the onPressed property. Ignore the code editor's red squiggly lines since you have not created the variables and method yet.

The duration argument takes a Duration() object to specify the type of time to use such as microseconds, milliseconds, seconds, minutes, hours, and days.

```
duration: Duration(milliseconds: 500),
```

The curve argument takes a Curves class and uses Curves.elasticOut. Some of the types of Curves available are bounceIn, bounceInOut, bounceOut, easeIn, easeInOut, easeOut, elasticIn, elasticInOut, and elasticOut.

```
curve: Curves.elasticOut,
```

Here's the full _AnimatedContainerWidget() widget class:

```
import 'package:flutter/material.dart';

class AnimatedContainerWidget extends StatefulWidget {
  const AnimatedContainerWidget({
    Key key,
  }) : super(key: key);

  @override
  _AnimatedContainerWidgetState createState() => _AnimatedContainerWidgetState();
}

class _AnimatedContainerWidgetState extends State<AnimatedContainerWidget> {
  double _height = 100.0;
  double _width = 100.0;

  void _increaseWidth() {
    setState(() {
      _width = _width >= 320.0 ? 100.0 : _width += 50.0;
    });
  }
```

```
    @override
    Widget build(BuildContext context) {
      return Row(
        children: <Widget>[
          AnimatedContainer(
            duration: Duration(milliseconds: 500),
            curve: Curves.elasticOut,
            color: Colors.amber,
            height: _height,
            width: _width,
            child: FlatButton(
              child: Text('Tap to\nGrow Width\n$_width'),
              onPressed: () {
                _increaseWidth();
              },
            ),
          ),
        ],
      );
    }
  }
```

5. Open the `home.dart` file and import the `animated_container.dart` file to the top of the page.

    ```
    import 'package:flutter/material.dart';
    import 'package:ch7_animations/widgets/animated_container.dart';
    ```

6. Add to the body a `SafeArea` widget with `Column` as a `child`. In the `Column` children, add the call to the widget class `AnimatedContainerWidget()`.

    ```
    body: SafeArea(
      child: Column(
        children: <Widget>[
          AnimatedContainerWidget(),
        ],
      ),
    ),
    ```

How It Works

The `AnimatedContainer` constructor takes a `duration` argument, and you use the `Duration` class to specify 500 milliseconds. The 500 milliseconds equals half a second. The `curve` argument gives the animation a spring effect by using `Curves.elasticOut`. The `onPressed` argument calls the `_increaseWidth()` method to change the `_width` variable dynamically. The `setState()` method notifies the Flutter framework that the internal state of the object changed and causes the framework to schedule a build for this `State` object. The `AnimatedContainer` widget automatically animates between the old `_width` value and the new `_width` value.

USING ANIMATEDCROSSFADE

The `AnimatedCrossFade` widget provides a great cross-fade between two children widgets. The `AnimatedCrossFade` constructor takes `duration`, `firstChild`, `secondChild`, `crossFadeState`, `sizeCurve`, and many other arguments.

TRY IT OUT Adding the AnimatedCrossFade Widget

This example creates a cross-fade between colors and size by tapping the widget. The widget will cross-fade the changing size and color from yellow to green.

1. Create a new Dart file in the `widgets` folder. Right-click the `widgets` folder, select New ⇨ Dart File, enter **animated_cross_fade.dart**, and click the OK button to save.

2. Import the `material.dart` library, add a new line, and start typing **st**. The autocompletion help opens. Select the `stful` abbreviation and give it a name of `AnimatedCrossFadeWidget`.

3. After the class `_AnimatedCrossFadeWidgetState extends State<AnimatedCrossFadeWidget>` and before `@override`, add a variable for `_crossFadeStateShowFirst` and the `_crossFade()` method.

The `_crossFadeStateShowFirst` variable is of type Boolean (`bool`).

```
bool _crossFadeStateShowFirst = true;
```

The `_crossFade()` method calls `setState()` to notify the framework that the `_crossFadeState-ShowFirst` value has changed and schedules a build for the state of this object to redraw the subtree. If you do not call `setState()`, the `_width` value still changes, but the `AnimatedCrossFade` widget will not redraw with the new value.

```
class _AnimatedCrossFadeWidgetState extends State<AnimatedCrossFadeWidget> {
  bool _crossFadeStateShowFirst = true;
```

```
void _crossFade() {
  setState(() {
    _crossFadeStateShowFirst = _crossFadeStateShowFirst ? false : true;
  });
}

@override
Widget build(BuildContext context) {
```

When the page is loaded, the `_crossFadeStateShowFirst` variable is initiated with a value of true. When `FlatButton` is tapped, the `onPressed` property calls the `_crossFade()` method.

To track which child (`firstChild`, `secondChild`) the `AnimatedCrossFade` widget should show and animate, use the ternary operator. If the `_crossFadeStateShowFirst` is true, then set the `_crossFadeStateShowFirst` value to `false`. Otherwise, set it to `true` since the current value is `false`.

4. To keep the UI clean, add each animation widget in a separate `Row`. Embed the `AnimatedCrossFade` widget in a `Row` with a `Stack` as a child. The reason to use a `Stack` is to add a `FlatButton` over the `AnimatedCrossFade` widget to give it a label and an `onPressed` event. You could also use a `GestureDetector` widget.

```
@override
Widget build(BuildContext context) {
  return Row(
    children: <Widget>[
      Stack(
        alignment: Alignment.center,
        children: <Widget>[
          AnimatedCrossFade(
            duration: Duration(milliseconds: 500),
            sizeCurve: Curves.bounceOut,
            crossFadeState: _crossFadeStateShowFirst ? CrossFadeState.showFirst :
CrossFadeState.showSecond,
            firstChild: Container(
              color: Colors.amber,
              height: 100.0,
              width: 100.0,
            ),
            secondChild: Container(
              color: Colors.lime,
              height: 200.0,
              width: 200.0,
            ),
          ),
          Positioned.fill(
            child: FlatButton(
              child: Text('Tap to\nFade Color & Size'),
              onPressed: () {
                _crossFade();
              },
            ),
          ),
        ),
      ],
```

```
            ),
         ],
      );
   }
```

5. Use a duration of 500 milliseconds like in the previous animation.

```
duration: Duration(milliseconds: 500),
```

6. For `sizeCurve`, use `Curves.bounceOut` to see how the `Curves` class affects animations.

```
sizeCurve: Curves.bounceOut,
```

7. To decide which `Container` widget to show when the animation is completed, set the `cross-FadeState` argument value by using the ternary operator to check whether the `_crossFadeState-ShowFirst` value is true; then show `CrossFadeState.showFirst`; otherwise, show `CrossFadeState.showSecond`.

```
crossFadeState: _crossFadeStateShowFirst ? CrossFadeState.showFirst :
CrossFadeState.showSecond,
```

8. The animation will cross-fade between colors and sizes; for `firstChild` and `secondChild`, use a `Container`. The `firstChild` `Container` has a `Colors.amber` color property and `height` and `width` values of 100.0 pixels. The `secondChild` `Container` has a `Colors.lime` color property and `height` and `width` values of 200.0 pixels.

```
firstChild: Container(
  color: Colors.amber,
  height: 100.0,
  width: 100.0,
),
secondChild: Container(
  color: Colors.lime,
  height: 200.0,
  width: 200.0,
),
```

9. Add the second `Stack` child and call the `Positioned.fill` constructor with a child of `FlatButton`. Using `Positioned.fill` allows the `FlatButton` widget to resize itself to the maximum size of the `Stack` widget. For the `onPressed` property, add a call to the `_crossFade()` method.

```
Positioned.fill(
  child: FlatButton(
    child: Text('Tap to\nFade Color & Size'),
    onPressed: () {
      _crossFade();
    },
  ),
),
```

Here's the full `_AnimatedCrossFadeWidget()` widget class:

```
import 'package:flutter/material.dart';

class AnimatedCrossFadeWidget extends StatefulWidget {
  const AnimatedCrossFadeWidget({
```

```
    Key key,
  }) : super(key: key);

  @override
  _AnimatedCrossFadeWidgetState createState() => _AnimatedCrossFadeWidgetState();
}

class _AnimatedCrossFadeWidgetState extends State<AnimatedCrossFadeWidget> {
  bool _crossFadeStateShowFirst = true;

  void _crossFade() {
    setState(() {
      _crossFadeStateShowFirst = _crossFadeStateShowFirst ? false : true;
    });
  }

  @override
  Widget build(BuildContext context) {
    return Row(
      children: <Widget>[
        Stack(
          alignment: Alignment.center,
          children: <Widget>[
            AnimatedCrossFade(
              duration: Duration(milliseconds: 500),
              sizeCurve: Curves.bounceOut,
              crossFadeState: _crossFadeStateShowFirst ? CrossFadeState.showFirst :
CrossFadeState.showSecond,
              firstChild: Container(
                color: Colors.amber,
                height: 100.0,
                width: 100.0,
              ),
              secondChild: Container(
                color: Colors.lime,
                height: 200.0,
                width: 200.0,
              ),
            ),
            Positioned.fill(
              child: FlatButton(
                child: Text('Tap to\nFade Color & Size'),
                onPressed: () {
                  _crossFade();
                },
              ),
            ),
          ],
        ),
      ],
    );
  }
}
```

10. Continue editing the `home.dart` file and import the `animated_cross_fade.dart` file to the top of the page.

```
import 'package:flutter/material.dart';
import 'package:ch7_animations/widgets/animated_container.dart';
import 'package:ch7_animations/widgets/animated_cross_fade.dart';
```

11. Just after the `AnimatedContainerWidget()` widget class, add a `Divider()` widget. On the next line, add a call to the widget class `AnimatedCrossFadeWidget()`.

```
body: SafeArea(
  child: Column(
    children: <Widget>[
      AnimatedContainerWidget(),
      Divider(),
      AnimatedCrossFadeWidget(),
    ],
  ),
),
```

Notice how clean the code looks and how it improves the readability by separating each major section of the widget tree. More importantly, only the widget class running is being rebuilt, and the other animation widget classes are not, giving you great performance.

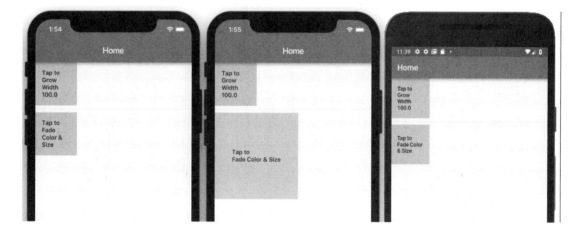

How It Works

The `AnimatedCrossFade` constructor takes a `duration` argument, and you use the `Duration` class to specify 500 milliseconds. The `sizeCurve` argument gives the animation between the two children's size a spring effect by using `Curves.bounceOut`. The `crossFadeState` argument sets the `child` widget to be shown once the animation is completed. By using the `_crossFadeStateShowFirst` variable, the correct `crossFadeState` child is displayed. The `firstChild` and `secondChild` arguments hold the two widgets to animate.

USING ANIMATEDOPACITY

If you need to hide or partially hide a widget, `AnimatedOpacity` is a great way to animate fading over time. The `AnimatedOpacity` constructor the takes `duration`, `opacity`, `curve`, and `child` arguments. For this example, you do not use a curve; since you want a smooth fade-out and fade-in, it's not necessary.

TRY IT OUT   Adding the AnimatedOpacity Widget

The example uses `opacity` to partially fade out a `Container` widget. The widget will animate the `opacity` value from fully visible to almost faded out.

1. Create a new Dart file in the `widgets` folder. Right-click the `widgets` folder, select New ⮑ Dart File, enter **animated_opacity.dart**, and click the OK button to save.

2. Import the `material.dart` library, add a new line, and then start typing **st**. The autocompletion help opens. Select the `stful` abbreviation and give it a name of `AnimatedOpacityWidget`.

3. After the class `_AnimatedOpacityWidgetState extends State<AnimatedOpacityWidget>` and before `@override`, add the variable for `_opacity` and the `_animatedOpacity()` method.

The `_opacity` variable is of type `double`.

```
double _opacity = 1.0;
```

The `_animatedOpacity()` method calls `setState()` to notify the framework that the `_opacity` value has changed and schedules a build for the state of this object to redraw the subtree. If you do not call `setState()`, the `_opacity` value still changes, but the `AnimatedOpacity` widget does not redraw with the new value.

```
class _AnimatedOpacityWidgetState extends State<AnimatedOpacityWidget> {
  double _opacity = 1.0;

  void _animatedOpacity() {
    setState(() {
      _opacity = _opacity == 1.0 ? 0.3 : 1.0;
    });
  }

  @override
  Widget build(BuildContext context) {
```

When the page is loaded, the `_opacity` variable is initiated with a value of 1.0, which is fully visible. When the `FlatButton` widget is tapped, the `onPressed` property calls the `_animatedOpacity()` method.

To calculate the widget opacity, use the ternary operator. If the `_opacity` value is `1.0`, then set `_opacity` to `0.3`. Otherwise, set it to `1.0` since the current value is `0.3`.

4. To keep the UI clean, add each animation widget in a separate Row. Embed the `AnimatedOpacity` widget in a Row.

```
@override
Widget build(BuildContext context) {
  return Row(
    children: <Widget>[
      AnimatedOpacity(
        duration: Duration(milliseconds: 500),
        opacity: _opacity,
        child: Container(
          color: Colors.amber,
          height: 100.0,
          width: 100.0,
          child: FlatButton(
            child: Text('Tap to Fade'),
            onPressed: () {
              _animatedOpacity();
            },
          ),
        ),
      ),
    ],
  );
}
```

5. Use a duration of 500 milliseconds like in the previous animations.

```
duration: Duration(milliseconds: 500),
```

6. The animation animates the `opacity` value of the `AnimatedOpacity` child widget, which is a `Container` in this case. Depending on the value of `opacity`, the `Container` widget fades out or fades in. An `opacity` value of 1.0 is fully visible, and an `opacity` value of 0.0 is invisible. You are going to animate the _opacity variable from 1.0 to 0.3, and vice versa.

```
opacity: _opacity,
```

7. Add a `Container` widget as a child of the `AnimatedOpacity` widget. Add a `FlatButton` widget as a child of the `Container` widget with `onPressed` calling the _animatedOpacity() method.

```
child: Container(
  color: Colors.amber,
  height: 100.0,
  width: 100.0,
  child: FlatButton(
    child: Text('Tap to Fade'),
    onPressed: () {
      _animatedOpacity();
    },
  ),
),
```

Here's the full `_buildAnimatedOpacity()` widget class:

```
import 'package:flutter/material.dart';

class AnimatedOpacityWidget extends StatefulWidget {
  const AnimatedOpacityWidget({
    Key key,
  }) : super(key: key);

  @override
  _AnimatedOpacityWidgetState createState() => _AnimatedOpacityWidgetState();
}

class _AnimatedOpacityWidgetState extends State<AnimatedOpacityWidget> {
  double _opacity = 1.0;

  void _animatedOpacity() {
    setState(() {
      _opacity = _opacity == 1.0 ? 0.3 : 1.0;
    });
  }

  @override
  Widget build(BuildContext context) {
    return Row(
      children: <Widget>[
        AnimatedOpacity(
          duration: Duration(milliseconds: 500),
          opacity: _opacity,
          child: Container(
            color: Colors.amber,
            height: 100.0,
            width: 100.0,
            child: FlatButton(
              child: Text('Tap to Fade'),
              onPressed: () {
                _animatedOpacity();
              },
            ),
          ),
        ),
      ],
    );
  }
}
```

8. Continue editing the `home.dart` file and import the `animated_opacity.dart` file to the top of the page.

```
import 'package:flutter/material.dart';
import 'package:ch7_animations/widgets/animated_container.dart';
```

```
import 'package:ch7_animations/widgets/animated_cross_fade.dart';
import 'package:ch7_animations/widgets/animated_opacity.dart';
```

9. Just after the `AnimatedCrossFadeWidget()` widget class, add a `Divider()` widget. On the next line, add the call to the widget class `AnimatedOpacityWidget()`.

```
body: SafeArea(
  child: Column(
    children: <Widget>[
      AnimatedContainerWidget(),
      Divider(),
      AnimatedCrossFadeWidget(),
      Divider(),
      AnimatedOpacityWidget(),
    ],
  ),
),
```

Again, notice how clean the code looks and how it improves the readability by separating each major section of the widget tree.

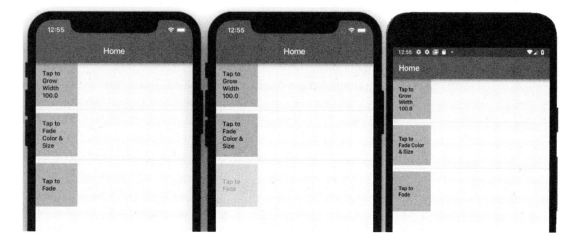

How It Works

The `AnimatedOpacity` widget takes a `duration` parameter, and you use the `Duration` class to specify 500 milliseconds. The `opacity` parameter is a value from 0.0 to 1.0. The `opacity` value of 1.0 is fully visible, and as the value changes toward zero, it starts to fade away. Once it reaches zero, it's invisible.

USING ANIMATIONCONTROLLER

The `AnimationController` class gives you increased flexibility in animation. The animation can be played forward or reverse, and you can stop it. The `fling` animation uses a physics simulation like a spring.

The `AnimationController` class produces linear values for a giving duration, and it tries to display a new frame at around 60 frames per second. The `AnimationController` class needs a `Ticker-Provider` class by passing the `vsync` argument in the constructor. The `vsync` prevents off-screen animations from consuming unnecessary resources. If the animation needs only one `AnimationCon-troller`, use `SingleTickerProviderStateMixin`. If the animation needs multiple `AnimationCon-trollers`, use `TickerProviderStateMixin`. The `Ticker` class is driven by the `ScheduleBinding.scheduleFrameCallback` reporting once per animation frame. It is trying to sync the animation to be as smooth as possible.

The `AnimationController` default object ranges from 0.0 to 1.0, but if you need a different range, you can use the `Animation` class (using `Tween`) to accept a different type of data. The `Animation` class is initiated by setting the `Tween` class (in-betweening) `begin` and `end` property values. For example, you have a balloon that floats from the bottom to the top of the screen, and you would set the `Tween` class `begin` value of 400.0, the bottom of the screen and the `end` value of 0.0, the top of the screen. Then you can chain the Tween `animate` method, which returns an `Animation` class. Simply put, it animates the Tween based on the animation, such as a `CurvedAnimation` class.

The `AnimationController` class at first can seem complex to use because of the different classes needed. The following are the basic steps that you take to create a custom animation (shown in Figure 7.1) or, eventually in the example, multiple animations running at the same time.

1. Add `AnimationController`.

2. Add `Animation`.

3. Initiate `AnimationController` with `Duration` (milliseconds, seconds, and so on).

4. Initiate `Animation` with `Tween` with `begin` and `end` values and chain the `animate` method with a `CurvedAnimation` (for this example).

5. Use the `AnimatedBuilder` with `Animation` using a `Container` with a balloon to start `Animation` by calling the `AnimationController.forward()` and `.reverse()` to run the animation backward. The `AnimatedBuilder` widget is used to create a widget that performs a reusable animation.

As you can see, once you break down the steps, it becomes more manageable and less complicated.

FIGURE 7.1: What you're building with AnimationController

Creating the AnimationController App

In this project, you'll animate a balloon that starts small at the bottom of the screen, and as it inflates, it floats toward the top, giving some nice spring animations. By using a GestureDetector tap on the balloon, the animation reverses, showing the balloon deflating and floating downward to the bottom of the screen. Every time the balloon is tapped, the animation starts again.

1. Create a new Flutter project and name it ch7_animation_controller. You can follow the instructions in Chapter 4. For this project, you need to create only the pages, widgets, and assets/images folders.

2. Open the `pubspec.yaml` file, and in `assets` add the `images` folder.

```
# To add assets to your application, add an assets section, like this:
assets:
  - assets/images/
```

Add the folder `assets` and subfolder `images` at the project's root and then copy the `Beginning-GoogleFlutter-Balloon.png` file to the `images` folder.

3. Click the Save button, and depending on the editor you are using, this automatically runs `flutter packages get`. Once finished, it shows a message of `Process finished with exit code 0`. It does not automatically run the command for you, though. Open the Terminal window (located at the bottom of your editor) and type **`flutter packages get`**.

4. Create a new Dart file in the `widgets` folder. Right-click the `widgets` folder, select New ⇨ Dart File, enter **`animated_balloon.dart`**, and click the OK button to save.

5. Import the `material.dart` library, add a new line, and then start typing **`st`**. The autocompletion help opens. Select the `stful` abbreviation and give it a name of `AnimatedBalloonWidget`.

6. It is appropriate to create the `AnimationController` and `Animation` variables before you can reference them in your code. Declare `TickerProviderStateMixin` to the `_AnimatedBalloonWidgetState` class by adding `with TickerProviderStateMixin`. The `AnimationController` vsync argument will use it. The vsync is referenced by `this`, meaning this reference of the `_AnimatedBalloonWidgetState` class.

```
class _AnimatedBalloonWidgetState extends State<AnimatedBalloonWidget> with
TickerProviderStateMixin {
```

7. After the class `_AnimatedBalloonWidgetState extends State<AnimatedBalloonWidget>` and before `@override`, create two `AnimationControllers` to handle the duration of the balloon floating upward and the inflation of the balloon inflating. Create two `Animations` to handle the actual movement range and inflation size. Override the `initState()` and `dispose()` methods to initiate `AnimationController` and dispose of them when the page closes.

An important note about using two `AnimationControllers` is that you could have used one `AnimationController` and made use of the `Interval()` curve to stagger `Animation`. A staggered animation uses `Interval()` to begin and end animations sequentially or to overlap one another. In the "Using Staggered Animations" section of this chapter, you'll create a staggered animation app.

```
class _AnimatedBalloonWidgetState extends State<AnimatedBalloonWidget> with
TickerProviderStateMixin {
  AnimationController _controllerFloatUp;
  AnimationController _controllerGrowSize;
  Animation<double> _animationFloatUp;
  Animation<double> _animationGrowSize;

  @override
  void initState() {
    super.initState();
```

```
    _controllerFloatUp = AnimationController(duration: Duration( seconds: 4),
vsync: this);
    _controllerGrowSize = AnimationController(duration: Duration(seconds: 2),
vsync: this);
  }

  @override
  void dispose() {

    _controllerFloatUp.dispose();
    _controllerGrowSize.dispose();
    super.dispose();
  }
```

Note that in the `initState()` method you could call the `Animation` class after the `Animation-Controller` to start the animation as the page loads, but you are going to place the `Animation` class in `Widget build(BuildContext context)` instead. The reason for this is to use the `Media-Query` class to obtain the screen size to place and size the balloon accordingly. The `initState()` method does not contain the `Widget context` object that `MediaQuery` requires. However, as `Widget build(BuildContext context)` is called, the animation starts on page load. If the user rotates the device, `Widget build(BuildContext context)` is called again, and the balloon will resize itself accordingly and run the animation if the balloon is located at the bottom of the screen.

8. After `Widget build(BuildContext context)`, create the balloon height, width, and page bottom position by using `MediaQuery.of(context).size`. I arrived at the following formulas for calculating the dimensions by testing different options to get the best look depending on different devices' screen size and orientation:

```
Widget build(BuildContext context) {
  double _balloonHeight = MediaQuery.of(context).size.height / 2;
  double _balloonWidth = MediaQuery.of(context).size.height / 3;
  double _balloonBottomLocation = MediaQuery.of(context).size.height -
_balloonHeight;
```

Create the `Animation` class by declaring a `Tween` with a `CurvedAnimation`. For the `_animation-FloatUp` value, the `begin` property is the `_balloonBottomLocation` variable with the `end` property at 0.0. This means the floating-upward animation starts at the bottom of the screen and moves all the way to the top.

For the `_animationGrowSize` value, the `begin` property is 50.0 pixels. Set the `end` value to the `_balloonWidth` variable. This means you can start the balloon width at 50.0 pixels and increase it to the maximum `_balloonWidth` value calculated by `MediaQuery`. Use the `elasticInOut` curve to give it a beautiful spring animation that looks like a quick inflation of air.

9. Call both `_controllerFloatUp.forward()` and `_controllerGrowSize.forward()` to start the animation.

```
    _animationFloatUp = Tween(begin: _balloonBottomLocation, end: 0.0).
  animate(CurvedAnimation(parent: _controllerFloatUp, curve: Curves.fastOutSlowIn));
    _animationGrowSize = Tween(begin: 50.0, end: _balloonWidth).
  animate(CurvedAnimation(parent: _controllerGrowSize, curve: Curves.elasticInOut));
```

```
    _controllerFloatUp.forward();
    _controllerGrowSize.forward();
}
```

10. Create `AnimatedBuilder` and let's take a look at a high-level structural breakdown for the `AnimatedBuilder` arguments that show how `AnimatedBuilder` child (`GestureDetector` with `Image`) is passed to the `builder`, which is the widget to receive the animation.

```
return AnimatedBuilder(
  animation: _animationFloatUp,
  builder: (context, child) {
    return Container(
      child: child,
    );
  },
  child: GestureDetector(/* Image*/) */
);
```

The `AnimatedBuilder` constructor passes the `animation` argument `_animationFloatUp`. For the `builder` argument, return a `Container` widget with the `child` property of `child`. I know that sounds weird for the `child` property, but this is the way the builder smartly redraws the `child` control being animated. The `child` widget being passed is declared next, and it will contain a `GestureDetector` widget and a `child` widget of `Image` (balloon).

The `AnimatedBuilder` constructor has the `animation`, `builder`, and `child` arguments.

Add to the `GestureDetector()` widget the `onTap` property. For the `GestureDetector()` widget, the `onTap` property checks for `_controllerFloatUp.isCompleted` (meaning the animation is done), and if yes, it starts the animation in reverse. This will deflate the balloon and start floating it down to the bottom of the page. The `else` portion handles the balloon already at the bottom of the screen and starts the animation forward by floating upward and inflating the balloon back to normal size.

11. Add to the `GestureDetector` child property a call to the `Image.asset()` constructor that loads the `BeginningGoogleFlutter-Balloon.png` file and sets `height` to `_balloonHeight` and `width` to `_balloonWidth`.

```
return AnimatedBuilder(
  animation: _animationFloatUp,
  builder: (context, child) {
    return Container(
      child: child,
      margin: EdgeInsets.only(
        top: _animationFloatUp.value,
      ),
```

```
      width: _animationGrowSize.value,
    );
  },
  child: GestureDetector(
    onTap: () {
      if (_controllerFloatUp.isComplctcd) {
        _controllerFloatUp.reverse();
        _controllerGrowSize.reverse();
      }
      else {
        _controllerFloatUp.forward();
        _controllerGrowSize.forward();
      }
    },
    child: Image.asset(
        'assets/images/BeginningGoogleFlutter-Balloon.png',
        height: _balloonHeight,
        width: _balloonWidth),
  ),
);
```

12. Open the `home.dart` file and import the `animated_balloon.dart` file to the top of the page.

```
import 'package:flutter/material.dart';
import 'package:ch7_animation_controller/widgets/animated_balloon.dart';
```

13. Add to the body a `SafeArea` with `SingleChildScrollView` as a child.

14. Add `Padding` as a child of the `SingleChildScrollView`.

15. Add a `Column` as a child of `Padding`.

16. In the `Column` children, add the call to the widget class `AnimatedBalloonWidget()`. Note I am using the `NeverScrollableScrollPhysics()` to stop the `SingleChildScrollView` to scroll content.

```
body: SafeArea(
  child: SingleChildScrollView(
    physics: NeverScrollableScrollPhysics(),
    child: Padding(
      padding: EdgeInsets.all(16.0),
      child: Column(
        children: <Widget>[
          AnimatedBalloonWidget(),
        ],
      ),
    ),
  ),
),
```

How It Works

Declaring `TickerProviderStateMixin` to the `AnimatedBalloonWidget` widget class allowed you to set the `AnimationController` vsync argument. You added `AnimationController` and declared the `_controllerFloatUp` variable to animate the floating upward and downward action. You declared the `AnimationController _controllerGrowSize` variable to animate the inflating and deflating actions. You declared the `_animationFloatUp` variable to hold the value from the `Tween` animation to show the balloon floating either upward or downward by setting the top margin of the `Container` widget. You declared the `_animationGrowSize` variable to hold the value from the `Tween` animation to show the balloon either inflating or deflating by setting the `width` value of the `Container` widget.

The `AnimatedBuilder` constructor takes the `animation`, `builder`, and `child` arguments. Next, you passed the `_animationFloatUp` animation to the `AnimatedBuilder` constructor. The `AnimatedBuilder` builder argument returns a `Container` widget with the child as an `Image` widget wrapped in a `GestureDetector` widget.

In the preceding example, I showed how you can use multiple `AnimationControllers` to run at the same time with different `Duration` values. In the next section, you'll use one `AnimationController` for a staggered animation.

Using Staggered Animations

A *staggered animation* triggers visual changes in sequential order. The animation changes can occur one after the other; they can have gaps without animations and overlap each other. One `AnimationController` class controls multiple `Animation` objects that specify the animation in a timeline (`Interval`). Now you'll walk through an example of using one `AnimationController` class and the `Interval()` curve property to start different animations at different times. As noted in the preceding section, a staggered animation uses `Interval()` to begin and end animations sequentially or to overlap one another.

TRY IT OUT Creating the Staggered Animations App

In this project, you'll re-create the balloon animation to duplicate the previous example but use only one `AnimationController` to take advantage of staggered animations. By using `Interval()`, you mark each animation's `begin` and `end` time to stagger the animations.

Like the previous project, you'll animate a balloon that starts small at the bottom of the screen, and as it inflates, it floats toward the top, giving some nice spring animations. By using a `GestureDetector` tap on the balloon, the animation reverses, showing the balloon deflating and floating downward to the bottom of the screen. Every time the balloon is tapped, the animation starts again.

1. Create a new Flutter project and name it `ch7_ac_staggered_animations`. You can follow the instructions in Chapter 4. For this project, you need to create only the `pages`, `widgets`, and `assets/images` folders.

2. Open the `pubspec.yaml` file, and under `assets`, add the `images` folder.

   ```
   # To add assets to your application, add an assets section, like this:
   assets:
     - assets/images/
   ```

   Add the folder `assets` and subfolder `images` at the project's root and then copy the `Beginning-GoogleFlutter-Balloon.png` file to the `images` folder.

3. Create a new Dart file under the `widgets` folder. Right-click the `widgets` folder, select New ⇨ Dart File, enter **animated_balloon.dart**, and click the OK button to save. Import the `material.dart` library, add a new line, and then start typing **st**. The autocompletion help opens. Select the `stful` abbreviation and give it a name of `AnimatedBalloonWidget`.

4. It is appropriate to create the `AnimationController` and `Animation` variables before you can reference them in the code. Declare `SingleTickerProviderStateMixin` to the `_HomeState` class by adding `with SingleTickerProviderStateMixin`. The `AnimationController` constructor takes the `vsync` argument. The `vsync` argument is referenced by `this`, meaning this reference of the `_HomeState` class.

   ```
   class _AnimatedBalloonWidgetState extends State<AnimatedBalloonWidget> with
   SingleTickerProviderStateMixin {
   ```

5. Create one `AnimationController` only to handle the animation duration. Create two `Animations` to handle the actual movement range and growing size. Override the `initState()` and `dispose()` methods to initiate the `AnimationController` and dispose of them when the page closes.

   ```
   class _HomeState extends State<Home> with SingleTickerProviderStateMixin {
     AnimationController _controller;
     Animation<double> _animationFloatUp;
     Animation<double> _animationGrowSize;

     @override
     void initState() {
       super.initState();
   ```

```
    _controller = AnimationController(duration: Duration(seconds: 4), vsync: this);
  }

  @override
  void dispose() {

    _controller.dispose();
    super.dispose();
  }
```

Note as stated in the previous section, in the `initState()` method you could call the `Animation` only after the `AnimationController` only to start the animation as page loads, but you are going to place it in the `_animatedBalloon()` method instead. The reason is to use the `MediaQuery` class to obtain the screen size to place and size the balloon accordingly. The `initState()` method does not contain the `Widget context` object that `MediaQuery` requires. However, as the `_animate-Balloon()` method is called, the animation starts on page load. If the user rotates the device, the `_animateBalloon()` method is called again, and the balloon resizes itself accordingly and runs the animation if the balloon is located at the bottom of the screen.

6. After `Widget build(BuildContext context)`, create the balloon height, width, and page bottom position by using `MediaQuery.of(context).size`. I arrived at the following formulas for calculating the dimensions by testing different options to get the best aesthetic look depending on different devices' screen size and orientation.

```
Widget build(BuildContext context) {
   double _balloonHeight = MediaQuery.of(context).size.height / 2;
   double _balloonWidth = MediaQuery.of(context).size.height / 3;
   double _balloonBottomLocation = MediaQuery.of(context).size.height -
_balloonHeight;
```

Creating an animation Tween is almost the same as the previous example except the `CurvedAnimation` parent is the `_controller`. The `curve` uses `Interval()` to mark each animation's begin and end time. Zero means `begin`, and 1.0 animation means `end`.

The `_controller` duration value is four seconds, `_animationGrowSize Interval begin` is 0.0, and `end` is 0.5. This means the balloon starts inflating as soon as the animation starts but finishes at 0.5, meaning two seconds. You can think of `Interval` `begin` and `end` as a percentage of the total duration of the animation.

```
void _animationFloatUp = Tween(begin: _balloonBottomLocation, end: 0.0).animate(
   CurvedAnimation(
     parent: _controller,
     curve: Interval(0.0, 1.0, curve: Curves.fastOutSlowIn),
   ),
 );
```

```
  void _animationGrowSize = Tween(begin: 50.0, end: _balloonWidth).animate(
    CurvedAnimation(
      parent: _controller,
      curve: Interval(0.0, 0.5, curve: Curves.elasticInOut),
    ),
  );
```

7. Create the `AnimatedBuilder` only, and let's look at the high-level structural breakdown for the `AnimatedBuilder` constructor that shows how the `AnimatedBuilder` child (`GestureDetector` with `Image`) argument is passed to the `builder`, which is the widget to receive the animation argument.

```
  return AnimatedBuilder(
    animation: _animationFloatUp,
    builder: (context, child) {
      return Container(
        child: child,
      );
    },
    child: GestureDetector(/* Image*/) */
  );
```

Using the `AnimatedBuilder` is almost the same as the previous example with the difference that you use only one `AnimationController` only to start animation in forward or reverse with the _controller variable.

The `AnimatedBuilder` constructor takes the `animation`, `builder`, and `child` arguments.

Add to the `GestureDetector()` widget the `onTap` property. For `GestureDetector()`, the `onTap` property callback checks for `_controllerFloatUp.isCompleted` (the animation is done), and if yes, it starts the animation in reverse. This will deflate the balloon and have it start floating down to the bottom of the page. The `else` portion handles the balloon already at the bottom of the screen; it starts the animation by floating the balloon upward and inflating it back to normal size. You'll notice that since you have only one `AnimationController`, you use the _controller variable to reverse or forward the animation.

8. Add to the `GestureDetector` child a call to the `Image.asset()` constructor that loads the `BeginningGoogleFlutter-Balloon.png` file and sets the `height` value to _balloonHeight and the `width` value to _balloonWidth.

```
  return AnimatedBuilder(
    animation: _animationFloatUp,
    builder: (context, child) {
      return Container(
        child: child,
        margin: EdgeInsets.only(
          top: _animationFloatUp.value,
        ),
```

```
                width: _animationGrowSize.value,
        );
      },
      child: GestureDetector(
        onTap: () {
          if (_controller.isCompleted) {
            _controller.reverse();
          } else {
            _controller.forward();
          }
        },
        child: Image.asset('assets/images/BeginningGoogleFlutter-Balloon.png',
            height: _balloonHeight, width: _balloonWidth),
      ),
    );
```

9.   Open the `home.dart` file and import the `animated_balloon.dart` file to the top of the page.:

```
import 'package:flutter/material.dart';
import 'package:ch7_ac_staggered_animations/widgets/animated_balloon.dart';
```

10.   Add to the body a `SafeArea` widget with `SingleChildScrollView` as a child.

11.   Add `Padding` as a child of `SingleChildScrollView`. Add a `Column` widget as a child of `Padding`.

12.   In the `Column` children, add the call to the method `_animateBalloon()`. Note that I am using `NeverScrollableScrollPhysics()` to stop the `SingleChildScrollView` to scroll content.

```
body: SafeArea(
  child: SingleChildScrollView(
    physics: NeverScrollableScrollPhysics(),
    child: Padding(
      padding: EdgeInsets.all(16.0),
      child: Column(
        children: <Widget>[
          AnimatedBalloonWidget(),
        ],
      ),
    ),
  ),
),
```

How It Works

Declaring `SingleTickerProviderStateMixin` to the `AnimatedBalloonWidget` widget class allows you to set the `AnimationController` vsync argument. The `SingleTickerProviderStateMixin` allows only one `AnimationController`. You added `AnimationController` and declared the `_controller` variable to animate both the floating upward or downward and the inflation or deflation of the balloon.

You declared the `_animationFloatUp` variable to hold the value from the Tween animation to show the balloon either floating upward or downward by setting the top margin of the `Container` widget. You also declared the `_animationGrowSize` variable to hold the value from the Tween animation to show the balloon either inflating or deflating by setting the `width` value of the `Container` widget.

The `AnimatedBuilder` constructor takes `animation`, `builder`, and `child` arguments. Next, you passed the `_animationFloatUp` animation to the `AnimatedBuilder` constructor. The `AnimatedBuilder` builder argument returns a `Container` widget with the child as an `Image` wrapped in a `GestureDetector` widget.

SUMMARY

In this chapter, you learned how to add animations to your app to improve the UX. You implemented `AnimatedContainer` to animate the width of a `Container` widget with a beautiful spring effect by using `Curves.elasticOut`. You added the `AnimatedCrossFade` widget to cross-fade between two children widgets. The color is animated from amber to green while at the same time the widget increased or decreased in width and height. To fade a widget in, out, or partially, you added the `AnimatedOpacity` widget. The `AnimatedOpacity` widget uses the `opacity` property passed over a period of time (`Duration`) to fade the widget. The `AnimationController` class allows the creation of custom animations.

You learned to use multiple `AnimationControllers` with different durations. You used two `Animation` classes to control the floating upward or downward and the inflation and deflation of the balloon at the same time. The animation is created by using `Tween` with `begin` and `end` values. You also used different `CurvedAnimation` class for a nonlinear effect like `Curves.fastOutSlowIn` to float upward or downward and `Curves.elasticInOut` to inflate or deflate the balloon. Lastly, you used one `AnimationController` class with multiple `Animation` classes to create staggered animations, which give a similar effect as the previous example.

In the next chapter, you'll learn the many ways of using navigation such as `Navigator`, `Hero Animation`, `BottomNavigationBar`, `BottomAppBar`, `TabBar`, `TabBarView`, and `Drawer`.

▶ **WHAT YOU LEARNED IN THIS CHAPTER**

TOPIC	KEY CONCEPTS
`AnimatedContainer`	This gradually changes values over time.
`AnimatedCrossFade`	This cross-fades between two child widgets.
`AnimatedOpacity`	This shows or hides widget visibility by animating fading over time.
`AnimatedBuilder`	This is used to create a widget that performs a reusable animation.
`AnimationController`	This creates custom animations by using `TickerProviderStateMixin`, `Single-TickerProviderStateMixin`, `AnimationController`, `Animation`, `Tween`, and `CurvedAnimation`.

8

Creating an App's Navigation

WHAT YOU WILL LEARN IN THIS CHAPTER

➤ How to use the `Navigator` widget to navigate between pages

➤ How hero animation allows a widget transition to fly into place from one page to another

➤ How to display a horizontal list of `BottomNavigationBarItems` containing an `icon` and a `title` at the bottom of the page

➤ How to enhance the look of a bottom navigation bar with the `BottomAppBar` widget, which allows enabling a notch

➤ How to display a horizontal row of tabs with `TabBar`

➤ How to use `TabBarView` in conjunction with `TabBar` to display the page of the selected tab

➤ How `Drawer` allows the user to slide a panel from left or right

➤ How to use the `ListView` constructor to build a short list of items quickly

➤ How to use the `ListView` constructor with the `Drawer` widget to show a menu list

In this chapter, you'll learn that navigation is a major component in a mobile application. Good navigation creates a great user experience (UX) by making it easy to access information. For example, imagine making a journal entry, and when trying to select a tag, it's not available, so you need to create a new one. Do you close the entry and go to Settings ➪ Tags to add a new one? That would be clunky. Instead, the user needs the ability to add a new tag on the fly and appropriately navigate to select or add a tag from their current position. When designing an app, always keep in mind how the user would navigate to different parts of the app with the least number of taps.

Animation while navigating to different pages is also important if it helps to convey an action, rather than simply being a distraction. What does this mean? Just because you can show fancy animations does not mean you should. Use animations to enhance the UX, not frustrate the user.

USING THE NAVIGATOR

The `Navigator` widget manages a stack of *routes* to move between pages. You can optionally pass data to the destination page and back to the original page. To start navigating between pages, you use the `Navigator.push`, `pushNamed`, and `pop` methods. (You'll learn how to use the `pushNamed` method in the "Using the Named Navigator Route" section of this chapter.) `Navigator` is incredibly smart; it shows native navigation on iOS or Android. For example, in iOS when navigating to a new page, you usually slide the next page from the right side of the screen toward the left. In Android when navigating to a new page, you typically slide the next page from the bottom of the screen toward the top. To summarize, in iOS, the new page slides in from the right, and in Android, it slides in from the bottom.

The following example shows you how to use the `Navigator.push` method to navigate to the About page. The `push` method passes the `BuildContext` and `Route` arguments. To push a new `Route` argument, you create an instance of the `MaterialPageRoute` class that replaces the screen with the appropriate platform (iOS or Android) animation transition. In the example, the `fullscreenDialog` property is set to `true` to present the About page as a full-screen modal dialog. By setting the `fullscreenDialog` property to `true`, the About page app bar automatically includes a close button. In iOS, the modal dialog transition presents the page by sliding from the bottom of the screen toward the top, and this is also the default for Android.

```
Navigator.push(
  context,
  MaterialPageRoute(
    fullscreenDialog: true,
    builder: (context) => About(),
  ),
);
```

The following example shows how to use the `Navigator.pop` method to close the page and navigate back to the previous page. You call the `Navigator.pop(context)` method by passing the `BuildContext` argument, and the page closes by sliding from the top of the screen toward the bottom. The second example shows how to pass a value back to the previous page.

```
// Close page
Navigator.pop(context);

// Close page and pass a value back to previous page
Navigator.pop(context, 'Done');
```

TRY IT OUT Creating the Navigator App, Part 1—The About Page

The project has a main home page with a `FloatingActionButton` to navigate to a gratitude page by passing a default selected `Radio` button value. The gratitude page shows three `Radio` buttons to select a value and then pass it back to the home page and update the `Text` widget with the appropriate value.

The `AppBar` has an `actions` `IconButton` that navigates to the about page by passing a `fullscreenDialog` argument set to `true` to create a full-screen modal dialog. The modal dialog shows a close button at the upper left of the page and animates from the bottom. In this first part, you'll develop the navigation from the main page to the About page and back.

1. Create a new Flutter project and name it `ch8_navigator`. Refer to the instructions in Chapter 4, "Creating a Starter Project Template." For this project, you need to create only the `pages` folder.

2. Open the `home.dart` file and add an `IconButton` to the `AppBar` `actions` `Widget` list.

    The `IconButton` `onPressed` property will call the method `_openPageAbout()` and pass `context` and `fullscreenDialog` arguments. Do not worry about the squiggly red lines under the method name; you'll create that method in later steps. The `context` argument is needed by the `Navigator` widget, and the `fullscreenDialog` argument is set to `true` to show the About page as a full-screen modal. If you set the `fullscreenDialog` argument to `false`, the About page shows a back arrow instead of a close button icon.

    ```
    appBar: AppBar(
      title: Text('Navigator'),
      actions: <Widget>[
        IconButton(
          icon: Icon(Icons.info_outline),
    ```

```
        onPressed: () => _openPageAbout(
          context: context,
          fullscreenDialog: true,
        ),
      ),
    ],
  ),
```

3. Add a `SafeArea` with `Padding` as a `child` to the body.

```
body: SafeArea(
  child: Padding(),
),
```

4. In the `Padding` child, add a `Text()` widget, with the text `'Grateful for: $_howAreYou'`. Notice the `$_howAreYou` variable, which will contain the returned value when navigating back (`Navigator.pop`) from the gratitude page. Add a `TextStyle` class with a `fontSize` value of 32.0 pixels.

```
body: SafeArea(
  child: Padding(
    padding: EdgeInsets.all(16.0),
    child: Text('Grateful for: $_howAreYou', style: TextStyle(fontSize: 32.0),),
  ),
),
```

5. To the `Scaffold floatingActionButton` property, add a `FloatingActionButton()` widget with an `onPressed` that calls the method `_openPageGratitude(context: context)`, which passes the `context` argument.

6. For the `FloatingActionButton()` child, add the icon called `sentiment_satisfied`, and for the `tooltip`, add the `'About'` description.

```
floatingActionButton: FloatingActionButton(
  onPressed: () => _openPageGratitude(context: context),
  tooltip: 'About',
  child: Icon(Icons.sentiment_satisfied),
),
```

7. On the first line after the `_HomeState` class definition, add a `String` variable called `_howAreYou` with a default value of `'...'`.

```
String _howAreYou = "...";
```

8. Continue by adding the `_openPageAbout()` method that accepts `BuildContext` and `bool` named parameters with the default values set to `false`.

```
void _openPageAbout({BuildContext context, bool fullscreenDialog = false}) {}
```

9. In the `openPageAbout()` method, add a `Navigator.push()` method with a `context` and a second argument of `MaterialPageRoute()`. The `MaterialPageRoute()` class passes the `fullscreen-Dialog` argument and a `builder` that calls the `About()` page that you'll create in later steps.

```
void _openPageAbout({BuildContext context, bool fullscreenDialog = false}) {
  Navigator.push(
```

```
      context,
      MaterialPageRoute(
        fullscreenDialog: fullscreenDialog,
        builder: (context) => About(),
      ),
    );
  }
```

10. On top of the home.dart page, import the about.dart page that you'll create next.

```
    import 'about.dart';
```

Navigator is simple to use but also powerful. Let's examine how it works. Navigator.push() passes two arguments: context and MaterialPageRoute. For the first argument, you pass the context argument. The second argument, MaterialPageRoute(), gives you the horsepower to navigate to another page using platform-specific animation. Only the builder is required to navigate with the optional fullscreenDialog argument.

11. Create a new file called about.dart in the lib/pages folder. Since this page only displays information, create a StatelessWidget class called About.

12. For the body, add the usual SafeArea with Padding and the child property as a Text widget.

```
    // about.dart
    import 'package:flutter/material.dart';

    class About extends StatelessWidget {
      @override
      Widget build(BuildContext context) {
        return Scaffold(
          appBar: AppBar(
            title: Text('About'),
          ),
          body: SafeArea(
            child: Padding(
              padding: const EdgeInsets.all(16.0),
              child: Text('About Page'),
            ),
          ),
        );
      }
    }
```

How It Works

You add to the AppBar an IconButton under the actions property. The icon property for the Icon-Button is set to Icons.info_outline, the _openPageAbout() method passes the context, and the fullscreenDialog argument is set to true. You also add to the Scaffold a FloatingActionButton that calls the _openPageGratitude() method. The _openPageAbout() method uses the Navigator.push() method to pass the context and the MaterialPageRoute. The MaterialPageRoute passes the fullscreenDialog argument set to true, and the builder calls the About() page. The About page class is a StatelessWidget with a Scaffold and AppBar; the body property has a SafeArea with Padding as a child that shows a Text widget with the "About Page" text.

TRY IT OUT Creating the Navigator App, Part 2—The Gratitude Page

The second part of the app is to navigate to the gratitude page by passing a default value to select the appropriate Radio button. Once you navigate back to the home page, the newly selected Radio button value is passed back and displayed in the Text widget.

1. Open the home.dart file, and after the _openPageAbout() method, add the _openPage-Gratitude() method. The _openPageGratitude() method takes two parameters: a context and a fullscreenDialog bool variable with a default value of false. In this case, the gratitude page is not a fullscreenDialog. Like the previous MaterialPageRoute, the builder opens the page. In this case, it is the gratitude page.

Note that when passing data to the gratitude page and waiting to receive a response, the method is marked as async to wait a response from Navigator.push by using the await keyword.

```
void _openPageGratitude(
    {BuildContext context, bool fullscreenDialog = false}) async {
  final String _gratitudeResponse = await Navigator.push(
```

The MaterialPageRoute builder builds the contents of the route. In this case, the content is the gratitude page, which accepts a radioGroupValue int parameter with a value of –1. The –1 value tells the Gratitude class page not to select any Radio buttons. If you pass a value like 2, it selects the appropriate Radio button that corresponds to this value.

```
builder: (context) => Gratitude(
    radioGroupValue: -1,
  ),
```

Once the user dismisses the gratitude page, the _gratitudeResponse variable is populated. Use the ?? (double question marks if null) operator to check the _gratitudeResponse for a valid value (not null) and populate the _howAreYou variable. The Text widget is populated with the _howAreYou value on the home page with the appropriate selected gratitude value or an empty string. In other words, if the _gratitudeResponse value is not null the _howAreYou variable is populated with the _gratitudeResponse value; otherwise the _howAreYou variable is populated by an empty string.

```
_howAreYou = _gratitudeResponse ?? '';
```

Here's the full _openPageGratitude() method code:

```
void _openPageGratitude(
    {BuildContext context, bool fullscreenDialog = false}) async {
  final String _gratitudeResponse = await Navigator.push(
    context,
    MaterialPageRoute(
      fullscreenDialog: fullscreenDialog,
      builder: (context) => Gratitude(
          radioGroupValue: -1,
        ),
```

```
      ),
    );
    _howAreYou = _gratitudeResponse ?? '';
  }
```

2. At the top of the home.dart page, add the gratitude.dart page that you'll create next.

```
import 'gratitude.dart';
```

3. Create a new file named gratitude.dart in the lib/pages folder. Since this page will modify data (state), create a StatefulWidget class called Gratitude.

To receive data passed from the home page, modify the Gratitude class by adding a final int variable named radioGroupValue. Note the final variable does not start with an underscore. Create a named constructor requiring this parameter. The radioGroupValue variable is accessed by the class _GratitudeState extends State<Gratitude> by calling widget.radioGroupValue.

```
class Gratitude extends StatefulWidget {
  final int radioGroupValue;

  Gratitude({Key key, @required this.radioGroupValue}) : super(key: key);

  @override
  _GratitudeState createState() => _GratitudeState();
}
```

4. For the Scaffold AppBar, add an IconButton to the actions list of Widget. Set the IconButton icon to Icons.check with the onPressed property calling the Navigator.pop, which returns the _selectedGratitude to the home page.

```
appBar: AppBar(
  title: Text('Gratitude'),
  actions: <Widget>[
    IconButton(
      icon: Icon(Icons.check),
      onPressed: () => Navigator.pop(context, _selectedGratitude),
    ),
  ],
),
```

5. For the body, add the usual SafeArea and Padding with child property as a Row.

The Row children list of Widget contains three alternating Radio and Text widgets. The Radio widget takes the value, groupValue, and onChanged properties. The value property is the ID value for the Radio button. The groupValue property holds the value of the currently selected Radio button. The onChanged passes the selected index value to the custom method _radioOnChanged() that handles which Radio button is currently selected. Following each Radio button, there is a Text widget that acts as a label for the Radio button.

Here's the full body source code:

```
body: SafeArea(
  child: Padding(
    padding: const EdgeInsets.all(16.0),
    child: Row(
      children: <Widget>[
        Radio(
          value: 0,
          groupValue: _radioGroupValue,
          onChanged: (index) => _radioOnChanged(index),
        ),
        Text('Family'),
        Radio(
          value: 1,
          groupValue: _radioGroupValue,
          onChanged: (index) => _radioOnChanged(index),
        ),
        Text('Friends'),
        Radio(
          value: 2,
          groupValue: _radioGroupValue,
          onChanged: (index) => _radioOnChanged(index),
        ),
        Text('Coffee'),
      ],
    ),
  ),
),
```

6. On the first line after the _HomeState class definition, add three variables—_gratitudeList, _selectedGratitude, and _radioGroupValue—and the _radioOnChanged() method.

➤ _gratitudeList is a List of String values.

```
List<String> _gratitudeList = List();
```

➤ _selectedGratitude is a String variable containing the selected Radio button value.

```
String _selectedGratitude;
```

➤ _radioGroupValue is an int containing the ID of the selected Radio button value.

```
int _radioGroupValue;
```

7. Create the _radioOnChanged() method taking an int for the selected index of the Radio button. In the method, call setState() to have the Radio widgets update with the selected value. The _radioGroupValue variable is updated with the index. The _selectedGratitude variable (example value Coffee) is updated by taking the _gratitudeList[index] list value by the selected index (position in the list).

```
void _radioOnChanged(int index) {
  setState(() {
    _radioGroupValue = index;
    _selectedGratitude = _gratitudeList[index];
    print('_selectedRadioValue $_selectedGratitude');
  });
}
```

8. Override `initState()` to initialize the _gratitudeList. Since the _radioGroupValue is passed from the home page, initialize it with `widget.radioGroupValue`, which is the final variable passed from the home page.

```
_gratitudeList..add('Family')..add('Friends')..add('Coffee');
_radioGroupValue = widget.radioGroupValue;
```

The following is the code that declares all variables and methods:

```
class _GratitudeState extends State<Gratitude> {
  List<String> _gratitudeList = List();
  String _selectedGratitude;
  int _radioGroupValue;

  void _radioOnChanged(int index) {
    setState(() {
      _radioGroupValue = index;
      _selectedGratitude = _gratitudeList[index];
      print('_selectedRadioValue $_selectedGratitude');
    });
  }

  @override
  void initState() {
    super.initState();

    _gratitudeList..add('Family')..add('Friends')..add('Coffee');
    _radioGroupValue = widget.radioGroupValue;
  }
```

Here's the entire `gratitude.dart` file source code:

```
import 'package:flutter/material.dart';

class Gratitude extends StatefulWidget {
  final int radioGroupValue;

  Gratitude({Key key, @required this.radioGroupValue}) : super(key: key);

  @override
  _GratitudeState createState() => _GratitudeState();
}

class _GratitudeState extends State<Gratitude> {
  List<String> _gratitudeList = List();
  String _selectedGratitude;
  int _radioGroupValue;

  void _radioOnChanged(int index) {
    setState(() {
      _radioGroupValue = index;
      _selectedGratitude = _gratitudeList[index];
      print('_selectedRadioValue $_selectedGratitude');
    });
  }
```

```
@override
void initState() {
  super.initState();

  _gratitudeList..add('Family')..add('Friends')..add('Coffee');
  _radioGroupValue = widget.radioGroupValue;
}

@override
Widget build(BuildContext context) {
  return Scaffold(
    appBar: AppBar(
      title: Text('Gratitude'),
      actions: <Widget>[
        IconButton(
          icon: Icon(Icons.check),
          onPressed: () => Navigator.pop(context, _selectedGratitude),
        ),
      ],
    ),
    body: SafeArea(
      child: Padding(
        padding: const EdgeInsets.all(16.0),
        child: Row(
          children: <Widget>[
            Radio(
              value: 0,
              groupValue: _radioGroupValue,
              onChanged: (index) => _radioOnChanged(index),
            ),
            Text('Family'),
            Radio(
              value: 1,
              groupValue: _radioGroupValue,
              onChanged: (index) => _radioOnChanged(index),
            ),
            Text('Friends'),
            Radio(
              value: 2,
              groupValue: _radioGroupValue,
              onChanged: (index) => _radioOnChanged(index),
            ),
            Text('Coffee'),
          ],
        ),
      ),
    ),
  );
}
}
```

How It Works

You have the entire app created with a home page that can navigate to the about page as a full-screenDialog. The fullscreenDialog gives the about page a default close action button. By tapping the home page's FloatingActionButton, the Navigator MaterialPageRoute builder builds the contents for the route, in this case the gratitude page. Through the Gratitude constructor, data is passed to unselected Radio buttons. From the gratitude page, a list of Radio buttons gives a choice to select a gratitude. By tapping the AppBar action button (checkbox IconButton), the Navigator.pop method passes the selected gratitude value back to the Home Text widget. From the home page, you called the Navigator.push method by using the await keyword, and the method has been waiting to receive a value. Once the About page's Navigator.pop method is called, it returns a value to the home page's _gratitudeResponse variable. Using the await keyword is a powerful and straightforward feature to implement.

Using the Named Navigator Route

An alternate way to use `Navigator` is to refer to the page that you are navigating to by the route name. The route name starts with a slash, and then comes the route name. For example, the About page route name is `'/about'`. The list of `routes` is built into the `MaterialApp()` widget. The `routes` have a Map of `String` and `WidgetBuilder` where the `String` is the route name, and the `WidgetBuilder` has a `builder` to build the contents of the route by the `Class` name (About) of the page to open.

```
routes: <String, WidgetBuilder>{
  '/about': (BuildContext context) => About(),
  '/gratitude': (BuildContext context) => Gratitude(),
},
```

To call the route, the `Navigator.pushNamed()` method is called by passing two arguments. The first argument is `context`, and the second is the `route` name.

```
Navigator.pushNamed(context, '/about');
```

USING HERO ANIMATION

The `Hero` widget is a great out-of-the-box animation to convey the navigation action of a widget flying into place from one page to another. The hero animation is a shared element transition (animation) between two different pages.

To visualize the animation, imagine seeing a superhero flying into action. For example, you have a list of journal entries with a photo thumbnail, the user selects an entry, and you see the photo thumbnail transition to the detail page by moving and growing to full size. The photo thumbnail is the superhero, and when tapped, it flies into action by moving from the list page to the detail page and lands perfectly on the correct location at the top of the detail page showing the full photo. When the detail page is dismissed, the `Hero` widget flies back to the original page, position, and size. In other words, the animation shows the photo thumbnail moving and growing into place from the list page to the detail page, and once the detail page is dismissed, the animation and size are reversed. The `Hero` widget has all of these features built in; there's no need to write custom code to handle the size and animation between pages.

To continue with the previous scenario, you wrap the list page `Image` widget as a `child` of the `Hero` widget and assign a `tag` property name. Repeat the same steps for the detail page and make sure the `tag` property value is the same in both pages.

```
// List page
Hero(
  tag: 'photo1',
  child: Image(
    image: AssetImage("assets/images/coffee.png"),
  ),
),

// Detail page
Hero(
```

```
      tag: 'photo1',
      child: Container(
        child: Image(
          image: AssetImage("assets/images/coffee.png"),
        ),
      ),
    ),
```

The `Hero child` widget is marked for hero animation. When the `Navigator` pushes or pops a `Page-Route`, the entire screen's content is replaced. This means during the animation transition the `Hero` widget is not shown in the original position in both the old and new routes, but it moves and resizes from one page to another. Each `Hero tag` must be unique and match on both the originating and landing pages.

TRY IT OUT Creating the Hero Animation App

In this example, the `Hero` widget has an `Icon` as a `child` wrapped in a `GestureDetector`. An `InkWell` could also be used instead of the `GestureDetector` to show a material tap animation. The `InkWell` widget is a Material Component that responds to touch gestures by displaying a splash (ripple) effect. You'll take a more in-depth look at `GestureDetector` and `InkWell` in Chapter 11, "Applying Interactivity." When the `Icon` is tapped, `Navigator.push` is called to navigate to the detail screen, called `Fly`. Since the `Hero` widget animation is like a superhero flying, the detail screen is named `Fly`.

1. Create a new Flutter project and name it `ch8_hero_animation`. Again, you can follow the instructions in Chapter 4. For this project, you need to create only the `pages` folder.

2. Open the `home.dart` file and add to the `body` a `SafeArea` with `Padding` as a child.

```
body: SafeArea(
  child: Padding(),
),
```

3. In the `Padding child`, add the `GestureDetector()` widget, which you will create next.

```
body: SafeArea(
  child: Padding(
    padding: const EdgeInsets.all(16.0),
    child: GestureDetector(),
  ),
),
```

4. Add to the `GestureDetector child` a `Hero` widget with tag `'format_paint'`; tag can be any unique ID. The `Hero` widget `child` is a `format_paint` icon with `lightGreen` color and a `size` value of 120.0 pixels. Note you could have used an `InkWell()` widget instead of `GestureDetector()`. The `InkWell()` widget shows a splash feedback where tapped, but the `GestureDetector()` widget will not show the touch feedback. For the `onTap` property, you call `Navigator.push` to open the detail page called `Fly`.

```
GestureDetector(
  child: Hero(
    tag: 'format_paint',
```

```
        child: Icon(
          Icons.format_paint,
          color: Colors.lightGreen,
          size: 120.0,
        ),
      ),
      onTap: () {
        Navigator.push(
          context,
          MaterialPageRoute(builder: (context) => Fly()),
        );
      },
    ),
  ),
```

5. At the top of the home.dart page, import the fly.dart page that you will create next.

```
import 'fly.dart';
```

Here's the entire Home.dart file source code:

```
import 'package:flutter/material.dart';
import 'fly.dart';

class Home extends StatelessWidget {
  @override
  Widget build(BuildContext context) {
    return Scaffold(
      appBar: AppBar(
        title: Text('Hero Animation'),
      ),
      body: SafeArea(
        child: Padding(
          padding: EdgeInsets.all(16.0),
          child: GestureDetector(
            child: Hero(
              tag: 'format_paint',
              child: Icon(
                Icons.format_paint,
                color: Colors.lightGreen,
                size: 120.0,
              ),
            ),
            onTap: () {
              Navigator.push(
                context,
                MaterialPageRoute(builder: (context) => Fly()),
              );
            },
          ),
        ),
      ),
    );
  }
}
```

6. Create a new file called `fly.dart` in the `lib/pages` folder. Since this page only displays information, create a `StatelessWidget` class called `Fly`. For the `body`, add the usual `SafeArea` with a `child` set to the `Hero()` widget.

```
body: SafeArea(
  child: Hero(),
),
```

7. To calculate the `width` of the `Icon`, after `Widget build(BuildContext context) {`, add a `double` variable called `_width` set by `MediaQuery.of(context).size.shortestSide / 2`. The `shortestSide` property returns the lesser of the width or height of the screen, and you divide by two to make it half the size.

The reason you calculate the width is only to resize the `Icon` `width` according to device size and orientation. If you used an `Image` instead, this calculation would not be necessary; it can be done by using `BoxFit.fitWidth`.

```
double _width = MediaQuery.of(context).size.shortestSide / 2;
```

8. Add to the `Hero` widget a `tag` of `'format_paint'` with a `Container` for the `child`. Note for the `Hero` widget to work properly, the `tag` needs to be the same name you gave in the `GestureDetector` child `Hero` widget in the `home.dart` file. The `Container` child is a `format_paint` icon with `lightGreen` `color` and a `size` value of the `width` variable. For the `Container` `alignment` property, use `Alignment.bottomCenter`. You can experiment using different `Alignment` values to see the hero animation variations at work.

```
Hero(
  tag: 'format_paint',
  child: Container(
    alignment: Alignment.bottomCenter,
    child: Icon(
      Icons.format_paint,
      color: Colors.lightGreen,
      size: _width,
    ),
  ),
)
```

Here's the entire `Fly.dart` file source code:

```
import 'package:flutter/material.dart';

class Fly extends StatelessWidget {
  @override
  Widget build(BuildContext context) {
    double _width = MediaQuery.of(context).size.shortestSide / 2;

    return Scaffold(
      appBar: AppBar(
        title: Text('Fly'),
      ),
```

```
      body: SafeArea(
        child: Hero(
          tag: 'format_paint',
          child: Container(
            alignment: Alignment.bottomCenter,
            child: Icon(
              Icons.format_paint,
              color: Colors.lightGreen,
              size: _width,
            ),
          ),
        ),
      ),
    );
  }
}
```

How It Works

The hero animation is a powerful built-in animation to convey an action by automatically animating a widget from one page to another to the correct size and position. On the home page, you declare a GestureDetector with the Hero widget as the child widget. The Hero widget sets an Icon as the child. The onTap calls the Navigator.push() method, which navigates to the page Fly. All you need to do on the Fly page is to declare the widget you're animating to as a child of the Hero widget. When you navigate back to the home page, the Hero animates the Icon to the original position.

USING THE BOTTOMNAVIGATIONBAR

BottomNavigationBar is a Material Design widget that displays a list of BottomNavigation-BarItems that contains an icon and a title at the bottom of the page (Figure 8.1). When the BottomNavigationBarItem is selected, the appropriate page is built.

FIGURE 8.1: Final BottomNavigationBar with icons and titles

TRY IT OUT Creating the BottomNavigationBar App

In this example, BottomNavigationBar has three BottomNavigationBarItems that replace the current page with the selected one. There are different ways to display the selected page; you use a Widget class as a variable.

1. Create a new Flutter project and name it ch8_bottom_navigation_bar. As always, you can follow the instructions in Chapter 4. For this project, you need to create only the pages folder.

2. Open the home.dart file, and add to the body a SafeArea with Padding as a child.

```
body: SafeArea(
  child: Padding(),
),
```

3. In the Padding child, add the variable Widget _currentPage, which you will create next. Note this time you are using a Widget class to create the _currentPage variable that holds each page that is selected, either the Gratitude, Reminders, or Birthdays StatelessWidget class.

```
body: SafeArea(
  child: Padding(
    padding: const EdgeInsets.all(16.0),
    child: _ currentPage,
  ),
),
```

4. Add to the Scaffold bottomNavigationBar property a BottomNavigationBar widget. For the currentIndex property, use the _currentIndex variable, which will be created later.

```
bottomNavigationBar: BottomNavigationBar(
        currentIndex: _currentIndex,
```

The items property is a List of BottomNavigationBarItems. Each BottomNavigationBarItem takes an icon property and a title property.

5. Add to the items property three BottomNavigationBarItems with icon cake, sentiment_satisfied, and access_alarm. The titles are 'Birthdays', 'Gratitude', and 'Reminders'.

```
items: [
  BottomNavigationBarItem(
    icon: Icon(Icons.cake),
    title: Text('Birthdays'),
  ),
```

6. For the onTap property, the callback returns the current index of the active item. Name the variable selectedIndex.

```
onTap: (selectedIndex) => _changePage(selectedIndex),
```

Here's the entire BottomNavigationBar code:

```
bottomNavigationBar: BottomNavigationBar(
  currentIndex: _currentIndex,
  items: [
    BottomNavigationBarItem(
      icon: Icon(Icons.cake),
      title: Text('Birthdays'),
    ),
```

```
      BottomNavigationBarItem(
        icon: Icon(Icons.sentiment_satisfied),
        title: Text('Gratitude'),
      ),
      BottomNavigationBarItem(
        icon: Icon(Icons.access_alarm),
        title: Text('Reminders'),
      ),
    ],
    onTap: (selectedIndex) => _changePage(selectedIndex),
  ),
```

7. Add the _changePage(int selectedIndex) method after Scaffold(). The _changePage() method accepts an int value of the selected index. The selectedIndex is used with the setState() method to set the _currentIndex and _currentPage variables.

The _currentIndex equals the selectedIndex, and the _currentPage equals the page from the List _listPages that corresponds to the selected index.

It's important to note that the Widget _currentPage variable displays each page selected without the need for a Navigator widget. This is a great example of the power of customizing widgets to your needs.

```
void _changePage(int selectedIndex) {
  setState(() {
    _currentIndex = selectedIndex;
    _currentPage = _listPages[selectedIndex];
  });
}
```

8. On the first line after the _HomeState class definition, add the variables _currentIndex, _listPages, and _currentPage. The _listPages List holds each page's Class name.

```
int _currentIndex = 0;
List _listPages = List();
Widget _currentPage;
```

9. Override initState() to add each page to the _listPages List and initialize the _currentPage with the Birthdays() page. Note the use of cascade notation; the double dots allow you to perform a sequence of operations on the same object.

```
@override
void initState() {
  super.initState();

  _listPages
    ..add(Birthdays())
    ..add(Gratitude())
    ..add(Reminders());
  _currentPage = Birthdays();
}
```

10. Add to the top of the `home.dart` file the imports for each page that will be created next.

```
import 'package:flutter/material.dart';
import 'gratitude.dart';
import 'reminders.dart';
import 'birthdays.dart';
```

Here's the entire `home.dart` file:

```
import 'package:flutter/material.dart';
import 'gratitude.dart';
import 'reminders.dart';
import 'birthdays.dart';

class Home extends StatefulWidget {
  @override
  _HomeState createState() => _HomeState();
}

class _HomeState extends State<Home> {
  int _currentIndex = 0;
  List _listPages = List();
  Widget _currentPage;

  @override
  void initState() {
    super.initState();

    _listPages
      ..add(Birthdays())
      ..add(Gratitude())
      ..add(Reminders());
    _currentPage = Birthdays();
  }

  void _changePage(int selectedIndex) {
    setState(() {
      _currentIndex = selectedIndex;
      _currentPage = _listPages[selectedIndex];
    });
  }

  @override
  Widget build(BuildContext context) {
    return Scaffold(
      appBar: AppBar(
        title: Text('BottomNavigationBar'),
      ),
      body: SafeArea(
        child: Padding(
          padding: EdgeInsets.all(16.0),
          child: _currentPage,
        ),
      ),
```

```
        bottomNavigationBar: BottomNavigationBar(
          currentIndex: _currentIndex,
          items: [
            BottomNavigationBarItem(
              icon: Icon(Icons.cake),
              title: Text('Birthdays'),
            ),
            BottomNavigationBarItem(
              icon: Icon(Icons.sentiment_satisfied),
              title: Text('Gratitude'),
            ),
            BottomNavigationBarItem(
              icon: Icon(Icons.access_alarm),
              title: Text('Reminders'),
            ),
          ],
          onTap: (selectedIndex) => _changePage(selectedIndex),
        ),
      );
    }
  }
```

11. Create three `StatelessWidget` pages and call them `Birthdays`, `Gratitude`, and `Reminders`. Each page will have a `Scaffold` with `Center()` for the `body`. The `Center` child is an `Icon` with a `size` value of 120.0 pixels and a `color` property. Here are the three Dart files, `birthdays.dart`, `gratitude.dart`, and `reminders.dart`:

```
// birthdays.dart
import 'package:flutter/material.dart';

class Birthdays extends StatelessWidget {
  @override
  Widget build(BuildContext context) {
    return Scaffold(
      body: Center(
        child: Icon(
          Icons.cake,
          size: 120.0,
          color: Colors.orange,
        ),
      ),
    );
  }
}

// gratitude.dart
import 'package:flutter/material.dart';

class Gratitude extends StatelessWidget {
  @override
  Widget build(BuildContext context) {
    return Scaffold(
      body: Center(
        child: Icon(
          Icons.sentiment_satisfied,
```

```
            size: 120.0,
            color: Colors.lightGreen,
          ),
        ),
      );
    }
  }

  // reminders.dart
  import 'package:flutter/material.dart';

  class Reminders extends StatelessWidget {
    @override
    Widget build(BuildContext context) {
      return Scaffold(
        body: Center(
          child: Icon(
            Icons.access_alarm,
            size: 120.0,
            color: Colors.purple,
          ),
        ),
      );
    }
  }
```

How It Works

The BottomNavigationBar items property has a List of three BottomNavigationBarItems. For each BottomNavigationBarItem, you set an icon property and a title property. The Bottom-

`NavigationBar onTap` passes the selected index value to the `_changePage` method. The `_changePage` method uses `setState()` to set the `_currentIndex` and `_currentPage` to display. The `_currentIndex` sets the selected `BottomNavigationBarItem`, and the `_currentPage` sets the current page to display from the `_listPages List`.

USING THE BOTTOMAPPBAR

The `BottomAppBar` widget behaves similarly to the `BottomNavigationBar`, but it has an optional notch along the top. By adding a `FloatingActionButton` and enabling the notch, the notch provides a nice 3D effect so it looks like the button is recessed into the navigation bar (Figure 8.2). For example, to enable the notch, you set the `BottomAppBar shape` property to a `Notched-Shape` class like the `CircularNotchedRectangle()` class and set the `Scaffold floatingActionButtonLocation` property to `FloatingActionButtonLocation.endDocked` or `center-Docked`. Add to the `Scaffold floatingActionButton` property a `FloatingActionButton` widget, and the result shows the `FloatingActionButton` embedded into the `BottomApp-Bar` widget, which is the notch.

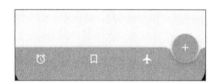

FIGURE 8.2: BottomAppBar with embedded FloatingActionButton creating a notch

```
BottomAppBar(
  shape: CircularNotchedRectangle(),
)

floatingActionButtonLocation: FloatingActionButtonLocation.endDocked,
floatingActionButton: FloatingActionButton(
  child: Icon(Icons.add),
),
```

TRY IT OUT   Creating the BottomAppBar App

In this example, the `BottomAppBar` has a `Row` as a child with three `IconButtons` to show selection items. The main objective is to use a `FloatingActionButton` to dock it to the `BottomAppBar` with a notch. The notch is enabled by the `BottomAppBar shape` property set to `CircularNotchedRectangle()`.

1. Create a new Flutter project and name it `ch8_bottom_app_bar`. Again, you can follow the instructions in Chapter 4. For this project, you only need to create the `pages` folder.

2. Open the `home.dart` file, and add to the `body` a `SafeArea` with a `Container` as a child.

    ```
    body: SafeArea(
      child: Container(),
    ),
    ```

3. Add a `BottomAppBar()` widget to the `Scaffold bottomNavigationBar` property.

    ```
    bottomNavigationBar: BottomAppBar(),
    ```

4. To enable the notch, you set two properties.

➤ First set the `BottomAppBar` shape property to `CircularNotchedRectangle()`. Set the `color` property to `Colors.blue.shade200` and add a `Row` as a child.

➤ Next set `floatingActionButtonLocation`, which you will handle in step 7.

```
bottomNavigationBar: BottomAppBar(
  color: Colors.blue.shade200,
  shape: CircularNotchedRectangle(),
  child: Row(),
),
```

5. Continue by adding to the `Row` a `mainAxisAlignment` property as `MainAxisAlignment.space-Around`. The spaceAround constant allows the `IconButtons` to have even spacing between them.

```
bottomNavigationBar: BottomAppBar(
  color: Colors.blue.shade200,
  shape: CircularNotchedRectangle(),
  child: Row(
    mainAxisAlignment: MainAxisAlignment.spaceAround,
    children: <Widget>[
    ],
  ),
),
```

6. Add three `IconButtons` to the `Row` children list. After the last `IconButton`, add a `Divider()` to add an even space to the right since `FloatingActionButton` is docked on the right side of the `BottomAppBar`. Instead of a `Divider()`, you could have used a `Container` with a `width` property.

```
bottomNavigationBar: BottomAppBar(
  color: Colors.blue.shade200,
  shape: CircularNotchedRectangle(),
  child: Row(
    mainAxisAlignment: MainAxisAlignment.spaceAround,
    children: <Widget>[
      IconButton(
        icon: Icon(Icons.access_alarm),
        color: Colors.white,
        onPressed: (){},
      ),
      IconButton(
        icon: Icon(Icons.bookmark_border),
        color: Colors.white,
        onPressed: (){},
      ),
      IconButton(
        icon: Icon(Icons.flight),
        color: Colors.white,
        onPressed: (){},
      ),
      Divider(),
    ],
  ),
),
```

7. Set the notch location of the `floatingActionButtonLocation` property to `FloatingActionButtonLocation.endDocked`. You could also set it to `centerDocked`.

```
floatingActionButtonLocation: FloatingActionButtonLocation.endDocked,
```

8. Add a `FloatingActionButton` to the `floatingActionButton` property.

```
floatingActionButton: FloatingActionButton(
  backgroundColor: Colors.blue.shade200,
  onPressed: () {},
  child: Icon(Icons.add),
),
```

Here's the entire `home.dart` file source code:

```dart
import 'package:flutter/material.dart';

class Home extends StatefulWidget {
  @override
  _HomeState createState() => _HomeState();
}

class _HomeState extends State<Home> {
  @override
  Widget build(BuildContext context) {
    return Scaffold(
      appBar: AppBar(
        title: Text('BottomAppBar'),
      ),
      body: SafeArea(
        child: Container(),
      ),
      bottomNavigationBar: BottomAppBar(
        color: Colors.blue.shade200,
        shape: CircularNotchedRectangle(),
        child: Row(
          mainAxisAlignment: MainAxisAlignment.spaceAround,
          children: <Widget>[
            IconButton(
              icon: Icon(Icons.access_alarm),
              color: Colors.white,
              onPressed: (){},
            ),
            IconButton(
              icon: Icon(Icons.bookmark_border),
              color: Colors.white,
              onPressed: (){},
            ),
            IconButton(
              icon: Icon(Icons.flight),
              color: Colors.white,
              onPressed: (){},
            ),
            Divider(),
          ],
```

```
            ),
          ),
      floatingActionButtonLocation: FloatingActionButtonLocation.endDocked,
      floatingActionButton: FloatingActionButton(
        backgroundColor: Colors.blue.shade200,
        onPressed: () {},
        child: Icon(Icons.add),
      ),
    );
  }
}
```

How It Works

To enable the notch, two properties need to be set for the `Scaffold` widget. The first is to use a `BottomAppBar` with the `shape` property set to `CircularNotchedRectangle()`. The second is to set the `floatingActionButtonLocation` property to `FloatingActionButtonLocation.endDocked` or `centerDocked`.

USING THE TABBAR AND TABBARVIEW

The `TabBar` widget is a Material Design widget that displays a horizontal row of tabs. The `tabs` property takes a `List` of `Widgets`, and you add tabs by using the `Tab` widget. Instead of using the `Tab` widget, you could create a custom widget, which shows the power of Flutter. The selected `Tab` is marked with a bottom selection line.

The `TabBarView` widget is used in conjunction with the `TabBar` widget to display the page of the selected tab. Users can swipe left or right to change content or tap each `Tab`.

Both the `TabBar` (Figure 8.3) and `TabBarView` widgets take a `controller` property of `TabController`. The `TabController` is responsible for syncing tab selections between a `TabBar` and a `TabBarView`. Since the `TabController` syncs the tab selections, you need to declare the `SingleTickerProviderStateMixin` to the class. In Chapter 7, "Adding Animation to an App," you learned how to implement the `Ticker` class that is driven by the `ScheduleBinding.scheduleFrameCallback` reporting once per animation frame. It is trying to sync the animation to be as smooth as possible.

FIGURE 8.3: TabBar in the Scaffold bottomNavigationBar property

TRY IT OUT   Creating the TabBar and TabBarView App

In this example, the `TabBar` widget is the child of a `bottomNavigationBar` property. This places the `TabBar` at the bottom of the screen, but you could also place it in the `AppBar` or a custom location. When you use a `TabBar` in combination with the `TabBarView`, once a `Tab` is selected, it automatically displays the appropriate content. In this project, the content is represented by three separate pages. You'll create the same three pages as you did in the `BottomNavigationBar` project.

1. Create a new Flutter project and name it `ch8_tabbar`. Once more, you can follow the instructions in Chapter 4. For this project, you need to create only the `pages` folder.

2. Open the `home.dart` file, and add to the `body` a `SafeArea` with `TabBarView` as a `child`. The `TabBarView` controller property is a `TabController` variable called `_tabController`. Add to the `TabBarView` children property the `Birthdays()`, `Gratitude()`, and `Reminders()` pages that you'll create in step 3.

```
body: SafeArea(
  child: TabBarView(
```

```
          controller: _tabController,
          children: [
            Birthdays(),
            Gratitude(),
            Reminders(),
          ],
        ),
      ),
```

3. This time you'll create the pages that you are navigating to first. Like in the `BottomNavigationBar` app, create three `StatelessWidget` pages and call them `Birthdays`, `Gratitude`, and `Reminders`. Each page has a `Scaffold` with `Center()` for the body. The `Center` child is an `Icon` with the size of 120.0 pixels and a `color`.

The following are the three Dart files, `birthdays.dart`, `gratitude.dart`, and `reminders.dart`:

```
// birthdays.dart
import 'package:flutter/material.dart';

class Birthdays extends StatelessWidget {
  @override
  Widget build(BuildContext context) {
    return Scaffold(
      body: Center(
        child: Icon(
          Icons.cake,
          size: 120.0,
          color: Colors.orange,
        ),
      ),
    );
  }
}

// gratitude.dart
import 'package:flutter/material.dart';

class Gratitude extends StatelessWidget {
  @override
  Widget build(BuildContext context) {
    return Scaffold(
      body: Center(
        child: Icon(
          Icons.sentiment_satisfied,
          size: 120.0,
          color: Colors.lightGreen,
        ),
      ),
    );
  }
}

// reminders.dart
import 'package:flutter/material.dart';
```

```
class Reminders extends StatelessWidget {
  @override
  Widget build(BuildContext context) {
    return Scaffold(
      body: Center(
        child: Icon(
          Icons.access_alarm,
          size: 120.0,
          color: Colors.purple,
        ),
      ),
    );
  }
}
```

4. Import each page in the home.dart file.

```
import 'package:flutter/material.dart';
import 'birthdays.dart';
import 'gratitude.dart';
import 'reminders.dart';
```

5. Declare the TickerProviderStateMixin to the _HomeState class by adding with TickerProviderStateMixin. The AnimationController vsync argument will use it.

```
class _HomeState extends State<Home> with SingleTickerProviderStateMixin {...}
```

6. Declare a TabController variable by the name of _tabController. Override the initState() method to initialize the _tabController with the vsync argument and a length value of 3. The vsync is referenced by this, meaning this reference of the _HomeState class. The length represents the number of Tabs to show. Add a Listener to the _tabController to catch when a Tab is changed. Then override the dispose() method for when the page closes to properly dispose of the _tabController.

Note in the _tabChanged method you check for indexIsChanging before showing which Tab is tapped. If you do not check for indexIsChanging, then the code runs twice.

```
class _HomeState extends State<Home> with SingleTickerProviderStateMixin {
  TabController _tabController;

  @override
  void initState() {
    super.initState();

    _tabController = TabController(vsync: this, length: 3);
    _tabController.addListener(_tabChanged);
  }

  @override
  void dispose() {
    super.dispose();

  @override
  void dispose() {
    _tabController.dispose();
```

```
    super.dispose();
  }
    _tabController.dispose();
  }

  void _tabChanged() {
    // Check if Tab Controller index is changing, otherwise we get the notice twice
    if (_tabController.indexIsChanging) {
      print('tabChanged: ${_tabController.index}');
    }
  }
}
```

7. Add a TabBar as a child of the bottomNavigationBar Scaffold property.

```
bottomNavigationBar: SafeArea(
  child: TabBar(),
),
```

8. Pass the _tabController for the TabBar controller property. I customized the labelColor and unselectedLabelColor by using, respectively, Colors.black54 and Colors.black38, but feel free to experiment using different colors.

```
bottomNavigationBar: SafeArea(
  child: TabBar(
    controller: _tabController,
    labelColor: Colors.black54,
    unselectedLabelColor: Colors.black38,
  ),
),
```

9. Add three Tab widgets to the tabs widget list. Customize each Tab icon and text.

```
bottomNavigationBar: SafeArea(
  child: TabBar(
    controller: _tabController,
    labelColor: Colors.black54,
    unselectedLabelColor: Colors.black38,
    tabs: [
      Tab(
        icon: Icon(Icons.cake),
        text: 'Birthdays',
      ),
      Tab(
        icon: Icon(Icons.sentiment_satisfied),
        text: 'Gratitude',
      ),
      Tab(
        icon: Icon(Icons.access_alarm),
        text: 'Reminders',
      ),
    ],
  ),
),
```

How It Works

When `TabBar` and `TabBarView` are used together, the correct associated page is automatically loaded. When the user swipes the `TabBarView` left or right, it scrolls to the correct page and selects the corresponding tab in the `TabBar`. All of these powerful features are built in; no custom coding is necessary.

How does it know which page belongs to which tab? The `TabController` is responsible for syncing tab selections between a `TabBar` and a `TabBarView`. Since the `TabController` syncs the tab selections, you need to declare the `SingleTickerProviderStateMixin` to the class.

Both the `TabBar` and `TabBarView` use the same `TabController`. The `TabController` is initiated by passing a `vsync` argument and a `length` argument. The `length` argument is the number of tabs to show. An optional `TabController Listener` is added to listen to `Tab` changes and take appropriate action if necessary, perhaps saving data before a `Tab` is switched. Each `Tab` is added to the `TabBar tabs` widget list by customizing each `icon` and `text`.

`TabBarView` is responsible for loading the appropriate page when `Tab` selection changes. The page views are listed as the `children` property of the `TabBarView` widget.

USING THE DRAWER AND LISTVIEW

You might be wondering why I'm covering the `ListView` in this navigation chapter. Well, it works great with the `Drawer` widget. `ListView` widgets are used quite often for selecting an item from a list to navigate to a detailed page.

Drawer is a Material Design panel that slides horizontally from the left or right edge of the Scaffold, the device screen. Drawer is used with the Scaffold drawer (left-side) property or endDrawer (right-side) property. Drawer can be customized for each individual need but usually has a header to show an image or fixed information and a ListView to show a list of navigable pages. Usually, a Drawer is used when the navigation list has many items.

To set the Drawer header, you have two built-in options, the UserAccountsDrawerHeader or the DrawerHeader. The UserAccountsDrawerHeader is intended to display the app's user details by setting the currentAccountPicture, accountName, accountEmail, otherAccountsPictures, and decoration properties.

```
// User details
UserAccountsDrawerHeader(
  currentAccountPicture: Icon(Icons.face,),
  accountName: Text('Sandy Smith'),
  accountEmail: Text('sandy.smith@domainname.com'),
  otherAccountsPictures: <Widget>[
    Icon(Icons.bookmark_border),
  ],
  decoration: BoxDecoration(
    image: DecorationImage(
      image: AssetImage('assets/images/home_top_mountain.jpg'),
      fit: BoxFit.cover,
    ),
  ),
),
```

DrawerHeader is intended to display generic or custom information by setting the padding, child, decoration, and other properties.

```
// Generic or custom information
DrawerHeader(
  padding: EdgeInsets.zero,
  child: Icon(Icons.face),
  decoration: BoxDecoration(color: Colors.blue),
),
```

The standard ListView constructor allows you to build a short list of items quickly. The next chapter will go into more depth on how to use the ListView. See Figure 8.4.

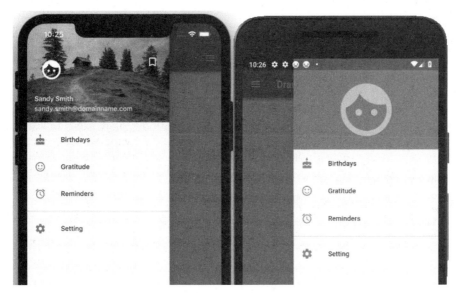

FIGURE 8.4: Drawer and ListView

TRY IT OUT   Creating the Drawer App

In this example, the Drawer is added to the drawer or endDrawer property of the Scaffold. The drawer and endDrawer properties slide the Drawer from either left to right (TextDirection.ltr) or right to left (TextDirection.rtl). In this example, you'll add both the drawer and the endDrawer to show how to use both. You use the UserAccountsDrawerHeader to the drawer (left-side) property and the DrawerHeader to the endDrawer (right-side) property.

You use the ListView to add the Drawer content and ListTile to align text and icons for the menu list easily. In this project, you use the standard ListView constructor since you have a small list of menu items.

1. Create a new Flutter project and name it ch8_drawer, following the instructions in Chapter 4. For this project, you need to create the pages, widgets, and assets/images folders. Copy the home_top_mountain.jpg image to the assets/images folder.

2. Open the pubspec.yaml file and under assets add the images folder.

    ```
    # To add assets to your application, add an assets section, like this:
    assets:
      - assets/images/
    ```

3. Add the folder `assets` and subfolder `images` at the project's root and then copy the `home_top_mountain.jpg` file to the `images` folder.

4. Click the Save button; depending on the editor you are using, it automatically runs the `flutter packages get`. Once finished, it shows a message of `Process finished with exit code 0`.

If it does not automatically run the command for you, open the Terminal window (located at the bottom of your editor) and type `flutter packages get`.

5. Create the pages that you are navigating to first. Create three `StatelessWidget` pages and call them `Birthdays`, `Gratitude`, and `Reminders`. Each page has a `Scaffold` with `Center()` for the body. The `Center` child is an `Icon` with the `size` value of 120.0 pixels and a `color` property.

```
class Birthdays extends StatelessWidget {
  @override
  Widget build(BuildContext context) {
    return Scaffold(
      body: Center(
        child: Icon(
          Icons.cake,
          size: 120.0,
          color: Colors.orange,
        ),
      ),
    );
  }
}
```

6. Add the `AppBar` to the `Scaffold`, which is needed for navigating back to the home page. The following shows the three Dart files, `birthdays.dart`, `gratitude.dart`, and `reminders.dart`:

```
// birthdays.dart
import 'package:flutter/material.dart';

class Birthdays extends StatelessWidget {
  @override
  Widget build(BuildContext context) {
    return Scaffold(
      appBar: AppBar(
        title: Text('Birthdays'),
      ),
      body: Center(
        child: Icon(
          Icons.cake,
          size: 120.0,
          color: Colors.orange,
        ),
      ),
    );
  }
}
```

```
// gratitude.dart
import 'package:flutter/material.dart';

class Gratitude extends StatelessWidget {
  @override
  Widget build(BuildContext context) {
    return Scaffold(
      appBar: AppBar(
        title: Text('Gratitude'),
      ),
      body: Center(
        child: Icon(
          Icons.sentiment_satisfied,
          size: 120.0,
          color: Colors.lightGreen,
        ),
      ),
    );
  }
}

// reminders.dart
import 'package:flutter/material.dart';

class Reminders extends StatelessWidget {
  @override
  Widget build(BuildContext context) {
    return Scaffold(
      appBar: AppBar(
        title: Text('Reminders'),
      ),
      body: Center(
        child: Icon(
          Icons.access_alarm,
          size: 120.0,
          color: Colors.purple,
        ),
      ),
    );
  }
}
```

7. The left and right Drawer widgets share the same menu list, and you'll write it first. Create a new Dart file in the widgets folder. Right-click the widgets folder and then select New ➪ Dart File, enter menu_list_tile.dart, and click the OK button to save.

8. Import the material.dart, birthdays.dart, gratitude.dart, and reminders.dart classes (pages). Add a new line and then start typing st; the autocompletion help opens, so select the stful abbreviation and give it a name of MenuListTileWidget.

```
import 'package:flutter/material.dart';
import 'package:ch8_drawer/pages/birthdays.dart';
import 'package:ch8_drawer/pages/gratitude.dart';
import 'package:ch8_drawer/pages/reminders.dart';
```

9. The `Widget build(BuildContext context)` returns a `Column`. The `Column children` widget list contains multiple `ListTiles` representing each menu item. Add a `Divider` widget with the `color` property set to `Colors.grey` before the last `ListTile` widget.

```
@override
Widget build(BuildContext context) {
  return Column(
    children: <Widget>[
      ListTile(),
      ListTile(),
      ListTile(),
      Divider(color: Colors.grey),
      ListTile(),
    ],
  );
}
```

10. For each `ListTile`, set the `leading` property as an `Icon` and the `title` property as a `Text`. For the `onTap` property, you first call `Navigator.pop()` to close the open `Drawer` and then call `Navigator.push()` to open the selected page.

```
@override
Widget build(BuildContext context) {
  return Column(
    children: <Widget>[
      ListTile(
        leading: Icon(Icons.cake),
        title: Text('Birthdays'),
        onTap: () {
          Navigator.pop(context);
          Navigator.push(
            context,
            MaterialPageRoute(
              builder: (context) => Birthdays(),
            ),
          );
        },
      ),
      ListTile(
        leading: Icon(Icons.sentiment_satisfied),
        title: Text('Gratitude'),
        onTap: () {
          Navigator.pop(context);
          Navigator.push(
            context,
            MaterialPageRoute(
              builder: (context) => Gratitude(),
            ),
          );
        },
      ),
      ListTile(
        leading: Icon(Icons.alarm),
        title: Text('Reminders'),
```

```
         onTap: () {
           Navigator.pop(context);
           Navigator.push(
             context,
             MaterialPageRoute(
               builder: (context) => Reminders(),
             ),
           );
         },
       ),
       Divider(color: Colors.grey),
       ListTile(
         leading: Icon(Icons.settings),
         title: Text('Setting'),
         onTap: () {
           Navigator.pop(context);
         },
       ),
     ],
   );
 }
```

11. Create a new Dart file in the `widgets` folder. Right-click the `widgets` folder and then select New ➪ Dart File, enter `left_drawer.dart`, and click the OK button to save.

12. Import the `material.dart` library and the `menu_list_tile.dart` class.

```
import 'package:flutter/material.dart';
import 'package:ch8_drawer/widgets/menu_list_tile.dart';
```

13. Add a new line and then start typing **st**; the autocompletion help opens. Select the `stful` abbreviation and give it a name of `LeftDrawerWidget`.

```
class LeftDrawerWidget extends StatelessWidget {
  const LeftDrawerWidget({
    Key key,
  }) : super(key: key);

  @override
  Widget build(BuildContext context) {
    return Drawer();
  }
}
```

14. The `Widget build(BuildContext context)` returns a `Drawer`. The `Drawer` child is a `ListView` children list widget of a `UserAccountsDrawerHeader` widget and a call to the `const` `MenuListTileWidget()` widget class. To fill the entire `Drawer` space, you set the `ListView` padding property to `EdgeInsets.zero`.

```
  @override
  Widget build(BuildContext context) {
    return Drawer(
      child: ListView(
        padding: EdgeInsets.zero,
```

```
        children: <Widget>[
          UserAccountsDrawerHeader(),
          const MenuListTileWidget(),
        ],
      ),
    );
}
```

15. For the `UserAccountsDrawerHeader`, set the `currentAccountPicture`, `accountName`, `account-Email`, `otherAccountsPictures`, and `decoration` properties.

```
@override
Widget build(BuildContext context) {
  return Drawer(
    child: ListView(
      padding: EdgeInsets.zero,
      children: <Widget>[
        UserAccountsDrawerHeader(
          currentAccountPicture: Icon(
            Icons.face,
            size: 48.0,
            color: Colors.white,
          ),
          accountName: Text('Sandy Smith'),
          accountEmail: Text('sandy.smith@domainname.com'),
          otherAccountsPictures: <Widget>[
            Icon(
              Icons.bookmark_border,
              color: Colors.white,
            )
          ],
          decoration: BoxDecoration(
            image: DecorationImage(
              image: AssetImage('assets/images/home_top_mountain.jpg'),
              fit: BoxFit.cover,
            ),
          ),
        ),
        const MenuListTileWidget(),
      ],
    ),
  );
}
```

16. Create a new Dart file in the `widgets` folder. Right-click the `widgets` folder and then select New ➪ Dart File, enter `right_drawer.dart`, and click the OK button to save. Import the `material.dart` library and the `menu_list_tile.dart` class.

```
import 'package:flutter/material.dart';
import 'package:ch8_drawer/widgets/menu_list_tile.dart';
```

17. Add a new line and then start typing **st**; the autocompletion help opens. Select the `stful` abbreviation and give it a name of `RightDrawerWidget`.

```
class RightDrawerWidget extends StatelessWidget {
  const RightDrawerWidget({
    Key key,
  }) : super(key: key);

  @override
  Widget build(BuildContext context) {
    return Drawer();
  }
}
```

18. The `Widget build(BuildContext context)` returns a `Drawer`. The `Drawer` child is a `ListView` children list of a `DrawerHeader` widget and a call to the const `MenuListTileWidget()` widget class. To fill the entire `Drawer` space, you set the `ListView` padding property to `EdgeInsets.zero`.

```
  @override
  Widget build(BuildContext context) {
    return Drawer(
      child: ListView(
        padding: EdgeInsets.zero,
        children: <Widget>[
          DrawerHeader(),
          const MenuListTileWidget(),
        ],
      ),
    );
  }
```

19. For the `DrawerHeader`, set the `padding`, `child`, and `decoration` properties.

```
  @override
  Widget build(BuildContext context) {
    return Drawer(
      child: ListView(
        padding: EdgeInsets.zero,
        children: <Widget>[
          DrawerHeader(
            padding: EdgeInsets.zero,
            child: Icon(
              Icons.face,
              size: 128.0,
              color: Colors.white54,
            ),
            decoration: BoxDecoration(color: Colors.blue),
          ),
          const MenuListTileWidget(),
        ],
      ),
    );
  }
```

20. Open the `home.dart` file and import the `material.dart`, `birthdays.dart`, `gratitude.dart`, and `reminders.dart` classes.

```
import 'package:flutter/material.dart';
import 'birthdays.dart';
import 'gratitude.dart';
import 'reminders.dart';
```

21. Add to the `body` a `SafeArea` with a `Container` as a child.

```
body: SafeArea(
  child: Container(),
),
```

22. Add to the `Scaffold drawer` property a call to the `LeftDrawerWidget()` widget class and for the `endDrawer` property a call to the `RightDrawerWidget()` widget class.

Note that you use the `const` keyword before calling each widget class to take advantage of caching and subtree rebuilding for better performance.

```
return Scaffold(
  appBar: AppBar(
    title: Text('Drawer'),
  ),
  drawer: const LeftDrawerWidget(),
  endDrawer: const RightDrawerWidget(),
  body: SafeArea(
    child: Container(),
  ),
);
```

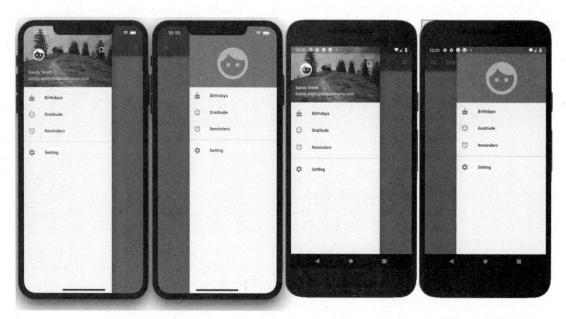

How It Works

To add a Drawer to an app, you set the Scaffold drawer or endDrawer property. The drawer and endDrawer properties slide the Drawer from either left to right (TextDirection.ltr) or right to left (TextDirection.rtl).

The Drawer widget takes a child property, and you passed a ListView. Using a ListView allows you to create a scrollable menu list of items. For the ListView children widget list, you created two widget classes, one to build the Drawer header and one to build the list of menu items. To set the Drawer header, you have two options, UserAccountsDrawerHeader or DrawerHeader. These two widgets easily allow you to set header content depending on the requirements. You looked at two examples for the Drawer header by calling the appropriate widget class LeftDrawerWidget() or RightDrawerWidget().

For the menu items list, you used the MenuListTileWidget() widget class. This class returns a Column widget that uses the ListTile to build your menu list. The ListTile widget allows you to set the leading Icon, title, and onTap properties. The onTap property calls Navigator.pop() to close Drawer and calls Navigator.push() to navigate to the selected page.

This app is an excellent example of creating a shallow widget tree by using widget classes and separating them into individual files for maximum reuse. You also nested widget classes with the left and right widget classes both calling the menu list class.

SUMMARY

In this chapter, you learned to use the Navigator widget to manage a stack of routes so as to allow navigation between pages. You optionally passed data to the navigation page and back to the original page. The hero animation allows a widget transition to fly into place from one page to another. The widget to animate from and to is wrapped in a Hero widget by a unique key.

You used the BottomNavigationBar widget to display a horizontal list of BottomNavigation-BarItems containing an icon and a title at the bottom of the page. When the user taps each BottomNavigationBarItem, the appropriate page is displayed. To enhance the look of a bottom navigation bar, you used the BottomAppBar widget and enabled the optional notch. The notch is the result of embedding a FloatingActionButton to a BottomAppBar by setting the BottomAppBar shape to a CircularNotchedRectangle() class and setting the Scaffold floatingActionButton-Location property to FloatingActionButtonLocation.endDocked.

The TabBar widget displays a horizontal row of tabs. The tabs property takes a List of widgets, and tabs are added by using the Tab widget. The TabBarView widget is used in conjunction with the TabBar widget to display the page of the selected tab. Users can swipe left or right to change content or tap each Tab. The TabController class handled the syncing of the TabBar and selected TabBar-View. The TabController requires the use of with SingleTickerProviderStateMixin in the class.

The Drawer widget allows the user to slide a panel from left or right. The Drawer widget is added by setting the Scaffold drawer or endDrawer property. To easily align menu items in a list, you pass a

ListView as a child of the Drawer. Since this menu list is short, you use the standard ListView constructor instead of a ListView builder, which is covered in the next chapter. You have two prebuilt drawer header options, UserAccountsDrawerHeader or DrawerHeader. When the user taps one of the menu items, the onTap property calls Navigator.pop() to close Drawer and calls Navigator.push() to navigate to the selected page.

In the next chapter, you'll learn to use different types of lists. You will take a look at the ListView, GridView, Stack, Card, and my favorite—CustomScrollView to use Slivers.

▶ **WHAT YOU LEARNED IN THIS CHAPTER**

TOPIC	KEY CONCEPTS
`Navigator`	The `Navigator` widget manages a stack of routes to move between pages.
Hero animation	The `Hero` widget is used to convey a navigation animation and size for a widget to fly into place from one page to another. When the second page is dismissed, the animation is reversed to the originating page.
`BottomNavigationBar`	`BottomNavigationBar` displays a horizontal list of `BottomNavigationBarItem` items containing an icon and a title at the bottom of the page.
`BottomAppBar`	The `BottomAppBar` widget behaves like the `BottomNavigationBar`, but it has an optional notch along the top.
`TabBar`	The `TabBar` widget displays a horizontal row of tabs. The `tabs` property takes a list of widgets, and tabs are added by using the `Tab` widget.
`TabBarView`	The `TabBarView` widget is used in conjunction with the `TabBar` widget to display the page of the selected tab.
`Drawer`	The `Drawer` widget allows the user to slide a panel from left or right.
`ListView`	The standard `ListView` constructor allows you to build a short list of items quickly.

Creating Scrolling Lists and Effects

In this chapter, you'll learn to create scrolling lists that help users view and select information. You'll start with the `Card` widget in this chapter because it is commonly used in conjunction with list-capable widgets to enhance the user interface (UI) and group data. In the previous chapter, you took a look at using the basic constructor for the `ListView`, and in this chapter, you'll use the `ListView.builder` to customize the data. The `GridView` widget is a fantastic widget that displays a list of data by a fixed number of tiles (groups of data) in the cross axis. The `Stack` widget is commonly used to overlap, position, and align widgets to create a custom look. A good example is a shopping cart with the number of items to purchase on the upper-right side.

The `CustomScrollView` widget allows you to create custom scrolling effects by using a list of slivers widgets. Slivers are handy, for instance, if you have a journal entry with an image on the top of the page and the diary description below. When the user swipes to read more, the description scrolling is faster than the image scrolling, creating a parallax effect.

USING THE CARD

The Card widget is part of the Material Design and has minimal rounded corners and shadows. To group and lay out data, the Card is a perfect widget to enhance the look of the UI. The Card widget is customizable with properties such as elevation, shape, color, margin, and others. The elevation property is a value of double, and the higher the number, the larger the shadow that is cast. You learned in Chapter 3, "Learning Dart Basics," that a double is a number that requires decimal point precision, such as 8.50. To customize the shape and borders of the Card widget, you modify the shape property. Some of the shape properties are StadiumBorder, Underline-InputBorder, OutlineInputBorder, and others.

```
Card(
    elevation: 8.0,
    color: Colors.white,
    margin: EdgeInsets.all(16.0),
    child: Column(
        mainAxisAlignment: MainAxisAlignment.center,
        children: <Widget>[
            Text('
                'Barista',
                textAlign: TextAlign.center,
                style: TextStyle(
                    fontWeight: FontWeight.bold,
                    fontSize: 48.0,
                    color: Colors.orange,
                ),
            '),
            Text(
                'Travel Plans',
                textAlign: TextAlign.center,
                style: TextStyle(color: Colors.grey),
            ),
        ],
    ),
),
```

The following are a few ways to customize the Card's shape property (Figure 9.1):

```
// Create a Stadium Border
shape: StadiumBorder(),

// Create Square Corners Card with a Single Orange Bottom Border
shape: UnderlineInputBorder(borderSide: BorderSide(color: Colors.deepOrange)),

// Create Rounded Corners Card with Orange Border
shape: OutlineInputBorder(borderSide: BorderSide(color: Colors.deepOrange.
withOpacity(0.5)),),
```

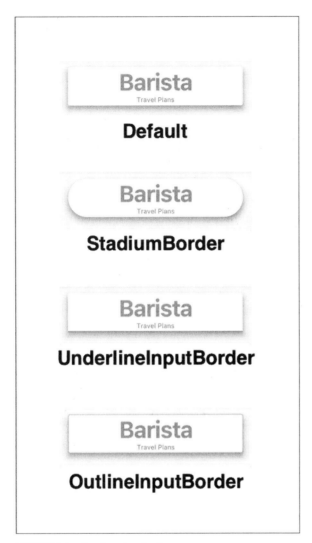

FIGURE 9.1: Card customizations

USING THE LISTVIEW AND LISTTILE

The constructor `ListView.builder` is used to create an on-demand linear scrollable list of widgets (Figure 9.2). When you have a large set of data, the `builder` is called only for visible widgets, which is great for performance. Within the `builder`, you use the `itemBuilder` callback to create the list of children widgets. Keep in mind the `itemBuilder` is called only if the `itemCount` argument is greater than zero, and it is called as many times as the `itemCount` value. Remember, the `List` starts at row 0, not 1. If you have 20 items in the `List`, it loops from row 0 to 19. The `scrollDirection` argument defaults to `Axis.vertical` but can be changed to `Axis.horizontal`.

The `ListTile` widget is commonly used with the `ListView` widget to easily format and organize icons, titles, and descriptions in a linear layout. Among the main properties are `leading`, `trailing`, `title`, and `subtitle` properties, but there are others. You can also use the `onTap` and `onLongPress` callbacks to execute an action when the user taps the `ListTile`. Usually the `leading` and `trailing` properties are implemented with icons, but you can add any type of widget.

In Figure 9.2, the first three `ListTiles` show an icon for the `leading` property, but for the `trailing` property, a `Text` widget shows a percentage value. The remaining `ListTiles` show both the `leading` and `trailing` properties as icons. Another scenario is to use the `subtitle` property to show a progress bar instead of additional text description since these properties accept widgets.

The first code example here shows a `Card` with the `child` property as a `ListTile` to give it a nice frame and shadow effect. The second example shows a base `ListTile`.

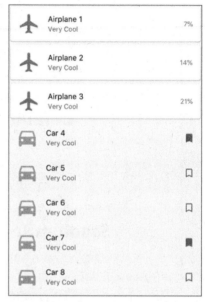

FIGURE 9.2: ListView linear layout using the ListTile

```
// Card with a ListTile widget
Card(
  child: ListTile(
    leading: Icon(Icons.flight),
    title: Text('Airplane $index'),
    subtitle: Text('Very Cool'),
    trailing: Text('${index * 7}%'),
    onTap: ()=> print('Tapped on Row $index'),
  ),
);

// ListTile
ListTile(
  leading: Icon(Icons.directions_car),
  title: Text('Car $index'),
  subtitle: Text('Very Cool'),
  trailing: Icon(Icons.bookmark),
  onTap: ()=> print('Tapped on Row $index'),
);
```

TRY IT OUT Creating the ListView App

In this example, the `ListView` widget uses the `builder` to display a `Card` for the header and two variations of the `ListTile` for the data list. The `ListTile` can display `leading` and `trailing` widgets. The `leading` property shows an `Icon` but could have displayed an `Image`. For the `trailing` property, the first type of `ListTile` shows data as a percentage, and the second `ListTile` shows a selected or unselected bookmark `Icon`. You also set a `title` and `subtitle`, and for the `onTap` you use the `print` statement to show the tapped row index value.

1. Create a new Flutter project and name it `ch9_listview`. You can follow the instructions in Chapter 4, "Creating a Starter Project Template." For this project, you need to create only the `pages` and `widgets` folders. Create the `Home Class` as a `StatelessWidget` since the data does not require changes.

2. Open the `home.dart` file and add to the body a `SafeArea` with `ListView.builder()` as a child.

```
body: SafeArea(
  child: ListView.builder(),
),
```

3. Set the `ListView.builder` with the `itemCount` argument set to 20. For this example, you specify 20 rows of data. For the `itemBuilder` callback, it passes the `BuildContext` and the widget `index` as an `int` value.

To show how to create different types of widgets to list each row of data, let's check the first row for the index value of zero and call the `HeaderWidget(index: index)` widget class. This class shows a `Card` with the text "Barista Travel Plan."

For the first, second, and third rows, the widget class `RowWithCardWidget(index: index)` is called to show a `ListTile` as a `child` of a `Card`. For the rest of the rows, you call the `RowWidget(index: index)` widget class to show a default `ListTile`.

It's important to understand that the widget classes you call from the `itemBuilder` create a unique widget with the index value passed. The `itemBuilder` loops the `itemCount` value, in this example 20 times.

You'll create the three widget classes in step 5.

```
body: SafeArea(
  child: ListView.builder(
    itemCount: 20,
    itemBuilder: (BuildContext context, int index) {
      if (index == 0) {
        return HeaderWidget(index: index);
      } else if (index >= 1 && index <= 3) {
        return RowWithCardWidget(index: index);
      } else {
        return RowWidget(index: index);
      }
    },
  ),
),
```

4. Add to the top of the file the `import` statements for the `header.dart`, `row_with_card.dart`, and `row.dart` widget classes that you'll create next.

```
import 'package:flutter/material.dart';
import 'package:ch9_listview/widgets/header.dart';
import 'package:ch9_listview/widgets/row_with_card.dart';
import 'package:ch9_listview/widgets/row.dart';
```

5. Create a new Dart file in the `widgets` folder. Right-click the `widgets` folder and then select New ⇨ Dart File, enter `header.dart`, and click the OK button to save.

6. Import the `material.dart` library, add a new line, and then start typing **st**; the autocompletion help opens, so select the `stless` (`StatelessWidget`) abbreviation and give it a name of `HeaderWidget`.

7. Modify the `HeaderWidget` widget class to return a `Container`. Import the `material.dart` library. The `Container` child is a `Card` with an `elevation` of 8.0 to show a deep shadow. The `Card` `children` list of widgets returns two `Text` widgets. I purposely left three `shape` types commented out for you to test and see how they change the `shape` and borders of the `Card`.

I wanted to point out that the `ListView itemBuilder` in the `main.dart` file calls this class, the `HeaderWidget(index: index)` for each row item. For every row, a `Widget` is created and added to the widget tree.

Note I commented out three different ways to customize the default `Card` shape for your testing.

```dart
import 'package:flutter/material.dart';

class HeaderWidget extends StatelessWidget {
  const HeaderWidget({
    Key key,
    @required this.index,
  }) : super(key: key);

  final int index;

  @override
  Widget build(BuildContext context) {
    return Container(
      padding: EdgeInsets.all(16.0),
      height: 120.0,
      child: Card(
        elevation: 8.0,
        color: Colors.white,
        //shape: StadiumBorder(),
        //shape: UnderlineInputBorder(borderSide: BorderSide(color: Colors
.deepOrange)),
        //shape: OutlineInputBorder(borderSide: BorderSide(color:
Colors.deepOrange.withOpacity(0.5)),),
        child: Column(
          mainAxisAlignment: MainAxisAlignment.center,
          children: <Widget>[
            Text(
              'Barista',
              textAlign: TextAlign.center,
              style: TextStyle(
                fontWeight: FontWeight.bold,
                fontSize: 48.0,
                color: Colors.orange,
              ),
            ),
            Text(
              'Travel Plans',
              textAlign: TextAlign.center,
              style: TextStyle(color: Colors.grey),
            ),
          ],
```

```
        ),
      ),
    );
  }
}
```

8. Create a new Dart file in the `widgets` folder. Right-click the `widgets` folder and then select New ⇨ Dart File, enter `row_with_card.dart`, and click the OK button to save.

9. Import the `material.dart` library, add a new line, and then start typing **st**; the autocompletion help opens, so select the `stless` (`StatelessWidget`) abbreviation and give it a name of `RowWithCardWidget`.

10. Modify the `RowWithCardWidget` class widget to return a `Card`. Import the `material.dart` library. The `Card` child is a `ListTile`, which is great to align content easily. For the `leading` property, return an `Icon`. The `trailing` property returns a `Text` widget with string interpolation that takes the `index` times seven to obtain a number. The `title` property returns a `Text` widget with the `index` value. The `subtitle` property returns a `Text` widget. For the `onTap` property, you use a `print` statement to show the tapped row `index`.

As a reminder, a widget is created and added to the widget tree for each row.

```dart
import 'package:flutter/material.dart';

class RowWithCardWidget extends StatelessWidget {
  const RowWithCardWidget({
    Key key,
    @required this.index,
  }) : super(key: key);

  final int index;

  @override
  Widget build(BuildContext context) {
    return Card(
      child: ListTile(
        leading: Icon(
          Icons.flight,
          size: 48.0,
          color: Colors.lightBlue,
        ),
        title: Text('Airplane $index'),
        subtitle: Text('Very Cool'),
        trailing: Text(
          '${index * 7}%',
          style: TextStyle(color: Colors.lightBlue),
        ),
        //selected: true,
        onTap: () {
          print('Tapped on Row $index');
        },
      ),
    );
  }
}
```

11. Create a new Dart file in the `widgets` folder. Right-click the `widgets` folder and then select New ➪ Dart File, enter `row.dart`, and click the OK button to save.

12. Import the `material.dart` library, add a new line, and then start typing **st**; the autocompletion help opens, so select the `stless` (`StatelessWidget`) abbreviation and give it a name of `RowWidget`.

13. Modify the `RowWidget` widget class to return a `ListTile`. Import the `material.dart` library.

14. For the `leading` property, return an `Icon`. For the `trailing` property, you return either a book-mark_border or a bookmark `Icon`. To randomize which `Icon` to return, use a ternary operator to calculate the `index modulus` (%) of 3 and check whether it's an even number. If the number is even or odd, the appropriate `Icon` is shown. The `title` property returns a `Text` widget with the `index` value. The `subtitle` property returns a `Text` widget.

For the `onTap`, you use a `print` statement to show the tapped row `index`.

Note that for each row a widget is added to the widget tree.

```
import 'package:flutter/material.dart';

class RowWidget extends StatelessWidget {
  const RowWidget({
    Key key,
    @required this.index,
  }) : super(key: key);

  final int index;

  @override
  Widget build(BuildContext context) {
    return ListTile(
      leading: Icon(
        Icons.directions_car,
        size: 48.0,
        color: Colors.lightGreen,
      ),
      title: Text('Car $index'),
      subtitle: Text('Very Cool'),
      trailing: (index % 3).isEven
          ? Icon(Icons.bookmark_border)
          : Icon(Icons.bookmark),
      selected: false,
      onTap: () {
        print('Tapped on Row $index');
      },
    );
  }
}
```

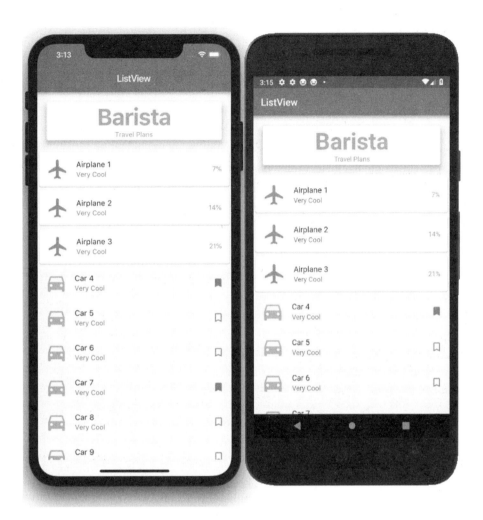

HOW IT WORKS

The `ListView.builder` constructor takes an `itemCount` and uses the `itemBuilder` to build a widget for each child record. Each child widget is added to the widget tree with the appropriate values. As each child widget is added, you can customize the `ListView` rows according to app specs.

Using the `ListTile` makes it extremely easy to align widgets. The `ListTile` takes a `leading`, `trailing`, `title`, `subtitle`, `onTap`, and other properties.

USING THE GRIDVIEW

The GridView (Figure 9.3) displays tiles of scrollable widgets in a grid format. The three constructors that I focus on are GridView.count, GridView.extent, and GridView.builder.

The GridView.count and GridView.extent are usually used with a fixed or smaller data set. Using these constructors means that all of the data, not just visible widgets, is loaded at init. If you have a large set of data, the user does not see the GridView until all data is loaded, which is not a great user experience (UX). Usually you use the GridView.count when you need a layout with a fixed number of tiles in the cross-axis. For example, it shows three tiles in portrait and land-scape modes. You use the GridView.extent when you need a layout with the tiles that need a maximum cross-axis extent. For example, two to three tiles fit in portrait mode, and five to six tiles fit in landscape mode; in other words, it fits as many tiles that it can depending on screen size.

The GridView.builder constructor is used with a larger, infinite, or unknown size set of data. Like our ListView.builder, when you have a large set of data, the builder is called only for visible widgets, which is great for performance. Within the builder, you use the itemBuilder callback to create the list of children widgets. Keep in mind the

FIGURE 9.3: GridView layout

itemBuilder is called only if the itemCount argument is greater than zero, and it is called as many times as the itemCount value. Remember, the List starts at row 0, not 1. If you have 20 items in the List, it loops from row 0 to 19. The scrollDirection argument defaults to Axis.vertical but can be changed to Axis.horizontal (Figure 9.3).

Using the GridView.count

The GridView.count requires setting the crossAxisCount and the children argument. The crossAxisCount sets the number of tiles to display (Figure 9.4), and children is a list of widgets. The scrollDirection argument sets the main axis direction for the Grid to scroll, either Axis .vertical or Axis.horizontal, and the default is vertical.

For the children, you use the List.generate to create your sample data, a list of values. Within the children argument, I added a print statement to show that the entire list of values is built at the same time, not just the visible rows like the GridView.builder. Note for the following sample code, 7,000 records are generated to show that the GridView.count does not show any data until all of the records are processed first.

```
GridView.count(
  crossAxisCount: 3,
  padding: EdgeInsets.all(8.0),
```

FIGURE 9.4: GridView count with three tiles in portrait and landscape mode

```
children: List.generate(7000, (index) {
  print('_buildGridView $index');

  return Card(
    margin: EdgeInsets.all(8.0),
    child: InkWell(
      child: Column(
        mainAxisAlignment: MainAxisAlignment.center,
        children: <Widget>[
          Icon(
            _iconList[0],
            size: 48.0,
            color: Colors.blue,
          ),
          Divider(),
          Text(
            'Index $index',
            textAlign: TextAlign.center,
            style: TextStyle(
              fontSize: 16.0,
            ),
          )
        ],
      ),
      onTap: () {
        print('Row $index');
      },
    ),
  );
},),
)
```

Using the GridView.extent

The `GridView.extent` requires you to set the `maxCrossAxisExtent` and `children` argument. The `maxCrossAxisExtent` argument sets the maximum size of each tile for the axis. For example, in portrait, it can fit two to three tiles, but when rotating to landscape, it can fit five to six depending on the screen size (Figure 9.5). The `scrollDirection` argument sets the main axis direction for the grid to scroll, either `Axis.vertical` or `Axis.horizontal`, and the default is `vertical`.

FIGURE 9.5: GridView extent showing the maximum number of tiles that can fit according to screen size

For the `children`, you use `List.generate` to create your sample data, which is a list of values. Within the `children` argument, I added a `print` statement to show that the entire list of values is built at the same time, not just the visible rows like the `GridView.builder`.

```
GridView.extent(
  maxCrossAxisExtent: 175.0,
  scrollDirection: Axis.horizontal,
  padding: EdgeInsets.all(8.0),
  children: List.generate(20, (index) {
    print('_buildGridViewExtent $index');

    return Card(
      margin: EdgeInsets.all(8.0),
      child: InkWell(
        child: Column(
          mainAxisAlignment: MainAxisAlignment.center,
          children: <Widget>[
            Icon(
              _iconList[index],
              size: 48.0,
              color: Colors.blue,
            ),
```

```
            Divider(),
            Text(
              'Index $index',
              textAlign: TextAlign.center,
              style: TextStyle(
                fontSize: 16.0,
              ),
            )
          ],
        ),
        onTap: () {
          print('Row $index');
        },
      ),
    );
  }),
)
```

Using the GridView.builder

The `GridView.builder` requires you to set the `itemCount`, `gridDelegate`, and `itemBuilder` arguments. The `itemCount` sets the number of tiles to build. The `gridDelegate` is a `SilverGrid-Delegate` responsible for laying out the children list of widgets for the `GridView`. The `gridDelegate` argument cannot be null; you need to pass the `maxCrossAxisExtent` size, for example, 150.0 pixels.

For example, to display three tiles across the screen you specify the `gridDelegate` argument with the `SliverGridDelegateWithFixedCrossAxisCount` class to create a grid layout with a fixed number of tiles for the cross axis. If you need to display tiles that have a maximum width of 150.0 pixels, you specify the `gridDelegate` argument with the `SliverGridDelegateWithMaxCrossAxisExtent` class to create a grid layout with tiles that have a maximum cross-axis extent, the maximum width of each tile.

The `GridView.builder` is used when you have a large set of data because the `builder` is called only for visible tiles, which is great for performance. Using the `GridView.builder` constructor results in lazily building a list for visible tiles, and when the user scrolls to the next visible tiles they are lazily built as needed.

TRY IT OUT Creating the GridView.builder App

In this example, the `GridView` widget uses the `builder` to display a `Card` that shows each `Grid` item with an `Icon` and a `Text` showing the index location. The `onTap` will print the index of the tapped `Grid` item.

1. Create a new Flutter project and name it `ch9_gridview`, following the instructions in Chapter 4. For this project, you need to create only the `pages`, `classes`, and `widgets` folders. Create the Home Class as a `StatelessWidget` since the data does not require changes.

2. Open the `home.dart` file and add to the `body` a `SafeArea` with the `GridViewBuilderWidget()` widget class as a `child`.

```
body: SafeArea(
  child: const GridViewBuildWidget(),
),
```

3. Add to the top of the file the `import` statement for the `gridview_builder.dart` widget class that you'll create next.

```
import 'package:flutter/material.dart';
import 'package:ch9_gridview/widgets/gridview_builder.dart';
```

4. Create a new Dart file in the `widgets` folder. Right-click the `classes` folder and then select New ⇨ Dart File, enter `grid_icons.dart`, and click the OK button to save.

5. Import the `material.dart` library, add a new line, and create the `GridIcons` Class. The `GridIcons` Class holds a List of IconData called `iconList`.

6. Create the `getIconList()` method that creates the List of IconData that is used later in the `GridView.builder`.

```
class GridIcons {
  List<IconData> iconList = [];

  List<IconData> getIconList() {
    iconList
      ..add(Icons.free_breakfast)
      ..add(Icons.access_alarms)
      ..add(Icons.directions_car)
      ..add(Icons.flight)
      ..add(Icons.cake)
      ..add(Icons.card_giftcard)
      ..add(Icons.change_history)
      ..add(Icons.face)
      ..add(Icons.star)
      ..add(Icons.headset_mic)
      ..add(Icons.directions_walk)
      ..add(Icons.sentiment_satisfied)
      ..add(Icons.cloud_queue)
      ..add(Icons.exposure)
      ..add(Icons.gps_not_fixed)
      ..add(Icons.child_friendly)
      ..add(Icons.child_care)
      ..add(Icons.edit_location)
      ..add(Icons.event_seat)
      ..add(Icons.lightbulb_outline);
    return iconList;
  }
}
```

7. Create a new Dart file under the `widgets` folder. Right-click the `widgets` folder and then select New ⇨ Dart File, enter `gridview_builder.dart`, and click the OK button to save.

8. Import the `material.dart` library, add a new line, and then start typing st; the autocompletion help opens, so select the `stless` (`StatelessWidget`) abbreviation and give it a name of `GridViewBuilderWidget`.

9. Modify the `GridViewBuilderWidget` widget class to return a `GridView.builder` with the `itemCount` argument set to 20. For this example, you specify to list 20 rows of data.

10. For the `gridDelegate` argument, use `SliverGridDelegateWithMaxCrossAxisExtent(maxCross AxisExtent: 150.0)`. Your other option is to use the `SliverGridDelegateWithFixedCrossAxisCount` instead, which works in the same manner as the `GridView.count` constructor, where you pass the number of tiles to display.

11. For the `itemBuilder` callback, it passes the `BuildContext` and the widget index as an `int` value. In the `itemBuilder` first line, place a `print` statement to show each item index being built according to the visible space.

12. Return a `Card` with the `child` as an `InkWell`. The `InkWell` `onTap` has a `print` statement to show the tapped `Card` item, with the `Row` selected.

13. For the `InkWell` child property, pass a `Column` with these `children`: `Icon`, `Divider`, and `Text` widgets. Note that the `itemBuilder` is called for each row item. For every row, a `Widget` is created and added to the widget tree.

The `onTap` will print the index of the tapped `Grid` item.

14. Add to the top of the file the `import` statement for the `grid_icons.dart` class.

```dart
import 'package:flutter/material.dart';
import 'package:ch9_gridview/classes/grid_icons.dart';

class GridViewBuilderWidget extends StatelessWidget {
  const GridViewBuilderWidget({
    Key key,
  }) : super(key: key);

  @override
  Widget build(BuildContext context) {
    List<IconData> _iconList = GridIcons().getIconList();

    return GridView.builder(
      itemCount: 20,
      padding: EdgeInsets.all(8.0),
      gridDelegate: SliverGridDelegateWithMaxCrossAxisExtent(maxCrossAxisExtent:
150.0),
      itemBuilder: (BuildContext context, int index) {
        print('_buildGridViewBuilder $index');

        return Card(
          color: Colors.lightGreen.shade50,
          margin: EdgeInsets.all(8.0),
          child: InkWell(
            child: Column(
              mainAxisAlignment: MainAxisAlignment.center,
              children: <Widget>[
                Icon(
                  _iconList[index],
                  size: 48.0,
                  color: Colors.lightGreen,
                ),
                Divider(),
                Text(
```

```
                            'Index $index',
                            textAlign: TextAlign.center,
                            style: TextStyle(
                              fontSize: 16.0,
                            ),
                          )
                        ],
                      ),
                    onTap: () {
                      print('Row $index');
                    },
                  ),
                );
              },
            );
          }
        }
```

HOW IT WORKS

The `GridView.builder` constructor takes an `itemCount` and uses the `itemBuilder` to build a widget for each child record. Each child widget is added to the widget tree with the appropriate values. As each child widget is added, you can customize the rows according to app specs. In this example, you used a `Card` to give each `Grid Row` item a nice look and used an `InkWell` to use the Material Design tap animation and the `onTap` property. The `InkWell` child is a `Column`, and its `children` items show an `Icon` and `Text`.

USING THE STACK

The Stack widget is commonly used to overlap, position, and align widgets to create a custom look. A good example is a shopping cart with the number of items to purchase on the upper-right side. The Stack children list of the widget is either positioned or nonpositioned. When you use a Positioned widget, each child widget is placed at the appropriate location.

The Stack widget resizes itself to accommodate all of the nonpositioned children. The nonpositioned children are positioned to the alignment property (Top-Left or Top-Right depending on the left-to-right or right-to-left environment). Each Stack child widget is drawn in order from bottom to top, like stacking pieces of paper on top of each other. This means the first widget drawn is at the bottom of the Stack, and then the next widget is drawn above the previous widget and so on. Each child widget is positioned on top of each other in the order of the Stack children list. The RenderStack class handles the stack layout.

To align each child in the Stack, you use the Positioned widget. By using the top, bottom, left, and right properties, you align each child widget within the Stack. The height and width properties of the Positioned widget can also be set (Figure 9.6).

FIGURE 9.6: Stack layout showing Image and Text widgets stacked over the background image

You'll also learn how to implement the FractionalTranslation class to position a widget fractionally outside the parent widget. You set the translation property with the Offset(dx, dy) (double type value for x-and y-axis) class that's scaled to the child's size, resulting in moving and positioning the widget. For example, to show a favorite icon moved a third of the way to the upper right of the parent widget, you set the translation property with the Offset(0.3, -0.3) value.

The following example (Figure 9.7) shows a Stack widget with a background image, and by using the FractionalTranslation class, you set the translation property to the Offset(0.3, -0.3) value, placing the star icon one-third to the right of the x-axis and a negative one-third (move icon upward) on the y-axis.

```
Stack(
  children: <Widget>[
    Image(image: AssetImage('assets/images/dawn.jpg')),
    Positioned(
```

```
          top: 0.0,
          right: 0.0,
          child: FractionalTranslation(
            translation: Offset(0.3, -0.3),
            child: CircleAvatar(
              child: Icon(Icons.star),
            ),
          ),
        ),
        Positioned(/* Eagle Image */),
        Positioned(/* Bald Eagle */),
      ],
    ),
```

FIGURE 9.7: FractionalTranslation class showing favorite icon moved to the upper right

TRY IT OUT Creating the Stack App

In this example, the Stack widget children list of widgets lays out a background Image and two Positioned widgets with CircleAvatar and Text widgets. To show an alternate layout, you use the same previous Stack layout and add a Positioned widget with the child property as a Fractional-Translation class to show a CircleAvatar pinned to the upper-right corner halfway outside the Stack. A ListView is used to create the sample list, and each row displays an alternate Stack widget.

1. Create a new Flutter project and name it ch9_stack. Again, follow the instructions in Chapter 4. For this project, you need to create the pages, widgets, and assets/images folders. Create the Home Class as a StatelessWidget since your data does not require changes.

2. Open the pubspec.yaml file to add resources. In the assets section, add the assets/ images/ folder.

```
# To add assets to your application, add an assets section, like this:
assets:
  - assets/images/
```

3. Click the Save button, and depending on the editor you are using, it automatically runs the `flutter packages get`, and once finished, it will show a message of `Process finished with exit code 0`. If it does not automatically run the command for you, open the Terminal window (located at the bottom of your editor) and type `flutter packages get`.

4. Add the folder `assets` and subfolder `images` at the project's root, and then copy the `dawn.jpg`, `eagle.jpg`, `lion.jpg`, and `tree.jpg` files to the `images` folder.

5. Open the `home.dart` file and add to the body a `SafeArea` with `ListView.builder()` as a child.

```
body: SafeArea(
  child: ListView.builder(),
),
```

6. Add to the top of the file the `import` statement for the `stack.dart` and `stack_favorite.dart` widget classes that you'll create next.

```
import 'package:flutter/material.dart';
import 'package:ch9_stack/widgets/stack.dart';
import 'package:ch9_stack/widgets/stack_favorite.dart';
```

7. Add to the `ListView.builder` the `itemCount` argument with a value set to 7. For this example, you specify to list seven rows of data. For the `itemBuilder` callback, it passes the `BuildContext` and the widget `index` as an `int` value.

With each `stack` layout, you alternate between them by checking whether the index value is even or odd and then call the widget classes `StackWidget()` and `StackFavoriteWidget()`, respectively.

I wanted to show that you can customize which widgets you present to the user. Let's say you have an app that you distribute as freeware and every ten records you show an advertisement or a tip embedded in the list. This technique is not as intrusive as a pop-up while the user views records.

```
body: SafeArea(
  child: ListView.builder(
    itemCount: 7,
    itemBuilder: (BuildContext context, int index) {
      if (index.isEven) {
        return const StackWidget();
      } else {
        return const StackFavoriteWidget();
      }
    },
  ),
),
```

8. Create a new Dart file in the `widgets` folder. Right-click the `widgets` folder and then select New ⇨ Dart File, enter `stack.dart`, and click the OK button to save.

9. Import the `material.dart` library, add a new line, and then start typing st; the autocompletion help opens, where you can select the `stless` (`StatelessWidget`) abbreviation and give it a name of `StackWidget`.

10. Modify the `StackWidget` widget class to return a `Stack`. The `Stack children` list of widgets consists of an `Image` with the `AssetImage tree.jpg`.

11. Add a `Positioned` widget with `bottom` and `left` properties with a value of `10.0`. The `child` is a `CircleAvatar` with a `radius` of `48.0` and has the `backgroundImage` property set to `AssetImage lion.jpg`.

12. Add another `Positioned` widget with `bottom` and `right` properties with a value of `16.0`. The `child` is a `Text` widget with a string value of `Lion`, and it has a `style` property with a `TextStyle` class with a `fontSize` set to `32.0` pixels, `color` set to `white30`, and `fontWeight` set to bold.

```
import 'package:flutter/material.dart';

class StackWidget extends StatelessWidget {
  const StackWidget({
    Key key,
  }) : super(key: key);

  @override
  Widget build(BuildContext context) {
    return Stack(
      children: <Widget>[
        Image(
          image: AssetImage('assets/images/tree.jpg'),
        ),
        Positioned(
          bottom: 10.0,
          left: 10.0,
          child: CircleAvatar(
            radius: 48.0,
            backgroundImage: AssetImage('assets/images/lion.jpg'),
          ),
        ),
        Positioned(
          bottom: 16.0,
          right: 16.0,
          child: Text(
            'Lion',
            style: TextStyle(
              fontSize: 32.0,
              color: Colors.white30,
              fontWeight: FontWeight.bold,
            ),
          ),
        ),
      ],
    );
  }
}
```

13. Create a new Dart file in the `widgets` folder. Right-click the `widgets` folder and then select New ⇨ Dart File, enter `stack_favorite.dart`, and click the OK button to save.

14. Import the `material.dart` library, add a new line, and then start typing **st**; autocompletion help opens, so select the `stless` (`StatelessWidget`) abbreviation and give it a name of `StackFavoriteWidget`.

15. Modify the `StackFavoriteWidget` widget class to return a `Container`. Use a `Container` to set color to `black87` and for the `child` use a `Padding` with `EdgeInsets.all(16.0)`. This will create a dark frame effect around the `Stack`.

16. For the `Stack` `children` list of widgets, add an `Image` set to `AssetImage dawn.jpg`.

17. Add a `Positioned` widget with `bottom` and `right` properties with the values `0.0`. The `child` is a `FractionalTranslation` class with a `translation` property of `Offset(0.3,-0.3)`. The `child` is a `CircleAvatar`, and by using the `Offset`, it shows it pinned to the upper-right corner halfway outside of the `Stack`.

18. Add a `Positioned` widget with `bottom` and `right` properties with a value of `10.0`. The `child` is a `CircleAvatar` with a radius of `48.0` and `backgroundImage` with the `AssetImage eagle.jpg`.

19. Add another `Positioned` widget with `bottom` and `right` properties that have values of `16.0`. The `child` is a `Text` widget with a string value of `Bald Eagle`, and it has a `style` property with a `TextStyle` with `fontSize` set to `32.0` pixels, `color` set to `white30`, and `fontWeight` set to bold.

```
import 'package:flutter/material.dart';

class StackFavoriteWidget extends StatelessWidget {
  const StackFavoriteWidget({
    Key key,
  }) : super(key: key);

  @override
  Widget build(BuildContext context) {
    return Container(
      color: Colors.black87,
      child: Padding(
        padding: const EdgeInsets.all(16.0),
        child: Stack(
          children: <Widget>[
            Image(
              image: AssetImage('assets/images/dawn.jpg'),
            ),
            Positioned(
              top: 0.0,
              right: 0.0,
              child: FractionalTranslation(
                translation: Offset(0.3, -0.3),
                child: CircleAvatar(
                  radius: 24.0,
                  backgroundColor: Colors.white30,
                  child: Icon(
                    Icons.star,
                    size: 24.0,
                    color: Colors.white,
                  ),
                ),
              ),
            ),
            Positioned(
              bottom: 10.0,
```

```
                        right: 10.0,
                        child: CircleAvatar(
                          radius: 48.0,
                          backgroundImage: AssetImage('assets/images/eagle.jpg'),
                        ),
                      ),
                      Positioned(
                        bottom: 16.0,
                        left: 16.0,
                        child: Text(
                          'Bald Eagle',
                          style: TextStyle(
                            fontSize: 32.0,
                            color: Colors.white30,
                            fontWeight: FontWeight.bold,
                          ),
                        ),
                      ),
                    ],
                  ),
                ),
              );
          }
        }
```

HOW IT WORKS

The Stack takes a children list of widgets and sizes itself to accommodate all of the nonpositioned widgets. When you use nonpositioned widgets in the Stack, they are automatically positioned to the setting of alignment (Top-Left or Top-Right depending on environment). Each Stack child widget is drawn in order from bottom to top, meaning each child widget is positioned on top of each other.

Using the `Positioned` widget allows each child widget to be aligned by using the `top`, `bottom`, `left`, and `right` properties. You learned how to position the favorite icon to the upper right of the parent widget by using the `FractionalTranslation` class's `translation` property with the `Offset(0.3,-03)` value.

CUSTOMIZING THE CUSTOMSCROLLVIEW WITH SLIVERS

The `CustomScrollView` widget creates custom scrolling effects by using a list of slivers. Slivers are a small portion of something larger. For example, slivers are placed inside a view port like the `CustomScrollView` widget. In the previous sections, you learned how to implement the `ListView` and `GridView` widgets separately. But what if you needed to present them together in the same list? The answer is that you can use a `CustomScrollView` with the `slivers` property list of widgets set to the `SliverSafeArea`, `SliverAppBar`, `SliverList`, and `SliverGrid` widgets (slivers). The order in which you place them in the `CustomScrollView` `slivers` property is the order in which they are rendered. Table 9.1 shows commonly used slivers and sample code.

TABLE 9.1: Slivers

SLIVER	DESCRIPTION	CODE
SliverSafeArea	Adds padding to avoid the device notch usually located on the top of the screen	<pre>SliverSafeArea(
    sliver: SliverGrid(),
)</pre>
SliverAppBar	Adds an app bar	<pre>SliverAppBar(
    expandedHeight: 250.0,
    flexibleSpace: FlexibleSpaceBar(
      title: Text('Parallax'),
    ),
)</pre>
SliverList	Creates a linear scrollable list of widgets	<pre>SliverList(
    delegate: SliverChildListDelegate(
      List.generate(3, (int index) {
        return ListTile();
      }),
    ),
)</pre>
SliverGrid	Displays tiles of scrollable widgets in a grid format	<pre>SliverGrid(
    delegate: SliverChildBuilderDelegate(
        (BuildContext context, int
index) {
          return Card();
        },
        childCount: _rowsCount,
      ),
    gridDelegate: SliverGridDelegateWithF
ixedCrossAxisCount(crossAxisCount: 3),
)</pre>

The `SliverList` and `SliverGrid` slivers use delegates to build the list of children explicitly or lazily. An explicit list builds all of the items first then displays them on the screen. A lazily built list only builds the visible items on the screen and when the user scrolls the next visible items are built (lazily) resulting in better performance. The `SliverList` has a `delegate` property and the `SliverGrid` has a `delegate` and a `gridDelegate` property.

The `SliverList` and `SliverGrid` `delegate` property can use the `SliverChildListDelegate` to build an explicit list or use the `SliverChildBuilderDelegate` to lazily build the list. The `SliverGrid` has an additional `gridDelegate` property to specify the size and position of the grid tiles. Specify the `gridDelegate` property with the `SliverGridDelegateWithFixed-CrossAxisCount` class to create a grid layout with a fixed number of tiles for the cross axis; for example, show three tiles across. Specify the `gridDelegate` property with the `SliverGrid-DelegateWithMaxCrossAxisExtent` class to create a grid layout with tiles that have a maximum cross-axis extent, the maximum width of each tile; for example, 150.0 pixels maximum width for each tile.

Table 9.2 shows the `SliverList` and `SliverGrid` delegates to help you build lists.

TABLE 9.2: Sliver Delegates

SLIVER	DESCRIPTION	CODE
| SliverList | SliverChildListDelegate builds a list of known number of rows (explicit). SliverChildBuilderDelegate lazily builds a list of unknown number of rows. | ```
SliverList(
    delegate:
SliverChildListDelegate(<Widget>[
      ListTile(title: Text('One')),
      ListTile(title: Text('Two')),
      ListTile(title: Text('Three')),
  ]),
 )
```<br><br>or<br><br>```
SliverList(
    delegate: SliverChildListDelegate(
    List.generate(30, (int index) {
      return ListTile();
    }),
  ),
 )
```<br><br>or<br><br>```
SliverList(
    delegate: SliverChildBuilderDeleg
ate((BuildContext context,
int index) {
      return ListTile();
    },
    childCount: _rowsCount,
  ),
 )
``` |
```

SLIVER	DESCRIPTION	CODE

SliverGrid	SliverChildListDelegate builds an explicit list. SliverChildBuilderDelegate lazily builds a list of unknown number of tiles. The gridDelegate property controls the position and size of the children widgets.	```SliverGrid(delegate: SliverChildListDelegate-(<Widget>[Card(), Card(), Card(),]), gridDelegate: SliverGridDelegateWithFixedCrossAxis-Count(crossAxisCount: 3),)```
		
		or
		
		```SliverGrid(delegate: SliverChildListDelegate(List.generate(30, (int index) { return Card(); }),), gridDelegate: SliverGridDelegateWithFixedCross-AxisCount(crossAxisCount: 3),)```
		
		or
		
		```SliverChildBuilderDelegate((BuildContext context, int index) { return Card(); }, childCount: _rowsCount,), gridDelegate: SliverGridDelegateWithFixedCross-AxisCount(crossAxisCount: 3),)```

The SliverAppBar widget can have a parallax (Figure 9.8) effect by using the expandedHeight and flexibleSpace properties. The parallax effect scrolls a background image slower than the content in the foreground. If you need to show the CustomScrollView initially scrolled at a particular position, use a controller and set the ScrollController.initialScrollOffset property. For example, you would set the initialScrollOffset by initializing the controller = ScrollController(initialScrollOffset: 10.0).

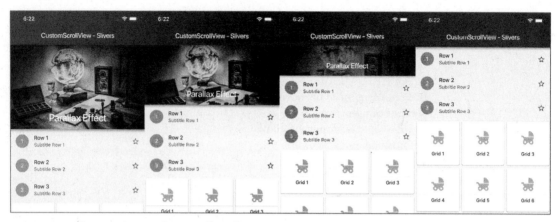

FIGURE 9.8: SliverAppBar scrolling parallax effect

TRY IT OUT   Creating the CustomScrollView Slivers App

In this example, the `CustomScrollView` children list of widgets contains a `SliverAppBar`, `SliverList`, `SliverSafeArea`, and `SliverGrid`. The `SliverAppBar` widget uses the `flexibleSpace` with a background `Image` that has a parallax effect while scrolling. The `SliverList` generates three items with the `List.generate` constructor. To account for the device notch, you use a `SliverSafeArea` to wrap the `SliverGrid`, and you generate 12 (sample value can be more or less) items.

1. Create a new Flutter project and name it `ch9_customscrollview_slivers`; you can follow the instructions in Chapter 4. For this project, you only need to create the `pages` and `assets/images` folders. Create the `Home Class` as a `StatelessWidget` since the data does not require changes.

2. Open the `pubspec.yaml` file to add resources. In the `assets` section, add the `assets/images/` folder.

```
# To add assets to your application, add an assets section, like this:
assets:
  - assets/images/
```

3. Click the Save button, and depending on the editor you are using, it automatically runs `flutter packages get`. Once finished, it will show a message of `Process finished with exit code 0`. If it does not automatically run the command for you, open the Terminal window (located at the bottom of your editor) and type `flutter packages get`.

4. Add the folder `assets` and subfolder `images` at the project's root and then copy the `desk.jpg` file to the `images` folder.

5. Open the `home.dart` file and add to the `body` a `CustomScrollView()`. For this project, set the `AppBar elevation` property to `0.0` because you enable the `SliverAppBar` shadow instead.

```
return Scaffold(
  appBar: AppBar(
    title: Text('CustomScrollView - Slivers'),
    elevation: 0.0,
  ),
```

```
    body: CustomScrollView(
      slivers: <Widget>[
      ],
    ),
  );
```

6. Add to the top of the file the `import` statement for the `sliver_app_bar.dart`, `sliver_list.dart`, and `sliver_grid.dart` widget classes that you'll create next.

```
import 'package:flutter/material.dart';
import 'package:ch9_customscrollview_slivers/widgets/sliver_app_bar.dart';
import 'package:ch9_customscrollview_slivers/widgets/sliver_list.dart';
import 'package:ch9_customscrollview_slivers/widgets/sliver_grid.dart';
```

7. Add calls to the `SliverAppBarWidget()`, `SliverListWidget()`, and `SliverGridWidget()` widget classes to the `CustomScrollView()` slivers property. Make sure the calls to the widget classes use the `const` keyword to take advantage of caching for performance gain.

```
return Scaffold(
  appBar: AppBar(
    title: Text('CustomScrollView - Slivers'),
    elevation: 0.0,
  ),
  body: CustomScrollView(
    slivers: <Widget>[
      const SliverAppBarWidget(),
      const SliverListWidget(),
      const SliverGridWidget(),
    ],
  ),
);
```

8. Create a new Dart file in the `widgets` folder. Right-click the `widgets` folder and then select New ⇨ Dart File, enter `sliver_app_bar.dart`, and click the OK button to save.

9. Import the `material.dart` library, add a new line, and then start typing **st**; the autocompletion help opens, so select the `stless` (`StatelessWidget`) abbreviation and give it a name of `SliverAppBarWidget`.

10. Modify the `SliverAppBarWidget` widget class to return a `SliverAppBar`.

11. To show a shadow at the bottom of the bar, set the `forceElevated` property to `true`.

12. To create a parallax effect while scrolling, set `expandedHeight` to `250.0` pixels and `flexible-Space` to `FlexibleSpaceBar`.

13. For the `FlexibleSpaceBar` background property, use the `Image` widget with the `desk.jpg` file and set `fit` to `BoxFit.cover`.

```
import 'package:flutter/material.dart';

class SliverAppBarWidget extends StatelessWidget {
  const SliverAppBarWidget({
    Key key,
  }) : super(key: key);
```

```
          @override
          Widget build(BuildContext context) {
            return SliverAppBar(
              backgroundColor: Colors.brown,
              forceElevated: true,
              expandedHeight: 250.0,
              flexibleSpace: FlexibleSpaceBar(
                title: Text(
                  'Parallax Effect',
                ),
                background: Image(
                  image: AssetImage('assets/images/desk.jpg'),
                  fit: BoxFit.cover,
                ),
              ),
            );
          }
        }
```

14. Create a new Dart file in the `widgets` folder. Right-click the `widgets` folder and then select New ⇨ Dart File, enter `sliver_list.dart`, and click the OK button to save.

15. Import the `material.dart` library, add a new line, and then start typing **st**; the autocompletion help opens, so select the `stless` (`StatelessWidget`) abbreviation and give it a name of `SliverListWidget`.

16. Modify the `SliverListWidget` widget class to return a `SliverList`. For the `SliverList` delegate property, pass the `SliverChildListDelegate`.

17. Use the `List.generate` constructor to build your sample data list. The constructor takes two arguments: the `length` of the list and the `index`. Return a `ListTile` with a `leading` `CircleAvatar` with the `child` as a `Text` widget with string interpolation set with `${index + 1}`.

18. Also, set the `ListTile` title, subtitle, and trailing properties.

```
      import 'package:flutter/material.dart';

      class SliverListWidget extends StatelessWidget {
        const SliverListWidget({
          Key key,
        }) : super(key: key);

        @override
        Widget build(BuildContext context) {
          return SliverList(
            delegate: SliverChildListDelegate(
              List.generate(3, (int index) {
                return ListTile(
                  leading: CircleAvatar(
                    child: Text("${index + 1}"),
                    backgroundColor: Colors.lightGreen,
                    foregroundColor: Colors.white,
                  ),
                  title: Text('Row ${index + 1}'),
```

```
                 subtitle: Text('Subtitle Row ${index + 1}'),
                 trailing: Icon(Icons.star_border),
              );
           }),
        ),
      );
    }
  }
```

19. Create a new Dart file in the `widgets` folder. Right-click the `widgets` folder and then select New ⇨ Dart File, enter `sliver_grid.dart`, and click the OK button to save.

20. Import the `material.dart` library, add a new line, and then start typing **st**; the autocompletion help opens, so select the `stless` (StatelessWidget) abbreviation and give it a name of `SliverGridWidget`.

21. Modify the `SliverGridWidget` widget class to return a `SliverSafeArea`. Since the `SliverGrid` does not handle the device notch automatically, you wrap it in a `SliverSafeArea`. The `SliverGrid` `delegate` property is a `SliverChildBuilderDelegate` taking the `BuildContext` and `int index`.

22. From the `SliverChildBuilderDelegate`, return a `Card` with the `child` as a `Column`. The `Column` children list of `Widget` has `Icon`, `Divider`, and `Text` widgets.

23. For the `childCount` property, pass `12` representing how many items the builder creates. The `gridDelegate` property is set to `SliverGridDelegateWithFixedCrossAxisCount(cross-AxisCount: 3)` showing three tiles.

```
import 'package:flutter/material.dart';

class SliverGridWidget extends StatelessWidget {
  const SliverGridWidget({
    Key key,
  }) : super(key: key);

  @override
  Widget build(BuildContext context) {
    return SliverSafeArea(
      sliver: SliverGrid(
        delegate: SliverChildBuilderDelegate(
            (BuildContext context, int index) {
          return Card(
            child: Column(
              mainAxisAlignment: MainAxisAlignment.center,
              children: <Widget>[
                Icon(Icons.child_friendly, size: 48.0, color: Colors.amber,),
                Divider(),
                Text('Grid ${index + 1}'),
              ],
            ),
          );
        },
        childCount: 12,
      ),
      gridDelegate:
```

```
                    SliverGridDelegateWithFixedCrossAxisCount(crossAxisCount: 3),
                  ),
                );
              }
            }
```

HOW IT WORKS

To create a custom scrolling effect, the CustomScrollView uses a list of slivers. You used the SliverAppBar to create a parallax scrolling effect by using a FlexibleSpaceBar. You also created a SliverList and set the delegate property to the SliverChildListDelegate class. To handle the device notch, the SliverGrid is wrapped in a SliverSafeArea widget. The SliverGrid delegate property uses the SliverChildBuilderDelegate, which takes a BuildContext and int index.

SUMMARY

In this chapter, you learned to use the Card to group information with the container having rounded corners and a shadow. You used the ListView to build a list of scrollable widgets and to align grouped data with the ListTile, and you used the GridView to display data in tiles, using the Card to group the data. You embedded a Stack in a ListView to show an Image as a background and stacked different widgets with the Positioned widget to overlap and position them at the appropriate locations by using the top, bottom, left, and right properties.

In the next chapter, you'll learn to build custom layouts by using SingleChildScrollView, SafeArea, Padding, Column, Row, Image, Divider, Text, Icon, SizedBox, Wrap, Chip, and CircleAvatar. You'll learn to take a high-level view as well as a detailed view to separate and nest widgets to create a custom UI.

▶ WHAT YOU LEARNED IN THIS CHAPTER

TOPIC	KEY CONCEPTS
`Card`	This groups and organizes information into a container with rounded corners and casts a drop shadow.
`ListView` and `ListTile`	This is a linear list of scrollable widgets with either vertical or horizontal scrolling. To easily format how the list of records is displayed in rows, you took advantage of the `ListTile` widget to align grouped data with leading and trailing icons.
`GridView`	This displays tiles of scrollable widgets in a grid format. Scrolling can be vertical or horizontal.
`Stack`	This is commonly used to overlap, position, and align its children widgets to create a custom look.
`CustomScrollView` and slivers	This allows you to create custom scrolling effects by using a list of slivers widgets like a `SliverSafeArea`, `SliverAppBar`, `SliverList`, `SliverGrid`, and more.

10

Building Layouts

- ➤ How to create simple and complex layouts
- ➤ How to combine and nest widgets
- ➤ How to combine vertical and horizontal widgets to create a custom layout
- ➤ How to build the UI layout by using widgets such as `SingleChildScrollView`, `SafeArea`, `Padding`, `Column`, `Row`, `Image`, `Divider`, `Text`, `Icon`, `SizedBox`, `Wrap`, `Chip`, and `CircleAvatar`

In this chapter, you'll learn how to take individual widgets and nest them to build a professional layout. This concept is known as *composition* and is a huge part of creating Flutter mobile apps. Most of the time you can build simple or complex layouts either using vertical or horizontal widgets or using a combination of both.

A HIGH-LEVEL VIEW OF THE LAYOUT

This chapter's goal is to create a journal entry page displaying details from top to bottom. The journal page shows the header image, title, diary detail, weather, (journal location) address, tags, and footer images. The weather, tags, and footer images sections are built by nesting widgets to build a custom layout (Figure 10.1).

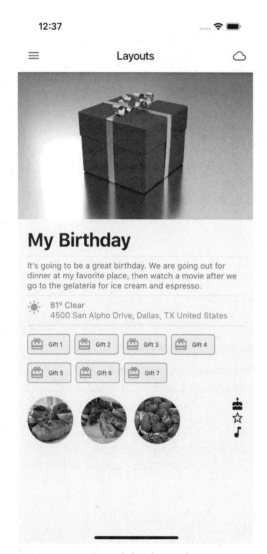
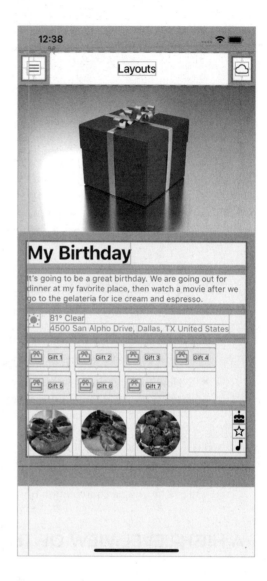

FIGURE 10.1: Journal detail page layout.

Starting with a high-level view, let's break down the main parts of the layout that forms the foundation. A great way to start laying out the journal entry is to add layers from the bottom toward the top, the same way you stack paper. Figure 10.2 shows the journal page layout structure.

1. Since mobile devices are available in different sizes, the layout starts by adding a `Single-ChildScrollView` to automatically handle scrolling for portions of the screen that are cut off by smaller devices.

2. Next a `Column` widget is used to align widgets vertically from the top toward the bottom of the screen.

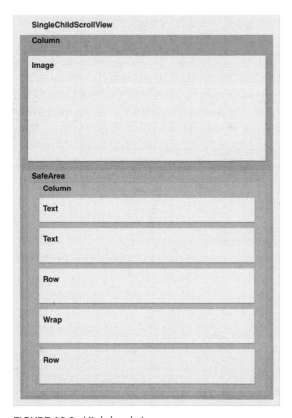

FIGURE 10.2: High-level view

3. For the wrapped gift image, the Image widget is added as the first child of the first Column, allowing the image to fill the full width of the device.

4. The first Column child is a SafeArea widget to handle the device notch for the journal entry content.

5. Add to the SafeArea child a second Column with children widgets composed of a Text widget for the journal entry title and a Text widget for the journal entry details.

6. Continue adding to the second Column children a Row widget that will contain the weather icon, the weather temperature, and the journal entry location address. In the "Weather Section Layout" section of this chapter, you will learn to add widgets to create the detailed layout.

7. Continue by adding to the second Column children a Wrap widget displaying the Chip widgets. You'll learn to add layout widgets in the "Tags Layout" section.

8. Lastly, you'll add to the second Column a Row widget to display images and icons, and you'll learn how to add layout widgets in the "Footer Images Layout" section of this chapter.

Weather Section Layout

Each journal entry records the weather, temperature, and location at the time of entry to recall the details at a later time. To provide that information, you're including a journal entry weather section. Using a Row, you add two Column widgets and one SizedBox widget. The first Column contains an Icon to show the weather symbol. The second Column contains two Row widgets. The first Row has a Text showing the weather temperature and description. The second Row has a Text showing the location address of the journal entry (Figure 10.3).

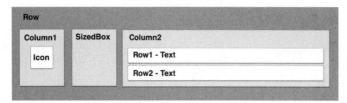

FIGURE 10.3: Weather section

Tags Layout

To organize each journal entry and facilitate searching, you use tags to add categories to the entry. Tags are items such as movie, family, birthday, vacation, and so on. The tags section uses a Wrap widget with a children list of Chip widgets. When you have a list of items that can be of different lengths and an unknown number of items, nesting them in a Wrap widget lays out each child automatically according to available space (Figure 10.4).

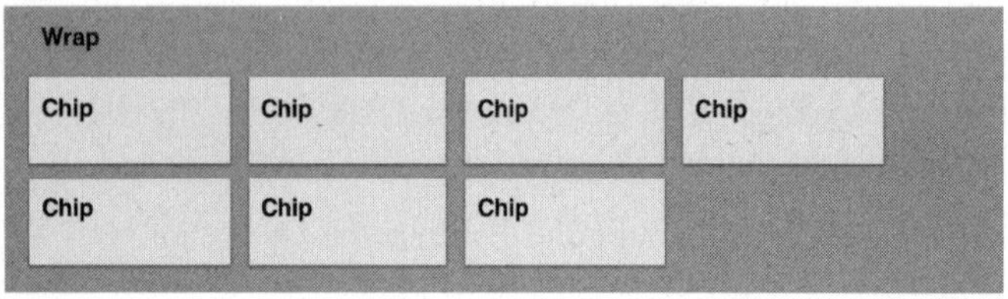

FIGURE 10.4: Tags section

The Chip widget is a great way to group information and customize the presentation look and feel. Setting the label property is the only requirement but most of the time it's used by setting the avatar property with an Icon or an Image widget. By default the Chip widget is a gray stadium (rectangle with large semicircles on the ends at opposite sides) shape but you can customize it by using the shape property and the backgroundColor property. The following sample code shows a customized Chip widget that displays the label and avatar in a rectangular shape with small rounded corners. The RoundedRectangleBorder class returns the rectangular border with rounded corners.

```
Chip(
  label: Text('Vacation'),
  avatar: Icon(Icons.local_airport),
  shape: RoundedRectangleBorder(
    borderRadius: BorderRadius.circular(4.0),
    side: BorderSide(color: Colors.grey),
  ),
  backgroundColor: Colors.grey.shade100,
);
```

Footer Images Layout

It is said that a picture is worth a thousand words, and the footer section allows you to add photos to each journal entry to bring back memories. The footer sections use a Row with a CircleAvatar widget showing different images. At the end of the Row, a SizedBox is used to space the child Column to the end. The Column shows vertically aligned Icons (Figure 10.5).

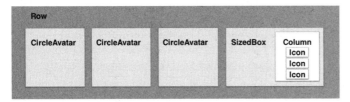

FIGURE 10.5: Footer section

Final Layout

You looked at how to lay out each section of the journal detail page. By nesting widgets, you build custom or complex layouts known as *composition*. The power of nesting widgets to create beautiful UIs is limited only by your imagination. Figure 10.6 shows the journal detail page and the three main customized sections for the weather, tags, and footer images.

CREATING THE LAYOUT

When creating the layout, it's good to start from a high-level view and then work your way down to each detailed section. By taking each section of the page, you start to analyze the requirements and format as needed. For example, if a particular section lays out the items horizontally, you start with a Row; if the section's layout is vertical, you start with a Column. Then you look at the display requirements and start breaking down data into its own sections by nesting widgets.

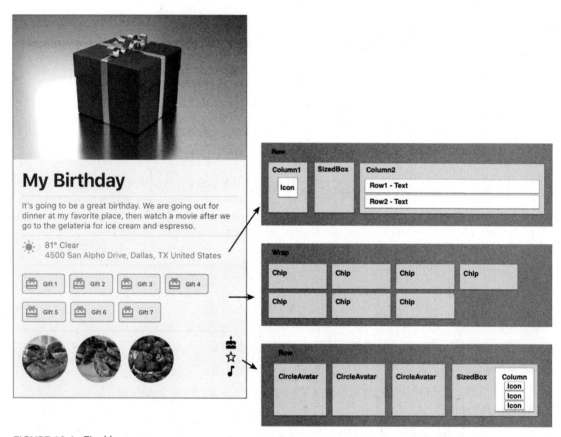

FIGURE 10.6: Final layout

TRY IT OUT Creating the Layout App

In our example, the main `body` contains a `SingleChildScrollView` with the `child` as a `Column`. The `Column` list of widgets contains a header `Image` followed by a `SafeArea` with `Padding` as a `child`. The `Image` fits the entire width of the device, but the journal entries are contained in the `SafeArea` with a `Padding` to format the entry.

The `Padding` `child` is a `Column` with a list of widgets breaking down each section of the journal entry separated by a `Divider` widget. Each separate section is called by the `_buildJournalHeaderImage()`, `_buildJournalEntry()`, `_buildJournalWeather()`, `_buildJournalTags()`, and `_buildJournal-FooterImages()` methods.

You are creating a journal entry page displaying details from top to bottom. The journal page shows the header image, title, diary detail, weather, address, tags, and footer images. The weather, tags, and footer images sections are built by nesting widgets to build a custom layout.

In this example, to keep the widget tree shallow, you'll use methods instead of widget classes. This is a great example of using the appropriate technique for each situation. The purpose of the journal entry is to view the details, and it does not require changes, which is why you use methods to keep the widget tree shallow. But if this page requires refreshing portions of the screen based on outside data changes, then using widget classes could be the better solution, because only the portion of the screen that changes is rebuilt.

1. Create a new Flutter project and name it `ch10_layouts`. You can follow the instructions in Chapter 4, "Creating a Starter Project Template." For this project, you need to create only the pages and `assets/images` folders. Create the `Home Class` as a `StatelessWidget` since the data does not require changes.

2. Open the `pubspec.yaml` file to add resources. In the `assets` section, add the `assets/images/` folder.

   ```
   # To add assets to your application, add an assets section, like this:
   assets:
     - assets/images/
   ```

3. Click the Save button, and depending on the Editor you are using, it automatically runs `flutter packages get`, and once finished, it will show a message of `Process finished with exit code 0`. If it does not automatically run the command for you, open the Terminal window (located at the bottom of your editor) and type **flutter packages get**.

4. Add the folder `assets` and subfolder `images` at the project's root, and then copy the `present.jpg`, `salmon.jpg`, `asparagus.jpg`, and `strawberries.jpg` files to the `images` folder. Since this example focuses on how to lay out a screen, the images are included in the `assets/images` folder, but in an actual application, the user would choose the images and they would be saved to the device instead.

5. Open the `home.dart` file and add to the `body` the `_buildBody()` method. For this project, customize the `AppBar` widget by changing the `backgroundColor`, `iconTheme`, `brightness`, `leading`, and `actions` properties, as shown in the following code. Making the `AppBar` changes is purely cosmetic to make the app look great. In Chapter 6, "Using Common Widgets," you learned that the `Icon` widget is drawn with a glyph from a font described in the `IconData`. You have available a full list of icons from the `MaterialIcons` font.

   ```dart
   Widget build(BuildContext context) {
     return Scaffold(
       appBar: AppBar(
         title: Text(
           'Layouts',
           style: TextStyle(color: Colors.black87),
         ),
         backgroundColor: Colors.white,
         iconTheme: IconThemeData(color: Colors.black54),
         brightness: Brightness.light,
         leading: IconButton(icon: Icon(Icons.menu), onPressed: () {}),
         actions: <Widget>[
           IconButton(icon: Icon(Icons.cloud_queue), onPressed: () {})
         ],
       ),
       body: _buildBody(),
     );
   }
   ```

6. Add the _buildBody() widget method after Widget build(BuildContext context) {...}.

7. Return a SingleChildScrollView with the child as a Column. The Column children list of widgets is calling all the methods to create each section of the page. Note that the first method, _buildJournalHeaderImage(), is positioned before the SafeArea and Padding, allowing the Image to fill the full width of the device.

8. Add a Column as a child of the Padding and then call the _buildJournalEntry(), _buildJournalWeather(), _buildJournalTags(), and _buildJournalFooterImages() methods.

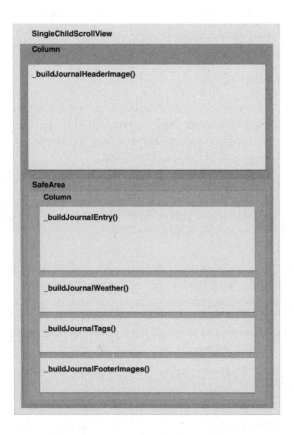

```
Widget _buildBody() {
  return SingleChildScrollView(
    child: Column(
      children: <Widget>[
        _buildJournalHeaderImage(),
        SafeArea(
          child: Padding(
            padding: EdgeInsets.all(16.0),
            child: Column(
```

```
                crossAxisAlignment: CrossAxisAlignment.start,
                children: <Widget>[
                  _buildJournalEntry(),
                  Divider(),
                  _buildJournalWeather(),
                  Divider(),
                  _buildJournalTags(),
                  Divider(),
                  _buildJournalFooterImages(),
                ],
              ),
            ),
          ),
        ],
      ),
    ),
  );
}
```

9. Create the _buildJournalHeaderImage() method, which returns an Image. The image property uses AssetImage present.jpg with fit set to BoxFit.cover, allowing the Image to fill the full width of the device.

```
Image _buildJournalHeaderImage() {
  return Image(
    image: AssetImage('assets/images/present.jpg'),
    fit: BoxFit.cover,
  );
}
```

10. Create the _buildJournalEntry() method, which returns a Column. The Column children list of widgets contains two Text widgets and one Divider() widget.

```
Column _buildJournalEntry() {
  return Column(
    crossAxisAlignment: CrossAxisAlignment.start,
    children: <Widget>[
      Text(
        'My Birthday',
        style: TextStyle(
          fontSize: 32.0,
          fontWeight: FontWeight.bold,
        ),
      ),
      Divider(),
      Text(
        'It's going to be a great birthday. We are going out for dinner at my
favorite place, then watch a movie after we go to the gelateria for ice cream and
espresso.',
        style: TextStyle(color: Colors.black54),
      ),
    ],
  );
}
```

11. Create the _buildJournalWeather() method, which returns a Row. The Row children list of widgets contains a Column, a SizedBox, and another Column. The second Column list of widgets contains two Row widgets.

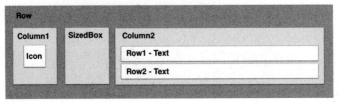

```
Row _buildJournalWeather() {
  return Row(
      crossAxisAlignment: CrossAxisAlignment.start,
      children: <Widget>[
        Column(
          crossAxisAlignment: CrossAxisAlignment.start,
          children: <Widget>[
            Icon(
              Icons.wb_sunny,
              color: Colors.orange,
            ),
          ],
        ),
        SizedBox(width: 16.0,),
        Column(
          crossAxisAlignment: CrossAxisAlignment.start,
          children: <Widget>[
            Row(
              children: <Widget>[
                Text(
                  '81° Clear',
                  style: TextStyle(color: Colors.deepOrange),
                ),
              ],
            ),
            Row(
              children: <Widget>[
                Text(
                  '4500 Alpho Drive, Dallas, TX United States',
                  style: TextStyle(color: Colors.grey),
                ),
              ],
            ),
          ],
        ),
      ],
  );
}
```

12. Create the _buildJournalTags() method, which returns a Wrap. The Wrap children use the List.generate constructor to build the sample data list to show seven sample tag values. The constructor takes two arguments, the length of the list and the index.

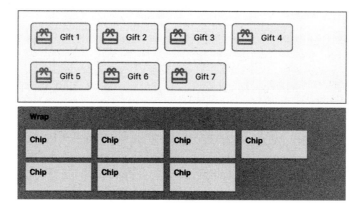

```
Wrap _buildJournalTags() {
  return Wrap(
    spacing: 8.0,
    children: List.generate(7, (int index) {
      return Chip(
        label: Text(
          'Gift ${index + 1}',
          style: TextStyle(fontSize: 10.0),
        ),
        avatar: Icon(
          Icons.card_giftcard,
          color: Colors.blue.shade300,
        ),
        shape: RoundedRectangleBorder(
          borderRadius: BorderRadius.circular(4.0),
          side: BorderSide(color: Colors.grey),
        ),
        backgroundColor: Colors.grey.shade100,
      );
    }),
  );
}
```

13. Create the _buildJournalFooterImages() method, which returns a Row. The Row children list of widgets contains three CircleAvatars and a SizedBox. The SizedBox child is a Column with a children list of Widget of three Icons. The main purpose of the SizedBox is adding extra spacing between the CircleAvatar and the vertically placed Icons.

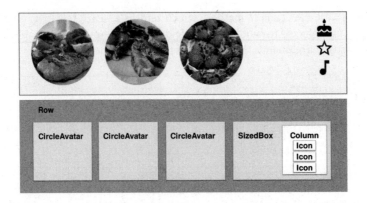

```
Row _buildJournalFooterImages() {
  return Row(
    mainAxisAlignment: MainAxisAlignment.spaceBetween,
    crossAxisAlignment: CrossAxisAlignment.start,
    children: <Widget>[
      CircleAvatar(
        backgroundImage: AssetImage('assets/images/salmon.jpg'),
        radius: 40.0,
      ),
      CircleAvatar(
        backgroundImage: AssetImage('assets/images/asparagus.jpg'),
        radius: 40.0,
      ),
      CircleAvatar(
        backgroundImage: AssetImage('assets/images/strawberries.jpg'),
        radius: 40.0,
      ),
      SizedBox(
        width: 100.0,
        child: Column(
          crossAxisAlignment: CrossAxisAlignment.end,
          children: <Widget>[
            Icon(Icons.cake),
            Icon(Icons.star_border),
            Icon(Icons.music_note),
            //Icon(Icons.movie),
          ],
        ),
      ),
    ],
  );
}
```

HOW IT WORKS

You first created a high-level view by breaking down the main sections of the page. At the base you used a `SingleChildScrollView` and consecutively built on top a `Column`, header `Image`, `SafeArea`, `Padding`, and a `Column` with a `children` list of `Widget` that build each section separately. You broke them down to four separate sections and built them by calling the `_buildJournalEntry()`, `_buildJournal-Weather()`, `_buildJournalTags()`, and `_buildJournalFooterImages()` methods. Each of these methods creates a custom layout by nesting widgets.

SUMMARY

In this chapter, you learned how to envision a high-level custom layout and break it down into its main sections. Then you took each main section and built the layout needed by nesting widgets.

In the next chapter, you'll learn to add interactivity by using the `GestureDetector`, `Draggable`, `DragTarget`, `InkWell`, and `Dismissable` widgets.

▶ **WHAT YOU LEARNED IN THIS CHAPTER**

TOPIC	KEY CONCEPTS
Getting a high-level view	Break down the page into main sections.
Creating simple and complex layouts	Separate and nest widgets.
Creating a custom layout	Lay out and use widgets such as `SingleChildScrollView`, `SafeArea`, `Padding`, `Column`, `Row`, `Image`, `Divider`, `Text`, `Icon`, `SizedBox`, `Wrap`, `Chip`, and `CircleAvatar`.

11

Applying Interactivity

WHAT YOU WILL LEARN IN THIS CHAPTER

➤ How to use `GestureDetector`, which recognizes gestures such as tap, double tap, long press, pan, vertical drag, horizontal drag, and scale.

➤ How to use the `Draggable` widget that is dragged to a `DragTarget`.

➤ How to use the `DragTarget` widget that receives data from a `Draggable`.

➤ How to use the `InkWell` and `InkResponse` widgets. You will learn that `InkWell` is a rectangular area that responds to touch and clips splashes within its area. You'll learn that `InkResponse` responds to touch and that splashes expand outside its area.

➤ How to use the `Dismissible` widget that is dismissed by dragging.

In this chapter, you'll learn how to add interactivity to an app by using gestures. In a mobile application, gestures are the heart of listening to user interaction. Making use of gestures can define an app with a great UX. Overusing gestures when they don't add value or convey an action creates a poor UX. You'll take a closer look at how to find a balance by using the correct gesture for the task at hand.

SETTING UP GESTUREDETECTOR: THE BASICS

The `GestureDetector` widget detects gestures such as tap, double tap, long press, pan, vertical drag, horizontal drag, and scale. It has an optional `child` property, and if a `child` widget is specified, the gestures apply only to the `child` widget. If the `child` widget is omitted, then the `GestureDetector` fills the entire parent instead. If you need to catch vertical drag and horizontal drag at the same time, use the pan gesture. If you need to catch a single-axis drag, then use either the vertical drag or horizontal drag gesture.

If you try to use vertical drag, horizontal drag, and pan gestures at the same time, you'll receive an `Incorrect GestureDetector Arguments` error. However, if you use either vertical or horizontal drag with a pan gesture, you'll not receive any errors. The reason you receive the error is that simultaneously having a vertical and horizontal drag gesture and a pan gesture results in the pan gesture being ignored since the other two (vertical and horizontal drag) will first catch all of the drags (Figure 11.1).

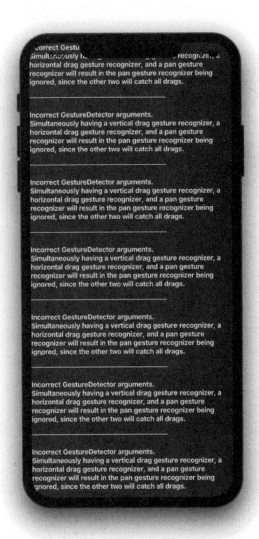

FIGURE 11.1: Vertical, horizontal, and pan gestures error

You'll get the same kind of error if you try to use vertical drag, horizontal drag, and scale gestures at the same time. However, if you use either vertical or horizontal drag with a scale gesture, you won't receive any errors.

Each pan, vertical drag, horizontal drag, and scale property has a callback for each start, update, and end drag. (See Table 11.1.) Each callback has access to the `details` object containing values about the gesture, which is rich in information and provides the touch position.

TABLE 11.1: GestureDetector Callbacks

PROPERTY/CALLBACK	DETAILS OBJECT FOR CALLBACK
onPanStart	DragStartDetails
onVerticalDragStart	DragStartDetails
onHorizontalDragStart	DragStartDetails
onScaleStart	ScaleStartDetails
onPanUpdate	DragUpdateDetails
onVerticalDragUpdate	DragUpdateDetails
onHorizontalDragUpdate	DragUpdateDetails
onScaleUpdate	ScaleUpdateDetails
onPanEnd	DragEndDetails
onVerticalDragEnd	DragEndDetails
onHorizontalDragEnd	DragEndDetails
onScaleEnd	ScaleEndDetails

For example, to check whether a user dragged on the screen from either left or right, you use the `onHorizontalDragEnd` callback that has access to the `DragEndDetails` `details` object. You use the `details.primaryVelocity` value to check whether it's negative, `'Dragged Right to Left'`, or if it's positive, `'Dragged Left to Right'`.

```
onHorizontalDragEnd: (DragEndDetails details) {
  print('onHorizontalDragEnd: $details');

  if (details.primaryVelocity < 0) {
    print('Dragged Right to Left: ${details.primaryVelocity}');
  } else if (details.primaryVelocity > 0) {
    print('Dragged Left to Right: ${details.primaryVelocity}');
  }
},

// print statement results
flutter: onHorizontalDragEnd: DragEndDetails(Velocity(-2313.4, -110.3))
flutter: Dragged Right to Left: -2313.4407865184226
flutter: onHorizontalDragEnd: DragEndDetails(Velocity(3561.4, 123.2))
flutter: Dragged Left to Right: 3561.4258553699615
```

The following are the `GestureDetector` gestures that you can listen for and take appropriate action:

- ➤ Tap
  - ➤ onTapDown
  - ➤ onTapUp
  - ➤ onTap
  - ➤ onTapCancel
- ➤ Double tap
  - ➤ onDoubleTap
- ➤ Long press
  - ➤ onLongPress
- ➤ Pan
  - ➤ onPanStart
  - ➤ onPanUpdate
  - ➤ onPanEnd
- ➤ Vertical drag
  - ➤ onVerticalDragStart
  - ➤ onVerticalDragUpdate
  - ➤ onVerticalDragEnd
- ➤ Horizontal drag
  - ➤ onHorizontalDragStart
  - ➤ onHorizontalDragUpdate
  - ➤ onHorizontalDragEnd
- ➤ Scale
  - ➤ onScaleStart
  - ➤ onScaleUpdate
  - ➤ onScaleEnd

TRY IT OUT Creating the Gesture, Drag-and-Drop App

In this section, you'll build the gesture area that catches drag events. To make the gesture area visible, you'll use a light green color and place an alarm clock icon for visual purposes only. In the next section, you'll add another area to this app to handle dragging capabilities.

In this example, the `Column` widget will vertically display a `GestureDetector` listening for the `onTap`, `onDoubleTap`, `onLongPress`, and `onPanUpdate` gestures. It will also display a `Draggable` widget and a `DragTarget` widget. The `Draggable Icon` will pass a `Color` to the `DragTarget` displaying a `Text` widget changing to the passed `Color`. In this example, to keep the widget tree shallow, you'll use methods instead of widget classes.

1. Create a new Flutter project and name it `ch11_gestures_drag_drop`. You can follow the instructions in Chapter 4, "Creating a Starter Project Template." For this project, you need to create only the `pages` folder.

2. Open the `main.dart` file. Change the `primarySwatch` property from `blue` to `lightGreen`.

   ```
   primarySwatch: Colors.lightGreen,
   ```

3. Open the `home.dart` file and add to the body a `SafeArea` with a `SingleChildScrollView` as a child. The reason for using a `SingleChildScrollView` is to handle device rotation and automatically be able to scroll to view hidden content. Add a `Column` as a child of the `SingleChildScrollView`. For the `Column children` list of `Widget`, add a method call to `_buildGestureDetector()`, `_buildDraggable()`, and `_buildDragTarget()` with `Divider` widgets between them.

   Note that you will implement `_buildDraggable()` and `_buildDragTarget()` in the next section. You can comment these methods out if you would like to test the project with just the `GestureDetector`.

   ```
   body: SafeArea(
     child: SingleChildScrollView(
       child: Column(
         children: <Widget>[
           _buildGestureDetector(),
           Divider(
             color: Colors.black,
   ```

```
              height: 44.0,
            ),
            _buildDraggable(),
            Divider(
              height: 40.0,
            ),
            _buildDragTarget(),
            Divider(
              color: Colors.black,
            ),
          ],
        ),
      ),
    ),
```

4. Add the `_buildGestureDetector()` `GestureDetector` method after the `Widget build(BuildContext context) {...}`.

5. Return a `GestureDetector` listening to the `onTap`, `onDoubleTap`, `onLongPress`, and `onPanUpdate` gestures.

6. To view captured gestures, add a `Container` as a `child` of the `GestureDetector`. The `Container` `child` is a `Column` displaying an `Icon` and a `Text` widget showing the gesture detected and pointer location on the screen. I have also added the `onVerticalDragUpdate` and `onHorizontalDragUpdate` gestures (properties) but commented them out for you to experiment.

Remember when using the `Pan` gesture that you can listen to only `onHorizontalDragUpdate` or `onVerticalDragUpdate`, not both, or you will receive an error (refer to Figure 11.1).

7. To update the screen with the pointer location and to have code reuse, create the `_displayGestureDetected(String gesture)` method. Each gesture passes the `String` representation of the gesture. The `onPanUpdate`, `onVerticalDragUpdate`, and `onHorizontalDragUpdate` gestures (properties) listen to `DragUpdateDetails`.

In this example, I'm using `onPanUpdate`, but I have left the `onVerticalDragUpdate`, `onHorizontalDragUpdate`, and `onHorizontalDragEnd` gestures (properties) commented out for you to experiment.

```
GestureDetector _buildGestureDetector() {
  return GestureDetector(
    onTap: () {
      print('onTap');
      _displayGestureDetected('onTap');
    },
    onDoubleTap: () {
      print('onDoubleTap');
```

```dart
            _displayGestureDetected('onDoubleTap');
        },
        onLongPress: () {
          print('onLongPress');
          _displayGestureDetected('onLongPress');
        },
        onPanUpdate: (DragUpdateDetails details) {
          print('onPanUpdate: $details');
          _displayGestureDetected('onPanUpdate:\n$details');
        },
        //onVerticalDragUpdate: ((DragUpdateDetails details) {
        //  print('onVerticalDragUpdate: $details');
        //  _displayGestureDetected('onVerticalDragUpdate:\n$details');
        //}),
        //onHorizontalDragUpdate: (DragUpdateDetails details) {
        //  print('onHorizontalDragUpdate: $details');
        //  _displayGestureDetected('onHorizontalDragUpdate:\n$details');
        //},
        //onHorizontalDragEnd: (DragEndDetails details) {
        //  print('onHorizontalDragEnd: $details');
        //  if (details.primaryVelocity < 0) {
        //    print('Dragging Right to Left: ${details.velocity}');
        //  } else if (details.primaryVelocity > 0) {
        //    print('Dragging Left to Right: ${details.velocity}');
        //  }
        //},
        child: Container(
          color: Colors.lightGreen.shade100,
          width: double.infinity,
          padding: EdgeInsets.all(24.0),
          child: Column(
            children: <Widget>[
              Icon(
                Icons.access_alarm,
                size: 98.0,
              ),
              Text('$_gestureDetected'),
            ],
          ),
        ),
      );
}

void _displayGestureDetected(String gesture) {
  setState(() {
    _gestureDetected = gesture;
  });
}
```

HOW IT WORKS

The GestureDetector listens to onTap, onDoubleTap, onLongPress, and onPanUpdate and for the app
the optional onVerticalDragUpdate and onHorizontalDragUpdate gestures (properties). As the
user taps and drags over the screen, the GestureDetector updates where the pointer begins and ends,
and while moving. To limit the area of detecting the gestures, you passed a Container as a child of the
GestureDetector.

IMPLEMENTING THE DRAGGABLE AND DRAGTARGET WIDGETS

To implement a drag-and-drop feature, you drag the Draggable widget to a DragTarget widget. You use the data property to pass any custom data and use the child property to display a widget like an Icon and remains visible while not being dragged as long as the childWhenDragging property is null. Set the childWhenDragging property to display a widget while dragging. Use the feedback property to display a widget showing the user visual feedback where the widget is being dragged. Once the user lifts their finger on top of the DragTarget, the target can accept the data. To reject accepting the data, the user moves away from the DragTarget without releasing touch. If you need to restrict the dragging vertically or horizontally, you optionally set the Draggable axis property. To catch a single axis drag, you set the axis property to either Axis.vertical or Axis.horizontal.

The DragTarget widget listens for a Draggable widget and receives data if dropped. The DragTarget builder property accepts three parameters: the BuildContext, List<dynamic> acceptedData (candidateData), and List<dynamic> of rejectedData. The acceptedData is the data passed from the Draggable widget, and it expects it to be a List of values. The rejectedData contains the List of data that will not be accepted.

TRY IT OUT   Gestures: Adding Drag and Drop

In this section you're going to add to the previous app an additional drag area that catches drag events. You'll create two widgets: a palette Icon widget that is draggable around the screen and a Text widget that receives data by accepting a drag gesture. When the Text widget receives data, it will change its text color from a light gray to a deep orange color but only if the drag is released on top of it.

To keep the example clean, the Draggable data property passes the deep color orange as an integer value. The DragTarget accepting an integer value checks whether a Draggable is over it. If not, a default label shows the message "Drag To and see the color change." If Draggable is over it and data has a value, you see a label with the data passed. The ternary operator (conditional statement) is used to check whether the data is passed.

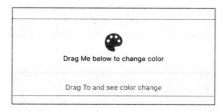

Continuing with the previous gestures project, let's add the Draggable and DragTarget methods.

1. Create the _buildDraggable() method, which returns a Draggable integer. The Draggable child is a Column with the children list of Widget consisting of an Icon and a Text widget. The feedback property is an Icon, and the data property passes the Color as an integer value. The data property can be any custom data needed, but to keep it simple, you are passing the integer value of the Color.

```
Draggable<int> _buildDraggable() {
  return Draggable(
    child: Column(
      children: <Widget>[
        Icon(
          Icons.palette,
          color: Colors.deepOrange,
          size: 48.0,
        ),
        Text(
          'Drag Me below to change color',
        ),
      ],
    ),
    childWhenDragging: Icon(
      Icons.palette,
      color: Colors.grey,
      size: 48.0,
    ),
    feedback: Icon(
      Icons.brush,
      color: Colors.deepOrange,
      size: 80.0,
    ),
    data: Colors.deepOrange.value,
  );
}
```

2. Create the _buildDragTarget() method, which returns a DragTarget integer. To accept data, set the DragTarget onAccept property value to colorValue and set the _paintedColor variable to the Color(colorValue). The Color(colorValue) constructs (converts) the integer value to a color.

3. Set the builder property to accept three parameters: BuildContext, List<dynamic> acceptedData, and List<dynamic> of rejectedData. Note that the data is a List, and to obtain the Color integer value, you read the first-row value by using acceptedData[0].

Use the arrow syntax with the ternary operator to check for acceptedData.isEmpty. If it's empty, it means no dragging over the DragTarget and shows a Text widget instructing the user to "Drag To and see color change." Otherwise, if there is dragging over, the DragTarget shows the Text widget displaying the 'Painting Color: $acceptedData'. For the same Text widget, set the color style property to the Color(acceptedData[0]) giving the user visual feedback of the color.

```
DragTarget<int> _buildDragTarget() {
  return DragTarget<int>(
    onAccept: (colorValue) {
```

```
            _paintedColor = Color(colorValue);
        },
        builder: (BuildContext context, List<dynamic> acceptedData, List<dynamic>
  rejectedData) => acceptedData.isEmpty
            ? Text(
        'Drag To and see color change',
        style: TextStyle(color: _paintedColor),
    )
            : Text(
        'Painting Color: $acceptedData',
        style: TextStyle(
          color: Color(acceptedData[0]),
          fontWeight: FontWeight.bold,
        ),
    ),
    );
  }
```

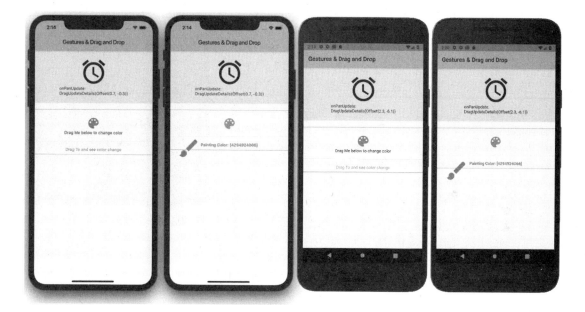

HOW IT WORKS

The `DragTarget` widget listens for a `Draggable` widget to drop. If the user releases over the `DragTarget`, the `onAccept` is called, as long as the `data` is acceptable. The `builder` property accepts three parameters: `BuildContext`, `List<dynamic>` `acceptedData` (`candidateData`), and `List<dynamic>` of `rejected-Data`. Using the `arrow syntax` with a ternary operator, you check for `acceptedData.isEmpty`. If it's empty, no `data` is passed, and a `Text` widget displays instructions. If `data` is valid and accepted, a `Text` widget is displayed with the `data` value and uses the `style` property to set the appropriate color.

USING THE GESTUREDETECTOR FOR MOVING AND SCALING

Now you'll build upon what you learned in the "Setting Up GestureDetector: The Basics" section, and by taking a more in-depth look, you'll learn how to scale widgets by using single or multitouch gestures. The goal is to learn how to implement multitouch scaling of an image by zooming in/out, double tap to increase zoom, and long press to reset the image to original size. The GestureDetector gives you the ability to accomplish scaling by using onScaleStart and onScaleUpdate. Use onDoubleTap to increase the zoom, and use onLongPress to reset the zoom to the original default size.

When the user taps the image, the image can be dragged around to change position or scaled by zooming in/out. To accomplish both requirements, you'll use the Transform widget. Use the Transform.scale constructor to resize the image, and use the Transform.translate constructor to move the image (Figure 11.2).

The Transform widget applies a transformation before the child is painted. Using the Transform default constructor, the transform argument is set by using the Matrix4 (4D Matrix) class, and this transformation matrix is applied to the child during painting. The benefits of using the default constructor are to use the Matrix4 to execute multiple cascading (..scale()..translate()) transformations. The double dots (..) are used to cascade multiple transformations. In Chapter 3, "Learning Dart Basics," you learned that the cascade notation allows you to make a sequence of operations on the same object. The following sample code shows how to use the Matrix4 class with the cascade notation to apply a scale and a translate transform to the same object:

FIGURE 11.2: Moving and scaling an image

```
Matrix4.identity()
  ..scale(1.0, 1.0)
  ..translate(30, 30);
```

The Transform widget has four different constructors.

➤ Transform: Default constructor taking a Matrix4 for the transform argument.

➤ Transform.rotate: Constructor to rotate a child widget around the center by using an angle. The angle argument rotates clockwise by radians. To rotate counterclockwise, pass a negative radian.

➤ Transform.scale: Constructor to evenly scale a child widget on the x-axis and y-axis. The widget is scaled by its center alignment. The scale argument value of 1.0 is the original widget size. Any values above 1.0 scale the widget larger, and values below 1.0 scale the widget smaller. A value of 0.0 makes the widget invisible.

➤ Transform.translate: Constructor to move/position a child widget by using a translation, an offset. The offset argument takes the Offset(double dx, double dy) class by positioning the widget on the x-axis and y-axis.

TRY IT OUT   Creating an App with Gestures for Moving and Scaling

In this example, the app presents a page showing an image that's the full device width. Imagine if this is a journal app and the user navigated to this page to view the selected image with the ability to zoom for more details. The image is moved by a single touch drag and can be zoomed in/out (pinching) by using multitouch. Double tapping allows the image to zoom in at the tapped location, and a single long press resets the image location and zoom level back to default values.

This example is the first part of the app where you lay out the widgets that handle the gestures moving and scaling the image. In the next exercise, you'll concentrate on adding the logic to handle the calculations necessary to keep track of the location and scale of the image.

The GestureDetector is the body (property) base widget and is listening for the onScaleStart, onScaleUpdate, onDoubleTap, and onLongPress gestures (properties). The GestureDetector child is a Stack that shows the image and a gesture status bar display. To apply the moving and scaling of the image, use the Transform widget. To show different ways to apply changes to a widget, you make use of three different Transform constructors: default, scale, and translate.

You'll take a look at two techniques to accomplish the same moving and scaling results. The first technique (beginning with step 13) involves nesting the scale and translate constructors. The second technique (starting at step 16) uses the default constructor with the Matrix4 to apply transformations.

Note in this example to keep the widget tree shallow, you'll use methods instead of widget classes.

1. Create a new Flutter project and name it `ch11_gestures_scale`. As usual, you can follow the instructions in Chapter 4. For this project, you need to create only the `pages` and `assets/images` folders.

2. Create the `Home Class` as a `StatefulWidget` since the data (state) requires changes.

3. Open the `pubspec.yaml` file to add resources. Under the `assets` section, add the `assets/images/` folder.

```
# To add assets to your application, add an assets section, like this:
assets:
  - assets/images/
```

4. Click the Save button, and depending on the Editor you are using, it automatically runs the `flutter packages get`; once finished, it will show a message of `Process finished with exit code 0`. If it does not automatically run the command for you, open the Terminal window (located at the bottom of your editor) and type `flutter packages get`.

5. Add the folder `assets` and subfolder `images` at the project's root, and then copy the `elephant.jpg` file to the `images` folder.

6. Open the `home.dart` file and add to the `body` a call to the `_buildBody(context)` method. The `context` is received by the `_buildBody()` method as a parameter for the method's `MediaQuery` to obtain the device `width`.

```
body: _buildBody(context),
```

7. Below the `class _HomeState extends State<Home>` and above `@override`, add the variables for `_startLastOffset`, `_lastOffset`, `_currentOffset`, `_lastScale`, and `_currentScale`.

The `_startLastOffset`, `_lastOffset`, and `_currentOffset` variables are of type `Offset` initialized to a value of `Offset.zero`. The `Offset.zero` is the same as `Offset(0.0, 0.0)`, meaning the default position for the image. These variables are used to keep track of the image position while it's dragged.

The `_lastScale` and `_currentScale` variables are of type `double`. They are initialized to a value of `1.0`, which is normal zoom size. These variables are used to keep track of the image while it's scaled. Values greater than `1.0` scale the image bigger, and values less than `1.0` scale the image smaller.

```
class _HomeState extends State<Home> {
  Offset _startLastOffset = Offset.zero;
  Offset _lastOffset = Offset.zero;
  Offset _currentOffset = Offset.zero;
  double _lastScale = 1.0;
  double _currentScale = 1.0;

  @override
  Widget build(BuildContext context) {
```

8. Add the _buildBody(BuildContext context) Widget method after the Widget build(BuildContext context) {...}. Return a GestureDetector with the child as a Stack. Note that the GestureDetector is at the root of the body property to intercept all gestures anywhere on the screen.

To show the image and the top gesture status bar display, you'll use the Stack widget.

9. Set the Stack fit property to StackFit.expand to expand to the biggest size allowed.

10. For the Stack children list of Widget, add three methods and name them _transformScale-AndTranslate(), _transformMatrix4(), and _positionedStatusBar(context). The _positionedStatusBar method passes the context for the MediaQuery to obtain the full width of the device.

11. Comment out the _transformMatrix4() method since you will be testing with the _transformScaleAndTranslate() first.

12. Add to the GestureDetector the onScaleStart, onScaleUpdate, onDoubleTap, and onLongPress gestures (properties) to listen for each gesture. Respectively pass the _onScaleStart, _onScaleUpdate, _onDoubleTap, and _onLongPress methods.

```
Widget _buildBody(BuildContext context) {
  return GestureDetector(
    child: Stack(
      fit: StackFit.expand,
      children: <Widget>[
        _transformScaleAndTranslate(),
        //_transformMatrix4(),
        _positionedStatusBar(context),
      ],
    ),
    onScaleStart: _onScaleStart,
    onScaleUpdate: _onScaleUpdate,
    onDoubleTap: _onDoubleTap,
    onLongPress: _onLongPress,
  );
}
```

13. In this step you implement the first technique (moving and scaling) by nesting the scale and translate constructors. Add the _transformScaleAndTranslate() Transform method after Widget build(BuildContext context) {...}. Return a Transform by nesting the scale and translate constructors.

14. For the Transform.scale constructor's scale argument, enter the variable _currentScale and set the child argument to the Transform.translate constructor.

15. For the Transform.translate constructor's offset argument, enter the variable _current_offset and set the child argument to an Image. This child widget is the image that is dragged around and scaled by nesting the two Transform widgets.

```
Transform _transformScaleAndTranslate() {
  return Transform.scale(
      scale: _currentScale,
      child: Transform.translate(
        offset: _currentOffset,
        child: Image(
          image: AssetImage('assets/images/elephant.jpg'),
        ),
      ),
    );
}
```

16. In this step, you implement the second technique (moving and scaling) by using the `default` constructor. Add the `_transformMatrix4()` `Transform` method. Return a `Transform` by using the `default` constructor.

17. For the `Transform` constructor's `transform` argument, use the `Matrix4`. Using the `Matrix4.identity()` creates the matrix from zero and sets default values. It is actually making a call to `Matrix4.zero()..setIdentity()`. From the `identity` constructor, use the double dots to cascade the scale and translate transformations. With this technique, there's no need to use multiple `Transform` widgets—you use only one and execute multiple transformations.

18. For the `scale` method, pass the `_currentScale` for both the x- and y-axes. The x-axis is mandatory, but the y-axis is optional. Since the image is scaled proportionally, both the x-axis and y-axis values are utilized.

19. For the `translate` method, pass the `_currentOffset.dx` for the x-axis and `_currentOffset.dy` for the y-axis. The x-axis is mandatory, but the y-axis is optional. In this app, the image is being dragged (moved) without restrictions, and both the x-axis and y-axis values are utilized.

20. To keep the image center-aligned during scaling, set the `alignment` property to use the `FractionalOffset.center`. If the center alignment is not used while the image scales, the translate `_currentOffset` moves the image. By keeping the image in the same location during scaling, it creates a great UX. If the image is moving away from the current location during scaling, that would not be a good UX.

Set the `child` property to an `Image` widget. The `image` property uses the `AssetImage` elephant.jpg.

```
Transform _transformMatrix4() {
  return Transform(
    transform: Matrix4.identity()
      ..scale(_currentScale, _currentScale)
      ..translate(_currentOffset.dx, _currentOffset.dy,),
    alignment: FractionalOffset.center,
    child: Image(
      image: AssetImage('assets/images/elephant.jpg'),
    ),
  );
}
```

21. Add the _positionedStatusBar(BuildContext context) Positioned method. Return a Positioned by using the default constructor. The purpose of this Positioned widget is to show a gesture status bar display on the top of the screen with the current scale and position.

22. Set the top property to 0.0 to position it on the top of the screen in the Stack widget. Set the width property by using the MediaQuery width to expand the full width of the device. The child is a Container with the color property set to a shade of Colors.white54. Set the Container height property to 50.0. Set the Container child to a Row with the mainAxisAlignment of MainAxisAlignment.spaceAround. For the Row children list of Widget, use two Text widgets. The first Text widget shows the current scale by using the _currentScale variable. To show only up to four decimal points precision, use _currentScale.toStringAsFixed(4). The second Text widget shows the current location by using the _currentOffset variable.

```
Positioned _positionedStatusBar(BuildContext context) {
  return Positioned(
    top: 0.0,
    width: MediaQuery.of(context).size.width,
    child: Container(
      color: Colors.white54,
      height: 50.0,
      child: Row(
        mainAxisAlignment: MainAxisAlignment.spaceAround,
        children: <Widget>[
          Text(
            'Scale: ${_currentScale.toStringAsFixed(4)}',
          ),
          Text(
            'Current: $_currentOffset',
          ),
        ],
      ),
    ),
  );
}
```

HOW IT WORKS

The GestureDetector listens to the onScaleStart, onScaleUpdate, onDoubleTap, and onLongPress gestures (properties). As the user taps and drags over the screen, the GestureDetector updates where the pointer begins and ends, as well as updating its location while moving. To maximize the gesture detecting area, the GestureDetector fills the entire screen by setting the child Stack widget fit property to StackFit.expand to expand to the biggest size allowed. Note that the GestureDetector fills the entire screen only if no child widget is used.

The _startLastOffset, _lastOffset, and _currentOffset variables are of type Offset and are used to track the image position. The _lastScale and _currentScale variables are of type double and are used to track the image scale.

Using the Stack widget allows you to place the Image and a Positioned widget to overlap each other. The Positioned widget is placed as the last widget in the Stack to allow the gesture status bar display to stay over the Image.

The `Transform` widget is used to move and scale the `Image` by implementing two different techniques. The first technique makes use of nesting the `Transform.scale` and `Transform.translate` constructors. The second technique uses the `Transform` default constructor by using the `Matrix4` to apply transformations. Both methods accomplish the same results.

TRY IT OUT Adding Logic and Calculations to the Moving and Scaling Project

Continue with the previous moving and scaling project and start adding the logic and calculations to handle the `GestureDetector` gestures. The `onScaleStart` and `onScaleUpdate` are responsible for handling moving and scaling gestures. The `onDoubleTap` is responsible for handling the double tapping gesture to increase the zoom. The `onLongPress` is responsible for handling a long press gesture to reset the zoom to the original default value.

1. Create the `_onScaleStart(ScaleStartDetails details)` method. This gesture is called once when the user starts to move or scale the image. This method populates the `_startLastOffset`, `_lastOffset`, and `_lastScale` variables, and the image position and scale calculations are based on these values.

```
void _onScaleStart(ScaleStartDetails details) {
  print('ScaleStartDetails: $details');

  _startLastOffset = details.focalPoint;
  _lastOffset = _currentOffset;
  _lastScale = _currentScale;
}
```

2. Create the `_onScaleUpdate(ScaleUpdateDetails details)` method. This gesture is called when the user is either moving or scaling the image.

By using the `details` (`ScaleUpdateDetails` from callback) object, different values such as the `scale`, `rotation`, and `focalPoint` (`Offset` of the contact position on the device screen) can be checked. The goal is to check whether the user is either moving or scaling the image by checking the `details.scale` value.

```
void _onScaleUpdate(ScaleUpdateDetails details) {
  print('ScaleUpdateDetails: $details - Scale: ${details.scale}');
}
```

3. Set up an `if` statement to check whether the user is scaling the image by evaluating `details.scale != 1.0`. If the `details.scale` is greater or less than `1.0`, it means the image is scaling. With values greater than `1.0`, the image is scaling larger, and with values less than `1.0`, the image is scaling smaller.

```
void _onScaleUpdate(ScaleUpdateDetails details) {
  print('ScaleUpdateDetails: $details - Scale: ${details.scale}');

  if (details.scale != 1.0) {
    // Scaling
  }
}
```

4. To calculate the current scale, create a local variable called `currentScale` of type `double` and calculate the value by taking the `_lastScale * details.scale`. The `_lastScale` was previously calculated from the `_onScaleStart()` method, and the `details.scale` is the current scale as the user continues to zoom the image.

```
double currentScale = _lastScale * details.scale;
```

5. To restrict the image not to scale down to more than half its size, check whether the `currentScale` is less than `0.5` (half the original size) and reset the value to `0.5`.

```
if (currentScale < 0.5) {
  currentScale = 0.5;
}
```

6. To have the `Image` widget refresh the current zoom, add the `setState()` method and populate the `_currentScale` value with the local `currentScale` variable. Remember that the `setState()` method tells the Flutter framework that the widget should redraw because the state has changed. It is recommended to place calculations that do not need state changes outside the `setState()` method. This best practice is why you created a local variable called `currentScale`.

```
setState(() {
  _currentScale = currentScale;
});
```

The following is the current `_onScaleUpdate()` method:

```
void _onScaleUpdate(ScaleUpdateDetails details) {
  print('ScaleUpdateDetails: $details - Scale: ${details.scale}');

  if (details.scale != 1.0) {
    // Scaling
    double currentScale = _lastScale * details.scale;
    if (currentScale < 0.5) {
      currentScale = 0.5;
    }
    setState(() {
      _currentScale = currentScale;
    });
    print('_scale: $_currentScale - _lastScale: $_lastScale');
  }
}
```

7. Continue adding to the `_onScaleUpdate()` method the logic to move the image around the screen.

8. Add an `else if` statement to check whether the `details.scale` is equal to `1.0`. If the scaling is `1.0`, it means the image is moving, not scaling.

```
} else if (details.scale == 1.0) {
```

Before the image can be moved, you need to take into account the current scale since it affects the `Offset` (position).

9. Create the local `offsetAdjustedForScale` variable as of type `Offset`. This variable holds the last offset by taking into consideration the scale factor. Take the `_startLastOffset` and subtract the `_lastOffset`; then divide the result by the `_lastScale`.

```
// Calculate offset depending on current Image scaling.
Offset offsetAdjustedForScale = (_startLastOffset - _lastOffset) / _lastScale;
```

10. Create the local `currentOffset` variable of type `Offset`. This variable holds the current offset (position) of the image. The `currentOffset` is calculated by taking the `details.focalPoint` minus the `offsetAdjustedForScale` times the `_currentScale`.

```
Offset currentOffset = details.focalPoint - (offsetAdjustedForScale *
_currentScale);
```

11. To have the `Image` widget refresh the current position, add the `setState()` method and populate the `_currentOffset` value with the local `currentOffset` variable.

```
setState(() {
  _currentOffset = currentOffset;
});
```

The following is the full `_onScaleUpdate()` method:

```
void _onScaleUpdate(ScaleUpdateDetails details) {
  print('ScaleUpdateDetails: $details - Scale: ${details.scale}');

  if (details.scale != 1.0) {
    // Scaling
    double currentScale = _lastScale * details.scale;
    if (currentScale < 0.5) {
      currentScale = 0.5;
    }
    setState(() {
      _currentScale = currentScale;
    });
    print('_scale: $_currentScale - _lastScale: $_lastScale');
  } else if (details.scale == 1.0) {
    // We are not scaling but dragging around screen
    // Calculate offset depending on current Image scaling.
    Offset offsetAdjustedForScale = (_startLastOffset - _lastOffset) /
_lastScale;
    Offset currentOffset = details.focalPoint - (offsetAdjustedForScale *
_currentScale);
    setState(() {
      _currentOffset = currentOffset;
    });
    print('offsetAdjustedForScale: $offsetAdjustedForScale - _currentOffset:
$_currentOffset');
  }
}
```

12. Create the _onDoubleTap() method. This gesture is called when the user is double tapping the screen. When a double tap is detected, the image is scaled twice as large.

13. Create the local currentScale variable of type double. The currentScale is calculated by taking the _lastScale times 2.0 (twice the size).

```
double currentScale = _lastScale * 2.0;
```

14. Add an if statement that checks whether the currentScale is greater than 16.0 (16 times the original size); then reset currentScale to 1.0. Add a call to the _resetToDefaultValues() (created in step 19) method that resets all variables to their default values. The result is that the image is recentered and scaled to the original size.

15. After the if statement, set the _lastScale variable to the local currentScale variable.

16. To have the Image widget refresh the current scale, add the setState() method and populate the _currentScale value with the local currentScale variable.

```
void _onDoubleTap() {
  print('onDoubleTap');

  // Calculate current scale and populate the _lastScale with currentScale
  // if currentScale is greater than 16 times the original image, reset scale
to default, 1.0
  double currentScale = _lastScale * 2.0;
  if (currentScale > 16.0) {
    currentScale = 1.0;
    _resetToDefaultValues();
  }
  _lastScale = currentScale;

  setState(() {
    _currentScale = currentScale;
  });
}
```

17. Create the _onLongPress() method. This gesture is called when the user is pressing and holding on the screen. When a long press is detected, the image is reset to its original position and scale.

18. To have the Image widget refresh to the default position and scale, add the setState() method and call the _resetToDefaultValues() method.

```
void _onLongPress() {
  print('onLongPress');

  setState(() {
    _resetToDefaultValues();
  });
}
```

19. Create the `_resetToDefaultValues()` method. The purpose of this method is to reset all values to default with the `Image` widget centered on the screen and scaled back to original size. Creating this method is a great way to share code reuse from anywhere in the page.

```
void _resetToDefaultValues() {
  _startLastOffset = Offset.zero;
  _lastOffset = Offset.zero;
  _currentOffset = Offset.zero;
  _lastScale = 1.0;
  _currentScale = 1.0;
}
```

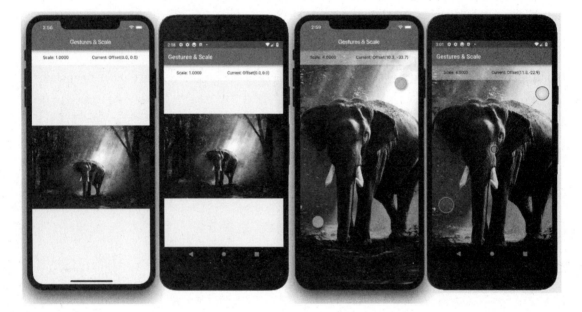

HOW IT WORKS

The `_onScaleStart()` method is called when a touch first begins to move or scale the image. The `_startLastOffset`, `_lastOffset`, and `_lastScale` variables are populated with values needed to properly position and scale the image by the `_onScaleUpdate()` method.

The `_onScaleUpdate()` method is called when the user is either moving or scaling the image. The details (`ScaleUpdateDetails`) object contains values such as the `scale`, `rotation`, and `focalPoint`. By using the `details.scale` value, you check whether the image is moving or scaling. If the `details.scale` is greater than `1.0`, the image is scaling larger, and if the `details.scale` is less than `1.0`, the image is scaling smaller. If the `details.scale` is equal to `1.0`, the image is moving.

The `_onDoubleTap()` method is called when the user is double tapping the screen. With each double tap, the image is scaled twice as large, and once it reaches 16 times the original size, the scale is reset to `1.0`, the original size.

The _onLongPress() method is called when the user is pressing and holding on the screen. When this gesture is detected, the image is reset to its original position and scale by calling the _resetToDefaultValues() method.

The _resetToDefaultValues() method is responsible for resetting all values back to default. The Image widget is moved back to the center of the screen and scaled to the original size.

USING THE INKWELL AND INKRESPONSE GESTURES

Both the InkWell and InkResponse widgets are Material Components that respond to touch gestures. The InkWell class extends (subclass) the InkResponse class. The InkResponse class extends a StatefulWidget class.

For the InkWell, the area that responds to touch is rectangular in shape and shows a "splash" effect—though it really looks like a ripple. The splash effect is clipped to the rectangular area of the widget (so as not go outside it). If you need to expand the splash effect outside the rectangular area, the InkResponse has a configurable shape. By default, the InkResponse shows a circular splash effect that can expand outside its shape (Figure 11.3).

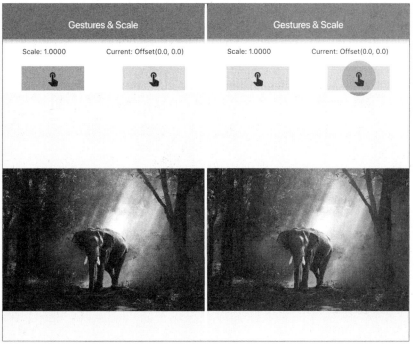

FIGURE 11.3: InkWell and InkResponse splash

Tapping the `InkWell` shows how the splash effect incrementally appears (Figure 11.4). In this scenario, the user tapped the left button, and it shows the splash effect gradually changing the button color from gray to a blue. The splash color stays inside the button's rectangular area.

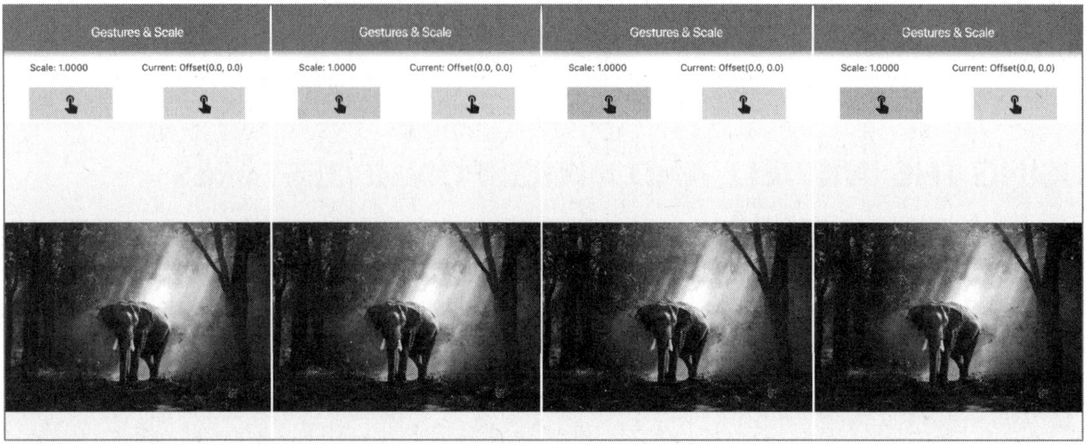

FIGURE 11.4: InkWell gradual splash inside rectangular area

Tapping the `InkResponse` shows how the splash effect incrementally appears (Figure 11.5). In this scenario the user tapped the right button, and it shows the circular splash effect gradually changing the button color from gray to a blue. The splash color circularly expands outside the button's rectangular area.

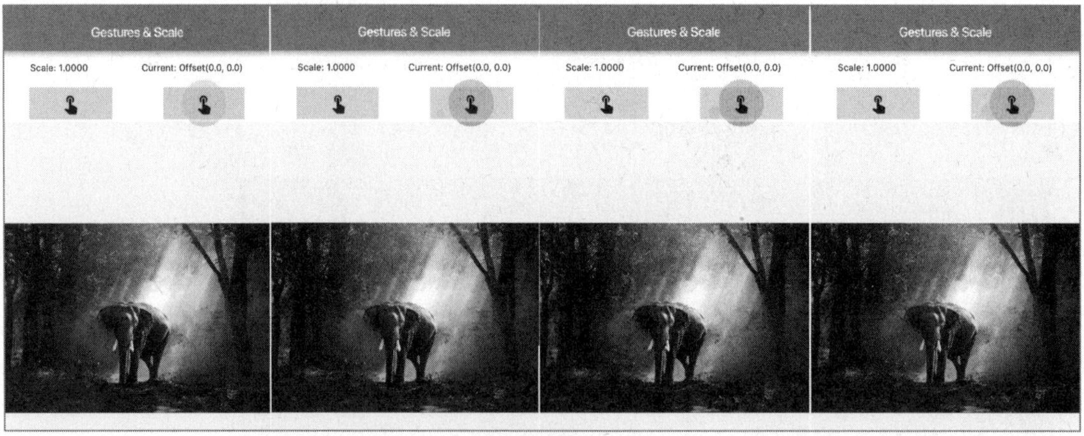

FIGURE 11.5: InkResponse gradual splash outside rectangular area

The following are the `InkWell` and `InkResponse` gestures that you can listen for and take appropriate action. The gestures captured are taps on the screen except for the `onHighlightChanged` property, which is called when part of the material starts or stops being highlighted.

➤ Tap

➤ `onTap`

➤ onTapDown

➤ onTapCancel

➤ Double tap

➤ onDoubleTap

➤ Long press

➤ onLongPress

➤ Highlight changed

➤ onHighlightChanged

TRY IT OUT Adding InkWell and InkResponse to the Gesture Status Bar

Continuing with the previous gestures project to compare how each widget performs, you'll add an `InkWell` and `InkResponse` to the current gesture status bar display.

1. In the `_buildBody(BuildContext context)` method, add a call to the `_positionedInkWellAndInkResponse(context)` method. Place this call after the `_positionedStatusBar(context)`
method.

```
Widget _buildBody(BuildContext context) {
  return GestureDetector(
    child: Stack(
      fit: StackFit.expand,
      children: <Widget>[
```

```
              //_transformScaleAndTranslate(),
              _transformMatrix4(),
              _positionedStatusBar(context),
              _positionedInkWellAndInkResponse(context),
            ],
          ),
          onScaleStart: _onScaleStart,
          onScaleUpdate: _onScaleUpdate,
          onDoubleTap: _onDoubleTap,
          onLongPress: _onLongPress,
        );
      }
```

2. Create the `_positionedInkWellAndInkResponse(BuildContext context)` `Positioned`
    method after the `_positionedStatusBar(BuildContext context)` method. Return a
    `Positioned` by using the `default` constructor. The purpose of this `Positioned` widget is to add to
    the current gesture status bar display the `InkWell` and `InkResponse` widgets.

3. Set the `top` property to `50.0` to position it below the previous `Positioned` widget (gesture status
    bar display) in the `Stack` widget.

4. Set the `width` property by using the `MediaQuery` width to expand the full width of the device. The
    `child` is a `Container` with the `color` property set to a shade of `Colors.white54`.

5. Set the `Container` `height` property to `56.0`. Set the `Container` `child` to a `Row` with the `mainAx-isAlignment` of `MainAxisAlignment.spaceAround`.

```
        Positioned _positionedInkWellAndInkResponse(BuildContext context) {
          return Positioned(
            top: 50.0,
            width: MediaQuery.of(context).size.width,
            child: Container(
              color: Colors.white54,
              height: 56.0,
              child: Row(
                mainAxisAlignment: MainAxisAlignment.spaceAround,
                children: <Widget>[

                ],
              ),
            ),
          );
        }
```

6. Add to the `Row` `children` list of `Widget` an `InkWell` and `InkResponse`. Since both widgets have the same properties, follow the same instructions for the `InkWell` and the `InkResponse`.

7. Set the `child` property to a `Container` with the `height` property set to `48.0`, the `width` property set to `128.0`, and the `color` property set to a light shade of `Colors.black12`. Set the `child` property to the `Icons.touch_app` with the `size` property of `32.0`.

8. To customize the splash color, set the `splashColor` property to `Colors.lightGreenAccent` and the `highlightColor` property to `Colors.lightBlueAccent`. The `splashColor` is displayed where the pointer first touched the screen, and the `highlightColor` is the splash (ripple) effect.

9. Add to the `InkWell` and `InkResponse` the `onTap`, `onDoubleTap`, and `onLongPress` to listen for each gesture. Respectively pass the `_setScaleSmall`, `_setScaleBig`, and `_onLongPress` methods.

```
Positioned _positionedInkWellAndInkResponse(BuildContext context) {
  return Positioned(
    top: 50.0,
    width: MediaQuery.of(context).size.width,
    child: Container(
      color: Colors.white54,
      height: 56.0,
      child: Row(
        mainAxisAlignment: MainAxisAlignment.spaceAround,
        children: <Widget>[
          InkWell(
            child: Container(
              height: 48.0,
              width: 128.0,
              color: Colors.black12,
              child: Icon(
                Icons.touch_app,
                size: 32.0,
              ),
            ),
            splashColor: Colors.lightGreenAccent,
            highlightColor: Colors.lightBlueAccent,
            onTap: _setScaleSmall,
            onDoubleTap: _setScaleBig,
            onLongPress: _onLongPress,
          ),
          InkResponse(
            child: Container(
```

```
            height: 48.0,
            width: 128.0,
            color: Colors.black12,
            child: Icon(
              Icons.touch_app,
              size: 32.0,
            ),
          ),
          splashColor: Colors.lightGreenAccent,
          highlightColor: Colors.lightBlueAccent,
          onTap: _setScaleSmall,
          onDoubleTap: _setScaleBig,
          onLongPress: _onLongPress,
        ),
      ],
    ),
   ),
  ),
 );
}
```

10. Create the _setScaleSmall() and _setScaleBig() methods after the _resetToDefault-
Values() method. For the _setScaleSmall() method, add a setState() to modify the
_currentScale variable to 0.5. When the onTap gesture is captured, it will decrease the image's
size to half of the original size.

For the _setScaleBig() method, add a setState() to modify the _currentScale variable to
16.0. When the onDoubleTap gesture is captured, it will increase the image size to 16 times the
original size.

```
void _setScaleSmall() {
  setState(() {
    _currentScale = 0.5;
  });
}

void _setScaleBig() {
  setState(() {
    _currentScale = 16.0;
  });
}
```

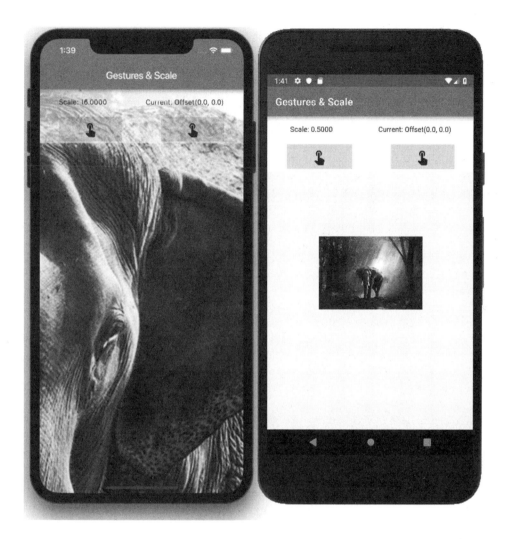

HOW IT WORKS

Both the InkWell and InkResponse widgets listen to the same gesture callbacks. The widgets capture the onTap, onDoubleTap, and onLongPress gestures (properties).

When a single tap is captured, the onTap calls the _setScaleSmall() method to scale the image to half the original size.

When a double tap is captured, the `onDoubleTap` calls the `_setScaleBig()` method to scale the image to 16 times the original size.

When a long press is captured, the `onLongPress` calls the `_onLongPress()` method to reset all values to the original positions and sizes.

The main benefits of using the `InkWell` and `InkResponse` are to capture taps on the screen and have a beautiful splash. This kind of reaction makes for a good UX, correlating an animation to a user's action.

USING THE DISMISSIBLE WIDGET

The `Dismissible` widget is dismissed by a dragging gesture. The direction of the drag can be changed by using `DismissDirection` for the `direction` property. (See Table 11.2 for `DismissDirection` options.) The `Dismissible child` widget slides out of view and automatically animates the height or width (depending on dismiss direction) down to zero. This animation happens in two steps; first the `Dismissible child` slides out of view, and second, the size animates down to zero. Once the `Dismissible` is dismissed, you can use the `onDismissed` callback to perform any necessary actions such as removing a data record from the database or marking a to-do item complete (Figure 11.6). If you do not handle the `onDismissed` callback, you'll receive the error "A dismissed `Dismissible` widget is still part of the tree." For example, if you use a `List` of items, once the `Dismissible` is removed you need to remove the item from the `List` by implementing the `onDismissed` callback. You'll take a detailed look at how to handle this in step 9 of the next exercise.

FIGURE 11.6: Dismissible widget showing the swiped row dismissed animation to complete the item

TABLE 11.2: `DismissDirection` Dismiss Options

DIRECTION	DISMISSED WHEN. . .
`startToEnd`	Dragging left to right.*
`endToStart`	Dragging right to left.*
`horizontal`	Dragging either left or right.
`up`	Dragging up.
`down`	Dragging down.
`vertical`	Dragging either up or down.

* Assuming reading direction is left to right; when reading direction is right to left, these work the opposite ways.

TRY IT OUT Creating the Dismissible App

In this example, you'll build a list of vacation trips, and when you drag from left to right, the `Dismissible` shows a checkbox icon with a green background to mark the trip completed. When swiping from right to left, the `Dismissible` shows a delete icon with a red background to remove the trip.

The `Dismissible` handles all the animations such as sliding, resizing to remove the selected row, and sliding the next item on the list upward.

You'll create a `Trip` class to hold the vacation details with an `id`, `tripName`, and `tripLocation` variables. You load a `List` to track the vacations by adding individual `Trip` details. The `body` property uses a `ListView.builder` that returns a `Dismissible` widget. You set the `Dismissible child` property to a `ListTile`, and the `background` and `secondaryBackground` properties return a `Container` with the child as a `Row` with a `children` list of `Widget` with an `Icon`.

Note that in this example to keep the widget tree shallow, you'll use methods instead of widget classes.

1. Create a new Flutter project and name it `ch11_dismissible`. Again, you can follow the instructions from Chapter 4. For this project, you only need to create the `pages` and `classes` folders. Create the `Home` `Class` as a `StatefulWidget` since the data (state) requires changes.

2. Open the `home.dart` file and add to the `body` a `ListView.builder()`.

```
body: ListView.builder(),
```

3. Add to the top of the file the import `trip.dart` package that you'll create next.

```
import 'package:flutter/material.dart';
import 'package:ch11_dismissible/classes/trip.dart';
```

4. Create a new Dart file under the `classes` folder. Right-click the `classes` folder, select New ⇨ Dart File, enter **trip.dart**, and click the OK button to save.

5. Create the `Trip` `Class`. The `Trip` `Class` holds the vacation details with an `id`, `tripName`, and `tripLocation` `String` variables. Create the `Trip` constructor with named parameters by entering the variable names `this.id`, `this.tripName`, and `this.tripLocation` inside the curly brackets ({}).

```
class Trip {
  String id;
  String tripName;
  String tripLocation;

  Trip({this.id, this.tripName, this.tripLocation});
}
```

6. Edit the `home.dart` file and after the `class _HomeState extends State<Home>` and before `@override`, add the `List` variable `_trips` initialized by an empty `Trip` `List`.

```
List _trips = List<Trip>();
```

7. Override the `initState()` to initialize the `_trips` `List`. You are going to add 11 items to the `_trips` `List`. Usually, this data would be read from a local database or a web server.

```
@override
void initState() {
  super.initState();
  _trips..add(Trip(id: '0', tripName: 'Rome', tripLocation: 'Italy'))
    ..add(Trip(id: '1', tripName: 'Paris', tripLocation: 'France'))
    ..add(Trip(id: '2', tripName: 'New York', tripLocation: 'USA - New York'))
    ..add(Trip(id: '3', tripName: 'Cancun', tripLocation: 'Mexico'))
    ..add(Trip(id: '4', tripName: 'London', tripLocation: 'England'))
    ..add(Trip(id: '5', tripName: 'Sydney', tripLocation: 'Australia'))
    ..add(Trip(id: '6', tripName: 'Miami', tripLocation: 'USA - Florida'))
    ..add(Trip(id: '7', tripName: 'Rio de Janeiro', tripLocation: 'Brazil'))
    ..add(Trip(id: '8', tripName: 'Cusco', tripLocation: 'Peru'))
    ..add(Trip(id: '9', tripName: 'New Delhi', tripLocation: 'India'))
    ..add(Trip(id: '10', tripName: 'Tokyo', tripLocation: 'Japan'));
}
```

8. Create two methods that simulate marking a `Trip` item completed or deleted in the database. Create the `_markTripCompleted()` and `_deleteTrip()` methods that act as placeholders to write to a database.

```
void _markTripCompleted() {
  // Mark trip completed in Database or web service
}

void _deleteTrip() {
  // Delete trip from Database or web service
}
```

9. Set the `ListView.builder` constructor with the `itemCount` argument set to `_trips.length`, which is the number of rows in the `_trips` List. For the `itemBuilder` argument, it takes the `BuildContext` and the widget `index` as an int value.

```
itemCount: _trips.length,
```

The `itemBuilder` returns a `Dismissible` with the `key` property as `Key(_trips[index].id)`. The `Key` is the identifier for each widget and must be unique, which is why you use the `_trips id` item. The `child` property is set to the `_buildListTile(index)` method, which passes the current widget `index`.

```
key: Key(_trips[index].id),
```

10. The `Dismissible` has a `background` (drag left to right) and the `secondaryBackground` (drag left to right) properties. Set the `background` property to the `_buildCompleteTrip()` method and set the `secondaryBackground` to the `_buildRemoveTrip()` method. Note that the `Dismissible` has an optional `direction` property that can set the restrictions on which direction to use.

```
child: _buildListTile(index),
background: _buildCompleteTrip(),
secondaryBackground: _buildRemoveTrip(),
```

The `onDismissed` callback (property) is called when the widget is dismissed, providing a function to run code by removing the dismissed widget item from the `_trips` List. In a real-world scenario, you would also update the database.

It's important that once the item is dismissed, it is removed from the `_trips` List or it will cause an error.

```
// A dismissed Dismissible widget is still part of the tree.
// Make sure to implement the onDismissed handler and to immediately remove the
Dismissible
// widget from the application once that handler has fired.
```

This makes sense since the item has been dismissed and removed. All of this is possible by using the unique `key` property.

The `onDismissed` passes the `DismissDirection` where you check with a ternary operator whether the direction is `startToEnd` and call the `_markTripCompleted()` method or otherwise call the _deleteTrip() method. The next step is to use the setState to remove the dismissed item from the _trips List by using the _trips.removeAt(index).

```
    body: ListView.builder(
      itemCount: _trips.length,
      itemBuilder: (BuildContext context, int index) {
        return Dismissible(
          key: Key(_trips[index].id),
          child: _buildListTile(index),
          background: _buildCompleteTrip(),
          secondaryBackground: _buildRemoveTrip(),
          onDismissed: (DismissDirection direction) {

direction == DismissDirection.startToEnd ? _markTripCompleted() : _deleteTrip();
          // Remove item from List
          setState(() {
            _trips.removeAt(index);
          });
        },
      );
    },
  ),
```

11. Add the _buildListTile(int index) Widget method after the Widget build(BuildContext context) {...}. Return a ListTile and set the title, subtitle, leading, and trailing properties.

12. Set the title property as a Text widget that shows the tripName and set the subtitle to tripLocation. Set the leading and trailing properties as Icons.

```
    ListTile _buildListTile(int index) {
      return ListTile(
          title: Text('${_trips[index].tripName}'),
          subtitle: Text(_trips[index].tripLocation),
          leading: Icon(Icons.flight),
          trailing: Icon(Icons.fastfood),
        );
    }
```

13. Add the _buildCompleteTrip() Widget method to return a Container with the color as green and the child property as a Padding. The Padding child is a Row with the alignment set to start (on the left side for left-to-right languages) with a children list of Widget of an Icon.

The background property is revealed when the user drags the item, and it's important to convey what action will take place. In this case, you are completing a trip, and you show a done (checkbox) Icon with a green background convening the action.

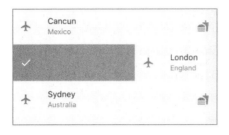

```
Container _buildCompleteTrip() {
  return Container(
        color: Colors.green,
        child: Padding(
          padding: const EdgeInsets.all(16.0),
          child: Row(
            mainAxisAlignment: MainAxisAlignment.start,
            children: <Widget>[
              Icon(
                Icons.done,
                color: Colors.white,
              ),
            ],
          ),
        ),
      );
}
```

14. Add the _buildRemoveTrip() Widget method to return a Container with the color as red and the child property as a Padding. The Padding child is a Row with the alignment set to end (on the right side for left-to-right languages) with a children list of Widget of an Icon.

The secondaryBackground property is revealed when the user drags the item, and it's important to convey what action will take place. In this case, you are deleting a trip, and you show a delete (trash can) Icon with a red background convening the action.

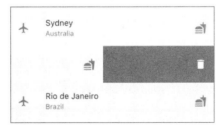

```
Container _buildRemoveTrip() {
    return Container(
        color: Colors.red,
```

```
            child: Padding(
              padding: const EdgeInsets.all(16.0),
              child: Row(
                mainAxisAlignment: MainAxisAlignment.end,
                children: <Widget>[
                  Icon(
                    Icons.delete,
                    color: Colors.white,
                  ),
                ],
              ),
            ),
          );
      }
```

HOW IT WORKS

You used a ListView to build a list of Trip details. The ListView itemBuilder returns a Dismissible with a key property set by using the Key class as a unique identifier for each widget. Using the key property is extremely important because the Dismissible uses it when it replaces one widget with another in the widget tree.

To convey the appropriate action when the user is dragging (left to right), you customized the background property to reveal a green background with a done Icon. When the user is dragging (right to left), you customized the secondaryBackground property to reveal a red background with a delete Icon.

You used the onDismissed callback (property) to check for the DismissDirection and take appropriate action. By using the ternary operator, you checked whether the direction was from startToEnd, and you called the _markTripCompleted() method; otherwise, you called the _deleteTrip() method. Next, you used the setState to remove the current item from the _trips List.

SUMMARY

In this chapter, you learned how to use a GestureDetector to handle onTap, onDoubleTap, onLongPress, and onPanUpdate gestures. The onPanUpdate is suitable to use when you need to track dragging in any direction. You took an in-depth look at using the GestureDetector to move, scale by zooming in/out, double tap to increase zoom, and long press to reset the elephant image to original size. For example, these techniques would be applied to a journaling app when a user selected an image and wanted to look closer at details. To accomplish this goal, you used the onScaleStart and onScaleUpdate to scale the image. Use the onDoubleTap to increase the zoom and onLongPress to reset the zoom to the original default size.

You learned two different techniques to scale and move the image when a gesture is detected. With the first technique, you used the Transform widget by nesting the Transform.scale constructor to resize the image and the Transform.translate constructor to move the image. For the second technique, you used the Transform default constructor by using the Matrix4 to apply the transformations. By using the Matrix4, you executed multiple cascading transformations (..scale()..translate()) without the need to nest multiple Transform widgets.

You used the InkWell and InkResponse to respond to touch gestures like tap, double tap, and long press. Both widgets are Material Components (Flutter material design widgets) that display a splashing effect when tapped.

You implemented the drag-and-drop feature by using the Draggable and DragTarget widgets. These widgets are used in conjunction. The Draggable widget has a data property that passes information to the DragTarget widget. The DragTarget widget can accept or refuse the data, which gives you the ability to check for the correct data format. In this example, you dragged the paint palette Icon (Draggable) over the Text (DragTarget) widget, and once you let go, the Text color changes to red.

The Dismissible widget listens to vertical and horizontal dragging gestures. By using the DismissDirection for the direction property, you can limit which dragging gestures you listen to, such as restricting to horizontal-only gestures. In this example, you created a List of Trip items that are displayed with the ListView.builder. When the user drags an item on the list from left to right, a green background with a checkbox Icon is revealed to convey the action that is about to be performed, completing the trip. But if the user drags on the list item from right to left, a red background with a trash can Icon is revealed to convey the action that the trip is going to be deleted. How does the `Dismissible` know which item to delete? By using the `Dismissible key` property, you passed a unique identifier for each item on the list, and once the `onDismissed` (callback) property is called, you checked the direction of the drag and took appropriate action. You then used the `setState` to make sure the dismissed item is removed from the `_trips` list. It is important to handle the `onDismissed` callback or you will receive the error "A dismissed Dismissible widget is still part of the tree."

In the next chapter, you'll learn how to write iOS and Android platform-specific code. You'll be using Swift for iOS and Kotlin for Android. These platform channels give you the ability to use native features such as accessing the device GPS location, local notifications, local file system, sharing, and many more.

▶ **WHAT YOU LEARNED IN THIS CHAPTER**

TOPIC	KEY CONCEPTS
Implementing `GestureDetector`	This widget recognizes gestures such as tap, double tap, long press, pan, vertical drag, horizontal drag, and scale.
Implementing `Draggable`	This widget is dragged to a `DragTarget`.
Implementing `DragTarget`	This widget receives data from a `Draggable`.
Implementing `InkWell` and `InkResponse`	The `InkWell` is a rectangular area that responds to touch and clips splashes within its area. The `InkResponse` responds to touch, and the splashes expand outside its area.
Implementing `Dismissible`	This widget is dismissed by dragging.

12

Writing Platform-Native Code

WHAT YOU WILL LEARN IN THIS CHAPTER

➤ How to use platform channels to send and receive messages from the Flutter app to iOS and Android to access specific API functionality

➤ How to write native platform code in iOS Swift and Android Kotlin to access device information

➤ How to use `MethodChannel` to send messages from the Flutter app (on the client side)

➤ How to use `FlutterMethodChannel` on iOS and `MethodChannel` on Android to receive calls and send back results (on the host side)

Platform channels give you the ability to use native features such as accessing the device information, GPS location, local notifications, local file system, sharing, and many more. In the "External Packages" section of Chapter 2, "Creating a Hello World App," you learned how to use third-party packages to add functionality to your apps. In this chapter, instead of relying on third-party packages, you'll learn how to add custom functionality to your apps by using platform channels and writing the API code yourself. You'll build an app that asks the iOS and Android platforms to return the device information.

UNDERSTANDING PLATFORM CHANNELS

When you need to access platform-specific APIs for iOS and Android, you use platform channels to send and receive messages. The Flutter app is the client, and the platform-native code for iOS and Android is the host. If needed, it is also possible to have the platform-native code to act as a client to call methods written in the Flutter app dart code.

The messages between the client and host are asynchronous, making sure that the UI remains responsive and not blocked. In Chapter 3, "Learning Dart Basics," you learned that `async` functions perform time-consuming operations without waiting for those operations to complete.

For the client side (Flutter app), you use the `MethodChannel` from an `async` method to send messages that contain the method call to be executed by the host side (iOS and Android). Once the host sends the response back, you can update the UI to display the information received.

For the host side, you use the `FlutterMethodChannel` on iOS and the `MethodChannel` on Android. Once the client call is received by the host, the native platform code executes the called method and then sends back the result (Figure 12.1).

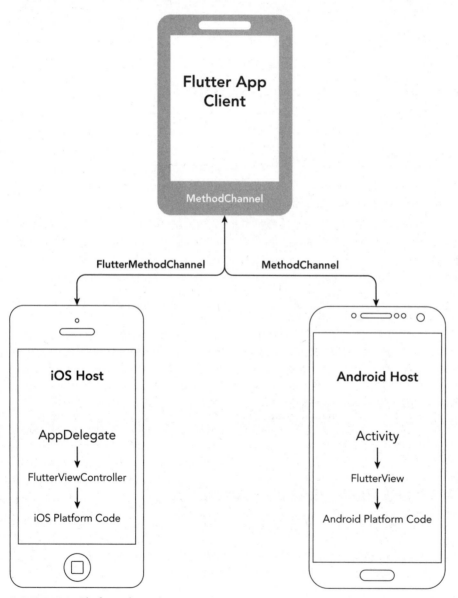

FIGURE 12.1: Platform channel messages

IMPLEMENTING THE CLIENT PLATFORM CHANNEL APP

To start communication from the Flutter client app to the iOS and Android platforms, you use the `MethodChannel`. A `MethodChannel` uses asynchronous method calls, and the channel requires a unique name. The channel name needs to be the same for the client as for the iOS and Android host. I suggest when you're creating a unique name for the channel that you use the app name, a domain prefix, and a descriptive name for the task such as `platformchannel.companyname.com/deviceinfo`.

```
// Name template
appname.domain.com/taskname
// Channel name
platformchannel.companyname.com/deviceinfo
```

At first, it seems that you are going overboard naming the channel, so why is it important for the name to be unique? If you have multiple named channels and they share the same name, they will cause conflicts with each other's messages.

To implement a channel, you create the `MethodChannel` through the default constructor by passing the unique channel name. The default constructor takes two arguments: the first is the channel name, and the second (which is optional) declares the default `MethodCodec`. The `MethodCodec` is the `StandardMethodCodec`, which uses Flutter's standard binary encoding; this means the serialization of data sent between the client and the host is automatically handled. Since you know the name of the channel at compile time and it will not change, you create the `MethodChannel` to a `static const` variable. Make sure you use the `static` keyword, or you will receive the error "Only static fields can be declared as const."

```
static const platform = const
MethodChannel('platformchannel.companyname.com/deviceinfo');
```

Table 12.1 displays the supported value types for Dart, iOS, and Android.

TABLE 12.1: StandardMessageCodec-Supported Value Types

DART	iOS	ANDROID
null	nil	null
bool	NSNumber numberWithBool:	java.lang.Boolean
int	NSNumber numberWithInt:	java.lang.Integer
int (bigger than 32 bits)	NSNumber numberWithLong:	java.lang.Long
double	NSNumber numberWithDouble:	java.lang.Double
String	NSString	java.lang.String
Uint8List	FlutterStandardTypedData typedDataWithBytes:	byte[]

continues

TABLE 12.1: *(continued)*

DART	iOS	ANDROID
Int32List	FlutterStandardTypedData typedDataWithInt32:	int []
Int64List	FlutterStandardTypedData typedDataWithInt64:	long []
Float64List	FlutterStandardTypedData typedDataWithFloat64:	double []
List	NSArray	java. util.ArrayList
Map	NSDictionary	java.util.HashMap

To call and specify which method to execute on the iOS and Android host, you use the invoke-Method constructor to pass the method name as a `String`. The invokeMethod is called from inside a Future method since the call is asynchronous.

```
String deviceInfo = await platform.invokeMethod('getDeviceInfo');
```

Once the client and the iOS and Android platform channels are implemented, the Flutter client side of the app will display the appropriate device information depending on the device (Figure 12.2).

TRY IT OUT Creating the Client Platform Channel App

In this example, you want to display the running device information such as the manufacturer, device model, name, operating system, and a few other details. The Flutter app client is written in Dart (as usual) and implements the MethodChannel to initiate a call to the iOS and Android host.

➤ The iOS host is written in Swift to access the platform API call to the UIDevice to query the device information and uses the FlutterMethodChannel to receive and return the requested information.

➤ The Android host is written in Kotlin to access the platform API call to the Build to query the device information and uses the MethodChannel to receive and return the requested information.

This app is divided into three different "Try It Out" exercises. In this first one, you'll concentrate on creating the client-side request. In the second one, "Creating the iOS Host Platform Channel," you'll build the iOS Host Platform Channel, and in the third exercise, "Creating the Android Host Platform Channel," you'll build the Android Host Platform Channel. If you run the app after this first section is completed, you will receive the error "Failed to get device info" since you have not written the iOS and Android host code yet. Note that the iOS and Android projects are independent of each other, and you can target both or only one, and you will receive the error on the platform that you run.

1. Create a new Flutter project and name it ch12_platform_channel; as always, you can follow the instructions in Chapter 4, "Creating a Starter Project Template." For this project, you need to create only the pages folder.

2. Open the home.dart file and add to the body a SafeArea with the child as a ListTile.

```
body: SafeArea(
   child: ListTile(),
),
```

3. After the class _HomeState extends State<Home> and before @override, add the static const variable _methodChannel initialized by the MethodChannel with the name platformchannel.companyname.com/deviceinfo.

```
static const _methodChannel = const MethodChannel('platformchannel.companyname.
com/deviceinfo');
```

4. Declare the _deviceInfo String variable that will receive the device information from the iOS and Android host call.

```
// Get device info
String _deviceInfo = '';
```

5. Create the _getDeviceInfo() async call that uses the _methodChannel.invokeMethod() to initiate the call to the iOS and Android host. This method is declared as a Future<void> and marked as async.

```
Future<void> _getDeviceInfo() async {
}
```

6. Create the local deviceInfo String variable that receives the device information.

```
String deviceInfo;
```

It's good practice to use the try-catch exception handling when calling the methodChannel .invokeMethod('getDeviceInfo') just in case the call fails. The invokeMethod takes the getDeviceInfo method name that needs to be the same one that you declare in both the iOS and Android host code.

```
try {
   deviceInfo = await methodChannel.invokeMethod('getDeviceInfo');
} on PlatformException catch (e) {
   deviceInfo = "Failed to get device info: '${e.message}'.";
}
```

7. Add the setState() method that populates the _deviceInfo (available class-wide) variable from the local deviceInfo value. In Chapter 3, "Learning Dart Basics," in the "Asynchronous Programming" section, you learned how to use the Future object.

```
Future<void> _getDeviceInfo() async {
   String deviceInfo;
   try {
      deviceInfo = await _methodChannel.invokeMethod('getDeviceInfo');
   } on PlatformException catch (e) {
      deviceInfo = "Failed to get device info: '${e.message}'.";
   }
}
```

```
            setState(() {
              _deviceInfo = deviceInfo;
            });
          }
```

8. Override the `initState()` to call the `_getDeviceInfo()` method. Once the app starts, it makes the `_getDeviceInfo()` call start retrieving device information.

```
          @override
          void initState() {
            super.initState();
            _getDeviceInfo();
          }
```

9. Let's go back to the `body` property and finish the `ListTile` widget to display the device information. For the `title` property, add a `Text` widget to show the Device Info heading, and set the `TextStyle` to `fontSize` 24.0 and `FontWeight.bold`.

10. For the `subtitle` property, add a `Text` widget with the `_deviceInfo` variable that shows the actual device information, and set the `TextStyle` to `fontSize` 18.0 and `FontWeight.bold`.

11. Add a `contentPadding` property to the `ListTile`, and set the `EdgeInsets.all()` to 16.0 to add some nice padding around the information.

```
          body: SafeArea(
            child: ListTile(
              title: Text(
                'Device info:',
                style: TextStyle(
                  fontSize: 24.0,
                  fontWeight: FontWeight.bold,
                ),
              ),
              subtitle: Text(
                _deviceInfo,
                style: TextStyle(
                  fontSize: 18.0,
                  fontWeight: FontWeight.bold,
                ),
              ),
              contentPadding: EdgeInsets.all(16.0),
            ),
          ),
```

HOW IT WORKS

In this client section of the app, you created the `MethodChannel` with a unique name to a `static const` `_methodChannel` variable. The `methodChannel` is used to communicate between the client and the host using the asynchronous method call. Using the `_getDeviceInfo()` `Future<void>` method, the `_methodChannel.invokeMethod('getDeviceInfo')` calls the host to execute the `getDeviceInfo` method in the iOS and Android platforms. Once the data is returned, the `setState()` method populates the `_deviceInfo` variable, and the `ListTile` `subtitle` is updated with the device information.

FIGURE 12.2: iOS and Android device information

IMPLEMENTING THE iOS HOST PLATFORM CHANNEL

The host is responsible for listening to incoming messages from the client. Once a message is received, the channel checks for a matching method name, executes the call method, and returns the appropriate result. In iOS, you use the `FlutterMethodChannel` for listening to incoming messages that take two parameters. The first parameter is the same platform channel name—`'platformchannel.` `companyname.com/deviceinfo'`—as the client. The second is the `FlutterViewController`, which is the main `rootViewController` of an iOS app. The `rootViewController` is the root view controller for the iOS app window that provides the content view of the window.

```
let flutterViewController: FlutterViewController = window?.rootViewController as!
FlutterViewController
let deviceInfoChannel = FlutterMethodChannel(name: "platformchannel.companyname.
com/deviceinfo", binaryMessenger: controller)
```

You then use the setMethodCallHandler (Future handler) to set up a callback for a matching method name that executes the iOS native platform code. Once completed, it sends back the result to the client.

```
deviceInfoChannel.setMethodCallHandler({
    (call: FlutterMethodCall, result: FlutterResult) -> Void in
    // Check for incoming method call name and return a result
})
```

Both the FlutterMethodChannel and the setMethodCallHandler will be placed in the didFinishLaunchingWithOptions method of the iOS app AppDelegate.swift file. The didFinishLaunchingWithOptions is responsible for notifying the app delegate that the app launch process is almost done.

```
override func application(
  _ application: UIApplication,
  didFinishLaunchingWithOptions launchOptions:
[UIApplicationLaunchOptionsKey: Any]?
) -> Bool {
  // Code
}
```

TRY IT OUT Creating the iOS Host Platform Channel

In this example, you want to retrieve the running device information such as the manufacturer, device model, name, operating system, and a few other details. The iOS host is written in Swift to access the platform API call to the UIDevice object to query the device information and uses the FlutterMethodChannel to receive communication from the client. Once the message is received, the setMethodCallHandler handles the request and returns the result.

In this section, you'll open Xcode and edit the native iOS Swift code.

1. If you closed the Flutter project ch12_platform_channel, reopen it. Click the Android Studio Tools menu bar and select Flutter ⇨ Open iOS module in Xcode. Note that this menu item selection opens the Xcode app with the iOS project, but you can also open the iOS project manually by double-clicking the Runner.xcworkspace file located in the ios folder. A Mac computer with Xcode installed is required to edit the iOS host project.

2. On the navigator area (left side), expand the `Runner` folder by clicking the arrow and then select the `AppDelegate.swift` file.

3. Edit the `didFinishLaunchingWithOptions` method; you'll be adding code before the line `GeneratedPluginRegistrant` call. Declare the `flutterViewController` variable as a `FlutterViewController` and initiate it with the `window?.rootViewController as!` `FlutterViewController`.

```
let flutterViewController: FlutterViewController = window?.rootViewController
as! FlutterViewController
```

4. In the next line, declare the `deviceInfoChannel` variable by initiating it with the `FlutterMethodChannel`.

5. For the `FlutterMethodChannel`'s first parameter, `name`, pass the Flutter channel name, the same one declared in the client. The second parameter, `binaryMessenger`, takes the `flutterViewController` variable.

```
let deviceInfoChannel = FlutterMethodChannel(name: "platformchannel
.companyname.com/deviceinfo", binaryMessenger: flutterViewController)
```

6. Add the `deviceInfoChannel.setMethodCallHandler` to set up a callback that matches the incoming method name of `getDeviceInfo` by using an `if-else` statement. If the `call.method` matches (`==`) the `getDeviceInfo`, then you call the `self.getDeviceInfo(result: result)` method (that you create in the next step) that retrieves the device information.

If the `call.method` does not match the incoming method name, the `else` statement returns the `result(FlutterMethodNotImplemented)`. The `FlutterMethodNotImplemented` is a constant that responds to the `call` that the method is unknown, or not implemented.

```
deviceInfoChannel.setMethodCallHandler({
    (call: FlutterMethodCall, result: FlutterResult) -> Void in
    if (call.method == "getDeviceInfo") {
        self.getDeviceInfo(result: result)
    }
    else {
        result(FlutterMethodNotImplemented)
    }
})
```

7. After the `didFinishLaunchingWithOptions` method, add the `getDeviceInfo(result:` `FlutterResult)` method that uses the iOS Swift `UIDevice.current` to query and retrieve the current device information.

8. Declare the `let device` variable by initializing it with the `UIDevice.current`. The `let` keyword is similar to the Dart `final` keyword, telling the compiler the value will not change. Declare the `deviceInfo String` variable and initialize it to an empty string by using double quotes (`""`).

To format the result to the `deviceInfo` variable, you use the `\n` characters to start a new line for each piece of information. By using string concatenation, you use the `=+` sign to add each line to the `deviceInfo` variable. In Swift, inside a `String`, you use the `\()` character combination to extract the value of the expression inside.

```
private func getDeviceInfo(result: FlutterResult) {
    let device = UIDevice.current
    var deviceInfo: String = ""
    deviceInfo = "\nName: \(device.name)"
```

```
        deviceInfo += "\nModel: \(device.model)"
        deviceInfo += "\nSystem: \(device.systemName) \(device.systemVersion)"
        deviceInfo += "\nProximity Monitoring Enabled: \(device.
isProximityMonitoringEnabled)"
        deviceInfo += "\nMultitasking Supported: \(device.isMultitaskingSupported)"
        result(deviceInfo)
    }
```

HOW IT WORKS

In the iOS host section of the app, you are listening for incoming messages by using the
`FlutterMethodChannel`. The `FlutterMethodChannel` expects two parameters, the `name` and the
`binaryMessenger`. The `name` parameter is the Flutter channel name declared in the client app
`platformchannel.companyname.com/deviceinfo`. The `binaryMessenger` parameter is the
`FlutterViewController` initiated by the iOS app `window?.rootViewController`.

You set up a callback with the `setMethodCallHandler` to match the incoming method name of `getDeviceInfo` by using an `if-else` statement. If the `call.method` matched the method name, you call the `getDeviceInfo` method to retrieve the device information and return a result. The device information is obtained by querying the `UIDevice.current` object. If the `call.method` does not match the incoming method name, the `else` statement returns the `FlutterMethodNotImplemented`.

IMPLEMENTING THE ANDROID HOST PLATFORM CHANNEL

The host is responsible for listening for incoming messages from the client. Once a message is received, the channel checks for a matching method name, executes the call method, and returns the appropriate result. In Android, you use the `MethodChannel` to listen to incoming messages that take two parameters. The first parameter is the `FlutterView`, which extends the `Activity` of an Android app screen and, by using the `flutterView` variable as the parameter, is the same as calling the `getFlutterView()` (`FlutterView`) method from the `FlutterActivity` class. The second parameter is the same platform channel name `platformchannel.companyname.com/deviceinfo` as the client.

```
private val DEVICE_INFO_CHANNEL = "platformchannel.companyname.com/deviceinfo"
val methodChannel = MethodChannel(flutterView, DEVICE_INFO_CHANNEL)
```

You then use the `setMethodCallHandler` (`Future handler`) to set up a callback for a matching method name that executes the Android native platform code. Once completed, it sends the result to the client.

```
methodChannel.setMethodCallHandler { call, result ->
    // Check for incoming method call name and return a result
}
```

Both the `MethodChannel` and the `setMethodCallHandler` are placed in the `onCreate` method of the Android app's `MainActivity.kt` file. The `onCreate` is called when the activity is first created.

```
override fun onCreate(savedInstanceState: Bundle?) {
    // Code
}
```

TRY IT OUT   Creating the Android Host Platform Channel

In this example, you want to retrieve the running device information such as the manufacturer, device model, name, operating system, and a few other details. The Android host is written in Kotlin to access the platform API call to the `Build` class to query the device information and uses the `MethodChannel` to receive communication from the client. Once the message is received, the `setMethodCallHandler` handles the request and returns the result.

In this section, you'll open another instance of Android Studio and edit the native Android Kotlin code.

1.   If you closed the Flutter project `ch12_platform_channel`, reopen it. Click on the Android Studio Tools menu bar and select Flutter ⇨ Open for Editing in Android Studio.

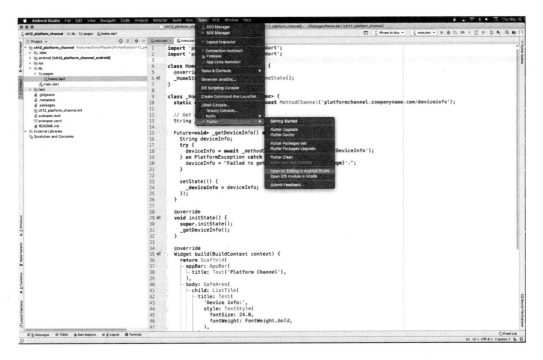

2. On the tool window area (on the left side), expand the `app` folder by clicking the arrow, open the `java` folder, open the `com.domainname.ch12platformchannel` folder, and then select the `MainActivity.kt` file. Note the `domainname` might be different depending on the name that you chose when creating the Flutter project.

3. Add two `import` statements before the `MainActivity` class. The first `import` statement adds support for the `MethodChannel`, and the second adds support to use the `Build` to query for the device information.

```
import io.flutter.plugin.common.MethodChannel
import android.os.Build
```

4. Edit the `onCreate` method, and you'll be adding code after the `GeneratedPluginRegistrant` call. Declare the `deviceInfoChannel` variable by initiating it with the `MethodChannel`.

5. For the `MethodChannel`'s first parameter, `BinaryMessenser`, pass the `flutterView` variable; note that you did not declare this variable. You do not need to declare it since it's the same as calling the `getFlutterView()` method from the `FlutterActivity` class.

6. For the second parameter, pass the Flutter channel name `platformchannel.companyname.com/deviceinfo`, the same one declared in the client.

```
val deviceInfoChannel = MethodChannel(flutterView, "platformchannel
.companyname.com/deviceinfo")
```

7. Add the `deviceInfoChannel.setMethodCallHandler` to set up a callback that matches the incoming method name of `getDeviceInfo` by using an `if-else` statement. If the `call.method` matches (`==`) the `getDeviceInfo`, then you call the `getDeviceInfo()` method (that you create in the next step) that retrieves the device information, and the result is saved to the `deviceInfo` variable. If the `call.method` does not match the incoming method name, the `else` statement returns the `result.notImplemented()`. The `notImplemented()` method responds to the `call` that the method is unknown, or not implemented.

```
deviceInfoChannel.setMethodCallHandler { call, result ->
    if (call.method == "getDeviceInfo") {
      val deviceInfo = getDeviceInfo()
      result.success(deviceInfo)
    } else {
      result.notImplemented()
    }
}
```

8. After the `onCreate` method, add the `getDeviceInfo(): String` method that uses the Android `Build` to query and retrieve the current device information.

To format the result, you use the `\n` characters to start a new line for each piece of information. By using string concatenation, you use the `+` sign to add each line and return the formatted result. The entire string concatenation is enclosed in open and close parentheses (`"..."`).

```
private fun getDeviceInfo(): String {
    return ("\nDevice: " + Build.DEVICE
      + "\nManufacturer: " + Build.MANUFACTURER
      + "\nModel: " + Build.MODEL
      + "\nProduct: " + Build.PRODUCT
      + "\nVersion Release: " + Build.VERSION.RELEASE
      + "\nVersion SDK: " + Build.VERSION.SDK_INT
      + "\nFingerprint : " + Build.FINGERPRINT)
}
```

HOW IT WORKS

In the Android host section of the app, you are listening for incoming messages by using the `MethodChannel`. The `MethodChannel` expects two parameters, the `binaryMessenger` and the `name`. The `binaryMessenger` parameter is the `flutterView`, which is the `getFlutterView()` method from the `FlutterActivity` class that extends the `Activity` of an Android app screen. The `name` parameter is the Flutter channel name declared in the client app `platformchannel.companyname.com/deviceinfo`.

You set up a callback with the `setMethodCallHandler` to match the incoming method name of `getDeviceInfo` by using an `if-else` statement. If the `call.method` matched the method name, you call the `getDeviceInfo` method to retrieve the device information and return a result. The device information is obtained by querying the `Build` class. If the `call.method` does not match the incoming method name, the `else` statement returns the `result.notImplemented()`.

SUMMARY

In this chapter, you learned how to access and communicate with iOS and Android platform-specific API code by implementing platform channels. Platform channels are a way for the Flutter app (client) to communicate (messages) with iOS and Android (host) to request and receive results specific to the operating system (OS). For the UI to remain responsive and not blocked, the messages between the client and host are asynchronous.

To start communicating from the Flutter app (client), you learned to use the `MethodChannel` that sends messages that contain method calls to be executed by the iOS and Android (host) side. Once the host processes the method requested, it then sends back a response to the client, and you update the UI to display the information. The `MethodChannel` uses a unique name, and you used a combination of the app name, the domain prefix, and the task name like `platformchannel.companyname.com/deviceinfo`. To start the call from the client and specify which method to execute on the host, you learned to use the `invokeMethod` constructor, and it is called from inside a `Future` method since calls are `asynchronous`.

For the iOS and Android host, you learned to use the Flutter `FlutterMethodChannel` on iOS and the `MethodChannel` on Android to start receiving communications from the client. The host is responsible for listening to incoming messages from the client. You used the `setMethodCallHandler` to set up a callback for an incoming matching method name that executes on the native platform-specific API code. Once the method completes, it sends the result to the client.

In the next chapter, you'll learn to use local persistence to save data locally to the device storage area.

▶ **WHAT YOU LEARNED IN THIS CHAPTER**

TOPIC	KEY CONCEPTS
Implementing `MethodChannel` (client)	This enables communication from the Flutter app (client) by sending messages that contain method calls to be executed by the iOS and Android (host).
Implementing `invokeMethod` (client)	This initiates (invokes) and specifies which method call to execute on the host side.
Implementing `FlutterMethodChannel` (iOS host) Implementing `MethodChannel` (Android host)	This enables communication from the host to receive method calls to execute platform-specific API code.
Implementing `setMethodCallHandler` (iOS and Android host)	This sets up a callback for incoming matching method names to execute platform-specific API code.

PART III
Creating Production-Ready Apps

13

Saving Data with Local Persistence

WHAT YOU WILL LEARN IN THIS CHAPTER

- ➤ How to persist saving and reading data locally
- ➤ How to structure data by using the JSON file format
- ➤ How to create model classes to handle JSON serialization
- ➤ How to access local iOS and Android filesystem locations using the path provider package
- ➤ How to format dates by using the internationalization package
- ➤ How to use the `Future` class with the `showDatePicker` to present a calendar to choose dates
- ➤ How to use the `Future` class to save, read, and parse JSON files
- ➤ How to use the `ListView.separated` constructor to section records with a `Divider`
- ➤ How to use `List().sort` to sort journal entries by date
- ➤ How to use `textInputAction` to customize keyboard actions
- ➤ How to use `FocusNode` and `FocusScope` with the keyboard `onSubmitted` to move the cursor to the next entry's `TextField`
- ➤ How to pass and receive data in a class by using the `Navigator`

In this chapter, you'll learn how to *persist* data—that is, save data on the device's local storage directory—across app launches by using the JSON file format and saving the file to the local iOS and Android filesystem. JavaScript Object Notation (JSON) is a common open-standard and language-independent file data format with the benefit of being human-readable text. Persisting data is a two-step process; first you use the `File` class to save and read data, and second, you parse the data from and to a JSON format. You'll create a class to handle saving and reading the data file that uses the `File` class. You'll also create a class to parse the full list of data by using `json.encode` and `json.decode` and a class to extract each record. And you'll create another class to handle passing an action and an individual journal entry between pages.

You'll build a journal app that saves and reads JSON data to the local iOS `NSDocumentDirectory` and Android `AppData` filesystem. The app uses a `ListView` to display a list of journal entries sorted by date, and you'll create a data entry screen to enter a date, mood, and note.

UNDERSTANDING THE JSON FORMAT

The JSON format is text-based and is independent of programming languages, meaning any of them can use it. It's a great way to exchange data between different programs because it is human-readable text. JSON uses the key/value pair, and the key is enclosed in quotation marks followed by a colon and then the value like `"id":"100"`. You use a comma (`,`) to separate multiple key/value pairs. Table 13.1 shows some examples.

TABLE 13.1: Key/Value Pairs

KEY	COLON	VALUE
`"id"`	:	`"100"`
`"quantity"`	:	3
`"in_stock"`	:	true

The types of values you can use are Object, Array, String, Boolean, and Number. Objects are declared by curly (`{}`) brackets, and inside you use the key/value pair and arrays. You declare arrays by using the square (`[]`) brackets, and inside you use the key/value or just the value. Table 13.2 shows some examples.

TABLE 13.2: Objects and Arrays

TYPE	SAMPLE

Object	`{`
	`  "id": "100",`
	`  "name": "Vacation"`
	`}`

Array with values only	`["Family", "Friends", "Fun"]`

TYPE	SAMPLE

Array with key/value	```json
	[
	    {
	        "id": "100",
	        "name": "Vacation"
	    },
	    {
	        "id": "102",
	        "name": "Birthday"
	    }
	]
	``

Object with array	```json
	{
	    "id": "100",
	    "name": "Vacation",
	    "tags": ["Family", "Friends", "Fun"]
	}
	``

Multiple objects with arrays	```json
	{
	    "journals":[
	        {
	            "id":"4710827",
	            "mood":"Happy"
	        },
	        {
	            "id":"427836",
	            "mood":"Surprised"
	        },
	    ],
	    "tags":[
	        {
	            "id": "100",
	            "name": "Family"
	        },
	        {
	            "id": "102",
	            "name": "Friends"
	        }
	    ]
	}
	``

The following is an example of the JSON file that you'll create for the journal application. The JSON file is used to save and read the journal data from the device local storage area, resulting in data persistence over app launches. You have the opening and closing curly brackets declaring an object. Inside the object, the journal's key contains an array of objects separated by a comma. Each object inside the array is a journal entry with key/value pairs declaring the id, date, mood, and note. The id key value is used to uniquely identify each journal entry and isn't displayed in the UI. How the value is obtained depends on the project requirement; for example, you can use sequential numbers or calculate a unique value by using characters and numbers (universally unique identifier [UUID]).

```
{
  "journals":[
    {
        "id":"470827",
        "date":"2019-01-13 00:27:10.167177",
        "mood":"Happy",
        "note":"Cannot wait for family night."
    },
    {
        "id":"427836",
        "date":"2019-01-12 19:54:18.786155",
        "mood":"Happy",
        "note":"Great day watching our favorite shows."
    },
  ],
}
```

USING DATABASE CLASSES TO WRITE, READ, AND SERIALIZE JSON

To create reusable code to handle the database routines such as writing, reading, and serializing (encoding and decoding) data, you'll place the logic in classes. You'll create four classes to handle local persistence, with each class responsible for specific tasks.

➤ The DatabaseFileRoutines class uses the File class to retrieve the device local document directory and save and read the data file.

➤ The Database class is responsible for encoding and decoding the JSON file and mapping it to a List.

➤ The Journal class maps each journal entry from and to JSON.

➤ The JournalEdit class is used to pass an action (save or cancel) and a journal entry between pages.

The DatabaseFileRoutines class requires you to import the dart:io library to use the File class responsible for saving and reading files. It also requires you to import the path_provider package to retrieve the local path to the document directory. The Database class requires you to import the dart:convert library to decode and encode JSON objects.

The first task in local persistence is to retrieve the directory path where the data file is located on the device. Local data is usually stored in the application documents directory; for iOS, the folder is called NSDocumentDirectory, and for Android it's AppData. To get access to these folders, you use the path_provider package (Flutter plugin). You'll be calling the getApplicationDocuments-Directory() method, which returns the directory giving you access to the path variable.

```
Future<String> get _localPath async {
  final directory = await getApplicationDocumentsDirectory();

  return directory.path;
}
```

Once you retrieve the path, you append the data filename by using the `File` class to create a `File` object. You import the `dart:io` library to use the `File` class, giving you a reference to the file location.

```
final path = await _localPath;
Final file = File('$path/local_persistence.json');
```

Once you have the `File` object, you use the `writeAsString()` method to save the file by passing the data as a `String` argument. To read the file, you use the `readAsString()` method without any arguments. Note that the file variable contains the documents folder's path and the data filename.

```
// Write the file
file.writeAsString('$json');
// Read the file
String contents = await file.readAsString();
```

As you learned in the "Understanding the JSON Format" section, you use a JSON file to save and read data from the device local storage. The JSON file data is stored as plain text (strings). To save data to the JSON file, you use serialization to convert an object to a string. To read data from the JSON file, you use deserialization to convert a string to an object. You use the `json.encode()` method to serialize and the `json.decode()` method to deserialize the data. Note that both the `json.encode()` and `json.decode()` methods are part of the `JsonCodec` class from the `dart:convert` library.

To serialize and deserialize JSON files, you import the `dart:convert` library. After calling the `readAsString()` method to read data from the stored file, you need to parse the string and return the JSON object by using the `json.decode()` or `jsonDecode()` function. Note that the `jsonDecode()` function is shorthand for `json.decode()`.

```
// String to JSON object
final dataFromJson = json.decode(str);
// Or
final dataFromJson = jsonDecode(str);
```

To convert values to a JSON string, you use the `json.encode()` or `jsonEncode()` function. Note that `jsonEncode()` is shorthand for `json.encode()`. It's a personal preference deciding which approach to use; in the exercises, you'll be using `json.decode()` and `json.encode()`.

```
// Values to JSON string
json.encode(dataToJson);
// Or
jsonEncode(dataToJson);
```

FORMATTING DATES

To format dates, you use the `intl` package (Flutter plugin) providing internationalization and localization. The full list of available date formats is available on the `intl` package page site at https://pub.dev/packages/intl. For our purposes, you'll use the `DateFormat` class to help you N format and parse dates. You'll use the `DateFormat` named constructors to format the date according to the specification. To format a date like Jan 13, 2019, you use the `DateFormat.yMMD()` constructor, and then you pass the date to the `format` argument, which expects a `DateTime`. If you pass the date as a `String`, you use `DateTime.parse()` to convert it to a `DateTime` format.

```
// Formatting date examples
print(DateFormat.d().format(DateTime.parse('2019-01-13')));
print(DateFormat.E().format(DateTime.parse('2019-01-13')));
print(DateFormat.y().format(DateTime.parse('2019-01-13')));
print(DateFormat.yMEd().format(DateTime.parse('2019-01-13')));
print(DateFormat.yMMMEd().format(DateTime.parse('2019-01-13')));
print(DateFormat.yMMMMEEEEd().format(DateTime.parse('2019-01-13')));
```

```
I/flutter (19337): 13
I/flutter (19337): Sun
I/flutter (19337): 2019
I/flutter (19337): Sun, 1/13/2019
I/flutter (19337): Sun, Jan 13, 2019
I/flutter (19337): Sunday, January 13, 2019
```

To build additional custom date formatting, you can chain and use the `add_*()` methods (substitute the * character with the format characters needed) to append and compound multiple formats. The following sample code shows how to customize the date format:

```
// Formatting date examples with the add_* methods
print(DateFormat.yMEd().add_Hm().format(DateTime.parse('2019-01-13 10:30:15')));
print(DateFormat.yMd().add_EEEE().add_Hms().format(DateTime.parse('2019-01-13
10:30:15')));
```

```
I/flutter (19337): Sun, 1/13/2019 10:30
I/flutter (19337): 1/13/2019 Sunday 10:30:15
```

SORTING A LIST OF DATES

You learned how to format dates easily, but how would you sort dates? The journal app that you'll create requires you to show a list of entries, and it would be great to be able to display the list sorted by date. In particular, you want to sort dates to show the newest first and oldest last, which is known as DESC (descending) order. Our journal entries are displayed from a `List`, and to sort them, you call the `List().sort()` method.

The `List` is sorted by the order specified by the function, and the function acts as a `Comparator`, comparing two values and assessing whether they are the same or whether one is larger than the other—such as the dates 2019-01-20 and 2019-01-22 in Table 13.3. The `Comparator` function returns an integer as negative, zero, or positive. If the comparison—for example, 2019-01-20 > 2019-01-22—is `true`, it returns 1, and if it's `false`, it returns -1. Otherwise (when the values are equal), it returns 0.

TABLE 13.3: Sorting Dates

COMPARE	TRUE	SAME	FALSE
date2.compareTo(date1)	1	0	-1
2019-01-20 > 2019-01-22			-1
2019-01-20 < 2019-01-22	1		
2019-01-22 = 2019-01-22		0	

Let's take a look by running the following sort with actual `DateTime` values sorted by DESC date. Note to sort by DESC, you start with the second date, comparing it to the first date like this: `comp2.date.compareTo(comp1.date)`.

```
_database.journal.sort((comp1, comp2) => comp2.date.compareTo(comp1.date));

// Results from print() to the log
I/flutter (10272): -1 - 2019-01-20 15:47:46.696727 - 2019-01-22 17:02:47.678590
I/flutter (10272): -1 - 2019-01-19 15:58:23.013360 - 2019-01-20 15:47:46.696727
I/flutter (10272): -1 - 2019-01-19 13:04:32.812748 - 2019-01-19 15:58:23.013360
I/flutter (10272):  1 - 2019-01-22 17:21:12.752577 - 2018-01-01 16:43:05.598094
I/flutter (10272):  1 - 2019-01-22 17:21:12.752577 - 2018-12-25 02:40:55.533173
I/flutter (10272):  1 - 2019-01-22 17:21:12.752577 - 2019-01-16 02:40:13.961852
```

I wanted to show you the longer way to the previous code's `sort()` to show how the compare result is obtained.

```
_database.journal.sort((comp1, comp2) {
  int result = comp2.date.compareTo(comp1.date);
  print('$result - ${comp2.date} - ${comp1.date}');
  return result;
});
```

If you would like to sort the dates by ASC (ascending) order, you can switch the compare statement to start with `comp1.date` to `comp2.date`.

```
_database.journal.sort((comp1, comp2) => comp1.date.compareTo(comp2.date));
```

RETRIEVING DATA WITH THE FUTUREBUILDER

In mobile applications, it is important not to block the UI while retrieving or processing data. In Chapter 3, "Learning Dart Basics," you learned how to use a `Future` to retrieve a possible value that is available sometime in the future. A `FutureBuilder` widget works with a `Future` to retrieve the latest data without blocking the UI. The three main properties that you set are `initialData`, `future`, and `builder`.

➤ `initialData`: Initial data to show before the snapshot is retrieved.

Sample code:

```
[]
```

➤ future: Calls a Future asynchronous method to retrieve data.

Sample code:

```
_ loadJournals()
```

➤ builder: The builder property provides the BuildContext and AsyncSnapshot (data retrieved and connection state). The AsyncSnapshot returns a snapshot of the data, and you can also check for the ConnectionState to get a status on the data retrieval process.

Sample code:

```
(BuildContext context, AsyncSnapshot snapshot)
```

➤ AsyncSnapshot: Provides the most recent data and connection status. Note that the data represented is immutable and read-only. To check whether data is returned, you use the snapshot.hasData. To check the connection state, you use the snapshot.connectionState to see whether the state is active, waiting, done, or none. You can also check for errors by using the snapshot.hasError property.

Sample code:

```
builder: (BuildContext context, AsyncSnapshot snapshot) {

return !snapshot.hasData

? CircularProgressIndicator()

: _ buildListView(snapshot);

},
```

The following is some FutureBuilder() sample code:

```
FutureBuilder(
  initialData: [],
  future: _loadJournals(),
  builder: (BuildContext context, AsyncSnapshot snapshot) {
    return !snapshot.hasData
        ? Center(child: CircularProgressIndicator())
        : _buildListViewSeparated(snapshot);
  },
),
```

BUILDING THE JOURNAL APP

You'll be building a journal app with the requirement of persisting data across app starts. The data is stored as JSON objects with the requirements of tracking each journal entry's id, date, mood, and note (Figure 13.1). As you learned in the "Understanding the JSON Format" section, the id key value is unique, and it's used to identify each journal entry. The id key is used behind the scenes to select the journal entry and is not displayed in the UI. The root object is a key/value pair with the key name of 'journal' and the value as an array of objects containing each journal entry.

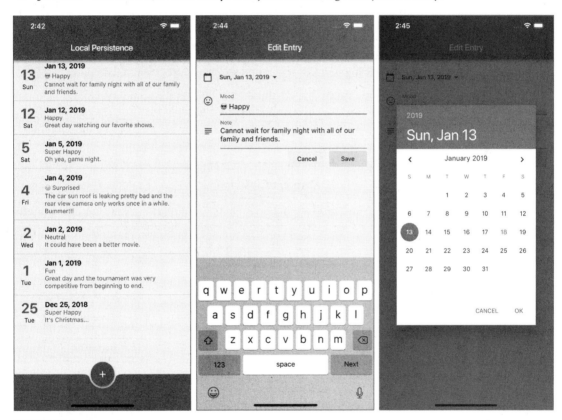

FIGURE 13.1: Journal app

The app has two separate pages; the main presentation page uses a ListView sorted by DESC date, meaning last entered record first. You utilize the ListTile widget to format how the List of records is displayed. The second page is the journal entry details where you use a date picker to select a date from a calendar and TextField widgets for entering the mood and note data. You'll create a database Dart file with classes to handle the file routines, database JSON parsing, a Journal class to handle individual records, and a JournalEdit class to pass data and actions between pages.

Figure 13.2 shows a high-level view of the journal app detailing how the database classes are used in the Home and Edit pages.

OVERVIEW OF JOURNAL APP

You'll be creating this app over the course of four Try It Out exercises:

Laying the Foundations of the Journal App: In the first section you add the `path_ provider` and `intl` packages to your `pubspec.yaml` file and set up the `home.dart` page with basic structure widgets.

Creating the Journal Database Classes: The second exercise focuses on creating the `database.dart` file with your classes to handle the file routines, database parsing, and `Journal` classes.

Creating the Journal Entry Page: The third exercise builds the `edit_entry.dart` file to handle creating and editing journal entries and selecting dates from a date picker.

Finishing the Journal Home Page: The fourth exercise finishes the `home.dart` page, which relies on the `database.dart` file by adding logic to build the `ListView` and save, read, sort data, and pass data to the edit journal page.

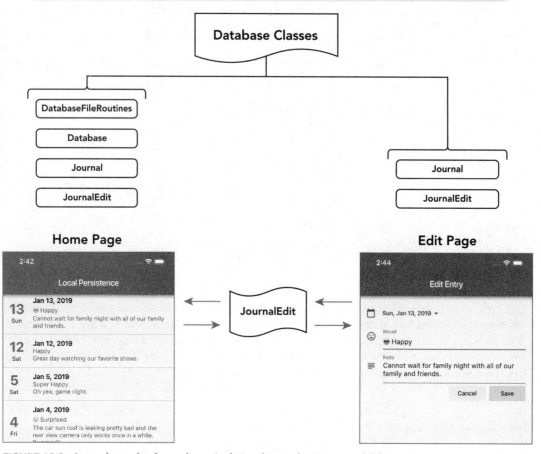

FIGURE 13.2: Journal app database classes' relationship to the Home and Edit pages

TRY IT OUT Laying the Foundations of the Journal App

In this series of steps, you'll do some essential setup for the journal app, which you'll build on over the remaining Try It Out sections in this chapter.

1. Create a new Flutter project and name it `ch13_local_persistence`. You can follow instructions in Chapter 4, "Creating a Starter Project Template." For this project, you need to create only the `pages` and `classes` folders.

2. Open the `pubspec.yaml` file to add resources. In the `dependencies:` section, add the `path_provider: ^1.1.0` and `intl: ^0.15.8` declarations. Note that your version might be higher.

```
dependencies:
  flutter:
    sdk: flutter

  # The following adds the Cupertino Icons font to your application.
  # Use with the CupertinoIcons class for iOS style icons.
  cupertino_icons: ^0.1.2

  path_provider: ^1.1.0
  intl: ^0.15.8
```

3. Click the Save button. Depending on the editor you are using, it automatically runs `flutter packages get`, and once finished, it will show a message of `Process finished with exit code 0`. If it does not automatically run the command for you, open the Terminal window (located at the bottom of your editor) and type `flutter packages get`.

4. Open the `main.dart` file. Add to the `ThemeData` the `bottomAppBarColor` property and set the color to `Colors.blue`.

```
return MaterialApp(
  debugShowCheckedModeBanner: false,
  title: 'Local Persistence',
  theme: ThemeData(
    primarySwatch: Colors.blue,
    bottomAppBarColor: Colors.blue,
  ),
  home: Home(),
);
```

5. Open the `home.dart` file and add to the `body` a `FutureBuilder()`. The `FutureBuilder()` `initialData` property is an empty `List` created with the open and close square brackets (`[]`). The `future` property calls the `_loadJournals()` `Future` method that you create in the "Finishing the Journal Home Page" exercise. For the `builder` property, you return a `CircularProgressIndicator()` if the `snapshot.hasData` is `false`, meaning no data has returned yet. Otherwise, you call the `_buildListViewSeparated(snapshot)` method to build the `ListView` showing the journal entries.

As you learned in the "Retrieving Data with the FutureBuilder" section, the `AsyncSnapshot` returns a snapshot of the data. The snapshot is immutable, meaning it's read-only.

```
body: FutureBuilder(
  initialData: [],
  future: _loadJournals(),
  builder: (BuildContext context, AsyncSnapshot snapshot) {
```

```
      return !snapshot.hasData
          ? Center(child: CircularProgressIndicator())
          : _buildListViewSeparated(snapshot);
    },
  ),
```

6. After the `body` property, add the `bottomNavigationBar` property and set it to a `BottomAppBar()`. Set the `shape` to a `CircularNotchedRectangle()` and set the `child` to a `Padding` of `24.0` pixels. Add the `floatingActionButtonLocation` property and set it to `FloatingActionButton-Location.centerDocked`.

```
bottomNavigationBar: BottomAppBar(
  shape: CircularNotchedRectangle(),
  child: Padding(padding: const EdgeInsets.all(24.0)),
),
floatingActionButtonLocation: FloatingActionButtonLocation.centerDocked,
```

7. Add the `floatingActionButton` property and set it to a `FloatingActionButton()`. Normally the `BottomAppBar()` is used to show a row of widgets to make a selection, but for our app you are using it for aesthetics looks by using it with the `FloatingActionButton` to show a notch. The `FloatingActionButton` is responsible for adding new journal entries. Set the `FloatingAction-Button()` `child` property to `Icon(Icons.add)` to show a plus sign that conveys the action to add a new journal entry.

```
floatingActionButton: FloatingActionButton(
  tooltip: 'Add Journal Entry',
  child: Icon(Icons.add),
),
```

8. Set the `FloatingActionButton()` `onPressed` property as an `async` callback that calls the `_addOrEditJournal()` method. Add a call to the `_addOrEditJournal()` method that takes three arguments: `add`, `index`, and `journal`. In "Finishing the Journal Home Page," you'll create the method that relies on the `database.dart` file creation.

When the user taps this button, it's to add a new entry, which is why you pass the arguments `add` as `true`, `index` as `-1`, and `journal` as a blank `Journal` (class) entry. Because you also use the same method to edit an entry (user taps the `ListView`, covered in the final exercise), you would pass the arguments `add` as `false`, `index` as the entry `index` from the `ListView`, and `journal` as the `Journal` selected.

```
bottomNavigationBar: BottomAppBar(
  shape: CircularNotchedRectangle(),
  child: Padding(padding: const EdgeInsets.all(24.0)),
),
floatingActionButtonLocation: FloatingActionButtonLocation.centerDocked,
floatingActionButton: FloatingActionButton(
  tooltip: 'Add Journal Entry',
  child: Icon(Icons.add),
  onPressed: () {
    _addOrEditJournal(add: true, index: -1, journal: Journal());
  },
),
```

HOW IT WORKS

You declared the `path_provider` and `intl` packages to your `pubspec.yaml` file. The `path_provider` gives you access to the local iOS and Android filesystem locations, and the `intl` gives you the ability to format dates. You added to the `body` property the `FutureBuilder` that calls a `Future` async method to return data, and you'll implement it in the fourth exercise, "Finishing the Journal Home Page."

You added a `BottomAppBar` and used the `FloatingActionButtonLocation` to dock the `FloatingAction-Button` on the bottom center. The `FloatingActionButton onPressed()` event is marked as async to call the `_addOrEditJournal()` method to add a new journal entry. You'll implement the `_addOrEditJour-nal()` method in "Finishing the Journal Home Page."

Adding the Journal Database Classes

You'll create four separate classes to handle the database routines and serialization to manage the journal data. Each class is responsible for handling specific code logic, resulting in code reusability. Collectively the database classes are responsible for writing (saving), reading, encoding, and decoding JSON objects to and from the JSON file.

➤ The **DatabaseFileRoutines class** handles getting the path to the device's local documents directory and saving and reading the database file by using the `File` class. The `File` class is used by importing the `dart:io` library, and to obtain the documents directory path, you import the `path_provider` package.

➤ The **Database class** handles decoding and encoding the JSON objects and converting them to a `List` of journal entries. You call `databaseFromJson` to read and parse from JSON objects. You call `databaseToJson` to save and parse to JSON objects. The `Database` class returns the `journal` variable consisting of a `List` of `Journal` classes, `List<Journal>`. The `dart:convert` library is used to decode and encode JSON objects.

➤ The **Journal class** handles decoding and encoding the JSON objects for each journal entry. The `Journal` class contains the `id`, `date`, `mood`, and `note` journal entry fields stored as `Strings`.

➤ The **JournalEdit class** handles the passing of individual journal entries between pages. The `JournalEdit` class contains the `action` and `journal` variables. The `action` variable is used to track whether the Save or Cancel button is pressed. The `journal` variable contains the individual journal entry as a `Journal` class containing the `id`, `date`, `mood`, and `note` variables.

TRY IT OUT   Creating the Journal Database Classes

In this section, you'll create the `DatabaseFileRoutines`, `Database`, `Journal`, and `JournalEdit` classes. Note that the default constructors use curly brackets (`{}`) to implement named parameters.

1.   Create a new Dart file under the `classes` folder. Right-click the `classes` folder, select New ➪ Dart File, enter **database.dart**, and click the OK button to save.

2.   Import the `path_provider.dart` package and the `dart:io` and `dart:convert` libraries. Add a new line and create the `DatabaseFileRoutines` class.

```
import 'package:path_provider/path_provider.dart'; // Filesystem locations
import 'dart:io'; // Used by File
import 'dart:convert'; // Used by json

class DatabaseFileRoutines {

}
```

3.   Inside the `DatabaseFileRoutines` class, add the `_localPath` async method that returns a `Future<String>`, which is the documents directory path.

```
Future<String> get _localPath async {
  final directory = await getApplicationDocumentsDirectory();

  return directory.path;
}
```

4.   Add the `_localFile` async method that returns a `Future<File>` with the reference to the `local_persistence.json` file, which is the `path`, combined with the filename.

```
Future<File> get _localFile async {
  final path = await _localPath;

  return File('$path/local_persistence.json');
}
```

5.   Add the `readJournals()` async method that returns a `Future<String>` containing the JSON objects. You'll use a `try-catch` just in case there is an issue with reading the file.

```
Future<String> readJournals() async {
  try {

  } catch (e) {

  }
}
```

6.   Use `file.existsSync()` to check whether the file exists; if not, you create it by calling the `writeJournals('{"journals": []}')` method by passing it an empty journals object. Next, `file.readAsString()` is called to load the contents of the file.

```
Future<String> readJournals() async {
  try {
    final file = await _localFile;

    if (!file.existsSync()) {
```

```
            print("File does not Exist: ${file.absolute}");
            await writeJournals('{"journals": []}');
        }

        // Read the file
        String contents = await file.readAsString();

        return contents;
    } catch (e) {
        print("error readJournals: $e");
        return "";
    }
}
```

7. Add the `writeJournals(String json)` async method returning a `Future<File>` to save the JSON objects to file.

```
Future<File> writeJournals(String json) async {
    final file = await _localFile;

    // Write the file
    return file.writeAsString('$json');
}
```

8. Following the `DatabaseFileRoutines` class, create two methods that call the `Database` class to handle the JSON decode and encode for the entire database. Create the `databaseFromJson-(String str)` method returning a `Database` by passing it the JSON string. By using `json .decode(str)`, it parses the JSON string and returns a JSON object.

```
// To read and parse from JSON data - databaseFromJson(jsonString);
Database databaseFromJson(String str) {
    final dataFromJson = json.decode(str);
    return Database.fromJson(dataFromJson);
}
```

9. Create the `databaseToJson(Database data)` method returning a `String`. By using the `json .encode(dataToJson)`, it parses the values to a JSON string.

```
// To save and parse to JSON Data - databaseToJson(jsonString);
String databaseToJson(Database data) {
    final dataToJson = data.toJson();
    return json.encode(dataToJson);
}
```

10. Create the `Database` class, and the first item to declare is the `journal` variable of a `List<Journal>` type, meaning it contains a list of journals. The `Journal` class contains each record, and you'll create it in step 13. Declare the `Database` constructor with the named parameter `this.journal` variable. Note you are using curly brackets (`{}`) to declare the constructor named parameter.

```
class Database {
    List<Journal> journal;

    Database({
        this.journal,
    });
}
```

11. To retrieve and map the JSON objects to a `List<Journal>` (list of Journal classes), create the factory `Database.fromJson()` named constructor. Note that the factory constructor does not always create a new instance but might return an instance from a cache. The constructor takes the argument of `Map<String, dynamic>`, which maps the `String` key with a `dynamic` value, the JSON key/value pair. The constructor returns the `List<Journal>` by taking the JSON `'journals'` key objects and mapping it from the `Journal` class that parses the JSON string to the `Journal` object containing each field such as the `id`, `date`, `mood`, and `note`.

```
factory Database.fromJson(Map<String, dynamic> json) => Database(
    journal: List<Journal>.from(json["journals"].map((x) => Journal.fromJson(x))),
);
```

12. To convert the `List<Journal>` to JSON objects, create the `toJson` method that parses each `Journal` class to JSON objects.

```
Map<String, dynamic> toJson() => {
    "journals": List<dynamic>.from(journal.map((x) => x.toJson())),
};
```

The following is the entire `Database` class:

```
class Database {
  List<Journal> journal;

  Database({
    this.journal,
  });

  factory Database.fromJson(Map<String, dynamic> json) => Database(
      journal: List<Journal>.from(json["journals"].map((x) => Journal.fromJson(x))),
  );

  Map<String, dynamic> toJson() => {
      "journals": List<dynamic>.from(journal.map((x) => x.toJson())),
  };
}
```

13. Create the `Journal` class and declare as `String` types the `id`, `date`, `mood`, and `note` variables. Declare the `Journal` constructor with the named parameters `this.id`, `this.date`, `this.mood`, and `this.note` variables. Note that you are using curly (`{ }`) brackets to declare the constructor named parameters.

```
class Journal {
  String id;
  String date;
  String mood;
  String note;

  Journal({
    this.id,
    this.date,
    this.mood,
    this.note,
  });
}
```

14. To retrieve and convert the JSON object to a `Journal` class, create the `factory Journal.fromJson()` named constructor. The constructor takes the argument of `Map<String, dynamic>`, which maps the `String` key with a `dynamic` value, the JSON key/value pair.

```
factory Journal.fromJson(Map<String, dynamic> json) => Journal(
  id: json["id"],
  date: json["date"],
  mood: json["mood"],
  note: json["note"],
);
```

15. To convert the `Journal` class to a JSON object, create the `toJson()` method that parses the `Journal` class to a JSON object.

```
Map<String, dynamic> toJson() => {
  "id": id,
  "date": date,
  "mood": mood,
  "note": note,
};
```

The following is the entire `Journal` class:

```
class Journal {
  String id;
  String date;
  String mood;
  String note;

  Journal({
    this.id,
    this.date,
    this.mood,
    this.note,
  });

  factory Journal.fromJson(Map<String, dynamic> json) => Journal(
    id: json["id"],
    date: json["date"],
    mood: json["mood"],
    note: json["note"],
  );

  Map<String, dynamic> toJson() => {
    "id": id,
    "date": date,
    "mood": mood,
    "note": note,
  };
}
```

16. Create the `JournalEdit` class that is responsible for passing the `action` and a `journal` entry between pages. Add a `String action` variable and a `Journal journal` variable. Add the default `JournalEdit` constructor.

```
class JournalEdit {
  String action;
```

```
    Journal journal;

    JournalEdit({this.action, this.journal});
}
```

HOW IT WORKS

You created a `database.dart` file containing four classes to handle the local persistence serialization and deserialization.

The `DatabaseFileRoutines` class handles locating the device's local document directory `path` through the `path_provider` package. You used the `File` class to handle the saving and reading of the database file by importing the `dart:io` library. The file is text-based containing the key/value pair of JSON objects.

The `Database` class uses `json.encode` and `json.decode` to serialize and deserialize JSON objects by importing the `dart:convert` library. You use the `Database.fromJson` named constructor to retrieve and map the JSON objects to a `List<Journal>`. You use the `toJson()` method to convert the `List<Journal>` to JSON objects.

The `Journal` class is responsible for tracking individual journal entries through the `String id`, `date`, `mood`, and `note` variables. You use the `Journal.fromJson()` named constructor to take the argument of `Map<String, dynamic>`, which maps the `String` key with a `dynamic` value, the JSON key/value pair. You use the `toJson()` method to convert the `Journal` class into a JSON object.

The `JournalEdit` class is used to pass data between pages. You declared a `String action` variable and a `Journal journal` variable. The `action` variable passes an action to `'Save'` or `'Cancel'`, editing an entry. You learn'll to use the `JournalEdit` class in the "Creating the Journal Entry Page" and "Finishing the Home Page" exercises. The `journal` variable passes the journal entry values.

Adding the Journal Entry Page

The entry page is responsible for adding and editing a journal entry. You might ask, how does it know when to add or edit a current entry? You created the `JournalEdit` class in the `database.dart` file for this reason—to allow you to reuse the same page for multiple purposes. The entry page extends a `StatefulWidget` with the constructor (Table 13.4) having the three arguments `add`, `index`, and `journalEdit`. Note that the index argument is used to track the selected journal entry location in the journal database list from the Home page. However, if a new journal entry is created, it does not exist in the list yet, so a value of -1 is passed instead. Any index numbers zero and up would mean the journal entry already exists in the list.

TABLE 13.4: EditEntry Class Constructor Arguments

VARIABLE	DESCRIPTION AND VALUE
`final bool add`	If the `add` variable value is `true`, it means you are adding a new journal. If the value is `false`, you are editing a journal entry.
`final int index`	If the index variable value is `-1`, it means you are adding a new journal entry. If the value is `0` or greater, you are editing a journal entry, and you need to track the index position in the `List<Journal>`.

VARIABLE	DESCRIPTION AND VALUE
final JournalEdit journalEdit String action Journal journal	The JournalEdit class passes two values. The action value is either 'Save' or 'Cancel'. The journal variable passes the entire Journal class, consisting of the id, date, mood, and note values.

The entry page has Cancel and Save buttons that call an action with the onPressed() method (Table 13.5). The onPressed() method sends back to the Home page the JournalEdit class with appropriate values depending on which button is pressed.

TABLE 13.5: Save or Cancel FlatButton

ONPRESSED()	RESULT
Cancel	The JournalEdit action variable is set to 'Cancel', and the class is passed back to the Home page with Navigator.pop(context, _journalEdit). The Home page receives the values and does not take any action since the editing was canceled.
Save	The JournalEdit action variable is set to 'Save', and the journal variable is set with the current Journal class values, the id, date, mood, and note. If the add value is equal to true, meaning adding a new entry, a new id value is generated. If the add value is equal to false, meaning editing an entry, the current journal id is used. The Home page receives the values and executes the 'Save' logic with received values.

To make it easy for the user to select a date, you use the built-in date picker that presents a calendar. To show the calendar, you call the showDatePicker() function (Table 13.6) and pass four arguments: context, initialDate, firstDate, and lastDate (Figure 13.3).

TABLE 13.6: showDatePicker

PROPERTY	VALUE
context	You pass the BuildContext as the context.
initialDate	You pass the journal date that is highlighted and selected in the calendar.
firstDate	The oldest date range available to be picked in the calendar from today's date.
lastDate	The newest date range available to be picked in the calendar from today's date.

Once the date is retrieved, you'll use the DateFormat.yMMMEd() constructor to show it in Sun, Jan 13, 2018 format. If you would like to show a time picker, call the showTimePicker() method and pass the context and initialTime arguments.

FIGURE 13.3: Date picker calendar

In Chapter 6, "Using Common Widgets," you learned how to use a Form with the TextFormField to create an entry form. Now let's use a different approach without a Form but use the TextField with a TextEditingController. You'll learn how to use the TextField TextInputAction with the FocusNode to customize the keyboard action button to execute a custom action (Figure 13.4). The keyboard action button is located to the right of the spacebar. You'll also learn how to customize the TextField capitalization options by using TextCapitalization that configures how the keyboard capitalizes words, sentences, and characters; the settings are words, sentences, characters, or none (default).

Keyboard Action Button

FIGURE 13.4: Keyboard action button for iOS and Android

TRY IT OUT Creating the Journal Entry Page

In this section, you'll create the EditEntry StatefulWidget with the constructor taking the arguments add, index, and journalEdit. Note that the default constructors use the curly brackets ({}) to implement named parameters. The following graphic is the final journal entry page that you'll create.

1. Create a new Dart file under the pages folder. Right-click the pages folder, select New ⇨ Dart File, enter **edit_entry.dart,** and click the OK button to save.

2. Import the material.dart class, the database.dart class, the intl.dart package, and the dart:math library. Add a new line and create the EditEntry class that extends a StatefulWidget.

```
import 'package:flutter/material.dart';
import 'package:ch13_local_persistence/classes/database.dart';
import 'package:intl/intl.dart'; // Format Dates
import 'dart:math'; // Random() numbers

class EditEntry extends StatefulWidget {
  @override
  _EditEntryState createState() => _EditEntryState();
}

class _EditEntryState extends State<EditEntry> {
  @override
  Widget build(BuildContext context) {
    return Container();
  }
}
```

3. After the class EditEntry extends StatefulWidget { and before the @override, add the three variables bool add, int index, and JournalEdit journalEdit and mark them as final.

```
class EditEntry extends StatefulWidget {
  final bool add;
  final int index;
  final JournalEdit journalEdit;

  @override
  _EditEntryState createState() => _EditEntryState();
}
```

4. Add the EditEntry constructor with Key key, this.add, this.index, and this.journalEdit as named parameters by enclosing them in curly brackets ({}).

```
class EditEntry extends StatefulWidget {
  final bool add;
  final int index;
  final JournalEdit journalEdit;

  const EditEntry({Key key, this.add, this.index, this.journalEdit})
      : super(key: key);

  @override
  _EditEntryState createState() => _EditEntryState();
}
```

5. Modify the _EditEntryState class and add the private JournalEdit _journalEdit, String _title, and DateTime _selectedDate variables. Note that the private _journalEdit variable is populated from the JournalEdit class value passed to the EditEntry constructor.

```
class _EditEntryState extends State<EditEntry> {
  JournalEdit _journalEdit;
  String _title;
  DateTime _selectedDate;

  @override
  Widget build(BuildContext context) {
    return Container();
  }
}
```

6. The mood and note use the TextField widget, which requires the TextEditingController to access and modify the values. Add _moodController and _noteController TextEditingController variables and initialize them with the TextEditingController() constructor. Note that this controller treats a null value as an empty string.

```
class _EditEntryState extends State<EditEntry> {
  JournalEdit _journalEdit;
  String _title;
  DateTime _selectedDate;
  TextEditingController _moodController = TextEditingController();
  TextEditingController _noteController = TextEditingController();
```

```
    @override
    Widget build(BuildContext context) {
      return Container();
    }
  }
```

7. Declare the _moodFocus and _noteFocus FocusNode variables and initialize them with the FocusNode() constructor. You'll use the FocusNode with the TextInputAction to customize the keyboard action button in steps 30 and 31.

```
class _EditEntryState extends State<EditEntry> {
  JournalEdit _journalEdit;
  String _title;
  DateTime _selectedDate;
  TextEditingController _moodController = TextEditingController();
  TextEditingController _noteController = TextEditingController();
  FocusNode _moodFocus = FocusNode();
  FocusNode _noteFocus = FocusNode();

  @override
  Widget build(BuildContext context) {
    return Container();
  }
}
```

8. Override the initState(), and let's initialize the variables with values passed to the EditEntry constructor and make sure you add the super.initState().

```
@override
void initState() {
  super.initState();
}
```

9. Initialize the _journalEdit variable by using the JournalEdit class constructor by defaulting the action to 'Cancel' and the journal to widget.journalEdit.journal value. Note that you use the widget to access the values from the EditEntry constructor. Also, note that you access the individual journal entry from the JournalEdit class by using the dot operator and then choosing the journal variable.

```
_journalEdit = JournalEdit(action: 'Cancel', journal: widget.journalEdit.journal);
```

10. Initialize the _title variable by using a ternary operator to check whether widget.add is true. If it is, set the value to 'Add', and if false, set the value to 'Edit'. By using the _title variable, you customize the AppBar's title to the action the user is taking. It's the little details that make an app great.

```
_title = widget.add ? 'Add' : 'Edit';
```

11. Initialize the _journalEdit.journal variable from the widget.journalEdit.journal variable.

```
_journalEdit.journal = widget.journalEdit.journal;
```

12. To populate the entry fields on the page, add an if-else statement. If the widget.add value is true, meaning adding a new journal record, then initialize the _selectedDate variable with the current date by using the DateTime.now() constructor and initialize the _moodController.text and _noteController.text to an empty string. If the widget.add value is false, meaning editing a current journal record, then initialize the _selectedDate variable with the _journal-Edit.journal.date and use the DateTime.parse to convert the date from String to a DateTime format. Also initialize the _moodController.text with the _journalEdit.journal.mood and the _noteController.text with the _journalEdit.journal.note. When you override the initState() method, make sure you *start* the method with a call to super.initState().

```
@override
void initState() {
  super.initState();

  _journalEdit = JournalEdit(action: 'Cancel', journal: widget.
journalEdit.journal);
  _title = widget.add ? 'Add' : 'Edit';
  _journalEdit.journal = widget.journalEdit.journal;
  if (widget.add) {
    _selectedDate = DateTime.now();
    _moodController.text = '';
    _noteController.text = '';
  } else {
    _selectedDate = DateTime.parse(_journalEdit.journal.date);
    _moodController.text = _journalEdit.journal.mood;
    _noteController.text = _journalEdit.journal.note;
  }
}
```

13. Override dispose(), and let's dispose the two TextEditingController and FocusNode; make sure you add super.dispose(). When you override the dispose() method, make sure you *end* the method with a call to super.dispose().

```
@override
dispose() {

  _moodController.dispose();
  _noteController.dispose();
  _moodFocus.dispose();
  _noteFocus.dispose();

  super.dispose();
}
```

14. Add the _selectDate(DateTime selectedDate) async method that returns a Future<DateTime>. This method is responsible for calling the Flutter built-in showDatePicker() that presents the user with a popup dialog displaying a Material Design calendar to choose dates.

```
// Date Picker
Future<DateTime> _selectDate(DateTime selectedDate) async {

}
```

15. Add the DateTime _initialDate variable and initialize it with the selectedDate variable passed in the constructor.

```
DateTime _initialDate = selectedDate;
```

16. Add a final `DateTime _pickedDate` (the date the user picks from the calendar) variable and initialize it by calling the `await showDatePicker()` constructor. Pass the `context`, `initialDate`, `firstDate`, and `lastDate` arguments. Note that for the `firstDate` you use today's date and subtract 365 days, and for the `lastDate`, you add 365 days, which tells the calendar a selectable dates range.

```
final DateTime _pickedDate = await showDatePicker(
  context: context,
  initialDate: _initialDate,
  firstDate: DateTime.now().subtract(Duration(days: 365)),
  lastDate: DateTime.now().add(Duration(days: 365)),
);
```

17. Add an `if` statement that checks that the `_pickedDate` (the date the user picked from the calendar) variable does not equal `null`, meaning the user tapped the calendar's Cancel button. If the user did pick a date, then modify the `selectedDate` variable by using the `DateTime()` constructor and pass the `_pickedDate` year, month, and day. For the time, pass the `_initialDate` hour, minute, second, millisecond, and microsecond. Note that since you are only changing the date and not the time, you use the original's created date time.

```
if (_pickedDate != null) {
  selectedDate = DateTime(
      _pickedDate.year,
      _pickedDate.month,
      _pickedDate.day,
      _initialDate.hour,
      _initialDate.minute,
      _initialDate.second,
      _initialDate.millisecond,
      _initialDate.microsecond);
}
```

18. Add a `return` statement to send back the `selectedDate`.

```
return selectedDate;
```

The following is the entire `_selectDate()` method:

```
// Date Picker
Future<DateTime> _selectDate(DateTime selectedDate) async {
  DateTime _initialDate = selectedDate;

  final DateTime _pickedDate = await showDatePicker(
    context: context,
    initialDate: _initialDate,
    firstDate: DateTime.now().subtract(Duration(days: 365)),
    lastDate: DateTime.now().add(Duration(days: 365)),
  );
  if (_pickedDate != null) {
    selectedDate = DateTime(
        _pickedDate.year,
        _pickedDate.month,
        _pickedDate.day,
        _initialDate.hour,
        _initialDate.minute,
```

```
          _initialDate.second,
          _initialDate.millisecond,
          _initialDate.microsecond);
    }
    return selectedDate;
  }
```

19. In the `Widget build()` method, replace the `Container()` with the UI widgets `Scaffold` and `AppBar`, and for the `body` property add a `SafeArea()` and `SingleChildScrollView()` with the `child` property as a `Column()`. Note that the `AppBar` `title` uses the `Text` widget with the `_title` variable to customize the `title` with either Add or Edit Entry.

```
@override
Widget build(BuildContext context) {]></line>
  return Scaffold(]
    appBar: AppBar(]
      title: Text('$_title Entry'),
      automaticallyImplyLeading: false,
    ),
    body: SafeArea(
      child: SingleChildScrollView(
        padding: EdgeInsets.all(16.0),
        child: Column(
          children: <Widget>[

          ],
        ),
      ),
    ),
  );
}
```

20. Add to the `Column` children a `FlatButton` widget that is used to show the formatted selected date, and when the user taps the button, it presents the calendar. Set the `FlatButton` padding property to `EdgeInsets.all(0.0)` to remove padding for better aesthetics and add to the `child` property a `Row()` widget.

```
FlatButton(
  padding: EdgeInsets.all(0.0),
  child: Row(
    children: <Widget>[
    ],
  ),
),
```

21. Add to the `Row` children property the `Icons.calendar_day` Icon with a size of `22.0` and a `color` property set to `Colors.black54`.

```
Icon(
  Icons.calendar_today,
  size: 22.0,
  color: Colors.black54,
),
```

22. Add a `SizedBox` with a `width` property set to `16.0` to add a spacer.

```
SizedBox(width: 16.0,),
```

23. Add a `Text` widget and format the `_selectedDate` with the `DateFormat.yMMMEd()` constructor.

```
Text(DateFormat.yMMMEd().format(_selectedDate),
  style: TextStyle(
      color: Colors.black54,
      fontWeight: FontWeight.bold),
),
```

24. Add the `Icons.arrow_drop_down` Icon with the `color` property set to `Colors.black54`.

```
Icon(
  Icons.arrow_drop_down,
  color: Colors.black54,
),
```

25. Add the `onPressed()` callback and mark it `async` since calling the calendar is a `Future` event.

```
onPressed: () async {
},
```

26. Add to `onPressed()` the `FocusScope.of().requestFocus()` method call to dismiss the keyboard if any of the `TextField` widgets have focus. (This step is optional, but I wanted to show you how it's accomplished.)

```
FocusScope.of(context).requestFocus(FocusNode());
```

27. Add a `DateTime` `_pickerDate` variable initialized by calling the `await _selectDate(_selectedDate)` `Future` method, which is why you add the `await` keyword. You added this method in step 14.

28. Add `setState()` and inside the call modify the `_selectedDate` variable with the `_pickerDate` value, which is the date selected from the calendar.

```
DateTime _pickerDate = await _selectDate(_selectedDate);
setState(() {
  _selectedDate = _pickerDate;
});
```

The following is the full `FlatButton` widget code:

```
FlatButton(
  padding: EdgeInsets.all(0.0),
  child: Row(
```

```
          children: <Widget>[
            Icon(
              Icons.calendar_today,
              size: 22.0,
              color: Colors.black54,
            ),
            SizedBox(width: 16.0,),
            Text(DateFormat.yMMMEd().format(_selectedDate),
              style: TextStyle(
                  color: Colors.black54,
                  fontWeight: FontWeight.bold),
            ),
            Icon(
              Icons.arrow_drop_down,
              color: Colors.black54,
            ),
          ],
        ),
        onPressed: () async {
          FocusScope.of(context).requestFocus(FocusNode());
          DateTime _pickerDate = await _selectDate(_selectedDate);
          setState(() {
            _selectedDate = _pickerDate;
          });
        },
      ),
```

29. Now it's time to add the two `TextField` widgets for the mood and note fields. How do you set which `TextField` belongs to the mood or note? It's the `controller`, of course.
For the mood `TextField`, set the controller to `_moodController`, and set `autofocus` to `true` to automatically set the focus and show the keyboard when the page opens.

```
TextField(
  controller: _moodController,
  autofocus: true,
),
```

30. Set `textInputAction` to `TextInputAction.next` telling the keyboard action button to move to the next field.

```
textInputAction: TextInputAction.next,
```

31. Set the `focusNode` to `_moodFocus` and `textCapitalization` to `TextCapitalization.words`, meaning every word is automatically capitalized.

```
focusNode: _moodFocus,
textCapitalization: TextCapitalization.words,
```

32. Set the `decoration` to `InputDecoration` with the `labelText` set to `'Mood'` and the `icon` set to `Icons.mood`.

```
decoration: InputDecoration(
  labelText: 'Mood',
  icon: Icon(Icons.mood),
),
```

33. For the onSubmitted property, enter the argument name as submitted and call the FocusScope
.of(context).requestFocus(_noteFocus) to have the keyboard action button change the focus
to the note TextField. Note that I named the argument submitted, but it can be any name, like
submittedValue or moodValue.

```
onSubmitted: (submitted) {
  FocusScope.of(context).requestFocus(_noteFocus);
},
```

The following is the full mood TextField widget:

```
TextField(
  controller: _moodController,
  autofocus: true,
  textInputAction: TextInputAction.next,
  focusNode: _moodFocus,
  textCapitalization: TextCapitalization.words,
  decoration: InputDecoration(
    labelText: 'Mood',
    icon: Icon(Icons.mood),
  ),
  onSubmitted: (submitted) {
    FocusScope.of(context).requestFocus(_noteFocus);
  },
),
```

34. For the note TextField, set the controller to _noteController, and set autofocus to true to
automatically set the focus and show the keyboard when the page opens.

```
TextField(
  controller: _noteController,
),
```

35. Set the textInputAction to TextInputAction.newline telling the keyboard action button to
insert a new line in the TextField.

```
textInputAction: TextInputAction.newline,
```

36. Set the `focusNode` to `_noteFocus` and `textCapitalization` to `TextCapitalization` `.sentences`, meaning every first word of a sentence is automatically capitalized.

```
focusNode: _noteFocus,
textCapitalization: TextCapitalization.sentences,
```

37. Set the `decoration` to `InputDecoration` with the `labelText` set to `'Note'` and the `icon` set to `Icons.subject`.

```
decoration: InputDecoration(
  labelText: 'Note',
  icon: Icon(Icons.subject),
),
```

38. Set the `maxLines` property to `null`, allowing the `TextField` to grow vertically to show the entire contents of the note. Using this technique is a great way to have a `TextField` automatically grow to the size of the content without writing any code logic.

```
maxLines: null,
```

The following is the full note `TextField` widget:

```
TextField(
  controller: _noteController,

  textInputAction: TextInputAction.newline,
  focusNode: _noteFocus,
  textCapitalization: TextCapitalization.sentences,
  decoration: InputDecoration(
    labelText: 'Note',
    icon: Icon(Icons.subject),
  ),
  maxLines: null,
),
```

39. The last part for the entry page is to add Cancel and Save buttons. Add a `Row` and set `mainAxisAlignment` to `MainAxisAlignment.end` to align buttons to the right side of the page.

```
Row(
  mainAxisAlignment: MainAxisAlignment.end,
```

```
    children: <Widget>[
    ],
  ),
```

40. Edit the `Row children` and add a `FlatButton` with the `child` set to a `Text` widget to display `'Cancel'`. Set the `color` property to `Colors.grey.shade100`, making the button not the main action focus.

```
FlatButton(
  child: Text('Cancel'),
  color: Colors.grey.shade100,
),
```

41. For the `onPressed` property, modify the `_journalEdit.action` to `'Cancel'` and call the `Navigator.pop(context, _journalEdit)` to dismiss the entry form and pass the value back to the calling page. You'll handle this action in the last Try It Out in this chapter ("Finishing the Journal Home Page").

```
FlatButton(
  child: Text('Cancel'),
  color: Colors.grey.shade100,
  onPressed: () {
    _journalEdit.action = 'Cancel';
    Navigator.pop(context, _journalEdit);
  },
),
```

42. Add a `SizedBox` with the `width` set to `8.0` to place a spacer between the two buttons.

```
SizedBox(width: 8.0),
```

43. Add the second `FlatButton` with the `child` set to a `Text` widget to display `'Save'`. Set the `color` property to `Colors.lightGreen.shade100`, making the button the main action focus.

```
FlatButton(
  child: Text('Save'),
  color: Colors.lightGreen.shade100,
),
```

44. For the `onPressed` property, modify the `_journalEdit.action` to `'Save'`.

```
onPressed: () {
  _journalEdit.action = 'Save';
},
```

45. Since you are saving the entry, declare a `String _id` variable and use the ternary operator to check that the `widget.add` variable is set to `true` and use the `Random().nextInt(9999999)` to generate a random number. If the `widget.add` is `false`, then use the current `_journalEdit.journal.id` since you are editing an existing entry.

Note that `nextInt()` sets the maximum number range from zero, and in our case, you set the maximum to 9999999. Note that for our purposes this works great, but in a production environment, I suggest you use a UUID, which is a 128-bit number that includes alphanumeric characters. A sample UUID looks like this: 409fg342-h34c-25c8-b311-51874523574e.

```
String _id = widget.add ? Random().nextInt(9999999).toString() : _journalEdit
.journal.id;
```

46. Modify the `_journalEdit.journal` value by using the `Journal()` class constructor and pass the `id` property with the `_id` variable, the `date` with the `_selectedDate.toString()` (date is saved as a `String`), the `mood` with the `_moodController.text`, and the `note` with the `_noteController.text`.

```
_journalEdit.journal = Journal(
  id: _id,
  date: _selectedDate.toString(),
  mood: _moodController.text,
  note: _noteController.text,
);
```

47. Call the `Navigator.pop(context, _journalEdit)` to dismiss the entry form and pass the value back to the calling page. You handle receiving this action in the "Finishing the Journal Home Page" exercise.

```
FlatButton(
  child: Text('Save'),
  color: Colors.lightGreen.shade100,
  onPressed: () {
    _journalEdit.action = 'Save';
    String _id = widget.add ? Random().nextInt(9999999).toString() : _journalEdit
.journal.id;
    _journalEdit.journal = Journal(
      id: _id,
      date: _selectedDate.toString(),
      mood: _moodController.text,
      note: _noteController.text,
    );
    Navigator.pop(context, _journalEdit);
  },
),
```

The following is the full `Row` widget code:

```
Row(
  mainAxisAlignment: MainAxisAlignment.end,
  children: <Widget>[
    FlatButton(
      child: Text('Cancel'),
      color: Colors.grey.shade100,
      onPressed: () {
        _journalEdit.action = 'Cancel';
        Navigator.pop(context, _journalEdit);
      },
    ),
    SizedBox(width: 8.0),
    FlatButton(
      child: Text('Save'),
      color: Colors.lightGreen.shade100,
      onPressed: () {
        _journalEdit.action = 'Save';
        String _id = widget.add ? Random().nextInt(9999999).toString() :
_journalEdit.journal.id;
        _journalEdit.journal = Journal(
```

```
        id: _id,
        date: _selectedDate.toString(),
        mood: _moodController.text,
        note: _noteController.text,
      );
      Navigator.pop(context, _journalEdit);
    },
  ),
 ],
),
```

HOW IT WORKS

You created the `edit_entry.dart` file with the `EditEntry` class extending a `StatefulWidget` to handle adding and editing journal entries. You customized the constructor to have the three arguments `add`, `index`, and `journalEdit`. The `add` variable is responsible for handling whether you are adding or modifying an entry; the `index` is -1 if adding a record or is the actual `List` index location if you are editing an entry. The `journalEdit` variable has an `action` value for `'Cancel'` or `'Save'` and the `Journal` class holding the journal entry values for the `id`, `date`, `mood`, and `note` values.

The `showDatePicker()` function displays a popup dialog that contains the Material Design date picker. You pass the `context`, `initialDate`, `firstDate`, and `lastDate` arguments to customize the pickable date range.

To format dates, you use the appropriate `DateFormat` named constructor. To further customize the date format, you can use the `add_*()` methods (substitute the * character with the format characters needed) to append and compound multiple formats.

The `TextEditingController` allows access to the value of the associated `TextField` widget. The `TextField` `TextInputAction` allows you to customize the device keyboard action button. The `FocusNode` is associated to the `TextField` widget, which allows you to set focus on the appropriate `TextField` programmatically. The `TextCapitalization` allows you to configure the `TextField` widget's capitalization by using `words`, `sentences`, and `characters`.

The `JournalEdit` class tracks the entry action and values. It uses the `action` variable to track whether the Save or Cancel button is tapped. It uses the `journal` variable to hold the `Journal` class field values for editing or creating new journal entries. The `Navigator.pop()` method returns the `JournalEdit` class values to the Home page.

Finishing the Journal Home Page

The Home page is responsible for showing a list of journal entries. In Chapter 9, "Creating Scrolling Lists and Effects," you learned how to use the `ListView.builder`, but for this app, you'll learn how to use the `ListView.separated` constructor. By using the `separated` constructor, you have the same benefits of the `builder` constructor because the builders are called only for the children who are visible on the page. You might have noticed I said *builders*, because you use two of them, the standard `itemBuilder` for the `List` of children (journal entries) and the `separatorBuilder` to show a separator between children. The `separatorBuilder` is extremely powerful for customizing the separator; it could be an `Image`, `Icon`, or custom widget, but for our purposes, you'll use a `Divider` widget. You'll use the `ListTile` to format your list of journal entries and customize the `leading` property with a `Column` to show the date and day of the week, making it easier to spot individual entries (Figure 13.5).

To delete journal entries, you'll use a `Dismissible`, which you learned about in Chapter 11, "Applying Interactivity." Keep in mind that for the `Dismissible` to work properly and delete the correct journal entry, you'll set the `key` property to the journal entry id field by using the `Key` class, which takes a `String` value like `Key(snapshot.data[index].id)`.

FIGURE 13.5: Journal entry list

You'll learn how to use the `FutureBuilder` widget, which works with a `Future` to retrieve the latest data without blocking the UI. You learned details in this chapter's "Retrieving Data with the `FutureBuilder`" section.

You'll use a `Future` that you learned how to use in Chapters 3 and 12 ("Learning Dart Basics" and "Writing Platform-Native Code") to retrieve the journal entries. Retrieving the journal entries requires multiple steps, and to help you manage them, you'll use the `database.dart` file classes that you created in the "Adding the Journal Database Classes" section of this chapter. The classes that you use are `DatabaseFileRoutines`, `Database`, `Journal`, and `JournalEdit`.

1. You call the `DatabaseFileRoutines` calls to read the JSON file located in the device documents folder.

2. You call the `Database` class to parse the JSON to a `List` format.

3. You use the `List sort` function to sort entries by DESC date.

4. The sorted `List` is returned to the `FutureBuilder`, and the `ListView` displays existing journal entries.

TRY IT OUT Finishing the Journal Home Page

In this section, you'll finish the Home page by adding methods to load, add, modify, and save journal entries. You'll create a method to build and use the `ListView.separated` constructor to customize your list of journal entries. In the `ListView itemBuilder`, you'll add a `Dismissible` to handle deleting journal entries.

You'll import the `database.dart` file to utilize the database classes to help you to serialize the JSON objects.

1. Import the `edit_entry.dart`, `database.dart` and `intl.dart` packages.

```
import 'package:flutter/material.dart';
import 'package:ch13_local_persistence/pages/edit_entry.dart';
```

```
import 'package:ch13_local_persistence/classes/database.dart';
import 'package:intl/intl.dart'; // Format Dates
```

2. After the class `_HomeState extends State<Home> {`, add the `Database _database` variable. The `_database` variable holds the parsed JSON objects of the `journal` JSON object, which is your list of journal entries.

```
class _HomeState extends State<Home> {
  Database _database;
```

3. Add the `_loadJournals()` async method that returns a `Future<List<Journal>>`, which is a `List` of the `Journal` class entries.

```
Future<List<Journal>> _loadJournals() async {
}
```

4. Add the `await DatabaseFileRoutines().readJournals()` call and add with the dot notation a call to `then((journalsJson) {})`.

What exactly is this call to `then()`? It registers a callback to be called when the `Future` completes. What this means is that once the `readJournals()` method completes and returns the value, `then()` executes the code inside. Note that the `journalsJson` parameter receives the value from the JSON objects read from the saved `local_persistence.json` file located in the device local documents folder.

```
await DatabaseFileRoutines().readJournals().then((journalsJson) {
});
```

5. Inside the `then()` callback, modify the `_database` variable with the value from the call to `databaseFromJson(journalsJson)`.

The `databaseFromJson` method in the `database.dart` class uses `json.decode()` to parse the JSON objects that are read from the saved file. `Database.fromJson()` is called, and it returns the JSON objects as a Dart `List`, which is extremely powerful. At this point, it's clear how separating the code logic to handle your data into the database classes becomes useful and straightforward.

```
_database = databaseFromJson(journalsJson);
```

6. Continue inside the `then()` callback, and let's sort the journal entries by DESC date, with newer entries first and older last. Use `_database.journal.sort()` to compare dates and sort them.

```
_database.journal.sort((comp1, comp2) => comp2.date.compareTo(comp1.date));
```

7. After the `then()` callback, add a new line with the `return` statement returning the variable `_database.journal`, which contains the sorted journal entries.

```
return _database.journal;
```

The following is the full `_loadJournals()` method:

```
Future<List<Journal>> _loadJournals() async {
  await DatabaseFileRoutines().readJournals().then((journalsJson) {
    _database = databaseFromJson(journalsJson);
    _database.journal.sort((comp1, comp2) => comp2.date.compareTo(comp1.date));
  });
  return _database.journal;
}
```

8. Add the _addOrEditJournal() method that handles presenting the edit entry page to either add or modify a journal entry. You use Navigator.push() to present the entry page and wait for the result of the user's actions. If the user pressed the Cancel button, nothing happens, but if they pressed Save, then you either add the new journal entry or save the changes to the current edited entry.

_addOrEditJournal() is an async method taking the named parameters of bool add, int index, and Journal journal. Refer to Table 13.4 for the arguments description. Initiate the JournalEdit _journalEdit variable with the JournalEdit class with the action value set to an empty string and the journal value set to the journal variable that is passed in from the constructor.

```
void _addOrEditJournal({bool add, int index, Journal journal}) async {
  JournalEdit _journalEdit = JournalEdit(action: '', journal: journal);
}
```

9. Add a new line; you are going to use the Navigator to pass the constructor values to the edit entry page by using the await keyword that passes the value back to the local _journalEdit variable. For the MaterialPageRoute builder, pass the constructor values to the EditEntry() class and set the fullscreenDialog property to true.

```
_journalEdit = await Navigator.push(
  context,
  MaterialPageRoute(
    builder: (context) => EditEntry(
      add: add,
      index: index,
      journalEdit: _journalEdit,
    ),
    fullscreenDialog: true
  ),
);
```

Once the edit entry page is dismissed, the switch statement executes next, and you'll take appropriate action depending on the user's selection. The switch statement evaluates the _journalEdit.action to check whether the Save button was pressed and then checks whether you are adding or saving the entry with an if-else statement.

```
switch (_journalEdit.action) {
}
```

10. Add the first switch case statement that checks for the 'Save' value.
If the add variable is set to true, meaning you are adding a new entry, then you use the setState() and call the _database.journal.add(_journalEdit.journal) by passing the journal values.

```
switch (_journalEdit.action) {
  case 'Save':
    if (add) {
      setState(() {
        _database.journal.add(_journalEdit.journal);
      });
    }
    break;
}
```

11. If the add variable is set to `false`, meaning you are saving an existing entry, then you use the `setState()` and modify the value of the `_database.journal[index]` = `_journalEdit.journal`. You are replacing the values from the current `_database.journal[index]` selected journal entry by the index value and replacing it with the `_journalEdit.journal` value passed from the edit entry page.

```
switch (_journalEdit.action) {
  case 'Save':
    if (add) {
      setState(() {
        _database.journal.add(_journalEdit.journal);
      });
    } else {
      setState(() {
        _database.journal[index] = _journalEdit.journal;
      });
    }
    break;
}
```

12. To save the journal entry values to the device local storage documents directory, you call `DatabaseFileRoutines().writeJournals(databaseToJson(_database))`. Add the second case statement that checks for the `'Cancel'` value, but there's no need to add any actions since the user canceled editing.

```
switch (_journalEdit.action) {
  case 'Save':
    if (add) {
      setState(() {
        _database.journal.add(_journalEdit.journal);
      });
    } else {
      setState(() {
        _database.journal[index] = _journalEdit.journal;
      });
    }
    DatabaseFileRoutines().writeJournals(databaseToJson(_database));
    break;
  case 'Cancel':
    break;
}
```

13. Add the `default` check just in case something else happened, but you also do not take any further action.

```
switch (_journalEdit.action) {
  case 'Save':
    if (add) {
      setState(() {
        _database.journal.add(_journalEdit.journal);
      });
    } else {
      setState(() {
        _database.journal[index] = _journalEdit.journal;
      });
    }
```

```
      DatabaseFileRoutines().writeJournals(databaseToJson(_database));
      break;
    case 'Cancel':
      break;
    default:
      break;
  }
}
```

The following is the full _addOrEditJournal method:

```
void _addOrEditJournal({bool add, int index, Journal journal}) async {
  JournalEdit _journalEdit = JournalEdit(action: '', journal: journal);
  _journalEdit = await Navigator.push(
    context,
    MaterialPageRoute(
      builder: (context) => EditEntry(
        add: add,
        index: index,
        journalEdit: _journalEdit,
      ),
      fullscreenDialog: true
    ),
  );
  switch (_journalEdit.action) {
    case 'Save':
      if (add) {
        setState(() {
          _database.journal.add(_journalEdit.journal);
        });
      } else {
        setState(() {
          _database.journal[index] = _journalEdit.journal;
        });
      }
      DatabaseFileRoutines().writeJournals(databaseToJson(_database));
      break;
    case 'Cancel':
      break;
    default:
      break;
  }
}
```

14. Add the _buildListViewSeparated(AsyncSnapshot snapshot) method that takes the
AsyncSnapshot parameter, which is the List of journal entries. The method is called from the
FutureBuilder() in the body property. The way to read the journal entry List is by accessing the
snapshot data property by using snapshot.data. Each journal entry is accessed by using the index
like snapshot.data[index]. To access each field, you use the snapshot.data[index].date or
snapshot.data[index].mood and so on.

```
Widget _buildListViewSeparated(AsyncSnapshot snapshot) {
}
```

15. The method returns a `ListView` by using the `separated()` constructor. Set the `itemCount` property to the `snapshot.data.length` and set the `itemBuilder` property to `(BuildContext context, int index)`.

```
Widget _buildListViewSeparated(AsyncSnapshot snapshot) {
  return ListView.separated(
    itemCount: snapshot.data.length,
    itemBuilder: (BuildContext context, int index) {
    },
  );
}
```

16. Inside the `itemBuilder`, initialize the `String _titleDate` with the `DateFormat.yMMMD()` constructor using the `format()` with the `snapshot.data[index].date`. Since the data is in a `String` format, use the `DateTime.parse()` constructor to convert it to a date.

```
String _titleDate = DateFormat.yMMMd().format(DateTime.parse(snapshot
.data[index].date));
```

17. Initialize the `String _subtitle` with the mood and note fields by using string concatenation and separate them with a blank line by using the `'\n'` character.

```
String _subtitle = snapshot.data[index].mood + "\n" + snapshot.data[index].note;
```

18. Add the `return Dismissible()`, and you'll complete it in step 20.

```
return Dismissible();
```

19. Add the `separatorBuilder` that handles the separator line between journal entries by using a `Divider()` with the `color` property set to `Colors.grey`.

```
Widget _buildListViewSeparated(AsyncSnapshot snapshot) {
  return ListView.separated(
    itemCount: snapshot.data.length,
    itemBuilder: (BuildContext context, int index) {
      String _titleDate = DateFormat.yMMMd().format(DateTime.parse(snapshot
.data[index].date));
      String _subtitle = snapshot.data[index].mood + "\n" + snapshot
.data[index].note;
      return Dismissible();
    },
    separatorBuilder: (BuildContext context, int index) {
      return Divider(
        color: Colors.grey,
      );
    },
  );
}
```

20. Finish the `Dismissible()` widget, which is responsible for deleting journal entries by swiping left or right on the entry itself. Set the `key` property to `Key(snapshot.data[index].id)`, which creates a `key` from the journal entry `id` field.

```
return Dismissible(
  key: Key(snapshot.data[index].id),
);
```

21. The `background` property is shown when the user swipes from left to right, and the `secondaryBackground` property is shown when the user swipes from right to left. For the `background` property, add a `Container` with the `color` set to `Colors.red`, the `alignment` set to `Alignment.centerLeft`, the `padding` set to `EdgeInsets.only(left: 16.0)`, and the `child` property set to `Icons.delete` with the `color` property set to `Colors.white`.

```
return Dismissible(
  key: Key(snapshot.data[index].id),
  background: Container(
      color: Colors.red,
      alignment: Alignment.centerLeft,
      padding: EdgeInsets.only(left: 16.0),
      child: Icon(
        Icons.delete,
        color: Colors.white,
      ),
  ),
);
```

22. For the `secondaryBackground`, use the same properties as the `background` but change the `alignment` property to `Alignment.centerRight`.

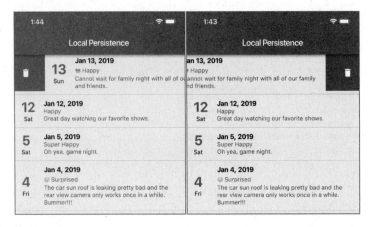

```
return Dismissible(
  key: Key(snapshot.data[index].id),
  background: Container(
      color: Colors.red,
      alignment: Alignment.centerLeft,
      padding: EdgeInsets.only(left: 16.0),
      child: Icon(
        Icons.delete,
        color: Colors.white,
      ),
  ),
  secondaryBackground: Container(
      color: Colors.red,
      alignment: Alignment.centerRight,
      padding: EdgeInsets.only(right: 16.0),
      child: Icon(
```

```
            Icons.delete,
            color: Colors.white,
          ),
        ),
      child: ListTile(),
      onDismissed: (direction) {
        setState(() {
          _database.journal.removeAt(index);
        });
        DatabaseFileRoutines().writeJournals(databaseToJson(_database));
      },
    );
```

23. Finish the `ListTile()` widget, which is responsible for displaying each journal entry. You are going to customize the `leading` property to show the date's day and weekday description. For the `leading` property, add a `Column()` with the `children` list of two `Text` widgets.

```
child: ListTile(
  leading: Column(
    children: <Widget>[
      Text(),
      Text(),
    ],
  ),
),
```

24. The first `Text` widget shows the day; let's format it with the `DateFormat.d()` constructor using the `format()` with the `snapshot.data[index].date`. Since the data is in a `String` format, use the `DateTime.parse()` constructor to convert it to a date.

```
Text(DateFormat.d().format(DateTime.parse(snapshot.data[index].date))),
  ),
```

25. Set the `style` property to `TextStyle` with a `fontWeight` of `FontWeight.bold`, `fontSize` of `32.0`, and `color` set to `Colors.blue`.

```
Text(DateFormat.d().format(DateTime.parse(snapshot.data[index].date))),
  style: TextStyle(
      fontWeight: FontWeight.bold,
      fontSize: 32.0,
      color: Colors.blue),
  ),
```

26. The second `Text` widget shows the weekday; let's format it with the `DateFormat.E()` constructor using the `format()` with the `snapshot.data[index].date`.
Since the data is in a `String` format, use the `DateTime.parse()` constructor to convert it to a date.

```
Text(DateFormat.E().format(DateTime.parse(snapshot.data[index].date))),
```

27. Set the `title` property to a `Text` widget with the `_titleDate` variable and the `style` property to `TextStyle` with the `fontWeight` set to `FontWeight.bold`.

```
title: Text(
  _titleDate,
  style: TextStyle(fontWeight: FontWeight.bold),
),
```

28. Set the `subtitle` property to a `Text` widget with the `_subtitle` variable.

```
subtitle: Text(_subtitle),
```

29. Add the `onTap` property that calls the `_addOrEditJournal()` method and pass the `add` property as `false`, meaning not adding a new entry but modifying the current entry. Set the `index` property to `index`, which is the current entry index in the `List`.
Set the `journal` property to the `snapshot.data[index]`, which is the `Journal` class with the entry details containing the `id`, `date`, `mood`, and `note` fields.

```
onTap: () {
  _addOrEditJournal(
      add: false,
      index: index,
      journal: snapshot.data[index],
  );
},
```

The following is the full `ListTile` widget:

```
child: ListTile(
  leading: Column(
    children: <Widget>[
      Text(DateFormat.d().format(DateTime.parse(snapshot.data[index].date)),
        style: TextStyle(
            fontWeight: FontWeight.bold,
            fontSize: 32.0,
            color: Colors.blue),
      ),
      Text(DateFormat.E().format(DateTime.parse(snapshot.data[index].date))),
    ],
  ),
  title: Text(
    _titleDate,
    style: TextStyle(fontWeight: FontWeight.bold),
  ),
  subtitle: Text(_subtitle),
  onTap: () {
    _addOrEditJournal(
        add: false,
        index: index,
```

```
                journal: snapshot.data[index],
        );
      },
    ),
```

The following is the full `_buildListViewSeparated()` method:

```
// Build the ListView with Separator
Widget _buildListViewSeparated(AsyncSnapshot snapshot) {
  return ListView.separated(
    itemCount: snapshot.data.length,
    itemBuilder: (BuildContext context, int index) {
      String _titleDate = DateFormat.yMMMd().format(DateTime.parse(snapshot
.data[index].date));
      String _subtitle = snapshot.data[index].mood + "\n" + snapshot
.data[index].note;
      return Dismissible(
        key: Key(snapshot.data[index].id),
        background: Container(
          color: Colors.red,
          alignment: Alignment.centerLeft,
          padding: EdgeInsets.only(left: 16.0),
          child: Icon(
            Icons.delete,
            color: Colors.white,
          ),
        ),
        secondaryBackground: Container(
          color: Colors.red,
          alignment: Alignment.centerRight,
          padding: EdgeInsets.only(right: 16.0),
          child: Icon(
            Icons.delete,
            color: Colors.white,
          ),
        ),
        child: ListTile(
          leading: Column(
            children: <Widget>[
              Text(DateFormat.d().format(DateTime.parse(snapshot.data[index].date)),
                style: TextStyle(
                    fontWeight: FontWeight.bold,
                    fontSize: 32.0,
                    color: Colors.blue),
              ),
              Text(DateFormat.E().format(DateTime.parse(snapshot.data[index].date))),
            ],
          ),
          title: Text(
            _titleDate,
            style: TextStyle(fontWeight: FontWeight.bold),
          ),
          subtitle: Text(_subtitle),
          onTap: () {
```

```
              _addOrEditJournal(
                  add: false,
                  index: index,
                  journal: snapshot.data[index],
              );
          },
        ),
        onDismissed: (direction) {
          setState(() {
            _database.journal.removeAt(index);
          });
          DatabaseFileRoutines().writeJournals(databaseToJson(_database));
        },
      );
    },
    separatorBuilder: (BuildContext context, int index) {
      return Divider(
        color: Colors.grey,
      );
    },
  );
}
```

HOW IT WORKS

You completed the home.dart file that is responsible for showing a list of journal entries with the ability to add, modify, and delete individual records.

The FutureBuilder() calls the _loadJournals() method that retrieves journal entries, and while the data is loading, a CircularProgressIndicator() is displayed, and when the data is returned, the builder calls the _buildListViewSeparated(snapshot) method by passing the snapshot, which is the journal entries List.

The _loadJournals() method retrieves journal entries by calling the database classes to read the local database file, convert JSON objects to a List, sort the entries by DESC date, and return the List of journal entries.

The _addOrEditJournal() method handles adding new entries or modifying a journal entry. The constructor takes three named parameters to aid you if you are adding or modifying an entry. It uses the JournalEdit database class to track the action to take depending on whether the user pressed the Cancel or Save button. To show the edit entry page, you pass the constructor arguments by calling Navigator.push() and use the await keyword to receive the action taken from the edit entry page to the _journalEdit variable. The switch statement is used to evaluate the action taken to save the journal entry or cancel the changes.

The _buildListViewSeparated(snapshot) method uses the ListView.separated() constructor to build the list of journal entries. The itemBuilder returns a Dismissible() widget that handles deleting journal entries by swiping left or right on the entry. The Dismissible() child property uses ListTile() to format each journal entry in the ListView. The separatorBuilder returns the Divider() widget to show a grey divider line between journal entries.

SUMMARY

In this chapter, you learned how to persist data by saving and reading locally to the iOS and Android device filesystem. For the iOS device, you used the NSDocumentDirectory, and for the Android device, you used the AppData directory. The popular JSON file format was used to store the journal entries to a file. You created a journaling mood app that sorts the list of entries by DESC date and allows adding and modifying records.

You learned how to create the database classes for handling local persistence to encode and decode JSON objects and write and read entries to a file. You learned how to create the DatabaseFile-Routines class to obtain the path of the local device documents directory and save and read the database file using the File class. You learned how to create the Database class handling decoding and encoding JSON objects and converting them to a List of journal entries. You learned how to use json.encode to parse values to a JSON string and json.decode to parse the string to a JSON object. The Database class returns a List of Journal classes, List<Journal>. You learned how to create the Journal class to handle decoding and encoding the JSON objects for each journal entry. The Journal class contains the id, date, mood, and note fields stored as String type. You learned how to create the JournalEdit class responsible for passing an action and individual Journal class entries between pages.

You learned how to create a journal entry page that handles both adding and modifying an existing journal entry. You learned how to use the `JournalEdit` class to receive a journal entry and return it to the Home page with an `action` and the modified entry. You learned how to call `showDatePicker()` to present a calendar to select a journal date. You learned to use the `DateFormat` class with different formatting constructors to display dates like 'Sun, Jan 13, 2019'. You learned how to use `DateTime.parse()` to convert a date saved as `String` to a `DateTime` instance. You learned how to use the `TextField` widget with the `TextEditingController` to access entry values. You learned how to customize the keyboard action button by setting the `TextField` `TextInput-Action`. You learned how to move the focus between `TextField` widgets by using the `FocusNode` and the keyboard action button.

You learned how to create the Home page to show a list of journal entries sorted by DESC date separated by a `Divider`. You learned how to use the `ListView.separated` constructor to easily separate each journal entry with a separator. `ListView.separated` uses two builders, and you learned how to use the `itemBuilder` for showing the `List` of journal entries and the `separatorBuilder` to add a `Divider` widget between entries. You used the `ListTile` to format the `List` of journal entries easily. You learned how to customize the `leading` property with a `Column` to show the day and weekday on the `leading` side of the `ListTile`. You used the `Dismissible` widget to make it easy to delete journal entries by swiping left or right on the entry itself (`ListTile`). You used the `Key('id')` constructor to set a unique `key` for each `Dismissible` widget to make sure the correct journal entry is deleted.

In the next chapter, you'll learn how to set up the Cloud Firestore backend NoSQL database. Cloud Firestore allows you to store, query, and synchronize data across devices without setting up your own servers.

▶ **WHAT YOU LEARNED IN THIS CHAPTER**

TOPIC	KEY CONCEPTS
Database classes	The four database classes collectively manage local persistence by writing, reading, encoding, and decoding JSON objects to and from the JSON file.
DatabaseFileRoutines class	This handles the File class to retrieve the device's local document directory and save and read the data file.
Database class	This handles decoding and encoding the JSON objects and converting them to a List of journal entries.
Journal class	This handles decoding and encoding the JSON objects for each journal entry.
JournalEdit class	This handles the passing of individual journal entries between pages and the action taken.
showDatePicker	This presents a calendar to select a date.
DateFormat	This formats dates by using different formatting constructors.
DateTime.parse()	This converts a String into a DateTime instance.
TextField	This allows text editing.
TextEditingController	This allows access to the value of the associated TextField.
TextInputAction	The TextField TextInputAction allows the customization of the keyboard action button.
FocusNode	This moves the focus between TextField widgets.
ListView.separated	This uses two builders, the itemBuilder and the separatorBuilder.
Dismissible	Swipe to dismiss by dragging. Use the onDismissed to call custom actions such as deleting a record.
List().sort	Sort a List by using a Comparator.
Navigator	This is used to navigate to another page. You can pass and receive data in a class by using the Navigator.
Future	You can retrieve possible values available sometime in the future.
FutureBuilder	This works with a Future to retrieve the latest data without blocking the UI.

TOPIC	KEY CONCEPTS
CircularProgressIndicator	This is a spinning circular progress indicator showing that an action is running.
path_provider package	You can access local iOS and Android filesystem locations.
intl package	You can use DateFormat to format dates.
dart:io library	You can use the File class.
dart:convert library	You can decode and encode JSON objects.
dart:math	This is used to call the Random() number generator.

14

Adding the Firebase and Firestore Backend

WHAT YOU WILL LEARN IN THIS CHAPTER

- ➤ How to create a Firebase project

- ➤ How to register the iOS and Android projects to use Firebase

- ➤ How to add a Cloud Firestore database

- ➤ How to structure and create a data model for the Cloud Firestore database

- ➤ How to enable and add Firebase authentication

- ➤ How to create Firestore security rules

- ➤ How to create the Flutter client app base structure

- ➤ How to add Firebase to iOS and how to add the Android projects with the Google service files

- ➤ How to add the Firebase and Cloud Firestore packages

- ➤ How to add the `intl` package to format dates

- ➤ How to customize the `AppBar` and `BottomAppBar` look and feel by using the `BoxDecoration` and `LinearGradient` widgets

In this chapter, in Chapter 15, and in Chapter 16, you'll use techniques that you have learned in previous chapters along with new concepts and tie them together to create a production-level mood-journaling app. In the previous chapters, you created many projects that taught you different ways to implement specific tasks and objectives. In a production-level app, you need to combine what you have learned to improve performance by redrawing only the widgets with data changes, pass state between pages and up the widget tree, handle the user authentication credentials, sync data between devices and the cloud, and create classes that handle platform-independent logic between mobile and web apps.

Because Google has open-sourced Flutter support for desktop and web apps, the Firebase backend services can be used for Flutter desktop and web apps, not just mobile. That's why in this chapter you'll learn how to develop a production-level mobile app.

Specifically, you'll learn how to use authentication and persist data to a cloud database by using Google's Firebase (backend server infrastructure), Firebase Authentication, and Cloud Firestore. You'll learn how to create and set up a Firebase project using Cloud Firestore as the cloud database. Cloud Firestore is a NoSQL document database to store, query, and sync data with offline support for mobile and web apps. Did I say offline? Yes, I did. The ability of a mobile app to function while an Internet connection is not available is a must-have feature that users expect. Another great feature of using Cloud Firestore is the ability to synchronize live data between devices automatically. The data syncing is fast, allowing collaboration between different devices and users. The amazing part of using these powerful features is that you don't have to deal with setting up and managing the server's infrastructure. This feature allows you to build serverless applications.

You'll configure the Firebase backend authentication provider, database, and security rules to sync data between multiple devices and platforms. To enable authentication and database services for the client-side Flutter project, you'll add the `firebase_auth` and `cloud_firestore` packages. In Chapter 15 and Chapter 16 you'll learn how to implement app-wide and local state management by using the `InheritedWidget` class and maximize platform code sharing by implementing the Business Logic Component pattern. You'll use app-wide and local state management to request data from different service classes.

WHAT ARE FIREBASE AND CLOUD FIRESTORE?

Before you start configuring, let's take a look at what Firebase encompasses. Firebase consists of one platform with a multitude of products that share and work together. Firebase handles the entire backend server infrastructure connecting iOS, Android, and web apps.

Build Apps

- ➤ **Cloud Firestore**—Store and sync NoSQL data in documents and collections between devices
- ➤ **Real-time database**—Store and sync NoSQL data as one large JSON tree between devices
- ➤ **Cloud storage**—Store and serve files
- ➤ **Cloud functions**—Run backend code
- ➤ **Authentication**—Secure user's authentication
- ➤ **Hosting**—Deliver web app assets

Ensure App Quality

> ➤ **Crashlytics**—Real-time crash reports

> ➤ **Performance monitoring**—App performance

> ➤ **Test lab**—Test apps on devices hosted by Google

Grow Business

> ➤ **In-app messaging**—Send users messages

> ➤ **Google Analytics**—Perform app analytics

> ➤ **Predictions**—User segmentation based on behavior

> ➤ **A/B testing**—Optimize app experience

> ➤ **Cloud messaging**—Send messages and notifications

> ➤ **Remote config**—Modify the app without deploying a new version

> ➤ **Dynamic links**—App deep links

> ➤ **App indexing**—Drive search traffic to a mobile app

Wow, this sounds amazing, but does it cost a fortune? Actually no; Google offers the Spark Plan, which gives you free access to the majority of the products, especially Cloud Firestore. You can view the details and restrictions at `https://firebase.google.com/pricing`.

In this chapter, I'll focus on using Cloud Firestore to store and sync data between devices. For general information on Firebase, you can browse `https://firebase.google.com`.

What is Cloud Firestore? It stores data in documents organized in collections, similar to JSON. It can scale complex and hierarchical data by using subcollections within documents. You'll take a detailed look at it in the next section, "Structuring and Data Modeling Cloud Firestore." It offers offline support for iOS, Android, and web apps. For the iOS and Android platforms, the offline persistence is enabled by default, but for the Web, the offline is disabled by default. To optimize querying data, it supports indexed queries with sorting and filtering. It can use transactions that automatically repeat until the task is completed. Data scaling is automatically handled for you. You use mobile SDKs to integrate different features of Firebase products into your apps.

Structuring and Data Modeling Cloud Firestore

To understand the Cloud Firestore data structure, let's compare it to a standard SQL Server database (see Table 14.1). The SQL Server database is a relational database management system (RDBMS) that supports table and row data modeling (Figure 14.1). The comparison is not a one-to-one but a guideline since the data structures differ.

TABLE 14.1: Data structure comparison

SQL SERVER DATABASE	CLOUD FIRESTORE
Table	Collection
Row	Document
Columns	Data

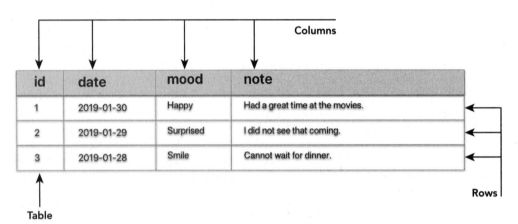

FIGURE 14.1: SQL Server Database Data Model

In Cloud Firestore, a collection can contain only documents. A document is a key-value pair and can optionally point to subcollections. Documents cannot point to another document and must be stored in collections (Figure 14.2).

What is the collection's responsibility? Collections are containers for documents; they hold them the same way a folder holds pages.

What is the document's responsibility? Documents hold data that is stored as a key-value pair similar to JSON. Documents support extra data types that JSON does not support. Each document is identified by name, and they are limited to 1MB in size (see Table 14.2).

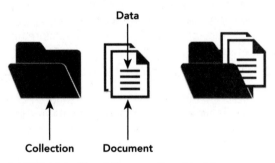

FIGURE 14.2: Cloud Firestore Data Model

TABLE 14.2: Cloud Firestore sample data

TYPE	VALUE
Collection	`journals`
Document	`R5NcTWAaWtHTttYtPoOd`
Document data as key-value pair	`date: "2019-0202T13:41:12.537285"` `mood: "Happy"` `note: "Great movie."` `uid: "F1GGeKiwp3jRpoCVskdBNmO4GUN4"`

Let's take a look at the Cloud Firestore sample data as JSON objects and in the Cloud Firestore console (Figure 14.3). Notice that the document name is a unique ID that can be automatically created by Cloud Firestore, or you can manually generate it.

```
{
    "journals":[
        {
            " R5NcTWAaWtHTttYtPoOd1":{
                "date": "2019-0202T13:41:12.537285",
                "mood":"Happy",
                "note":"Great movie."
                "uid": " F1GGeKiwp3jRpoCVskdBNmO4GUN4",
            }
        }
    ]
}
```

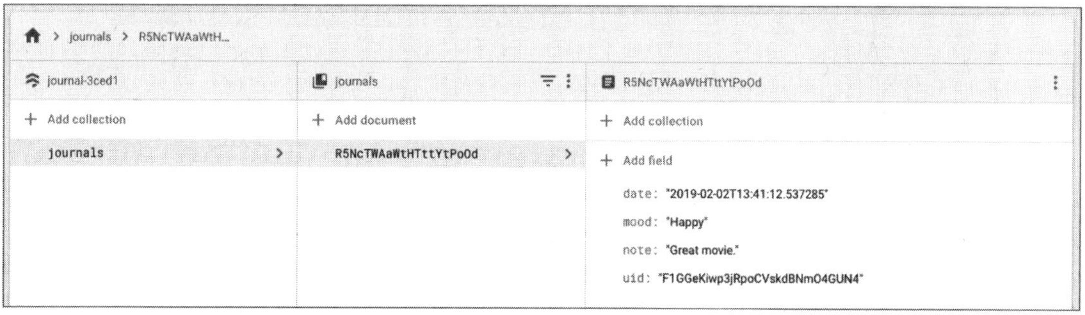

FIGURE 14.3: Collection and Document

Cloud Firestore supports many data types such as array, Boolean, byte, date and time, floating-point number, geographical point, integer, map, reference, text string, and null. One of the major advantages of using Cloud Firestore is the automatic syncing of data between devices and the ability of the client app to continue working offline while the Internet is not available.

Viewing Firebase Authentication Capabilities

Adding security to an app is extremely important in keeping the information private and safe. Firebase Authentication provides built-in backend services accessible from the client's SDK to support full authentication. The following is a list of the currently available authentication sign-in providers:

- ➤ Email/Password
- ➤ Phone
- ➤ Google
- ➤ Play Games (Google)
- ➤ Game Center (Apple)
- ➤ Facebook
- ➤ Twitter
- ➤ GitHub
- ➤ Anonymous

Each authentication sign-in provider is disabled by default, and you enable the providers needed for your app specs (Figure 14.4). I'll walk you through how to enable a sign-in provider later in this chapter.

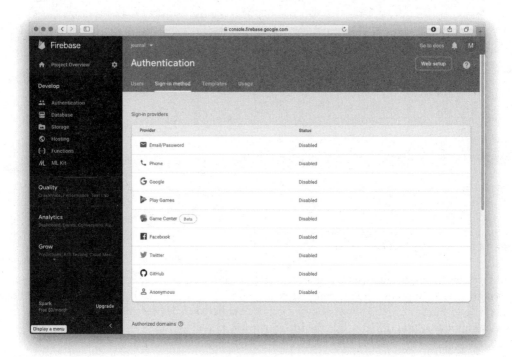

FIGURE 14.4: Firebase Authentication's Sign-In Providers

An important note on using the Anonymous provider is that if the user deletes the app from the device and reinstalls it, a new anonymous user is created and will not have access to the previous data. The data from the original anonymous user is still stored on the backend, but the client app has no way of knowing the original anonymous user ID since the app was deleted from the device. One example of using the Anonymous sign-in provider is to allow the user free access to the app and allow a paid upgrade path to advanced features.

From your mobile app, you retrieve the user's authentication credentials from any of the available sign-in providers. You pass these credentials to the client Firebase Authentication SDK, and the Firebase backend services verify whether credentials are valid and return a response to the client app. If the credentials are valid, you allow the user to access the data and pages in the app depending on the security rules that you will learn about in the next section, "Viewing Cloud Firestore Security Rules."

Once a particular sign-in provider is enabled, you use the Firebase Authentication SDK to create a Firebase User object saved on the Firebase backend. The Firebase User object has a set of properties that you can customize, except for the unique ID. You can customize the primary email address, name, and a photo URL (usually the user's photo or an avatar). By using the Firebase User object's unique ID, you bind all the data that the user has created to the ID.

Viewing Cloud Firestore Security Rules

To secure access to collections and documents, you implement Cloud Firestore security rules. In the previous section, you learned that you create a Firebase User object through the Firebase Authentication SDK. Once you have the Firebase User object's unique ID, you use it with Cloud Firestore security rules to secure and lock data to each user. The following code shows the security rules that you'll create for securing the Cloud Firestore database:

```
service cloud.firestore {
  match /databases/{database}/documents {
    match /journals/{document=**} {
      allow read, write: if resource.data.uid == request.auth.uid;
      allow create: if request.auth.uid != null;
    }
  }
}
```

The rules are editable from the database rules page on the Firebase console website. The rules consist of using the match statements to identify documents, with the allow expressions to control access to the documents. Every time you change the rules and save them, a history of changes is automatically created, allowing you to revert changes if needed (Figure 14.5).

Let's take a look at an example that requires rules to allow a user to read and write documents assigned to them. The first match /databases/{database}/documents declaration tells the rules to match any Cloud Firestore Database in the project.

```
match /databases/{database}/documents
```

The second and the main part of understanding is to use the match statement to point to the collection and expression to evaluate, as in match /journals/{document=**}. The journals declaration is the container name, and the expression to evaluate is document=** (all documents for the journals collection) wrapped inside curly brackets. Inside this particular match, you use the allow expression for the read and write privileges by using the if statement to see whether the resource .data.uid value equals the request.auth.uid. The resource.data.uid is the uid field inside the document, and the request.auth.uid is the logged-in user's unique ID.

```
match /journals/{document=**} {
    allow read, write: if resource.data.uid == request.auth.uid;
}
```

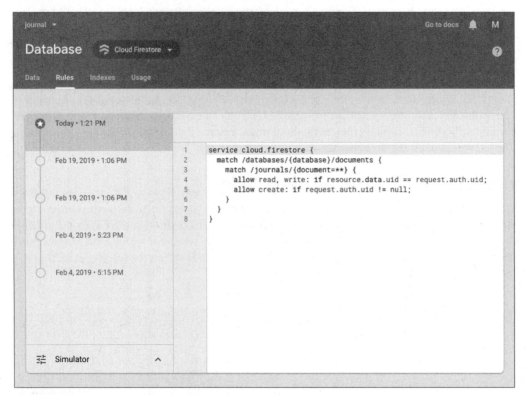

FIGURE 14.5: Cloud Firestore Rules

You can break down the rules even further by using a match statement for each read or write action. For the read rule, it can be broken into get and list. For the write rule, it can be broken into create, update, and delete.

```
// Read
allow get: if <condition>;
allow list: if <condition>;

// Write
allow create: if <condition>;
allow update: if <condition>;
allow delete: if <condition>;
```

The following example uses the `create` rule to allow only authenticated users to add new records by checking whether the `request.auth.id` value is not equal to a `null` value:

```
allow create: if request.auth.uid != null;
```

CONFIGURING THE FIREBASE PROJECT

You now understand how Cloud Firestore stores data and the benefits of syncing multiple devices with offline data persistence. The offline feature works by caching a copy of the app's active data, making it accessible when the device is offline. Before you can use Cloud Firestore in your app, you need to create a Firebase project.

A Firebase project is backed by the Google Cloud Platform, which allows apps to scale. The Firebase project is a container that supports sharing features such as the database, notifications, users, remote config, crash reports, and analytics (many more) between the iOS, Android, and web apps. Each account can have multiple projects, for example to separate different and unrelated applications.

TRY IT OUT Creating the Firebase Project

You need to create a Firebase project that sets up a container to start adding your Cloud Firestore database and enabling authentication. You will start by adding the iOS app, and then you'll continue by adding the Android app.

1. Navigate to `https://console.firebase.google.com` and log in to Google Firebase with your Google account. If you do not have a Google account, you can create one at `https://accounts .google.com/SignUp`.

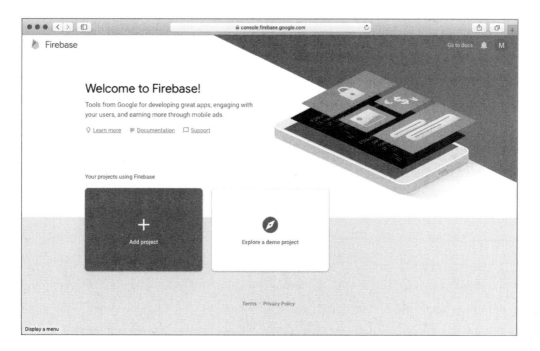

2. Click the Add Project button in Firebase; the Add A Project dialog will open. For the project name, enter journal; the project ID is automatically created for you. Notice it takes the project name and adds a unique identifier to it like journal-aa2f3. (Your ID will be different because each project name must be unique.)

The location of the Cloud Firestore project is automatically selected for you, but you can change it if you like. You will need to select each checkbox to accept the Google Analytics terms; then click the Create Project button.

3. When you are presented with the dialog showing that the new project is ready, click the Continue button.

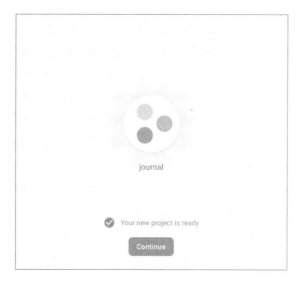

IOS

4. From the main Firebase project page, click the iOS button to add Firebase to the iOS app that you created in the section "Adding Authentication and Cloud Firestore Packages to the Client App."

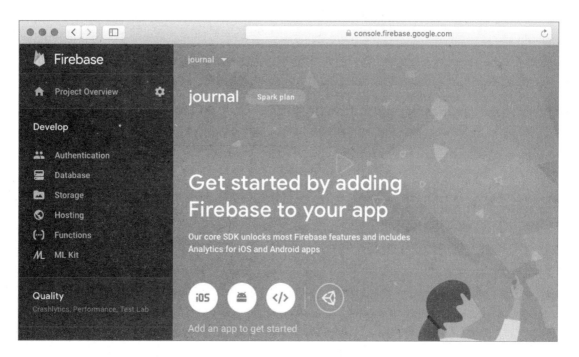

5. Enter the iOS bundle ID, as in com.domainname.journal. The bundle ID is the reverse domain name, *com.domainname*, combined with the Flutter app name of *journal*.

6. Enter the optional app nickname Journal and skip the optional App Store ID since this is obtained once an app is created from Apple's iTunes Connect to submit an app for distribution approval. Click the Register App button.

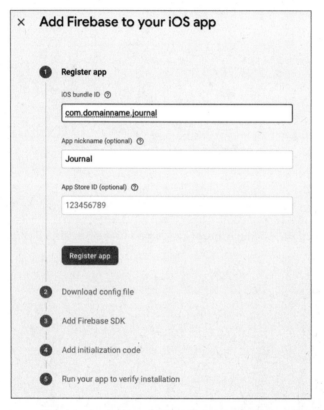

7. Click the Download GoogleService-Info.plist button. (You'll add the downloaded `GoogleService-Info.plist` file to your Xcode project in the section "Adding Authentication and Cloud Firestore Packages to the Client App.")

8. Click the Next button, and skip the Add Firebase SDK and Add Initialization Code steps. You are skipping these steps because the Firebase SDK is added in the section "Adding Authentication and Cloud Firestore Packages to the Client App."

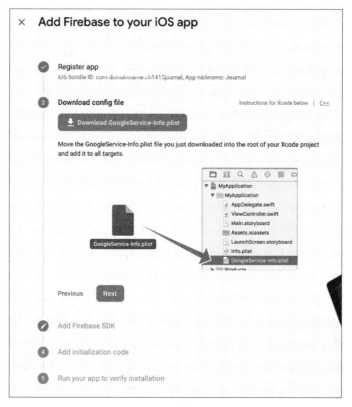

9. Click Skip This Step in the Run Your App To Verify Installation step.

10. On the main Firebase project page, click the Add App button.

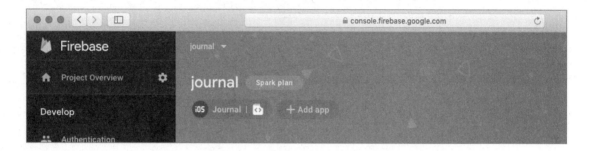

ANDROID

11. Click the Android button to add Firebase to the Android project that you created in the section "Adding Authentication and Cloud Firestore Packages to the Client App."

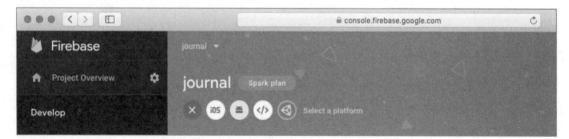

12. Enter the Android package name, such as com.domainname.journal. The bundle ID is the reverse domain name, *com.domainname*, combined with a Flutter app name of *journal*. You'll create the Flutter app in the section "Adding Authentication and Cloud Firestore Packages to the Client App."

13. Enter the optional app nickname Journal and skip the step of optional debug signing certificate SHA-1. Click the Register App button.

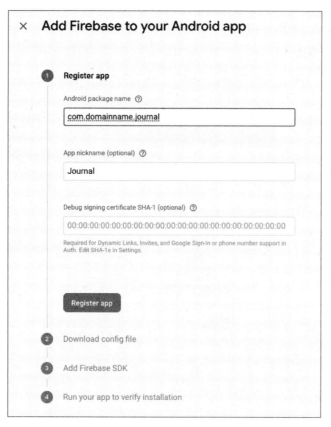

14. Click the Download googleservices.json button. (You'll add the downloaded `googleservices` `.json` file to your Android project in the section "Adding Authentication and Cloud Firestore Packages to the Client App.")

15. Click the Next button and skip the Add Firebase SDK step. You are skipping this step because the Firebase SDK is added in the section "Adding Authentication and Cloud Firestore Packages to the Client App."

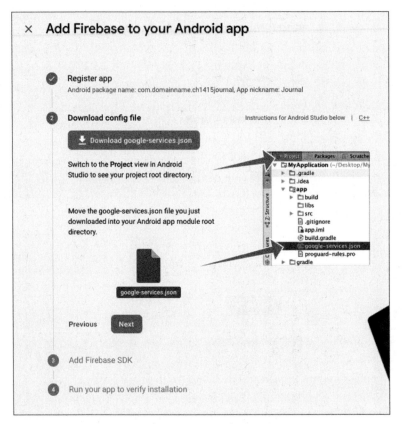

16. Click Skip This Step in the Run Your App To Verify Installation step.

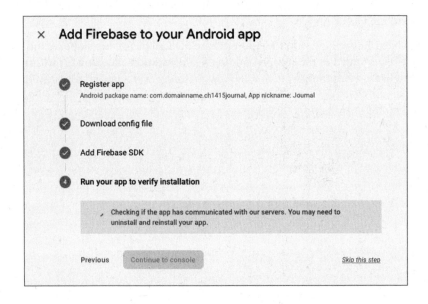

You will be automatically brought to the main Firebase project page, showing the iOS and Android projects you just added.

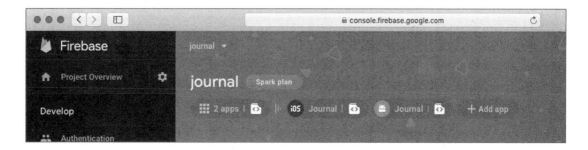

HOW IT WORKS

Navigate to the Firebase console panel at `https://console.firebase.google.com` to add or select existing projects. When you add a project and give it a name, a unique project ID is automatically created with the option to rename it. Once the project is created, the project ID cannot be changed. The server's location is automatically chosen, but you have the option to change it.

Once a Firebase project is created, you register the iOS and Android projects to use Firebase. To register each project, you enter **com.domainname.journal** for the iOS bundle ID and the Android package name. For the iOS project, you download the `GoogleService-Info.plist` file and for the Android project the `googleservices.json` file. These files are added to the Flutter app in the Xcode and Android projects in the section "Adding Authentication and Cloud Firestore Packages to the Client App."

ADDING A CLOUD FIRESTORE DATABASE AND IMPLEMENTING SECURITY

You've learned how to create a Firebase project, making it possible to add the Cloud Firestore database and Firebase Authentication. You learned about the different available sign-in methods, and in this section, you'll walk through how to implement security rules and enable an authentication sign-in method—specifically, an email/password authentication provider.

TRY IT OUT Creating the Cloud Firestore Database and Enabling Authentication

In this exercise, you'll learn how to enable Firebase Authentication, create a Cloud Firestore database, and implement security rules to keep the data private for each user.

1. Navigate to `https://console.firebase.google.com` and select the journal project.

2. From the menu on the left, click the Authentication link in the Develop section. If the Develop section is closed, click the Develop link to open the submenu. Click the Sign-in Method tab showing a list of available sign-in providers.

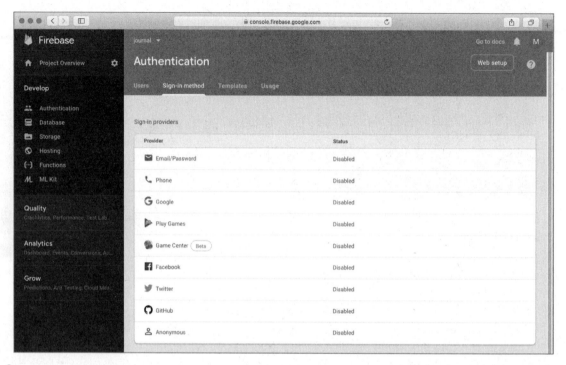

3. Click the Email/Password option, click Enable to turn on the feature, and click the Save button.

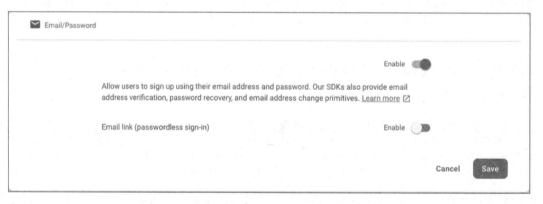

4. In the left menu, click the Database link and click the Create Database (Cloud Firestore) button.

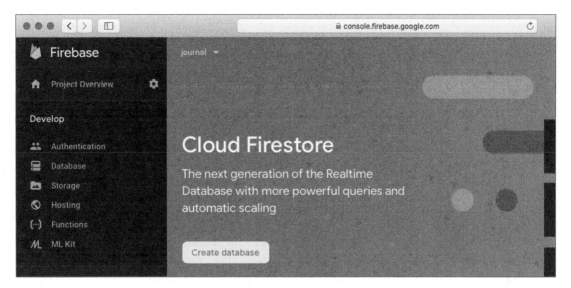

5. In the Security Rules For Cloud Firestore dialog, leave the locked mode radio button selected and click the Enable button. The locked mode creates the basic security rules with the access locked for reading and writing privileges.

The following code shows the default security rules that are automatically created when you click the Enable button. The current security rules deny all read and write requests, making it completely safe but also inaccessible, which you will modify in step 6.

```
service cloud.firestore {
  match /databases/{database}/documents {
    match /{document=**} {
      allow read, write: if false;
    }
  }
}
```

6. Tap the Rules tab to edit the default locked rules and change `match /{document=**}` to `match /journals/{document=**}`. `{document=**}` matches any document, but you are going to use a granular approach by matching the `journals` collection and `document` to the logged-in user ID. This approach allows you to restrict each document to each user ID, keeping the data secure for the rightful owner of the data.

7. Change `allow read, write: if false;` to `allow read, write: if resource.data.uid == request.auth.uid;`, restricting the data field `uid` to match the logged-in `uid`. The `resource.data.uid` is the `uid` field inside the document, and the `request.auth.uid` is the logged-in user unique ID. Add `allow create: if request.auth.uid != null;` to allow creating new records if the user is authenticated.

```
service cloud.firestore {
  match /databases/{database}/documents {
    match /journals/{document=**} {
      allow read, write: if resource.data.uid == request.auth.uid;
      allow create: if request.auth.uid != null;
    }
  }
}
```

Note that a history log of changes is automatically created, allowing the reverting of changes if needed.

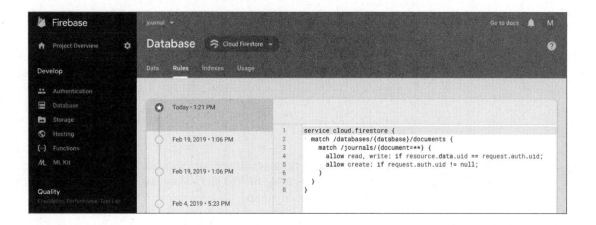

HOW IT WORKS

Navigate to `https://console.firebase.google.com` and select the journal project. Navigate to the Authentication page and select the Sign-in Method tab to enable and disable sign-in providers. Navigate to the Database page to create or edit databases and in this case Cloud Firestore. From the Database page, select the Rules tab to view or modify current security rules. With every saved edit, the history of changes is automatically created, making it easy to revert changes if needed.

BUILDING THE CLIENT JOURNAL APP

The process of creating the mood-journaling app spans from this chapter to Chapter 16. In this section, you'll create the base structure of the app and configure the iOS and Android projects to use Firebase Authentication and the Cloud Firestore database. You'll modify the basic look and feel of the app by using color gradients.

The goal of the mood-journaling app is to have the ability to list, add, and modify journal entries by collecting a date, a mood, a note, and the user's ID. You'll learn to create a login page to authenticate users through the email/password Firebase Authentication sign-in provider. The main presentation page implements a `ListView` widget by using the `separated` constructor sorted by DESC (descending) date, meaning last entered record first. The `ListTile` widget easily formats how you'll display the `List` of records. The journal entry page uses the `showDatePicker` widget to select a date from a calendar, a `DropdownButton` widget to select from a list of moods, and a `TextField` widget to enter the note.

Adding Authentication and Cloud Firestore Packages to the Client App

It's time to create the Flutter app and add the Firebase Authentication and Cloud Firestore SDKs by installing the Firebase Flutter packages. The Flutter team authors the different Firebase packages, and like other packages, the full package source code is available on the appropriate package's GitHub page.

You'll install the `firebase_auth`, `cloud_firestore`, and `intl` packages. You'll download the Google service files (config) for iOS and Android that contain properties needed to access the Firebase products from the client app.

TRY IT OUT Creating the Journal App

In this example, you'll build a production-level journal app similar to the one in Chapter 13, but instead, it uses Firebase Authentication for security and the Cloud Firestore database for storing and syncing data. The structure of how you read and save data is completely different. You'll also add mood tracking to each journal entry. You'll use some new and familiar packages in this exercise.

➤ To add security to your journal app, you'll use the `firebase_auth` package, which provides authentication.

➤ To add data-storage capabilities, you'll use the `cloud_firestore` package, which provides cloud syncing and storing.

➤ To format dates, you'll use the `intl` package, which provides internationalization and localization. You learned how to use it in Chapter 13 in the "Formatting Dates" section.

1. Create a new Flutter project and name it `journal`. You can follow the instructions in Chapter 4, "Creating a Starter Project Template."

Note that since this app continues in the next two chapters, to keep things simple, the project name does not start with the chapter number. Naming the project `journal` also results in the package name `com.domainname.journal`, matching the iOS bundle ID and Android package name. Since you are using Cloud Firestore, the package name must exactly match what you entered when you registered the iOS and Android projects in the Firebase console. As a side note, you can also manually change the package name when creating a new Flutter project.

For this project, you need to create the `pages`, `classes`, `services`, `models`, and `blocs` folders.

2. Open the `pubspec.yaml` file to add resources. In the `dependencies:` section, add the `firebase_auth:^0.11.1+6` and `cloud_firestore:^0.12.5` and `intl:^0.15.8` declarations. Note that your package's version may be higher.

```
dependencies:
  flutter:
    sdk: flutter

  # The following adds the Cupertino Icons font to your application.
  # Use with the CupertinoIcons class for iOS style icons.
  cupertino_icons: ^0.1.2

  firebase_auth: ^0.11.1+6
  cloud_firestore: ^0.12.5
  intl: ^0.15.8
```

3. Click the Save button, and depending on the editor you are using, it automatically runs the `flutter packages get`; once finished, it shows the message `Process finished with exit code 0`. If it does not automatically run the command for you, open the Terminal window (located at the bottom of your editor) and type **`flutter packages get`**.

4. From the Flutter project, open the iOS Xcode project to add Firebase. From Android Studio, click the menu bar and select Tools ⇨ Flutter ⇨ Open iOS Module In Xcode.

5. Drag the downloaded `GoogleService-Info.plist` file to the `Runner` folder in the Xcode project.

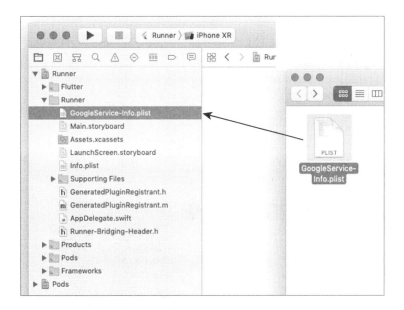

6. In the next dialog, finish adding the `GoogleService-Info.plist` file and make sure Copy Items If Needed is checked, the Create Folder References radio button is selected, and the Add To Targets ⇨ Runner option is checked. The iOS Xcode project is now configured to handle Firebase and Firestore. Once the file is copied, close Xcode.

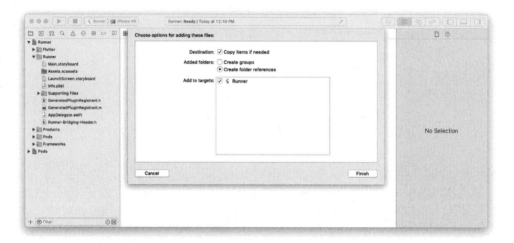

7. From the Flutter project, open the Android Studio project to add Firebase. From Android Studio, click the menu bar and select Tools ⇨ Flutter ⇨ Open For Editing In Android Studio.

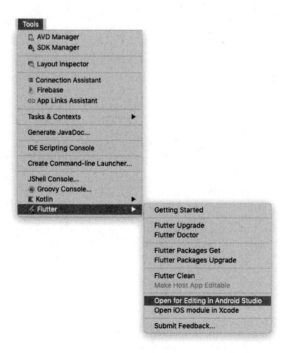

8. Drag the downloaded `google-services.json` file to the `App` folder in the Android project. If you do not see the `App` folder, make sure in the Android Studio tool window that the Project view (top left) is selected, not the Android view.

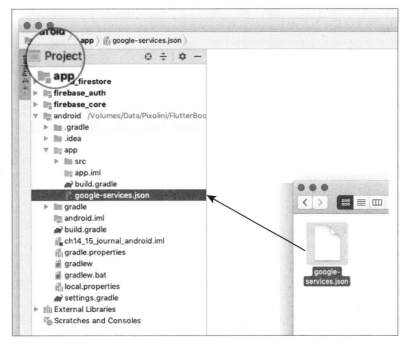

9. Finish adding the `google-services.json` file and click the OK button.

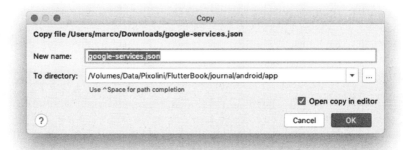

10. For the Android project, you need to edit two files manually. For the first file, open the app-level `build.gradle` file located at `android/app/build.gradle`. Add to the bottom of the file the google-services gradle plugin by specifying `apply plugin: 'com.google.gms.google-services'`. In this app-level `build.gradle` file, make sure you are using `compileSdkVersion 28`, `minSdkVersion 16`, and `targetSdkVersion 28` and save.

11. To avoid receiving ".dex file cannot exceed 64 error" when you try to run the Flutter app for Android, you need to add the `multiDexEnabled true` in the `defaultConfig` section and save. Note that this step may not be needed in future updates. You can review the Android Studio multidex user guide page at `https://developer.android.com/studio/build/multidex`.

```
android {
    compileSdkVersion 28

    sourceSets {...}

    lintOptions {...}

    defaultConfig {
        applicationId "com.domainname.journal"
        minSdkVersion 16
        targetSdkVersion 28
        // ...
        // Enable if you get error in Flutter app - .dex file cannot exceed 64K
        multiDexEnabled true // Enable
    }

    buildTypes {...}
}

flutter {...}

dependencies {
    // ...}

// Add at the bottom of the file
apply plugin: 'com.google.gms.google-services'
```

```
24  apply plugin: 'com.android.application'
25  apply plugin: 'kotlin-android'
26  apply from: "$flutterRoot/packages/flutter_tools/gradle/flutter.gradle"
27
28  android {
29      compileSdkVersion 28
30
31      sourceSets {
32          main.java.srcDirs += 'src/main/kotlin'
33      }
34
35      lintOptions {
36          disable 'InvalidPackage'
37      }
38
39      defaultConfig {
40          // TODO: Specify your own unique Application ID (https://developer.android.com
41          applicationId "com.domainname.journal"
42          minSdkVersion 16
43          targetSdkVersion 28
44          versionCode flutterVersionCode.toInteger()
45          versionName flutterVersionName
46          testInstrumentationRunner "android.support.test.runner.AndroidJUnitRunner"
47          // Enable if you get error in Flutter app - .dex file cannot exceed 64K
48          multiDexEnabled true // Enable
49      }
50
51      buildTypes {...}
58  }
59
60  flutter {source '../..'}
63
64  dependencies {
65      implementation "org.jetbrains.kotlin:kotlin-stdlib-jdk7:$kotlin_version"
66      testImplementation 'junit:junit:4.12'
67      androidTestImplementation 'com.android.support.test:runner:1.0.2'
68      androidTestImplementation 'com.android.support.test.espresso:espresso-core:3.0.2'
69      // Add if you get error in Flutter app - .dex file cannot exceed 64K
70      // The multidex library as a dependency
71      implementation 'com.android.support:multidex:1.0.3'
72  }
73
74  apply plugin: 'com.google.gms.google-services'
```

12. For the second file, open the project-level `build.gradle` file located at `android/build.gradle`. Add to the `dependencies` the `classpath` of the `google-services` plugin and save.

```
buildscript {
  // ...
  dependencies {
    // ...
    // Add the following line:
    classpath 'com.google.gms:google-services:4.2.0' // googleservices plugin
  }
}
```

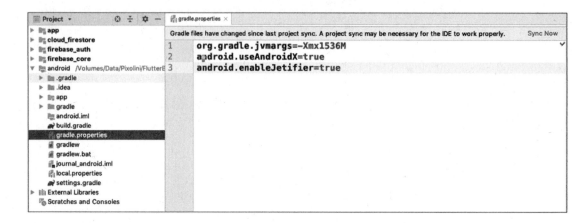

13. To avoid receiving AndroidX errors, edit the project-level `gradle.properties` file by adding the following two lines and save the file. Note that this manual step may not be needed in future updates. Enabling AndroidX compatibility depends on the plugins requirement.

    ```
    android.useAndroidX=true
    android.enableJetifier=true
    ```

14. You will see a yellow bar with a notice that the gradle files have changed. Click the Sync Now button, and once the process is done, close the Android project.

HOW IT WORKS

You declared the `firebase_auth`, `cloud_firestore`, and `intl` packages in your `pubspec.yaml` file. The `firebase_auth` package gives you the ability to use Firebase Authentication to secure the application. The `cloud_firestore` package gives you the ability to use the Cloud Firestore database to sync and store data on the cloud. The `intl` package gives you the ability to format dates.

You used Xcode to import the `GoogleService-info.plist` file to the iOS project. You used Android Studio to import the `google-services.json` file to the Android project. For the Android project, you modified the project and app-level `build.gradle` files to enable the Firebase plugins. The Google service files import all the properties needed to access the Firebase project products.

From the Firebase console, you registered the iOS and Android projects with the iOS bundle ID and Android package name of `com.domainname.journal`, matching exactly the Flutter's project package name of `com.domainname.journal`.

Adding Basic Layout to the Client App

In the previous section, you learned how to add and configure Firebase Authentication and the Cloud Firestore database. The next step is to work on the Flutter project to customize the look and feel of the journal app.

You'll customize the app's background color by setting the `MaterialApp canvasColor` property to a light shade of green. The `AppBar` and `BottomAppBar` customizations show a color gradient from light green to a *very* light shade of green, merging with the app's background color. To achieve the color effect, set the `BoxDecoration gradient` property by using a `LinearGradient` widget that you learned in Chapter 6, "Using Common Widgets."

TRY IT OUT Adding a Basic Layout to the Journal App

In this section, continue to edit the `journal` project by customizing the app's colors and look and feel, giving it that professional look.

1. Open the `main.dart` file. Modify the `MaterialApp title` property to `Journal` and modify the `ThemeData primarySwatch` property to `Colors.lightGreen`. Add the `canvasColor` property and set the color to `Colors.lightGreen.shade50`. Add the `bottomAppBarColor` property and set the color to `Colors.lightGreen`.

```
return MaterialApp(
  debugShowCheckedModeBanner: false,
  title: 'Journal',
  theme: ThemeData(
    primarySwatch: Colors.lightGreen,
    canvasColor: Colors.lightGreen.shade50,
    bottomAppBarColor: Colors.lightGreen,
  ),
  home: Home(),
);
```

2. Open the `home.dart` file, set the `AppBar title` property's `Text` widget to `Journal`, and set the `TextStyle color` property to `Colors.lightGreen.shade800`.

3. To customize the `AppBar` background color with a gradient, remove the `AppBar` widget shadow by setting the `elevation` property to `0.0`. To increase the `AppBar`'s height, set the `bottom` property to a `PreferredSize` widget with the `child` property as a `Container` widget and the `preferredSize` property to `Size.fromHeight(32.0)`.

4. Set the `flexibleSpace` property to a `Container` widget, with the `decoration` property set to a `BoxDecoration` widget.

5. Set the `BoxDecoration gradient` property to a `LinearGradient` with the `colors` property set to a list of `[Colors.lightGreen, Colors.lightGreen.shade50]`.

6. Set the `begin` property to `Alignment.topCenter` and the `end` property to `Alignment.bottom-Center`. The `LinearGradient` effect draws the `AppBar` color from a `lightGreen` and gradually fades to a `lightGreen.shade50` color.

```
appBar: AppBar(
  title: Text('Journal',
      style: TextStyle(color: Colors.lightGreen.shade800)),
  elevation: 0.0,
  bottom: PreferredSize(
      child: Container(), preferredSize: Size.fromHeight(32.0)),
  flexibleSpace: Container(
    decoration: BoxDecoration(
      gradient: LinearGradient(
        colors: [Colors.lightGreen, Colors.lightGreen.shade50],
        begin: Alignment.topCenter,
        end: Alignment.bottomCenter,
      ),
    ),
  ),
),
```

7. Add an `IconButton` widget to the `AppBar` `actions` property. Set the `icon` property to `Icons.exit_to_app`, with the `color` property set to `Colors.lightGreen.shade800`.

8. Add to the `onPressed` property a `TODO:` comment with a reminder to add a method to sign out the current user.

```
actions: <Widget>[
  IconButton(
    icon: Icon(
      Icons.exit_to_app,
      color: Colors.lightGreen.shade800,
    ),
    onPressed: () {
      // TODO: Add signOut method
    },
  ),
],
```

9. Add the `Scaffold bottomNavigationBar` property and set it to a `BottomAppBar` widget. To customize the `BottomAppBar` background color with a gradient, remove the `BottomAppBar` widget shadow by setting the `elevation` property to `0.0`. Set the `BottomAppBar` `child` property to a `Container` widget with the `height` property set to `44.0`.

10. Set the `Container decoration` property to a `BoxDecoration` widget. Set the `BoxDecoration` `gradient` property to a `LinearGradient`, with the `colors` property set to a list of `[Colors .lightGreen.shade50, Colors.lightGreen]`.

11. Set the `begin` property to `Alignment.topCenter`, and set the `end` property to `Alignment .bottomCenter`. The `LinearGradient` effect draws the `AppBar` color from a `lightGreen. shade50` and gradually fades to a `lightGreen` color.

```
bottomNavigationBar: BottomAppBar(
  elevation: 0.0,
  child: Container(
    height: 44.0,
    decoration: BoxDecoration(
      gradient: LinearGradient(
        colors: [Colors.lightGreen.shade50, Colors.lightGreen],
        begin: Alignment.topCenter,
        end: Alignment.bottomCenter,
      ),
    ),
  ),
),
```

12. Add the `Scaffold floatingActionButtonLocation` property and set it to `FloatingActionButtonLocation.centerDocked`.

```
floatingActionButtonLocation: FloatingActionButtonLocation.centerDocked,
```

13. The `FloatingActionButton` is responsible for adding new journal entries. Add the `Scaffold` `floatingActionButton` property and set it to a `FloatingActionButton` widget, with the `tooltip` property set to `Add Journal Entry` and with the `backgroundColor` property set to `Colors.lightGreen.shade300`. Set the `child` property to `Icons.add`.

14. Add the `FloatingActionButton onPressed` property and mark it with the `async` keyword and a `TODO:` comment with a reminder to add a method to add journal entries.

```
floatingActionButton: FloatingActionButton(
  tooltip: 'Add Journal Entry',
  backgroundColor: Colors.lightGreen.shade300,
  child: Icon(Icons.add),
  onPressed: () async {
    // TODO: Add _addOrEditJournal method
  },
),
```

HOW IT WORKS

You modified the `MaterialApp ThemeData canvasColor` property to light green and a `bottomAppBar-Color` property to light green. You customized the home page `AppBar` and `BottomAppBar` widgets to show a light green color gradient. You customized the `BoxDecoration gradient` property to use a `Lin-earGradient` to achieve smooth gradient color shading. You added to the `AppBar actions` property an `IconButton` that is used to log out a user. To dock the `FloatingActionButton` to the `BottomAppBar` widget, you added a `floatingActionButtonLocation` property set to `centerDocked`. You added a `FloatingActionButton` widget that is used to add a new journal entry.

Adding Classes to the Client App

You'll need to create two classes to handle formatting dates and tracking the mood icons. The `FormatDates` class uses the `intl` package to format dates. The `MoodIcons` class stores reference to the mood icons `title`, `color`, `rotation`, and `icon`.

TRY IT OUT   Adding the FormatDates and MoodIcons Classes

In this section, continue to edit the `journal` project by adding the `FormatDates` and `MoodIcons` classes.

1. Create a new Dart file in the `classes` folder. Right-click the `classes` folder, select New ⇨ Dart File, enter **`FormatDates.dart`**, and click the OK button to save.

2. Import the `intl.dart` package and create the `FormatDates` class. You learned how to use the `DateFormat` class in Chapter 13's "Formatting Dates" section. Add the `dateFormatShortMonth-DayYear`, `dateFormatDayNumber`, and `dateFormatShortDayName` methods.

```dart
import 'package:intl/intl.dart';

class FormatDates {
  String dateFormatShortMonthDayYear(String date) {
    return DateFormat.yMMMd().format(DateTime.parse(date));
  }

  String dateFormatDayNumber(String date) {
    return DateFormat.d().format(DateTime.parse(date));
  }

  String dateFormatShortDayName(String date) {
    return DateFormat.E().format(DateTime.parse(date));
  }
}
```

3. Create a new Dart file in the `classes` folder. Right-click the `classes` folder, select New ⇨ Dart File, enter `mood_icons.dart`, and click the OK button to save. Import the `material.dart` package and create the `MoodIcons` class.

```dart
class MoodIcons {
}
```

4. Add the `title`, `color`, `rotation`, and `icon` variables and mark them `final`. Depending on the mood, each icon is shown by a different color and rotation; for example, the happy icon is rotated toward the left, and the sad icon is rotated toward the right.

5. Add a new line and enter the `MoodIcons` constructor with named parameters by enclosing them in the curly brackets (`{}`). Reference each `title`, `color`, `rotation`, and `icon` variable by using syntactic sugar to access the values with the `this` keyword, referring to the current state in the class.

```dart
class MoodIcons {
  final String title;
  final Color color;
  final double rotation;
  final IconData icon;

  const MoodIcons({this.title, this.color, this.rotation, this.icon});
}
```

6. You'll finish adding methods to the MoodIcons class in step 8 because they need access to the _moodIconsList variable containing the list of mood-setting icons. The list contains five mood configurations containing title, color, rotation, and icon.

Add a line after the MoodIcons class and declare the _moodIconsList variable as a List<MoodIcons> using the const keyword for performance gain since the list will not change. Initialize the _moodIconsList with the list of MoodIcons using the const keyword.

7. Add five MoodIcons() classes using the const keyword and populate the constructor with the following values:

```
const List<MoodIcons> _moodIconsList = const <MoodIcons>[
  const MoodIcons(title: 'Very Satisfied', color: Colors.amber, rotation: 0.4,
icon: Icons.sentiment_very_satisfied),
  const MoodIcons(title: 'Satisfied', color: Colors.green, rotation: 0.2, icon:
Icons.sentiment_satisfied),
  const MoodIcons(title: 'Neutral', color: Colors.grey, rotation: 0.0, icon: Icons.
sentiment_neutral),
  const MoodIcons(title: 'Dissatisfied', color: Colors.cyan, rotation: -0.2, icon:
Icons.sentiment_dissatisfied),
  const MoodIcons(title: 'Very Dissatisfied', color: Colors.red, rotation: -0.4,
icon: Icons.sentiment_very_dissatisfied),
];
```

8. Go back inside the MoodIcons class and add the getMoodIcons, getMoodColor, getMoodRotation, and getMoodIconsList methods to retrieve the appropriate icon attribute values. The first three methods use the List object's indexWhere method to find the matching icon attributes. The last method returns the full list of mood icons.

```
IconData getMoodIcon(String mood) {
  return _moodIconsList[_moodIconsList.indexWhere((icon) => icon.title == mood)]
.icon;
}

Color getMoodColor(String mood) {
  return _moodIconsList[_moodIconsList.indexWhere((icon) => icon.title == mood)]
.color;
}

double getMoodRotation(String mood) {
  return _moodIconsList[_moodIconsList.indexWhere((icon) => icon.title == mood)]
.rotation;
}

List<MoodIcons> getMoodIconsList() {
  return _moodIconsList;
}
```

SUMMARY

In this chapter, you learned how to persist and secure data over app launches by using Google's Firebase, Firebase Authentication, and Cloud Firestore. Firebase is the infrastructure that doesn't require the developer to set up or maintain backend servers. The Firebase platform allows you to connect and share data between iOS, Android, and web apps. You configure the Firebase project with the online web console. In this chapter, you registered both the iOS and Android projects with the com .domainname.journal package name to connect the client app to the Firebase products.

You created a Cloud Firestore database that safely stores the client app's data in a cloud database. Cloud Firestore is a NoSQL document database to store, query, and sync data with offline support for mobile and web apps. You structure and data model Cloud Firestore databases by using a collection to store documents that contain data as a key-value pair similar to JSON.

Securing the Cloud Firestore database is done by creating Cloud Firestore security rules. The security rules consist of using the match statements to identify documents, with the allow expression to control access.

Firebase Authentication provides built-in backend services that are accessible from the client's SDK, which supports full user authentication. Enabling the email/password authentication sign-in provider allows users to register and log in to the app. By passing the user credentials (email/password) to the client's Firebase Authentication SDK, the Firebase backend services verify whether the credentials are valid and return a response to the client app.

You created the base structure of the client mood-journaling app and connected it to the Firebase services by installing the firebase_auth and cloud_firestore packages. You configured the client iOS and Android projects to use Firebase. You added the GoogleService-Info.plist file to the iOS project and the google-services.json file to the Android project. The Google service files contain properties needed to access the Firebase products from the client app. You modified the base look and feel of the app by using the BoxDecoration widget, with the gradient property set to a Linear-Gradient to create a smooth light green color gradient.

In the next chapter, you'll learn how to implement app-wide and local state management by using the InheritedWidget class and how to maximize platform code sharing and separation by implementing the Business Logic Component pattern. You'll use state management to implement Firebase Authentication, access the Cloud Firestore database, and implement service classes.

▶ **WHAT YOU LEARNED IN THIS CHAPTER**

TOPIC	KEY CONCEPTS
Google's Firebase	Firebase consists of one platform with many products that work together as a backend server infrastructure connecting iOS, Android, and web apps.
Cloud Firestore	You learned how to structure and data model the Cloud Firestore database. Cloud Firestore is a NoSQL document database to store, query, and sync data with offline support.
Firebase Authentication	Firebase Authentication provides built-in backend services accessible from the client's SDK, supporting full authentication.
Cloud Firestore Security Rules	To secure access to data, you learned how to implement Cloud Firestore security rules. Rules consist of using the `match` statements to identify documents with the `allow` expressions.
Cloud Firestore collection	A collection can contain only documents.
Cloud Firestore document	A document is a key-value pair and can optionally point to subcollections. Documents cannot point to another document and must be stored in collections.
`firebase_auth` package	You learned how to add the `firebase_auth` package to enable authentication in the Flutter app.
`cloud_firestore` package	You learned how to add the `cloud_firestore` package to provide database storing and cloud syncing in the Flutter app.
`GoogleService-Info .plist` file	You learned how to add the `google-services.json` file to the iOS Xcode project to connect the client app to the Firebase services.
`google-services .json` file	You learned how to add the `google-services.json` file to the Android project to connect the client app to the Firebase services. For the Android project, you also learned how to modify the project and app-level gradle files to use Firebase Authentication and Cloud Firestore.
Flutter app base layout	You learned how to use the `BoxDecoration` widget by setting the `gradient` property to a `LinearGradient` list of colors to enhance the look and feel of the app.

15

Adding State Management to the Firestore Client App

WHAT YOU WILL LEARN IN THIS CHAPTER

➤ How to use state management to control Firebase Authentication and the Cloud Firestore database

➤ How to use the BLoC pattern to separate business logic

➤ How to use the `InheritedWidget` class as a provider to manage and pass state

➤ How to implement `abstract` classes

➤ How to use `StreamBuilder` to receive the latest data from Firebase Authentication and the Cloud Firestore database

➤ How to use `StreamController`, `Stream`, and `Sink` to handle Firebase Authentication and Cloud Firestore data events

➤ How to create service classes to handle Firebase Authentication and Cloud Firestore API calls with `Stream` and `Future` classes

➤ How to create a model class for individual journal entries and convert Cloud Firestore `QuerySnapshot` and map it to the `Journal` class

➤ How to use the optional Firestore Transaction to save data to the Firestore database

➤ How to create a class to handle mood icons, descriptions, and rotation

➤ How to create a class to handle date formatting

➤ How to use the `ListView.separated` named constructor

In this chapter, you'll continue to edit the mood journaling app created in Chapter 14. For your convenience, you can use the `ch14_final_journal` project as your starting point and make sure you add your `GoogleService-Info.plist` file to the Xcode project and the `google-services.json` file to the Android project that you downloaded in Chapter 14 from your Firebase console.

You'll learn how to implement app-wide and local-state management that uses the `InheritedWidget` class as a provider to manage and pass `State` between widgets and pages.

You'll learn how to use the Business Logic Component (BLoC) pattern to create BLoC classes, for example managing access to the Firebase Authentication and Cloud Firestore database service classes. You'll learn how to use a reactive approach by using `StreamBuilder`, `StreamController`, and `Stream` to populate and refresh data.

You'll learn how to create a service class to manage the Firebase Authentication API by implementing an `abstract` class that manages the user login credentials. You'll create a separate service class to handle the Cloud Firestore database API. You'll learn how to create a `Journal` model class to handle the mapping of the Cloud Firestore `QuerySnapshot` to individual records. You'll learn how to create a mood icons class to manage a list of mood icons, a description, and an icon rotation position according to the selected mood. You'll learn how to create a date formatting class using the `intl` package.

IMPLEMENTING STATE MANAGEMENT

Before you dive into state management, let's take a look at what state means. At its most basic, *state* is data that is read synchronously and can change over time. For example, a `Text` widget value is updated to show the latest game score, and the state for the `Text` widget is the value. *State management* is the way to share data (state) between pages and widgets.

You can have app-wide state management to share the state between different pages. For example, the authentication state manager monitors the logged-in user and when the user logs out, it takes the appropriate action to redirect to the login page. Figure 15.1 shows the home page getting the state from the main page; this is app-wide state management.

You can have local-state management confined to a single page or a single widget. For example, the page displays a selected item, and the purchase button needs to be enabled only if the item is in-stock. The button widget needs to access the state of the in-stock value. Figure 15.2 shows an Add button getting state up the widget tree; this is local-state management.

There are many different techniques for handling state management, and there isn't a right or wrong answer on which approach to take because it depends on your needs and personal preference. The beauty is that you can create a custom approach to state management. You have already mastered one of the state-management techniques, the `setState()` method. In Chapter 2 you learned how to use the `StatefulWidget` and call the `setState()` method to propagate changes to the UI. Using the `setState()` method is the default way that a Flutter app manages state changes, and you have used it for all of the example apps that you've created from this book.

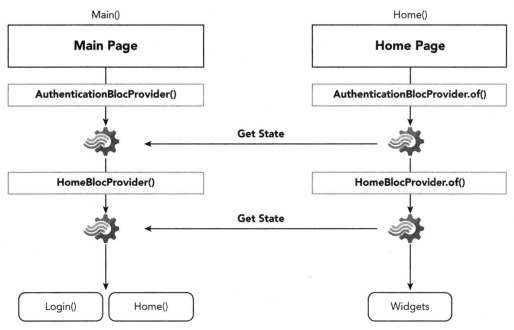

FIGURE 15.1: App-wide state management

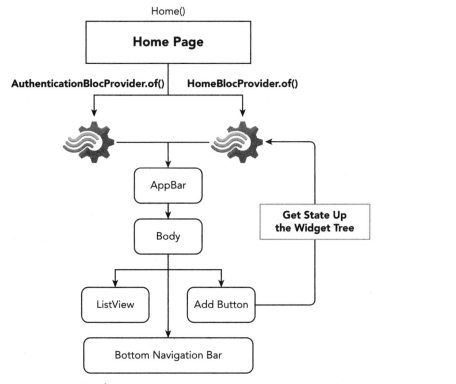

FIGURE 15.2: Local-state management

To show different state management approaches, the journal app uses a combination of an `abstract` class and an `InheritedWidget` class as providers, plus a service class, a mood utility class, a date utility class, and the BLoC pattern to separate the business code logic from the UI.

Implementing an Abstract Class

One of the main benefits of using an abstract class is to separate the interface methods (called from the UI) from the actual code logic. In other words, you declare the methods without any implementation (code). Another benefit is that the abstract class cannot be directly instantiated, meaning an object cannot be created from it unless you define a factory constructor. Abstract classes help you to program to interfaces, not the implementation. Concrete classes implement the methods of the abstract class.

By default (concrete) classes define an interface containing all of the members and methods that it implements. The following example shows the `AuthenticationService` class declaring a variable and methods containing the code logic:

```
class AuthenticationService {
    final FirebaseAuth _firebaseAuth = FirebaseAuth.instance;

    Future<void> sendEmailVerification() async {
      FirebaseUser user = await _firebaseAuth.currentUser();
      user.sendEmailVerification();
    }

    Future<bool> isEmailVerified() async {
      FirebaseUser user = await _firebaseAuth.currentUser();
      return user.isEmailVerified;
    }
}
```

You are going to use an `abstract` class to define your authentication interface in this section. The `abstract` class has callable methods without containing the actual code (implementation), and they are called *abstract methods*. To declare an `abstract` class, you use the `abstract` modifier before the class declaration like `abstract class Authentication {}`. The abstract methods work with a class that implements one or more interfaces and is declared by using the `implements` clause like this example: `class AuthenticationService implements Authentication {}`. Note that the abstract method is declared by using a semicolon (`;`) instead of the body declared by curly brackets (`{}`). The code logic for the abstract methods is implemented (concrete implementation) in the class that implements the `abstract` class.

The following example declares the `Authentication` class as an `abstract` class by using the `abstract` modifier and contains two abstract methods. The `AuthenticationService` class uses the `implements` clause to implement the methods declared by the `Authentication` class.

```
abstract class Authentication {
  Future<void> sendEmailVerification();
  Future<bool> isEmailVerified();
}
```

```
class AuthenticationService implements Authentication {
  final FirebaseAuth _firebaseAuth = FirebaseAuth.instance;

  Future<void> sendEmailVerification() async {
    FirebaseUser user = await _firebaseAuth.currentUser();
    user.sendEmailVerification();
  }

  Future<bool> isEmailVerified() async {
    FirebaseUser user = await _firebaseAuth.currentUser();
    return user.isEmailVerified;
  }
}
```

Why use an abstract class instead of declaring a class with variables and methods? Of course, you can use the class without creating an abstract class for the interface since the class already declares them by default. But one of the benefits of using an abstract class is to impose implementation and design constraints.

For the journal app, the main benefits of using abstract classes are to use them in the BLoC classes, and with *dependency injection* you inject the platform-dependent implementation classes, making the BLoC classes platform-agnostic. Dependency injection is a way to make a class independent of its dependencies. The class does not contain platform-specific code (libraries), but it is passed (injected) at runtime. You'll learn about the BLoC pattern in the "Implementing the BLoC Pattern" section of this chapter.

Implementing the InheritedWidget

One of the ways to pass State between pages and the widget tree is to use the InheritedWidget class as a provider. A provider holds an object and provides it to its child widgets. For example, you use the InheritedWidget class as the provider of a BLoC class responsible for making API calls to the Firebase Authentication API. As a reminder, the BLoC pattern is covered in the "Implementing the BLoC Pattern" section. In the example we'll go through now, I cover how to use the Inherited-Widget class with a BLoC class, but you could also use it with a regular service class instead. You'll learn how to create service classes in the "Implementing the Service Class" section.

For the journal app, the relationship between the InheritedWidget class and the BLoC class is one to one, meaning one InheritedWidget class for one BLoC class. You'll use the of(context) to get a reference to the BLoC class; for example, AuthenticationBlocProvider.of(context). authenticationBloc.

The following example shows the AuthenticationBlocProvider class that *extends* (subclasses) the InheritedWidget class. The BLoC authenticationBloc variable is marked as final, which references the AuthenticationBloc BLoC class. The AuthenticationBlocProvider constructor takes a Key, Widget, and this.authenticationBloc variable.

```
// authentication_provider.dart
class AuthenticationBlocProvider extends InheritedWidget {
  final AuthenticationBloc authenticationBloc;
```

```
   const AuthenticationBlocProvider({Key key, Widget child, this.authenticationBloc})
 : super(key: key, child: child);

   static AuthenticationBlocProvider of(BuildContext context) {
      return (context.inheritFromWidgetOfExactType(AuthenticationBlocProvider) as
 AuthenticationBlocProvider);
   }

   @override
   bool updateShouldNotify(AuthenticationBlocProvider old) => authenticationBloc !=
 old.authenticationBloc;
   }
```

To access the `AuthenticationBlocProvider` class from a page, you use the `of()` method. When a page loads, the `InheritedWidget` needs to be called from the `didChangeDependencies` method, not the `initState` method. If the inherited values change, they would not be called again from the `initState`, but to make sure the widget updates when the values change, you need to use the `didChangeDependencies` method.

```
// page.dart
@override
void didChangeDependencies() {
   super.didChangeDependencies();
   _authenticationBloc = AuthenticationBlocProvider.of(context).authenticationBloc;
}

// Logout a user from a button widget
_authenticationBloc.logoutUser.add(true);
```

Implementing the Model Class

The model class is responsible for modeling the data structure. The data model represents the data structure for how the data is stored in the database or data storage. The data structure declares the data type for each variable as a `String` or `Boolean`. You can also implement methods that perform a specific function like mapping data from one format to another.

The following example shows a model class declaring the data structure and a method to map and convert data:

```
class Journal {
   String documentID;
   String date;

   Journal({
      this.documentID,
      this.date
   });

   factory Journal.fromDoc(dynamic doc) => Journal(
        documentID: doc.documentID,
        date: doc["date"]
   );
}
```

Implementing the Service Class

The journal app uses Firebase Authentication to verify user credentials and the Cloud Firestore database for storing data to the cloud. The services are invoked by making the appropriate API call.

Creating a class to group all of the same type services together is a great option. Another benefit of separating services in service classes is that this makes it easier to create separate classes to implement additional or alternative services. For the journal app, you'll learn how to implement the service classes as abstract classes, but for this example, I wanted to show you how to implement the basic service class.

The following example shows a `DbFirestoreService` class that implements methods to call the Cloud Firestore database API:

```
class DbFirestoreService {
  Firestore _firestore = Firestore.instance;
  String _collectionJournals = 'journals';

  DbFirestoreService() {
    _firestore.settings(timestampsInSnapshotsEnabled: true);
  }

  Stream<List<Journal>> getJournalList(String uid) {
    return _firestore
        .collection(_collectionJournals)
        .where('uid', isEqualTo: uid)
        .snapshots()
        .map((QuerySnapshot snapshot) {
      List<Journal> _journalDocs = snapshot.documents.map((doc) => Journal
.fromDoc(doc)).toList();
      _journalDocs.sort((comp1, comp2) => comp2.date.compareTo(comp1.date));
      return _journalDocs;
    });
  }

  Future<bool> addJournal(Journal journal) async {}
  void updateJournal(Journal journal) async {}
  void updateJournalWithTransaction(Journal journal) async {}
  void deleteJournal(Journal journal) async {}
}
```

Implementing the BLoC Pattern

BLoC stands for Business Logic Component, and it was conceived to define a platform-agnostic interface for the business logic. The BLoC pattern was developed internally by Google to maximize code sharing between Flutter mobile and AngularDart web apps. It was first publicly presented by Paolo Soares at the DartConf 2018 conference. The BLoC pattern exposes streams and sinks to handle data flow, making the pattern reactive. In its simplest form, reactive programming handles the data flow with asynchronous streams and the propagation of data changes. The BLoC pattern omits how the data store is implemented; that is up to the developer to choose according to project requirements. By separating the business logic, it does not matter which infrastructure you use to build your app; other parts of the app can change, and the business logic remains intact.

Paolo Soares shared the following BLoC pattern guidelines at the DartConf 2018 conference.

The BLoC pattern has design guidelines to adhere to:

➤ Inputs and outputs are Streams and Sinks only

➤ Platform agnostic and dependencies must be injectable

➤ No platform branching allowed

➤ Implementation is up to the developer like reactive programming

The BLoC pattern has UI design guidelines to adhere to:

➤ Create a BLoC for each complex enough component

➤ Components should send inputs as is

➤ Components should show outputs as close as possible to as is

➤ All branching should be based on simple BLoC Boolean outputs

You'll learn to use the `InheritedWidget` as a provider to access and pass the BLoC classes between pages. You'll also learn how to instantiate a BLoC without a provider for pages that do not require sharing a reference between them—for example, the login page.

The following summarizes the BLoC pattern guidelines presented at the DartConf 2018 conference.

➤ Move business logic to BLoCs

➤ Keep UI components simple

➤ Design rules aren't negotiable

Let's take a look at a BLoC class structure. Although it's not required, I name the class with a descriptive name and the word *Bloc* like `HomeBloc`. The following example `HomeBloc` class handles the database calls to the `DbFirestoreService` API service class, retrieves the list of converted journal entries, and then sends it back to the widget (UI). The `DbFirestoreService` is injected to the `HomeBloc()` constructor, making it platform independent. In the `HomeBloc` class, the `DbApi` abstract class is platform independent and receives the injected `DbFirestoreService` class. The Business Logic Component processes, formats, and sends the output back to the widget, and the receiving client app could be mobile, web, or desktop, resulting in business logic separation and maximum code sharing between platforms.

The following example shows how the platform-dependent `DbFirestoreService()` class is injected to the `HomeBloc(DbFirestoreService())` constructor, resulting in the `HomeBloc()` class remaining platform independent.

```
// Inject the DbFirestoreService() to the HomeBloc() from UI widgets page
// by using dependency injection
HomeBloc(DbFirestoreService());

// BLoC pattern class
// The HomeBloc(this.dbApi) constructor receives
// the injected DbFirestoreService() class
```

```
class HomeBloc {
  final DbApi dbApi;

  final StreamController<List<Journal>> _journalController =
StreamController<List<Journal>>();
  Sink<List<Journal>> get _addJournal => _journalController.sink;
  Stream<List<Journal>> get listJournal => _journalController.stream;

  // Constructor
  HomeBloc(this.dbApi) {
    _startListeners();
  }

  // Close StreamControllers when no longer needed
  void dispose() {
    _journalController.close();
  }

  void _startListeners() {
    // Retrieve Firestore Journal Records as List<Journal> not DocumentSnapshot
    dbApi.getJournalList().listen((journalDocs) {
      _addListJournal.add(journalDocs);
    });
  }
}
```

Implementing StreamController, Streams, Sinks, and StreamBuilder

The StreamController is responsible for sending data, done events, and errors on the stream property. The StreamController has a sink (input) property and a stream (output) property. To add data to the stream, you use the sink property, and to receive data from the stream, you listen to the stream events by setting up listeners. The Stream class is asynchronous data events, and the Sink class allows the adding of data values to the StreamController stream property.

The following example shows how to use the StreamController class. You use the Sink class to add data with the sink property and the Stream class to send data with the stream property of the StreamController. Note the use of the get keyword for the _addUser (Sink) and the user (Stream) declarations. The get keyword is called a getter, and it's a special method that provides read and write access to the object's properties.

```
final StreamController<String> _authController = StreamController<String>();
Sink<String> get _addUser => _authController.sink;
Stream<String> get user => _authController.stream;
```

To add data to the stream property, you use the sink property's add(event) method.

```
_addUser.add(mood);
```

To listen to stream events, you use the listen() method to subscribe to the stream. You also use the StreamBuilder widget to listen for stream events.

```
_authController.listen((mood) {
  print('My mood: $mood');
})
```

When you need multiple listeners to the `StreamController` stream property, use the `Stream-Controller` broadcast constructor. For example, you might have a `StreamBuilder` widget and a listener listening to the same `StreamController` class.

```
final StreamController<String> _authController = StreamController<String>
.broadcast();
```

The `StreamBuilder` widget rebuilds itself based on the latest `snapshot` of new events from a `Stream` class, and you'll use it to build your reactive widgets to display data. In other words, the `Stream-Builder` rebuilds every time it receives a new event from a `stream`.

```
StreamBuilder(
  initialData: '',
  stream: user,
  builder: (BuildContext context, AsyncSnapshot snapshot) {
    return Text('Hello $snapshot.data');
  },
)
```

Use the `initialData` property to set the initial data `snapshot` before the `stream` sends the latest data events. The `builder` is always called before the `stream` listener has a chance to process data, and by setting the `initialData`, a default value is shown instead of a blank value.

```
initialData: '',
```

The `stream` property is set to the `stream` responsible for the latest data events, for example, the `StreamController` stream property.

```
stream: user,
```

The `builder` property is used to add your logic to build a widget according to the results of the `stream` data events. The `builder` property takes the `BuildContext` and `AsyncSnapshot` parameters. The `Async-Snapshot` contains the connection and data information that you learned in Chapter 13's "Retrieving Data with the FutureBuilder" section. Make sure that the `builder` returns a widget; otherwise, you'll receive an error that the build functions returned a `null`. In Flutter the build functions must never return a `null` value.

```
builder: (BuildContext context, AsyncSnapshot snapshot) {
  return Text('Hello $snapshot.data');
},
```

The following example shows how to use the `StreamBuilder` widget to reactively change the UI widget depending on the `stream` property value. This reactive programming results in performance gain since only this widget in the widget tree rebuilds to redraw a new value when the stream changes. Note that the `user` stream is configured from the previous `StreamController` example.

```
StreamBuilder(
  initialData: '',
  stream: user,
  builder: (BuildContext context, AsyncSnapshot snapshot) {
    if (snapshot.connectionState == ConnectionState.waiting) {
      return Container(color: Colors.yellow,);
    } else if (snapshot.hasData) {
      return Container(color: Colors.lightGreen);
    } else {
      return Container(color: Colors.red);
    }
  },
),
```

BUILDING STATE MANAGEMENT

Before implementing state management for the client journal app that you created in Chapter 14, let's go over the overall plan and priority steps. In order of creation, you'll create the model class, service classes, utility classes, validator classes, BLoC classes, and `InheritedWidget` class as a provider, and finally you'll add state management and BLoCs for all pages. You begin by modifying the main page, creating the login page, modifying the home page, and creating the entry page.

Note that from the UI widget pages you'll inject the platform-specific `authentication.dart` and `db_firestore.dart` service classes to the BLoC class constructor. The BLoC class uses the API abstract class to receive the injected platform-specific service class, making the BLoC class platform-agnostic. If you were also creating a web version of the journal app, you would inject the web appropriate authentication and database service classes to the BLoC classes, and they would just work; these are some the benefits of using the BLoC pattern.

Table 15.1 lists the folders and pages structure for the journal app.

TABLE 15.1: Folders and files structure

FOLDERS	FILES
blocs	authentication_bloc.dart
	authentication_bloc_provider.dart
	home_bloc.dart
	home_bloc_provider.dart
	journal_edit_bloc.dart
	journal_edit_bloc_provider.dart
	login_bloc.dart
classes	format_dates.dart
	mood_icons.dart
	validators.dart
models	journal.dart
pages	edit_entry.dart
	home.dart
	login.dart
services	authentication.dart
	authentication_api.dart
	db_firestore.dart
	db_firestore_api.dart
Root folder	main.dart

To help you visualize the app that you are developing, Figure 15.3 shows the final design for the mood journaling app. From left to right, it shows the login page, home page, journal-entry deletion, and edit entry page.

FIGURE 15.3: The final mood journal app

Adding the Journal Model Class

For the journal app, you'll create a `Journal` model class that is responsible for holding individual journal entries and mapping a Cloud Firestore document to a `Journal` entry. The `Journal` class holds the `documentID`, `date`, `mood`, `note`, and `uid String` fields. The `documentID` variable stores a reference to the Cloud Firestore database document unique ID. The `uid` variable stores the logged-in user unique ID. The `date` variable is formatted as an ISO 8601 standard, for example, 2019-03-18T13:56:54.985747. The mood variable stores the mood name like `Satisfied`, `Neutral`, and so on. The note variable stores the detailed journal description for the entry.

TRY IT OUT   Creating the Journal Model Class

In this section, continue to edit the `journal` project that you created in Chapter 14. You'll be adding the `Journal` model class.

1. Create a new Dart file under the `models` folder. Right-click the `models` folder, select New ⇨ Dart File, enter **journal.dart,** and click the OK button to save.

2. Create the `Journal` class structure.

```
class Journal {

}
```

3. Inside the `Journal` class add the declarations for the `documentID`, `date`, `mood`, `note`, and `uid` `String` variables.

```
String documentID;
String date;
String mood;
String note;
String uid;
```

4. Add a new line and enter the `Journal` constructor with named parameters by enclosing them in curly brackets (`{}`). Reference each `documentID`, `date`, `mood`, `note`, and `uid` variable by using the syntactic sugar to access the values with the `this` keyword, referring to the current state in the class.

```
Journal({
  this.documentID,
  this.date,
  this.mood,
  this.note,
  this.uid
});
```

5. Add a new line and enter the `factory Journal.fromDoc()` method that is responsible for converting and mapping a Cloud Firestore database document record to an individual Journal entry.

```
factory Journal.fromDoc(dynamic doc) => Journal(
    documentID: doc.documentID,
    date: doc["date"],
    mood: doc["mood"],
    note: doc["note"],
    uid: doc["uid"]
);
```

The following is the full Journal class:

```
class Journal {
  String documentID;
  String date;
  String mood;
  String note;
  String uid;

  Journal({
    this.documentID,
    this.date,
    this.mood,
    this.note,
    this.uid
  });

  factory Journal.fromDoc(dynamic doc) => Journal(
      documentID: doc.documentID,
```

```
        date: doc["date"],
        mood: doc["mood"],
        note: doc["note"],
        uid: doc["uid"]
    );
}
```

HOW IT WORKS

You created the `journal.dart` file containing the `Journal` class that is responsible for tracking individual journal entries with the `documentID`, date, mood, note, and uid `String` variables. You created the `Journal.fromDoc()` method that maps a Cloud Firestore database document record to an individual `Journal` entry.

Adding the Service Classes

They are called service classes because they send and receive calls to a service. The journal app has two service classes to handle the Firebase Authentication and Cloud Firestore database API calls.

The `AuthenticationService` class implements the `AuthenticationApi abstract` class. The `DbFirestoreService` class implements the `DbApi abstract` class. The following is a sample call to the Cloud Firestore database to query records; Table 15.2 describes the details:

```
Firestore.instance
    .collection("journals")
    .where('uid', isEqualTo: uid)
    .snapshots()
```

TABLE 15.2: How to query the database

CALL	DESCRIPTION
`Firestore.instance`	Obtain the `Firestore.instance` reference.
`.collection('journals')`	Specify the collection name.
`.where('uid', isEqualTo: uid)`	The `where()` method filters by the specified field.
`.snapshots()`	The `snapshots()` method returns a `Stream` of a `QuerySnapshot` containing the record(s).

Cloud Firestore supports using transactions. One of the benefits of using transactions is to group multiple operations (add, update, delete) in one transaction. Another case is concurrent editing: when multiple users are editing the same record, the transaction is run again, making sure the latest data is used before updating. If one of the operations fails, the transaction will not do a partial update. However, if the transaction is successful, all of the updates are executed.

The following is a sample transaction that takes the _docRef document reference and calls the run-Transaction() method to update the document's data:

```
DocumentReference _docRef = _firestore.collection('journals').document('Cf409us32');
var journalData = {
  'date': journal.date,
  'mood': journal.mood,
  'note': journal.note,
};
_firestore.runTransaction((transaction) async {
  await transaction
      .update(_docRef, journalData)
      .catchError((error) => print('Error updating: $error'));
});
```

TRY IT OUT Creating the Authentication Service Classes

In this section, continue to edit the journal project. You'll be adding the AuthenticationApi and Authentication classes to handle the Firebase Authentication API.

1. Create a new Dart file in the services folder. Right-click the services folder, select New ⇨ Dart File, enter authentication_api.dart, and click the OK button to save.

2. Create the AuthenticationApi class and use the abstract modifier before the class declaration.

```
abstract class AuthenticationApi {

}
```

3. Inside the AuthenticationApi class, add the following interface methods:

```
getFirebaseAuth();
Future<String> currentUserUid();
Future<void> signOut();
Future<String> signInWithEmailAndPassword({String email, String password});
Future<String> createUserWithEmailAndPassword({String email, String password});
Future<void> sendEmailVerification();
Future<bool> isEmailVerified();
```

4. Create a new Dart file in the services folder. Right-click the services folder, select New ⇨ Dart File, enter authentication.dart, and click the OK button to save. Import the firebase_auth.dart package and the authentication_api.dart abstract class.

5. Add a new line and create the AuthenticationService class that implements the AuthenticationApi abstract class.

6. Declare the final FirebaseAuth _firebaseAuth variable that has a reference to the FirebaseAuth.instance.

7. Add the `_getFirebaseAuth()` method and return the `_firebaseAuth` variable. The FirebaseAuth is the entry point of the Firebase Authentication SDK.

```
import 'package:firebase_auth/firebase_auth.dart';
import 'package:journal/services/authentication_api.dart';

class AuthenticationService implements Authentication {
  final FirebaseAuth _firebaseAuth = FirebaseAuth.instance;

  FirebaseAuth getFirebaseAuth() {
    return _firebaseAuth;
  }
}
```

8. Add the `Future<String> currentUserUid()` async method responsible for retrieving the currently logged-in `user.uid`.

```
Future<String> currentUserUid() async {
  FirebaseUser user = await _firebaseAuth.currentUser();
  return user.uid;
}
```

9. Add the `Future<void> signOut()` async method responsible for logging out the current user.

```
Future<void> signOut() async {
  return _firebaseAuth.signOut();
}
```

10. Add the `Future<String> signInWithEmailAndPassword` method accepting the named parameters `email` and `password` as `String`. This method is responsible for logging in a `user` by email/password authentication provider by calling the `_firebaseAuth.signInWithEmailAndPassword` method, and it returns the `user.uid`.

```
Future<String> signInWithEmailAndPassword({String email, String password}) async {
  FirebaseUser user = await _firebaseAuth.signInWithEmailAndPassword(email: email,
password: password);
  return user.uid;
}
```

11. Add the `Future<String> createUserWithEmailAndPassword` method accepting the named parameters `email` and `password` as `String`. This method is responsible for creating a `user` by email/password authentication provider by calling the `_firebaseAuth.createUserWithEmailAndPassword` method, and it returns the newly created `user.uid`.

```
Future<String> createUserWithEmailAndPassword({String email, String password}) async {
  FirebaseUser user = await _firebaseAuth.createUserWithEmailAndPassword(email:
email, password: password);
  return user.uid;
}
```

12. Add the `Future<void> sendEmailVerification` method that retrieves the current logged-in user by calling the `_firebaseAuth.currentUser` method. Once the `user` is retrieved, it calls the `user.sendEmailVerification` method to send an email to the user to verify it was them creating the account.

```
Future<void> sendEmailVerification() async {
  FirebaseUser user = await _firebaseAuth.currentUser();
  user.sendEmailVerification();
}
```

13. Add the `Future<bool> isEmailVerified` method that calls the `_firebaseAuth.currentUser` method to retrieve the current logged-in user. Once the `user` is retrieved, it returns the `user.isEmailVerified` bool value to verify the `user` has verified their email.

```
Future<bool> isEmailVerified() async {
  FirebaseUser user = await _firebaseAuth.currentUser();
  return user.isEmailVerified;
}
```

HOW IT WORKS

You created the `authentication_api.dart` file with the `AuthenticationApi` abstract class containing the interface methods.

To implement the code logic that calls the Firebase Authentication API, you created the `authentication.dart` file containing the `AuthenticationService` class that `implements` the `AuthenticationApi` abstract class. Each method in the `AuthenticationService` class calls the Firebase Authentication API.

TRY IT OUT   Creating the DbFirestoreService Service Classes

In this section, continue to edit the `journal` project. You'll be adding the `DbApi` and `DbFirestoreService` classes to handle the Cloud Firestore database API.

1. Create a new Dart file in the `services` folder. Right-click the `services` folder, select New ⇨ Dart File, enter `db_firestore_api.dart`, and click the OK button to save.

2. Create the `DbApi` class and use the `abstract` modifier before the class declaration. Import the `journal.dart` class.

```
import 'package:journal/models/journal.dart';

abstract class DbApi {

}
```

3. Inside the `DbApi` class, add the following interface methods:

```
Stream<List<Journal>> getJournalList(String uid);
Future<Journal> getJournal(String documentID);
```

```
Future<bool> addJournal(Journal journal);
void updateJournal(Journal journal);
void updateJournalWithTransaction(Journal journal);
void deleteJournal(Journal journal);
```

4. Create a new Dart file in the `services` folder. Right-click the `services` folder, select New ⇨ Dart File, enter `db_firestore.dart`, and click the OK button to save. Import the `cloud_firestore` `.dart` package, the `journal.dart` class, and the `db_firestore_api.dart` class.

5. Add a new line and create the `DbFirestoreService` class that implements the `DbApi` abstract class.

6. Declare the `final Firestore _firestore` variable that has a reference to the `Firestore` `.instance`. Add the `final _collectionJournals` `String` variable that holds the Firestore collection name initialized to `journals`.

7. Add a new line and add the `DbFirestoreService()` constructor that uses the `_firestore` instance to call the `settings()` method to enable the `timestampsInSnapshotsEnabled` by setting the value to `true`. In the future, Cloud Firestore will enable the value to `true` by default, and it's good to opt in to this new behavior.

```
import 'package:cloud_firestore/cloud_firestore.dart';
import 'package:journal/models/journal.dart';
import 'package:journal/services/db_firestore_api.dart';

class DbFirestoreService implements DbApi {
  Firestore _firestore = Firestore.instance;
  String _collectionJournals = 'journals';

  DbFirestoreService() {
    _firestore.settings(timestampsInSnapshotsEnabled: true);
  }
}
```

8. Add the `Stream<List<Journal>> getJournalList` method, taking the `uid` `String` parameter. Note that the `uid` value is the logged-in user ID. This method is responsible for retrieving journal entries. Use the `_firestore` instance with the dot (`.`) operator to set the `_firestore` member property values. Refer to Table 15.2 to see how to query a Cloud Firestore database.

9. Set the value of the collection to the `_collectionJournals` variable, and set the `where()` method to filter by the `uid` field. The `snapshots()` method returns a `QuerySnapshot` `Stream`.

10. Continue with the dot operator and add the `map()` method by passing the received `snapshot`. Inside the `map()` method you convert the snapshot's `documents` and map them to `Journal` classes by using the `Journal` class `fromDoc(doc)` method and converting it to a `List()` by using the `toList()` method.

11. Take the `_journalDocs` variable that is populated with the `List` of `Journal` classes and use the `sort()` method to sort dates in descending order. For the last line, return the `_journalDocs` `List` of `Journal` classes.

```
Stream<List<Journal>> getJournalList(String uid) {
  return _firestore
    .collection(_collectionJournals)
```

```
      .where('uid', isEqualTo: uid)
      .snapshots()
      .map((QuerySnapshot snapshot) {
    List<Journal> _journalDocs = snapshot.documents.map((doc) => Journal.
  fromDoc(doc)).toList();
      _journalDocs.sort((comp1, comp2) => comp2.date.compareTo(comp1.date));
      return _journalDocs;
    });
  }
```

12. Add the `Future<bool> addJournal(Journal journal)` async method that takes the `Journal` class parameter. This method is responsible for adding a new journal entry.

13. Declare the `DocumentReference _documentReference` variable that holds the new document added. Use the `await` keyword with the `_firestore` instance, specify the `collection` with the `_collectionJournals` variable, and call the `add()` method.

14. The `add()` method takes the journal entry fields `date`, `mood`, `note`, and `uid` variables.

15. Add a new line to return a `bool` value if the record was successfully created by checking whether `_documentReference.documentID != null`. If the `documentID` is not `null`, the record was created and returns a `true` value; otherwise, it returns a `false` value.

```
Future<bool> addJournal(Journal journal) async {
  DocumentReference _documentReference =
    await _firestore.collection(_collectionJournals).add({
    'date': journal.date,
    'mood': journal.mood,
    'note': journal.note,
    'uid': journal.uid,
  });
  return _documentReference.documentID != null;
}
```

16. Add the `updateJournal(Journal journal)` async method taking the `Journal` class parameter. This method is responsible for updating an existing journal entry.

17. Use the `_firestore` instance with the dot (`.`) operator to set the `_firestore` member property values. Set the value of the `collection` to the `_collectionJournals` variable, and set the `document` variable to the `journal.documentID`, which is the Cloud Firestore document ID.

18. Continue with the dot operator and add the `updateData()` method, passing the `date`, `mood`, and `note` values from the `journal` variable. Add the `catchError()` method to intercept any errors and print them to the console.

```
void updateJournal(Journal journal) async {
  await _firestore
    .collection(_collectionJournals)
    .document(journal.documentID)
    .updateData({
      'date': journal.date,
      'mood': journal.mood,
      'note': journal.note,
    })
    .catchError((error) => print('Error updating: $error'));
}
```

19. Add the `deleteJournal(Journal journal)` async method, taking the `Journal` class parameter. This method is responsible for deleting a journal entry.

20. Use the `_firestore` instance with the dot (`.`) operator to set the `_firestore` member property values. Set the value of the `collection` to the `_collectionJournals` variable, and set the `document` variable to the `journal.documentID`.

21. Continue with the dot operator and add the `delete()` method. Add the `catchError()` method to intercept any errors and print them to the console.

```
void deleteJournal(Journal journal) async {
  await _firestore
    .collection(_collectionJournals)
    .document(journal.documentID)
    .delete()
    .catchError((error) => print('Error deleting: $error'));
}
```

HOW IT WORKS

You created the `db_firestore_api.dart` file with the `DbApi abstract` class containing the interface methods.

You created the `db_firestore.dart` file containing the `DbFirestoreService` class that `implements` the `DbApi abstract` class. Each method in the `DbFirestoreService` class calls the Cloud Firestore database API.

Adding the Validators Class

The `Validators` class uses the `StreamTransformer` to validate whether the email is in the correct format by using at least one @ sign and a period. The password validator checks for a minimum of six characters entered. The `Validators` class is used with the BLoC classes.

The `StreamTransformer` transforms a `Stream` that is used to validate and process values inside a `Stream`. The incoming data is a `Stream`, and the outgoing data after processing is a `Stream`. For example, once the incoming data is processed, you can use the `sink.add()` method to add data to the `Stream` or use the `sink.addError()` method to return a validation error. The `StreamTransformer.fromHandlers` constructor is used to delegate events to a given function.

The following is an example that shows how to use the `StreamTransformer` by using the `fromHandlers` constructor to validate whether the email is in the correct format:

```
StreamTransformer<String, String>.fromHandlers(handleData: (email, sink) {
  if (email.contains('@') && email.contains('.')) {
    sink.add(email);
  } else if (email.length > 0) {
    sink.addError('Enter a valid email');
  }
});
```

TRY IT OUT Creating the Validators Class

In this section, continue to edit the `journal` project by adding the `Validators` class.

1. Create a new Dart file in the `classes` folder. Right-click the `classes` folder, select New ➪ Dart File, enter `validators.dart`, and click the OK button to save.

2. Import the `async.dart` library and create the `Validators` class.

```
import 'dart:async';

class Validators {

}
```

3. Add the `validateEmail` variable and use the `final` keyword. This method is responsible for checking whether the email is formatted correctly by having at least one @ sign and one period.

4. Initialize the `validateEmail` variable by calling the `StreamTransformer.fromHandlers` constructor.

5. Inside the handler, add an `if` statement to check whether `email.contains('@') && email.contains('.')`, and when both expressions validate to `true`, add the `sink.add(email)` method.

6. Add an `else if` statement to check whether the `email.length > 0`, meaning if the user has typed at least one character, then add the `sink.addError('Enter a valid email')`.

```
final validateEmail =
StreamTransformer<String, String>.fromHandlers(handleData: (email, sink) {
  if (email.contains('@') && email.contains('.')) {
    sink.add(email);
  } else if (email.length > 0) {
    sink.addError('Enter a valid email');
  }
});
```

7. Add the `validatePassword` variable and use the `final` keyword. This method is responsible for checking whether the password length is at least 6 characters.

8. Initialize the `validatePassword` variable by calling the `StreamTransformer.fromHandlers` constructor.

9. Inside the handler, add an `if` statement to check whether `password.length >= 6`, and if the expression validates to `true`, add the `sink.add(password)` method.

10. Add an `else if` statement to check whether the `password.length > 0`, meaning if the user has typed at least one character, then add the `sink.addError(Password needs to be at least 6 characters ')`.

```
final validatePassword = StreamTransformer<String, String>.fromHandlers(
  handleData: (password, sink) {
    if (password.length >= 6) {
```

```
      sink.add(password);
    } else if (password.length > 0) {
      sink.addError('Password needs to be at least 6 characters');
    }
  });
}
```

HOW IT WORKS

You created the `validators.dart` file containing the `Validators` class. The `StreamTransformer` is used to validate that emails and passwords pass a minimum standard. If the expressions' values are `true`, the email or password is added to the `Stream` by using the `sink.add()` method. If the expressions validate to `false`, the `sink.addError()` method sends back the error description.

Adding the BLoC Pattern

In this section, you'll create the authentication BLoC, authentication BLoC provider, login BLoC, home BLoC, home BLoC provider, journal edit BLoC, and journal edit BLoC provider. The login BLoC doesn't need a provider class because it does not rely on receiving data from other pages.

I want to remind you of this important concept: BLoC classes are platform-agnostic and do not rely on platform-specific packages or classes. For example, the Login page injects the platform-specific (Flutter) `AuthenticationService` class to the `LoginBloc` class constructor. The receiving BLoC class has the `abstract` `AuthenticationApi` class that receives the injected `AuthenticationService` class, making the BLoC class platform-agnostic.

Adding the AuthenticationBloc

The `AuthenticationBloc` is responsible for identifying logged-in user credentials and monitoring user authentication login status. When the `AuthenticationBloc` is instantiated, it starts a `StreamController` listener that monitors the user's authentication credentials, and when changes occur, the listener updates the credential status by calling a `sink.add()` method event. If the user is logged in, the `sink` events send the user `uid` value, and if the user logs out, the `sink` events sends a `null` value, meaning no user is logged in.

TRY IT OUT Creating the AuthenticationBloc

In this section, continue to edit the `journal` project. You'll be adding the `AuthenticationBloc` class to handle calling the Firebase Authentication service to log in or log out a user.

1. Create a new Dart file in the `blocs` folder. Right-click the `blocs` folder, select New ➪ Dart File, enter `authentication_bloc.dart`, and click the OK button to save.

2. Import the `async.dart` library and `authentication_api.dart` class and create the `AuthenticationBloc` class.

```
import 'dart:async';
import 'package:journal/services/authentication_api.dart';
```

```
class AuthenticationBloc {

}
```

3. Inside the `AuthenticationBloc` class, declare the `final AuthenticationApi authentication-Api` variable. The BLoC pattern requires that you inject the platform-specific classes, and you'll pass the `AuthenticationService` class in the BLoC's constructor. The `authenticationApi` variable receives the injected `AuthenticationService` class.

```
final AuthenticationApi authenticationApi;
```

4. Add the `_authenticationController` variable as a `String StreamController`, add the `addUser` variable getter as a `String Sink`, and add the `user` getter as a `String Stream`. Every time the user logs in or logs out, the `_authenticationController StreamController` is updated with the `addUser` getter.

```
final StreamController<String> _authenticationController = StreamController<String>();
Sink<String> get addUser => _authenticationController.sink;
Stream<String> get user => _authenticationController.stream;
```

5. Add the `_logoutController` variable as a `bool StreamController`, the `logoutUser` variable getter as a `bool Sink`, and the `listLogoutUser` getter as a `bool Stream`. Every time the user logs out, the `_logoutController StreamController` is updated with the `logoutUser` getter.

```
final StreamController<bool> _logoutController = StreamController<bool>();
Sink<bool> get logoutUser => _logoutController.sink;
Stream<bool> get listLogoutUser => _logoutController.stream;
```

6. Add a new line and enter the `AuthenticationBloc` constructor receiving the injected `this.authenticationApi` parameter. Note that the injected parameter is the `AuthenticationService` class. Inside the constructor add a call to the `onAuthChanged()` method that you create in step 8.

```
AuthenticationBloc(this.authenticationApi) {
  onAuthChanged();
}
```

7. Add the `dispose()` method and call the `_authenticationController.close()` and `_logout-Controller.close()` methods to close the `StreamController`'s stream when it's not needed. Note that for the `AuthenticationBloc` class the `close()` method will not be called because authentication needs to be accessible throughout the lifetime of the app.

```
void dispose() {
  _authenticationController.close();
  _logoutController.close();
}
```

8. Add the `onAuthChanged()` method that is responsible for setting up a listener to check when the user logs in and logs out. Inside the method, call the `authenticationApi.getFirebaseAuth()` to get the `FirebaseAuth.instance` from the authentication service class. Continue by using the dot operator to call the `onAuthStateChanged.listen((user))` to set up the listener. When the user

logs in, the user variable returns the `FirebaseUser` class with the user information. When the user logs out, the user variable returns a `null` value.

9. Inside the listener, add the `final String uid` variable initialized by using the ternary operator to check whether `user != null` and retrieve the `user.uid` value; otherwise, return a `null` value.

10. Add a new line and call the `_addUser.add(uid)` method to add the value to the `sink` with either the user `uid` or the `null` value.

11. Add a new line and call the `_logoutController.stream.listen((logout))` listener that is called when the user logs out.

12. Inside the listener, add an `if` statement to check whether `logout == true` and call the `_signOut()` method that you'll create in step 13.

```
void onAuthChanged() {
  authenticationApi
      .getFirebaseAuth()
      .onAuthStateChanged
      .listen((user) {
    final String uid = user != null ? user.uid : null;
    addUser.add(uid);
  });
  _logoutController.stream.listen((logout) {
    if (logout == true) {
      _signOut();
    }
  });
}
```

13. Add the `void _signOut()` method that calls the authentication service's `authenticationService.signOut()` method to log out the user.

```
void _signOut(){
  authenticationApi.signOut();
}
```

HOW IT WORKS

To identify the logged-in user credentials and to monitor the login status, you created the `authentication_bloc.dart` file containing the `AuthenticationBloc` class. You declared a reference to the `AuthenticationApi` class to gain access to the Firebase Authentication API. The `authenticationApi` variable receives the injected `AuthenticationService` class. To add data to the `StreamController`'s `stream` property, you used the `sink.add()` method, and the `stream` property emits the latest `stream` events. You added methods that call the authentication service to log in, to log out, and to create new users.

Adding the AuthenticationBlocProvider

The `AuthenticationBlocProvider` class is responsible for passing the `State` between widgets and pages by using the `InheritedWidget` class as a provider. The `AuthenticationBlocProvider` constructor takes a `Key`, `Widget`, and the `this.authenticationBloc` variable, which is the `AuthenticationBloc` class.

TRY IT OUT Creating the AuthenticationBlocProvider

In this section, continue to edit the `journal` project. You'll be adding the `AuthenticationBlocProvider` class as the provider for the `AuthenticationBloc` class to handle the logging in and logging out and to monitor a user's credentials. The `AuthenticationBloc` class calls the `AuthenticationService` service class Firebase Authentication API.

1. Create a new Dart file in the `blocs` folder. Right-click the `blocs` folder, select New ⇨ Dart File, enter `authentication_bloc_provider.dart`, and click the OK button to save.

2. Import the `material.dart` package and the `authentication_bloc.dart` package and create the `AuthenticationBlocProvider` class that extends the `InheritedWidget` class.

```
import 'package:flutter/material.dart';
import 'package:journal/blocs/authentication_bloc.dart';

class AuthenticationBlocProvider extends InheritedWidget {

}
```

3. Inside the `AuthenticationBlocProvider` class, declare the `final AuthenticationBloc authenticationBloc` variable.

```
final AuthenticationBloc authenticationBloc;
```

4. Add the `AuthenticationBlocProvider` constructor with the `const` keyword. Add to the constructor the `key`, `child`, and `this.authenticationBloc` parameters.

```
const AuthenticationBlocProvider(
    {Key key, Widget child, this.authenticationBloc})
    : super(key: key, child: child);
```

5. Add the `AuthenticationBlocProvider of(BuildContext context)` method with the `static` keyword.

6. Inside the method, return the `AuthenticationBlocProvider` by using the `inheritFromWidgetOfExactType` method that allows children widgets to get the instance of the `AuthenticationBlocProvider` provider.

```
static AuthenticationBlocProvider of(BuildContext context) {
  return (context.inheritFromWidgetOfExactType(AuthenticationBlocProvider)
      as AuthenticationBlocProvider);
}
```

7. Add and override the `updateShouldNotify` method to check whether the `authenticationBloc` does not equal the `old` `AuthenticationBlocProvider` `authenticationBloc`. If the expression returns `true`, the framework notifies widgets that hold the inherited data that they need to rebuild.

```
@override
bool updateShouldNotify(AuthenticationBlocProvider old) =>
    authenticationBloc != old.authenticationBloc;
```

HOW IT WORKS

To pass the `State` between widgets and pages, you created the `authentication_bloc_provider.dart` file containing the `AuthenticationBlocProvider` class as the provider for the `AuthenticationBloc` class. The `AuthenticationBlocProvider` class constructor takes the key, `widget`, and `this.authenticationBloc` parameters. The `of()` method returns the result of the `inheritFromWidgetOfExactType` method that allows children widgets to get the instance of the `AuthenticationBlocProvider` provider. The `updateShouldNotify` method checks whether the value has changed, and the framework notifies widgets to rebuild.

Adding the LoginBloc

The `LoginBloc` is responsible for monitoring the login page to check for a valid email format and password length. When the `LoginBloc` is instantiated, it starts the `StreamController`'s listeners that monitor the user's email and password, and once they pass validation, the login and create account buttons are enabled. Once the login and password values pass validation, the authentication service is called to log in or create a new user. The `Validators` class is responsible for validating the email and password values.

TRY IT OUT   Creating the LoginBloc

In this section, continue to edit the `journal` project. You'll be adding the `LoginBloc` class to handle the login page's email, password, login, and create account buttons. The `LoginBloc` is also responsible for calling the Firebase Authentication service to log in or create a new user.

1. Create a new Dart file in the `blocs` folder. Right-click the `blocs` folder, select New ⇨ Dart File, enter `login_bloc.dart`, and click the OK button to save.

2. Import the `async.dart` library, import the `validators.dart` and `authentication_api.dart` classes, and create the `LoginBloc` class by using the `with` keyword and the `Validators` class.

```
import 'dart:async';
import 'package:journal/classes/validators.dart';
import 'package:journal/services/authentication_api.dart';

class LoginBloc with Validators {

}
```

3. Inside the `LoginBloc` class, declare the `final AuthenticationApi authenticationApi` variable. Add the `String _email` and `_password` private variables and the `bool _emailValid` and `_passwordValid` private variables.

```
final AuthenticationApi authenticationApi;
String _email;
String _password;
bool _emailValid;
bool _passwordValid;
```

4. Add the `_emailController` variable as a `String StreamController`, add the `emailChanged` variable getter as a `String Sink`, and add the `email` getter as a `String Stream`. Note that the `StreamController` is initialized with the `broadcast()` stream since we'll have multiple listeners. After the `stream` property, add the `transform(validateEmail)` method that calls the `Validators` class `StreamTransformer` and validates the email address. The `StreamTransformer` adds to the `sink` property either the email address value if it passes validation or an error if it fails.

```
final StreamController<String> _emailController = StreamController<String>
.broadcast();
Sink<String> get emailChanged => _emailController.sink;
Stream<String> get email => _emailController.stream.transform(validateEmail);
```

5. By following the previous steps, add the additional `StreamControllers` to handle the password, enable the login or create account buttons, and add the login or create account calls to the Cloud Firestore service.

```
final StreamController<String> _passwordController = StreamController<String>
.broadcast();
Sink<String> get passwordChanged => _passwordController.sink;
Stream<String> get password => _passwordController.stream.transform
(validatePassword);

final StreamController<bool> _enableLoginCreateButtonController =
StreamController<bool>.broadcast();
Sink<bool> get enableLoginCreateButtonChanged => _enableLoginCreateButton-
Controller.sink;
Stream<bool> get enableLoginCreateButton => _enableLoginCreateButtonCon-
troller.stream;

final StreamController<String> _loginOrCreateButtonController =
StreamController<String>();
Sink<String> get loginOrCreateButtonChanged => _loginOrCreateButtonController.sink;
Stream<String> get loginOrCreateButton => _loginOrCreateButtonController.stream;

final StreamController<String> _loginOrCreateController =
StreamController<String>();
Sink<String> get loginOrCreateChanged => _loginOrCreateController.sink;
Stream<String> get loginOrCreate => _loginOrCreateController.stream;
```

6. Add a new line and enter the `LoginBloc` constructor receiving the injected `this.authentica-tionApi` parameter. Note that the injected parameter is the `AuthenticationService` class. Inside the constructor, call the `_startListenersIfEmailPasswordAreValid()` method that you create in step 8.

```
LoginBloc(this.authenticationApi) {
  _startListenersIfEmailPasswordAreValid();
}
```

7. Add the `dispose()` method and call the `_passwordController`, `_emailController`, `_enable-LoginCreateButtonController`, and `_loginOrCreateButtonController` `close()` methods to close the `StreamController`'s stream when they are not needed.

```
void dispose() {
  _passwordController.close();
  _emailController.close();
  _enableLoginCreateButtonController.close();
  _loginOrCreateButtonController.close();
  _loginOrCreateController.close();
}
```

8. Add the `_startListenersIfEmailPasswordAreValid()` method that is responsible for setting up three listeners that check the email, password, and login or create button streams.

9. Inside the method, add the `email.listen((email))` listener. Inside the listener, set the `_email = email` and the `_emailValid = true` values.

10. By using the dot operator, add the `onError((error))` event handler and set the `_email = ''` and the `_emailValid = false` values.

11. For both scenarios, call the `_updateEnableLoginCreateButtonStream()` method that you'll create in step 14.

12. Add a new line, and by following the previous steps, enter the `password.listen((password))` listener.

13. Add the `loginOrCreate.listen((action)` listener, and by using a ternary operator, set the action variable to either `_login()` or `_createAccount()`, depending on whether the user has chosen to log in or create a new account.

```
void _startListenersIfEmailPasswordAreValid() {
  email.listen((email) {
    _email = email;
    _emailValid = true;
    _updateEnableLoginCreateButtonStream();
  }).onError((error) {
    _email = '';
    _emailValid = false;
    _updateEnableLoginCreateButtonStream();
  });
  password.listen((password) {
    _password = password;
    _passwordValid = true;
```

```
      _updateEnableLoginCreateButtonStream();
    }).onError((error) {
      _password = '';
      _passwordValid = false;
      _updateEnableLoginCreateButtonStream();
    });
    loginOrCreate.listen((action) {
      action == 'Login' ? _logIn() : _createAccount();
    });
  }
```

14. Add the `_updateEnableLoginCreateButtonStream()` method that checks whether the `_emailValid` and `_passwordValid` variables evaluate to `true`, and call the `enableLogin-CreateButtonChanged.add(true)` to add a `true` value to the `sink` property. Otherwise, add a `false` value to the `sink` property. The results of the value being added to the `sink` property either enable or disable the login or create account buttons.

```
void _updateEnableLoginCreateButtonStream() {
  if (_emailValid == true && _passwordValid == true) {
    enableLoginCreateButtonChanged.add(true);
  }
  else {
    enableLoginCreateButtonChanged.add(false);
  }
}
```

15. Add the `Future<String> _logIn()` async method that is responsible for logging in a user with the email/password credentials.

16. Inside the method, add `String _result = ''` variable that tracks if the login is successful or fails.

17. Add an `if` statement checking whether the `_emailValid` and `_passwordValid` variables evaluate to a `true` value. If the expression evaluates to `true`, add the `await authenticationApi` call to the `signInWithEmailAndPassword()` by passing the `_email` and `_password` values.

18. By using the dot operator, add the `then((user))` callback that sets the `_result = 'Success'` variable.

19. Add the `catchError((error))` callback that sets the `_result = error` variable.

20. Add the `return _result` statement to return a status that the login has been successful or return the login error.

21. Add an `else` statement to check whether the `_emailValid` and `_passwordValid` variables evaluate to a `false` value and `return 'Email and Password are not valid'` since validation failed.

```
Future<String> _logIn() async {
  String _result = '';
  if(_emailValid && _passwordValid) {
    await authenticationApi.signInWithEmailAndPassword(email: _email, password:
_password).then((user) {
      _result = 'Success';
```

```
      }).catchError((error) {
        print('Login error: $error');
        _result = error;
      });
      return _result;
    } else {
      return 'Email and Password are not valid';
    }
  }
}
```

22. Add the `Future<String> _createAccount()` async method that is responsible for creating a new account and if successful automatically logging in the new user. When a new account is created, it's a good practice to automatically log in the new user.

    Follow the previous steps and add the `createUserWithEmailAndPassword` and `signInWithEmailAndPassword` methods.

```
Future<String> _createAccount() async {
  String _result = '';
  if(_emailValid && _passwordValid) {
    await authenticationApi.createUserWithEmailAndPassword(email: _email, password:
_password).then((user) {
      print('Created user: $user');
      _result = 'Created user: $user';
      authenticationApi.signInWithEmailAndPassword(email: _email, password:
_password).then((user) {
      }).catchError((error) async {
        print('Login error: $error');
        _result = error;
      });
    }).catchError((error) async {
      print('Creating user error: $error');
    });
    return _result;
  } else {
    return 'Error creating user';
  }
}
```

HOW IT WORKS

To monitor the login to check for a valid email format and password length, you created the `login_bloc.dart` file containing the `LoginBloc` class that works with the `Validators` class. You declared a reference to the `AuthenticationApi` class to gain access to the Firebase Authentication API. The `authenticationApi` variable receives the injected `AuthenticationService` class. To add data to the `StreamController`'s stream property, you used the `sink.add()` method, and the `stream` property emits the latest `stream` events. You added methods that call the Firebase Authentication service to log in or create a new account by using the email/password authentication provider.

Adding the HomeBloc

The HomeBloc is responsible for identifying logged-in user credentials and monitoring user authentication login status. When the HomeBloc is instantiated, it starts a StreamController listener that monitors the user's authentication credentials, and when changes occur, the listener updates the credential status by calling a sink.add() method event. If the user is logged in, the sink events send the user uid value, and if the user logs out, the sink events send a null value, meaning no user is logged in.

TRY IT OUT Creating the HomeBloc

In this section, continue to edit the journal project. You'll be adding the HomeBloc class to handle calling the Cloud Firestore database service.

1. Create a new Dart file in the blocs folder. Right-click the blocs folder, select New ⇨ Dart File, enter home_bloc.dart, and click the OK button to save.

2. Import the async.dart library; import the authentication.dart class, db_firestore_api .dart class, and journal.dart class; and create the HomeBloc class.

```
import 'dart:async';
import 'package:journal/services/authentication_api.dart';
import 'package:journal/services/db_firestore_api.dart';
import 'package:journal/models/journal.dart';

class HomeBloc {

}
```

3. Inside the HomeBloc class, declare the final DbApi dbApi variable and the final AuthenticationApi authenticationApi variable.

```
final DbApi dbApi;
final AuthenticationApi authenticationApi;
```

4. Add the _journalController variable as a String StreamController, add the _addListJournal (private) variable getter as a List<Journal> Sink, and add the listJournal getter as a List<Journal> Stream.

```
final StreamController<List<Journal>> _journalController =
StreamController<List<Journal>>.broadcast();
Sink<List<Journal>> get _addListJournal => _journalController.sink;
Stream<List<Journal>> get listJournal => _journalController.stream;
```

5. Add the _journalDeleteController variable as a Journal StreamController, and add the deleteJournal variable getter as a Journal Sink. Since this StreamController is responsible for deleting journals, you will not need a list of deleted journals Stream.

```
final StreamController<Journal> _journalDeleteController =
StreamController<Journal>.broadcast();
Sink<Journal> get deleteJournal => _journalDeleteController.sink;
```

6. Add a new line and enter the `HomeBloc` constructor, taking the `this.dbApi` and the `this.authen-ticationApi` parameters. Note that the injected parameters are, respectively, the `DbFirestoreService` and `AuthenticationService` classes.

7. Inside the `HomeBloc` constructor, call the `_startListeners()` method that you will create in step 9.

```
HomeBloc(this.dbApi , this.authenticationApi) {
  _startListeners();
}
```

8. Add the `dispose()` method and call the `_journalController.close()` and `_journalDelete-Controller.close()` methods to close the `StreamController`'s stream when they are not needed.

```
void dispose() {
  _journalController.close();
  _journalDeleteController.close();
}
```

9. Add the `_startListeners()` method responsible for setting up two listeners to retrieve a list of journals and to delete an individual journal entry.

10. Before you start the listeners, you need to retrieve the currently logged-in user `uid`. Inside the method, call the `authenticationApi.getFirebaseAuth().currentUser()` method, and with the dot operator add the `then((user))` callback that returns the `user.uid` value.

11. Inside the `currentUser()` method, call the `dbApi.getJournalList()` method to get the list of journals filtered by the user's `uid` from the Cloud Firestore service class.

12. Continue by using the dot operator to call the `listen((journalDocs))` to set up the listener.

13. Inside the listener, call the `_addListJournal.add(journalDocs)` sink to add the list of journals to the `_journalController` stream.

14. Add a new line and enter the `_journalDeleteController.stream.listen((journal))` listener that returns a `journal` to be deleted. Inside the listener, call the `DbApi` class `dbApi.deleteJournal(journal)` method to delete the journal from the database.

```
void _startListeners() {
  // Retrieve Firestore Journal Records as List<Journal> not DocumentSnapshot
  authenticationApi.getFirebaseAuth().currentUser().then((user) {
    dbApi.getJournalList(user.uid).listen((journalDocs) {
    _addListJournal.add(journalDocs);
    });

    _journalDeleteController.stream.listen((journal) {
      dbApi.deleteJournal(journal);
    });
  });
}
```

HOW IT WORKS

To identify the logged-in user credentials and to monitor the user authentication login status, you created the home_bloc.dart file containing the HomeBloc class. You declared a reference to the DbApi class to gain access to the Cloud Firestore database API. You also declared a reference to the AuthenticationApi class to gain access to the Firebase Authentication API. The dbApi variable receives the injected DbFirestoreService class. The authenticationApi variable receives the injected AuthenticationService class. To add data to the StreamController's stream property, you used the sink.add() method, and the stream property emits the latest stream events. You added methods that call the Cloud Firestore service to retrieve a list of filtered journals by the user's uid and to delete individual journal entries.

Adding the HomeBlocProvider

The HomeBlocProvider class is responsible for passing the State between widgets and pages by using the InheritedWidget class as a provider. The HomeBlocProvider constructor takes a Key, Widget, and the this.authenticationBloc variable, which is the HomeBloc class.

TRY IT OUT Creating the HomeBlocProvider

In this section, continue to edit the journal project. You'll be adding the HomeBlocProvider class as the provider for the HomeBloc class to retrieve the list of journals and delete individual entries. The Home-Bloc class calls the DbFirestoreService service class Cloud Firestore database API.

1. Create a new Dart file in the blocs folder. Right-click the blocs folder, select New ⇨ Dart File, enter home_bloc_provider.dart, and click the OK button to save.

2. Import the material.dart package and home_bloc.dart package and create the HomeBlocProvider class that extends the InheritedWidget class.

```
import 'package:flutter/material.dart';
import 'package:journal/blocs/home_bloc.dart';

class HomeBlocProvider extends InheritedWidget {

}
```

3. Inside the HomeBlocProvider class, declare the final HomeBloc homeBloc and the final String uid variables.

```
final HomeBloc homeBloc;
final String uid;
```

4. Add the HomeBlocProvider constructor with the const keyword.

5. Add to the constructor the key, child, this.homeBloc, and this.uid parameters.

```
const HomeBlocProvider(
    {Key key, Widget child, this.homeBloc, this.uid})
    : super(key: key, child: child);
```

6. Add the `HomeBlocProvider of (BuildContext context)` method with the `static` keyword.

7. Inside the method, return the `HomeBlocProvider` by using the `inheritFromWidgetOfExactType` method that allows children widgets to get the instance of the `HomeBlocProvider` provider.

```
static HomeBlocProvider of (BuildContext context) {
    return (context.inheritFromWidgetOfExactType(HomeBlocProvider)
        as HomeBlocProvider);
}
```

8. Add and override the `updateShouldNotify` method to check whether the `homeBloc` does not equal the `old HomeBlocProvider homeBloc`. If the expression returns `true`, the framework notifies widgets that hold the inherited data that they need to rebuild. If the expression returns a `false` value, the framework does not send a notification since there is no need to rebuild widgets.

```
@override
bool updateShouldNotify(HomeBlocProvider old) =>
    homeBloc != old.homeBloc;
```

HOW IT WORKS

To pass the `State` between widgets and pages, you created the `home_bloc_provider.dart` file containing the `HomeBlocProvider` class as the provider for the `HomeBloc` class. The `HomeBlocProvider` class constructor takes the key, `widget`, `this.homeBloc`, and `this.uid` parameters. The `of ()` method returns the result of the `inheritFromWidgetOfExactType` method that allows children widgets to get the instance of the `HomeBlocProvider` provider. The `updateShouldNotify` method checks whether the value has changed, and the framework notifies widgets to rebuild.

Adding the JournalEditBloc

The `JournalEditBloc` is responsible for monitoring the journal edit page to either add a new or save an existing entry. When the `JournalEditBloc` is instantiated, it starts the `StreamController`'s listeners that monitor the date, mood, note, and save button streams.

TRY IT OUT   **Creating the JournalEditBloc**

In this section, continue to edit the `journal` project. You'll be adding the `JournalEditBloc` class to handle the journal entry page date, mood, note, and save button. The `JournalEditBloc` is also responsible for calling the Cloud Firestore database service to save the entry.

1. Create a new Dart file in the `blocs` folder. Right-click the `blocs` folder, select New ⇨ Dart File, enter `journal_entry_bloc.dart`, and click the OK button to save.

2. Import the `async.dart` library; import the `journal.dart`, `db_firestore_api.dart` classes; and create the `JournalEditBloc` class that accepts the `this.add`, `this.selectedJournal`, and `this.dbApi` parameters. When the `add` variable is `true`, a new entry is created, and when the value is `false`, an existing entry is edited. The `selectedJournal` parameter contains the `Journal` class variables that contain the selected entry values. The `this.dbApi` receives the injected `DbFirestoreService` class.

```
import 'dart:async';
import 'package:journal/models/journal.dart';
import 'package:journal/services/db_firestore_api.dart';

JournalEditBloc(this.add, this.selectedJournal, this.dbApi) {

}
```

3. Inside the `JournalEditBloc` class, declare the `final DbApi dbApi` variable. Add the `final bool add` variable and the `Journal selectedJournal` variable.

```
final DbApi dbApi;
final bool add;
Journal selectedJournal;
```

4. Add the `_dateController` variable as a `String StreamController`, add the `dateEditChanged` variable getter as a `String Sink`, and add the `dateEdit` getter as a `String Stream`. Note that `StreamController` is initialized with the `broadcast()` stream since we'll have multiple listeners.

```
final StreamController<String> _dateController = StreamController<String>
.broadcast();
Sink<String> get dateEditChanged => _dateController.sink;
Stream<String> get dateEdit => _dateController.stream;
```

5. By following the previous steps, add the additional `StreamControllers` to handle the mood, note, and save journal call to the Cloud Firestore service.

```
final StreamController<String> _moodController = StreamController<String>
.broadcast();
Sink<String> get moodEditChanged => _moodController.sink;
Stream<String> get moodEdit => _moodController.stream;

final StreamController<String> _noteController = StreamController<String>
.broadcast();
Sink<String> get noteEditChanged => _noteController.sink;
Stream<String> get noteEdit => _noteController.stream;

final StreamController<String> _saveJournalController = StreamController<String>
.broadcast();
Sink<String> get saveJournalChanged => _saveJournalController.sink;
Stream<String> get saveJournal => _saveJournalController.stream;
```

6. Add a new line and enter the `JournalEditBloc` constructor receiving the injected `this.add`, `this.selectedJournal`, and `this.dbApi` parameters. Note that the injected `this.dbApi` parameter receives the `DbFirestoreService` class.

7. Inside the `JournalEditBloc` constructor, call the `_startEditListeners()` method that you will create in step 10.

8. By using the dot operator, add the `then((finished))` callback that calls the `_getJournal()` method that you create in step 12, and pass the `add` and `selectedJournal` variables.

```
JournalEditBloc(this.add, this.selectedJournal, this.dbApi) {
  _startEditListeners().then((finished) => _getJournal(add, selectedJournal));
}
```

9. Add the `dispose()` method and call the `_dateController`, `_moodController`, `_noteController`, and `_saveJournalController` `close()` methods to close the `StreamController`'s stream when they are not needed.

```
void dispose() {
  _dateController.close();
  _moodController.close();
  _noteController.close();
  _saveJournalController.close();
}
```

10. Add the `Future<bool> _startEditListeners()` async method that is responsible for setting up four listeners to monitor the date, mood, note, and save streams.

11. Inside each `listen()` listener, the `selectedJournal` `date`, `mood`, `note` values are maintained. When the `_saveJournalController` listener is called, it checks whether the `action == 'Save'` and calls the `_saveJournal()` method that you will create in step 10. The last line of the method adds the `return true` statement signaling that all listeners have been started.

```
Future<bool> _startEditListeners() async {
  _dateController.stream.listen((date) {
    selectedJournal.date = date;
  });
  _moodController.stream.listen((mood) {
    selectedJournal.mood = mood;
  });
  _noteController.stream.listen((note) {
    selectedJournal.note = note;
  });
  _saveJournalController.stream.listen((action) {
    if (action == 'Save') {
      _saveJournal();
    }
  });
  return true;
}
```

12. Add the `_getJournal` method that takes the `bool add` and `Journal journal` parameters.

13. Add an `if` statement to check whether the `add` value is true, meaning a new entry is going to be created, and set the default values for the `selectedJournal` variable.

14. Add an `else` statement to handle editing an existing entry and set the default values from the passed-in existing `journal` variable.

15. After the `if-else` statement, notify the `StreamControllers` by adding the date, mood, and note values through each `sink.add()` method.

```
void _getJournal(bool add, Journal journal) {
  if (add) {
    selectedJournal = Journal();
    selectedJournal.date = DateTime.now().toString();
    selectedJournal.mood = 'Very Satisfied';
    selectedJournal.note = '';
    selectedJournal.uid = journal.uid;
  } else {
    selectedJournal.date = journal.date;
    selectedJournal.mood = journal.mood;
    selectedJournal.note = journal.note;
  }
  dateEditChanged.add(selectedJournal.date);
  moodEditChanged.add(selectedJournal.mood);
  noteEditChanged.add(selectedJournal.note);
}
```

16. Add the `_saveJournal()` method to create a `Journal journal` variable that holds the entry values.

17. Call the `DateTime.parse()` constructor to convert the `date` to the ISO 8601 standard.

18. Add a ternary operator to check whether the `add` variable equals `true` and call the `dbApi.addJournal(journal)` method to create a new journal entry. Otherwise, call the `dbApi.updateJournal(journal)` method to update the current entry.

```
void _saveJournal() {
  Journal journal = Journal(
    documentID: selectedJournal.documentID,
    date: DateTime.parse(selectedJournal.date).toIso8601String(),
    mood: selectedJournal.mood,
    note: selectedJournal.note,
    uid: selectedJournal.uid,
  );
  add ? dbApi.addJournal(journal) : dbApi.updateJournal(journal);
}
```

HOW IT WORKS

To monitor the journal edit page to add a new entry or save an existing entry, you created the `journal_edit_bloc.dart` file containing the `JournalEditBloc` class. You declared a reference to the `DbApi` class to gain access to the Cloud Firestore database API. The `dbApi` variable receives the injected `DbFirestoreService` class. To add data to the `StreamController`'s stream property, you used the `sink.add()` method, and the `stream` property emits the latest `stream` events. You added methods that call the Cloud Firestore service to create a new entry or save an existing entry.

Adding the JournalEditBlocProvider

The `JournalEditBlocProvider` class is responsible for passing the `State` between widgets and pages by using the `InheritedWidget` class as a provider. The `JournalEditBlocProvider` constructor takes a `Key`, `Widget`, and `this.journalEditBloc` variables. Note that the `this.journalEditBloc` variable is the `JournalEditBloc` class.

TRY IT OUT Creating the JournalEditBlocProvider

In this section, continue to edit the `journal` project. You'll be adding the `JournalEditBlocProvider` class as the provider for the `JournalEditBloc` class to add or edit individual entries. The `JournalEdit-Bloc` class calls the `DbFirestoreService` service class Cloud Firestore database API.

1. Create a new Dart file in the `blocs` folder. Right-click the `blocs` folder, select New ⇨ Dart File, enter `journal_edit_bloc_provider.dart`, and click the OK button to save.

2. Import the `material.dart` package, the `journal_edit_bloc.dart` package, and the `journal.dart` class, and create the `JournalEditBlocProvider` class that extends the `InheritedWidget` class.

```
import 'package:flutter/material.dart';
import 'package:journal/blocs/journal_edit_bloc.dart';

class JournalEditBlocProvider extends InheritedWidget {

}
```

3. Inside the `JournalEditBlocProvider` class, declare the `final JournalEditBloc journalEdit-Bloc`, `final bool add`, and `final Journal journal` variables.

```
final JournalEditBloc journalEditBloc;
```

4. Add the `JournalEditBlocProvider` constructor with the `const` keyword.

5. Add to the constructor the `key`, `child`, `this.journalEditBloc`, `this.add`, and `this.journal` parameters.

```
const JournalEditBlocProvider(
    {Key key, Widget child, this.journalEditBloc})
    : super(key: key, child: child);
```

6. Add the `JournalEditBlocProvider of(BuildContext context)` method with the `static` keyword.

7. Inside the method, return the `JournalEditBlocProvider` by using the `inheritFromWidgetOf-ExactType` method that allows children widgets to get the instance of the `JournalEditBlocProvider` provider.

```
static JournalEditBlocProvider of(BuildContext context) {
  return (context.inheritFromWidgetOfExactType(JournalEditBlocProvider) as
  JournalEditBlocProvider);
}
```

8. Add and override the `updateShouldNotify` method to check whether the `journalEditBloc` does not equal the `old JournalEditBlocProvider journalEditBloc`. If the expression returns `true`, the framework notifies widgets that hold the inherited data that they need to rebuild.

```
@override
bool updateShouldNotify(JournalEditBlocProvider old) => false;
```

HOW IT WORKS

To pass the `State` between widgets and pages, you created the `journal_edit_bloc_provider.dart` file containing the `JournalEditBlocProvider` class as the provider for the `JournalEditBloc` class. The `JournalEditBlocProvider` class constructor takes the `key`, `widget`, and `this.journalEditBloc` parameters. The `of()` method returns the result of the `inheritFromWidgetOfExactType` method that allows children widgets to get the instance of the `JournalEditBlocProvider` provider. The `updateShouldNotify` method checks whether the value has changed, and the framework notifies widgets to rebuild.

SUMMARY

In this chapter, you implemented the client app's app-wide and local-state management. You learned how to implement the BLoC pattern to separate business logic from the UI pages. You created an `abstract` class to define the authentication interface and the authentication service class to implement the `abstract` class. By using the `abstract` class, you can impose implementation and design constraints. You used the `abstract` class with the BLoC class to inject at runtime the appropriate platform-dependent class, resulting in the BLoC class being platform-agnostic.

You implemented an `InheritedWidget` class as a provider to pass `State` between widgets and pages. You used the `of()` method to access reference to the provider. You created the `Journal` model class to structure the individual journal records and used the `fromDoc()` method to convert and map a Cloud Firestore database document to an individual `Journal` entry. You created service classes to manage sending and receiving the service API calls. You created the `AuthenticationService` class implementing the `AuthenticationApi` `abstract` class to access the Firebase Authentication API. You created the `DbFirestoreService` class implementing the `DbApi` `abstract` class to access the Cloud Firestore database API.

You implemented the BLoC pattern to maximize separation of the UI widgets and the business logic components. You learned that the pattern exposes sinks to input data and exposes streams to output data. You learned how to inject the platform-aware service classes to the BLoC's constructor, making the BLoC classes platform independent. By separating the business logic from the UI, it does not matter if you are using Flutter for the mobile apps, AngularDart for web apps, or any other platform. You implemented the `StreamController` to send data, done events, and errors on the `stream` property. You implemented the `Sink` class to add data with the `sink` property and the `Stream` class to send data with the `stream` property of the `StreamController`.

In the next chapter, you'll learn how to implement reactive pages to communicate with the BLoCs. You'll modify the main page to implement the app-wide state management by using the authentication BLoC provider. You'll create the login page and implement the BLoC to validate the email and password, log in, and create a new user account. You'll modify the home page to implement the database BLoC and use the `ListView.separated` constructor. You'll create the journal edit entry page and implement the BLoC to create and update existing entries.

▶ **WHAT YOU LEARNED IN THIS CHAPTER**

TOPIC	KEY CONCEPTS
App-wide and local-state management	You learned how to apply state management by creating the `InheritedWidget` class as a provider to pass `State` between widgets and pages.
`abstract` class	You learned how to implement an `abstract` class and `abstract` methods to define the authentication interface. You created the `AuthenticationService` class that implements the `abstract` class.
Model class	You learned how to create the `Journal` model class responsible for modeling the data structure and map Cloud Firestore database `QuerySnapshot` to individual `Journal` entries.
Service classes	You learned how to create service classes that call different services API. You created the `AuthenticationService` class to call the Firebase Authentication API and the `DbFirestoreService` class to call the Cloud Firestore database API.
`Validator` class	You learned how to create the `Validators` class that uses the `StreamTransformer` to validate the email and password to pass minimum requirements.
`StreamController`, `Streams`, `Sinks`, and `StreamBuilder`	You learned how to use the `StreamController` to send data, done events, and errors on the `stream` property. The `StreamController` has a `sink` (input) property and a `stream` (output) property.
BLoC pattern	The BLoC acronym stands for Business Logic Component, and it was created to define a platform-agnostic interface for the business logic. In other words, it separates the business logic from the UI widgets/components.
BLoC classes	You learned how to create the `AuthenticationBloc`, `LoginBloc`, `HomeBloc`, and `JournalEditBloc` BLoC classes.
BLoC dependency injection	You learned how to use `abstract` classes with the BLoC classes and how to inject platform-dependent classes to the BLoC classes, making the BLoC classes platform-agnostic.

TOPIC	KEY CONCEPTS
`InheritedWidget` class as a provider	You learned how to create the `AuthenticationBlocProvider`, `HomeBlocProvider`, and `JournalEditBlocProvider` classes that extend the `InheritedWidget` class to act as providers for the `AuthenticationBloc`, `HomeBloc`, and `JournalEditBloc` classes.

16

Adding BLoCs to Firestore Client App Pages

WHAT YOU WILL LEARN IN THIS CHAPTER

➤ How to pass app-wide state management between pages

➤ How to apply local-state management in the widget tree

➤ How to apply the `InheritedWidget` as a provider to pass state between widgets and pages

➤ How to use dependency injection to inject service classes to the BLoC classes to achieve platform independence

➤ How to apply the `LoginBloc` class to the Login page

➤ How to apply the `AuthenticationBloc` class to manage user credentials for app-wide state management

➤ How to apply the `HomeBloc` class to the home page to list, add, and delete journal entries

➤ How to apply the `JournalEditBloc` to the journal edit page to add or modify an existing entry

➤ How to build reactive widgets by implementing the `StreamBuilder` widget

➤ How to use the `ListView.separated` constructor to build a list of journal entries with a divider line by using the `Divider()` widget

➤ How to use the `Dismissible` widget to swipe and delete an entry

➤ How to use the `Dismissible` widget `confirmDismiss` property to prompt a delete confirmation dialog

➤ How to use the `DropdownButton()` widget to present a list of moods with the title, color, and icon rotation

➤ How to apply the `MoodIcons` class to retrieve the mood title, color, rotation, and icon

➤ How to apply the `Matrix4 rotateZ()` method to rotate icons according to the mood in conjunction with the `MoodIcons` class

➤ How to apply the `FormatDates` class to format dates

In this chapter, you'll continue to edit and complete the mood journaling app you've worked on in Chapters 14 and 15. For your convenience, you can use the `ch15_final_journal` project as your starting point and make sure you add your `GoogleService-Info.plist` file to the Xcode project and the `google-services.json` file to the Android project that you downloaded in Chapter 14 from your Firebase console.

You'll learn how to apply the BLoC, service, provider, model, and utility classes to the UI widget pages. The benefit of using the BLoC pattern allows for separation of the UI widgets from the business logic. You'll learn how to use dependency injection to inject service classes into the BLoC classes. By using dependency injection, the BLoCs remain platform-agnostic.

You'll also learn how to apply app-wide state management by implementing the `Authentication-BlocProvider` class to the main page. You'll learn how to pass state between pages and the widget tree by implementing the `HomeBlocProvider` and `JournalEditBlocProvider` classes. You'll learn how to create a Login page that implements the `LoginBloc` class to validate emails, passwords, and user credentials. You'll modify the home page and learn how to implement the `HomeBloc` class to handle the journal entries list and add and delete individual entries. You'll learn how to create the journal edit page that implements the `JournalEditBloc` class to add, modify, and save existing entries.

ADDING THE LOGIN PAGE

The Login page contains a `TextField` for entering the email address and a `TextField` for entering the password by obscuring the characters for privacy. You'll also add a button to log in the user and a button to create a new user account. You'll learn how to implement the `LoginBloc` class by using the `StreamBuilder` widget. You'll learn how to use dependency injection to inject the `AuthenticationService()` class to the `LoginBloc` class constructor, resulting in the `LoginBloc` being platform-agnostic. See Figure 16.1 for an idea of how the final Login page will look.

FIGURE 16.1: Final Login page

TRY IT OUT   Creating the Login Page

In this section, you'll continue to edit the `journal` project. You'll be adding the `LoginBloc` class to handle the validation of the email and password values. You'll use the `LoginBloc` class to log in the user or create a new user account and log in with the new authentication credentials.

1. Create a new Dart file in the `pages` folder. Right-click the `pages` folder, select New ➪ Dart File, enter `login.dart`, and click the OK button to save.

2. Import the `material.dart`, `login_bloc.dart`, and `authentication.dart` classes. Add a new line and create the `Login` class that extends a `StatefulWidget`.

```
import 'package:flutter/material.dart';
import 'package:journal/blocs/login_bloc.dart';
import 'package:journal/services/authentication.dart';
```

```
class Login extends StatefulWidget {
  @override
  _LoginState createState() => _LoginState();
}

class _LoginState extends State<Login> {
  @override
  Widget build(BuildContext context) {
    return Container();
  }
}
```

3. Modify the `_LoginState` class and add the private `LoginBloc _loginBloc` variable.

4. Override the `initState()` and initialize the `_loginBloc` variable with the `LoginBloc(Authenti-cationService())` class by injecting the `AuthenticationService()` in the constructor.

Note that the reason you initialized the `_loginBloc` variable from the `initState()` and not the `didChangeDependencies()` is because the `LoginBloc` does not need a provider (`Inher-itedWidget`).

```
class _LoginState extends State<Login> {
  LoginBloc _loginBloc;

  @override
  void initState() {
    super.initState();
    _loginBloc = LoginBloc(AuthenticationService());
  }

  @override
  Widget build(BuildContext context) {
    return Container();
  }
}
```

5. Override the `dispose()` method and dispose the `_loginBloc` variable. The `LoginBloc` class's `dispose()` method is called and closes all of the `StreamControllers`.

```
  @override
  void dispose() {
    _loginBloc.dispose();
    super.dispose();
  }
```

6. In the `Widget build()` method, replace the `Container()` with the UI widgets `Scaffold` and `AppBar` and for the `body` property add a `SafeArea()` and `SingleChildScrollView()` with the `child` property as a `Column()`. Set the `Column crossAxisAlignment` property to stretch.

7. For the `AppBar bottom` property, add a `PreferredSize` widget with the `child` property set to the `Icons.account_circle` and set the `size` property to `88.0` pixels and the `color` property to `Colors.white`.

```
  @override
  Widget build(BuildContext context) {
    return Scaffold(
      appBar: AppBar(
```

```
            bottom: PreferredSize(
                child: Icon(
                    Icons.account_circle,
                    size: 88.0,
                    color: Colors.white,
                ),
                preferredSize: Size.fromHeight(40.0)),
            ),
        ),
        body: SafeArea(
            child: SingleChildScrollView(
                padding: EdgeInsets.all(16.0, 32.0, 16.0, 16.0),
                child: Column(
                    crossAxisAlignment: CrossAxisAlignment.stretch,
                    children: <Widget>[

                    ],
                ),
            ),
        ),
    );
}
```

8. Add to the `Column` `children` property two `StreamBuilder` widgets. The first `StreamBuilder` handles the email `TextField` and sets the `stream` property to the `_loginBloc.email` stream. Add to the `builder` property the `TextField` widget, and for the `InputDecoration` `errorText` property set it to the `snapshot.error`. The `onChanged` property calls the `_loginBloc` `.emailChanged.add` sink that passes the current email address.

Add the second `StreamBuilder` by following the previous steps to handle the password `TextField`. Add a `SizedBox` with the `height` property set to `48.0` pixels and add a call to the `_buildLoginAndCreateButtons()` method that you will create in step 9.

```
Column(
    crossAxisAlignment: CrossAxisAlignment.stretch,
    children: <Widget>[
        StreamBuilder(
            stream: _loginBloc.email,
            builder: (BuildContext context, AsyncSnapshot snapshot) => TextField(
                keyboardType: TextInputType.emailAddress,
                decoration: InputDecoration(
                    labelText: 'Email Address',
                    icon: Icon(Icons.mail_outline),
                    errorText: snapshot.error),
                onChanged: _loginBloc.emailChanged.add,
            ),
        ),
        StreamBuilder(
            stream: _loginBloc.password,
            builder: (BuildContext context, AsyncSnapshot snapshot) =>
                TextField(
                    obscureText: true,
                    decoration: InputDecoration(
                        labelText: 'Password',
```

```
                    icon: Icon(Icons.security),
                    errorText: snapshot.error),
                  onChanged: _loginBloc.passwordChanged.add,
                ),
              ),
            SizedBox(height: 48.0),
            _buildLoginAndCreateButtons(),
          ],
        ),
      ),
```

9. Add a new line after the `Widget build(BuildContext context)` method and add the `_build-LoginAndCreateButtons()` that returns a `Widget`. Add the `StreamBuilder` to handle which set of buttons is active, for example Login button and then Create Account, or in reverse order. The `StreamBuilder` checks whether the `snapshot.data == 'Login'` and calls the `_buttonsLogin()` method; otherwise, it calls the `_buttonsCreateAccount()` method. You will create each method, respectively, in steps 10 and 11.

```
Widget _buildLoginAndCreateButtons() {
  return StreamBuilder(
    initialData: 'Login',
    stream: _loginBloc.loginOrCreateButton,
    builder: ((BuildContext context, AsyncSnapshot snapshot) {
      if (snapshot.data == 'Login') {
        return _buttonsLogin();
      } else if (snapshot.data == 'Create Account') {
        return _buttonsCreateAccount();
      }
    }),
  );
}
```

10. Add the `_buttonsLogin()` method that handles returning the button's combination with `Login` first and `Create Account` second. Since the `Login` button is the default, add the `RaisedButton` widget, and for the `Create Account` button add the `FlatButton` widget.

```
Column _buttonsLogin() {
  return Column(
    crossAxisAlignment: CrossAxisAlignment.stretch,
    children: <Widget>[
      StreamBuilder(
        initialData: false,
        stream: _loginBloc.enableLoginCreateButton,
```

```
builder: (BuildContext context, AsyncSnapshot snapshot) =>
    RaisedButton(
      elevation: 16.0,
      child: Text('Login'),
      color: Colors.lightGreen.shade200,
      disabledColor: Colors.grey.shade100,
      onPressed: snapshot.data
          ? () => _loginBloc.loginOrCreateChanged.add('Login')
          : null,
    ),
  ),
  FlatButton(
    child: Text('Create Account'),
    onPressed: () {
      _loginBloc.loginOrCreateButtonChanged.add('Create Account');
    },
  ),
 ],
);
}
```

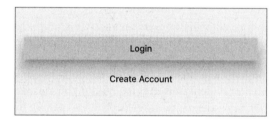

11. Add the _buttonsCreateAccount() method that handles returning the button's combination with Create Account first and Login second. Since the Create Account button is the default, add the RaisedButton widget, and for the Login button add the FlatButton widget.

```
Column _buttonsCreateAccount() {
  return Column(
    crossAxisAlignment: CrossAxisAlignment.stretch,
    children: <Widget>[
      StreamBuilder(
        initialData: false,
        stream: _loginBloc.enableLoginCreateButton,
        builder: (BuildContext context, AsyncSnapshot snapshot) =>
            RaisedButton(
              elevation: 16.0,
              child: Text('Create Account'),
              color: Colors.lightGreen.shade200,
              disabledColor: Colors.grey.shade100,
              onPressed: snapshot.data
                  ? () =>
                      _loginBloc.loginOrCreateChanged.add('Create Account')
                  : null,
            ),
      ),
```

```
        FlatButton(
          child: Text('Login'),
          onPressed: () {
            _loginBloc.loginOrCreateButtonChanged.add('Login');
          },
        ),
      ],
    );
}
```

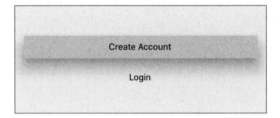

HOW IT WORKS

The login.dart file contains the Login class that extends a StatefulWidget to handle logging in a user or creating a new user account. You instantiate the LoginBloc class by injecting the Authenti-cationService() class by overriding the initState() method. Note that the reason you initialized the _loginBloc variable from the initState() and not the didChangeDependencies() is because the LoginBloc does not need a provider (InheritedWidget). You closed the LoginBloc Stream-Controllers listeners by overriding the dispose() method and calling the _loginBloc.dispose() method. It's good practice to close the StreamController listeners when they aren't needed.

The StreamBuilder widget is used to monitor the email and password values. You used the TextField widget's onChanged property to call the _loginBloc.emailChanged.add sink and the _loginBloc. passwordChanged.add sink to send the values to the LoginBloc Validators class to validate that the minimum formatting requirements are met. You learned in Chapter 15's "Adding the Validators Class" section how the StreamTransformer transforms a Stream that is used to validate and process values inside a Stream.

The StreamBuilder widget is used to listen to the _loginBloc.loginOrCreateButton stream to tog-gle showing Login or Create Account as the default button.

MODIFYING THE MAIN PAGE

The main page is the control center responsible for monitoring app-wide state management. You'll learn how to implement the AuthenticationBlocProvider class as the main provider to the AuthenticationBloc class. You'll learn how to implement the HomeBlocProvider class as the provider to the HomeBloc class with the child property as the Home class and also to hold the state for the user uid. You'll learn how to apply the StreamBuilder widget to monitor the user's authentication status. When the user logs in, the widget directs the user to the home page, and when the user logs out, it directs the user to the Login page. See Figure 16.2 for the main page BLoC flow.

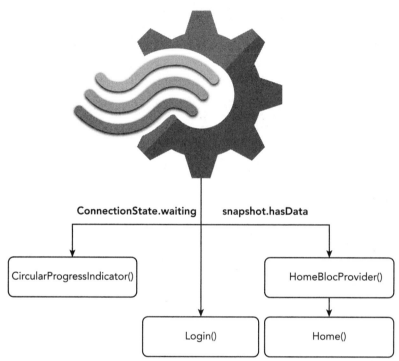

FIGURE 16.2: Main page BLoC flow

TRY IT OUT Modifying the Main Page

In this section, you'll continue to edit the journal project. You'll be modifying the main.dart file to handle app-wide state management by using the StreamBuilder and BLoCs.

1. Open the main.dart file and add the following packages and classes:

```
import 'package:flutter/material.dart';
import 'package:journal/blocs/authentication_bloc.dart';
import 'package:journal/blocs/authentication_bloc_provider.dart';
import 'package:journal/blocs/home_bloc.dart';
import 'package:journal/blocs/home_bloc_provider.dart';
import 'package:journal/services/authentication.dart';
import 'package:journal/services/db_firestore.dart';
import 'package:journal/pages/home.dart';
import 'package:journal/pages/login.dart';
```

2. Inside the `Widget build()` method, add the `final _authenticationService` variable initialized by the `AuthenticationService()`.

```
@override
Widget build(BuildContext context) {
    final AuthenticationService _authenticationService = AuthenticationService();
```

3. Add the `final _authenticationBloc` variable initialized by the `AuthenticationBloc()` and inject the `_authenticationService` dependency. The `AuthenticationBloc` class remains platform-agnostic by using dependency injection of the `AuthenticationService()` class.

```
final AuthenticationBloc _authenticationBloc = AuthenticationBloc
(_authenticationService);
```

4. Refactor the `MaterialApp()` widget to a method by placing the mouse over the word `MaterialApp` and right-clicking. Then select Refactor ⇨ Extract ⇨ Method ⇨ Method.

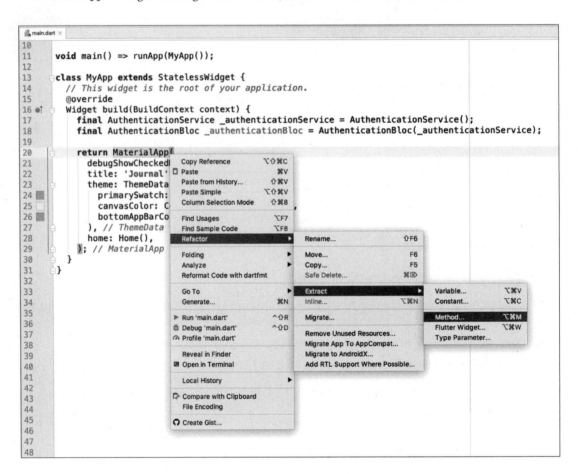

5. In the Extract Method dialog, enter **_buildMaterialApp** for the method name and click the Refactor button.

6. Add to the _buildMaterialApp() constructor the Widget homePage parameter. When this method is called, the page widget is passed to the homePage parameter, for example, the Login() or Home() class page. Change the home property to the homePage widget.

```
MaterialApp _buildMaterialApp(Widget homePage) {
  return MaterialApp(
    debugShowCheckedModeBanner: false,
    title: 'Security Inherited',
    theme: ThemeData(
      primarySwatch: Colors.lightGreen,
      canvasColor: Colors.lightGreen.shade50,
      bottomAppBarColor: Colors.lightGreen,
    ),
    home: homePage,
  );
}
```

7. Go back to the Widget build method and replace the return _buildMaterialApp() call with the AuthenticationBlocProvider() class.

8. For the authenticationBloc property, pass the _authenticationBloc variable, and for the child property, pass the StreamBuilder() widget.

```
return AuthenticationBlocProvider(
  authenticationBloc: _authenticationBloc,
  child: StreamBuilder(),
);
```

9. Set the `StreamBuilder()` widget's `initialData` property to a null value, meaning no user is logged in. Set the `stream` property to the `_authenticationBloc.user stream`.

10. While the snapshot connection status is waiting, it's good practice to show a progress indicator. Otherwise, the user thinks the app stopped working. Inside the `builder` property, add an `if` statement checking that `snapshot.connectionState == ConnectionState.waiting` and return a `Container` widget with the `color` property set to `Colors.lightGreen` and the `child` property to the `CircularProgressIndicator()` widget.

11. When the user logs in with the correct credentials, you need to navigate to the `Home()` class page. Add an `else if` statement checking whether the `snapshot.hasData` equals `true` and add the `return HomeBlocProvider()` class.

12. Set the `HomeBlocProvider()` class's `homeBloc` property to the `HomeBloc(DbFirestoreService()`, `_authenticationService)` class; note that you are injecting the Flutter platform service classes.

13. For the `child` property, call the `_buildMaterialApp(Home())` method to navigate to the `Home()` class page.

14. Add the last `else` statement and add the `return _buildMaterialApp(Login())` method to navigate to the `Login()` class page.

```
StreamBuilder(
  initialData: null,
  stream: _authenticationBloc.user,
  builder: (BuildContext context, AsyncSnapshot snapshot) {
    if (snapshot.connectionState == ConnectionState.waiting) {
      return Container(
        color: Colors.lightGreen,
        child: CircularProgressIndicator(),
      );
    } else if (snapshot.hasData) {
      return HomeBlocProvider(
        homeBloc: HomeBloc(DbFirestoreService(), _authenticationService),
        uid: snapshot.data,
        child: _buildMaterialApp(Home()),
      );
    } else {
      return _buildMaterialApp(Login());
    }
  },
),
```

HOW IT WORKS

You edited the `main.dart` file that contains the `MyApp` class that extends a `StatelessWidget` to handle app-wide authentication state management. The root of the `MyApp` class is the `Authentication-BlocProvider` class with the `child` property set to the `StreamBuilder` widget. This `StreamBuilder` widget monitors the `_authenticationBloc.user stream`, and the `builder` rebuilds every time the user's authentication status changes and navigates the user to the appropriate login or home page.

MODIFYING THE HOME PAGE

The home page is responsible for showing a list of journal entries filtered by the logged-in user `uid` and the ability to add, modify, and delete individual entries. In this section, you'll learn how to implement the `AuthenticationBlocProvider` as the provider for the `AuthenticationBloc` class. You'll learn how to implement the `HomeBlocProvider` class as the provider for the `HomeBloc` class. You'll learn how to apply the `StreamBuilder` widget to build the journal entries list by calling the `ListView` `.separated` constructor. The `Dismissible` widget is used to swipe on an item to delete the entry. You'll learn how to use the `Dismissible` widget `confirmDismiss` property to prompt the user with a delete confirmation dialog. You'll learn how to call the `MoodIcons` class to color and rotate icons according to the selected mood. You'll learn how to call the `FormatDates` class to format dates.

Note that I purposely didn't inject the `MoodIcons` and `FormatDates` classes into the `HomeBloc` and `EditJournalBLoc` classes to show that you can decide not to include certain utility classes in the BLoC. If you were to include them in these BLoCs, you would duplicate the `MoodIcons` and `FormatDates` methods into two different BLoCs. In Chapter 15's "Implementing the BLoC Pattern" section, you learned in the UI design guidelines to create a BLoC for each complex enough component. Another option is to create a `MoodAndDatesBloc` class to handle the `MoodIcons` and `FormatDates` classes (as abstract classes) and use the `MoodAndDatesBloc` class in both the home and edit entry pages. See Figure 16.3 for an idea of how the final home page will look.

FIGURE 16.3: Final home page

Modifying the Home Page

In this section, you'll continue to edit the `journal` project. You'll be modifying the `home.dart` file to handle listing the journal entries, as well as adding, modifying, and deleting them. You'll use the `MoodIcons` class to retrieve the correct mood `title`, `color`, `rotation`, and `icon`. You'll use the `FormatDates` class to format dates.

1. Open the `home.dart` file and add the following packages and classes:

```
import 'package:flutter/material.dart';
import 'package:journal/blocs/authentication_bloc.dart';
import 'package:journal/blocs/authentication_bloc_provider.dart';
import 'package:journal/blocs/home_bloc.dart';
import 'package:journal/blocs/home_bloc_provider.dart';
import 'package:journal/blocs/journal_edit_bloc.dart';
import 'package:journal/blocs/journal_edit_bloc_provider.dart';
import 'package:journal/classes/format_dates.dart';
import 'package:journal/classes/mood_icons.dart';
import 'package:journal/models/journal.dart';
import 'package:journal/pages/edit_entry.dart';
import 'package:journal/services/db_firestore.dart';
```

2. Modify the `_HomeState` class and add the private `_authenticationBloc`, `_homeBloc`, `_uid`, `_moodIcons`, and `_formatDates` variables. Override the `initState()` and initialize the `_login-Bloc` variable with the `LoginBloc(AuthenticationService())` class by injecting the `AuthenticationService()` in the constructor.

```
AuthenticationBloc _authenticationBloc;
HomeBloc _homeBloc;
String _uid;
MoodIcons _moodIcons = MoodIcons();
FormatDates _formatDates = FormatDates();
```

3. Override the `didChangeDependencies()` method and initialize the variables from the provider classes. Note that the `InheritedWidget` classes need to be accessed from the `didChangeDependencies()` method and not the `initState()` method. Note that the `_uid` variable state is initialized from the `HomeBlocProvider`, and the value is passed to the `Journal` class for adding journal entries.

```
@override
void didChangeDependencies() {
   super.didChangeDependencies();
   _authenticationBloc = AuthenticationBlocProvider.of(context).
authenticationBloc;
   _homeBloc = HomeBlocProvider.of(context).homeBloc;
   _uid = HomeBlocProvider.of(context).uid;
}
```

4. Override the `dispose()` method and dispose the `_homeBloc` variable. The `HomeBloc` class `dispose()` method is called and closes all of the `StreamControllers`.

```
@override
void dispose() {
   _homeBloc.dispose();
```

```
      super.dispose();
   }
```

5. Add the _addOrEditJournal() method receiving the add and journal named parameters.

6. Inside the method add the Navigator.push() method that navigates to the EditEntry() page as a child property of the JournalEditBlocProvider class.

7. For the journalEditBloc property, inject the JournalEditBloc class with the add, journal, and DbFirestoreService() class.

8. Add the fullscreenDialog property and set it to true.

Note that you input values to the BLoC through sinks, but for this case, it makes sense to avoid adding unnecessary StreamContollers and listeners since it doesn't require the user to input this data. Instead, you pass the add and journal variables through the JournalEditBloc() constructor.

```
// Add or Edit Journal Entry and call the Show Entry Dialog
void _addOrEditJournal({bool add, Journal journal}) {
  Navigator.push(
    context,
    MaterialPageRoute(
        builder: (BuildContext context) => JournalEditBlocProvider(
          journalEditBloc: JournalEditBloc(add, journal, DbFirestoreService()),
          child: EditEntry(),
        ),
        fullscreenDialog: true
    ),
  );
}
```

9. Add the _confirmDeleteJournal() method that returns the showDialog() method. The dialog shows a delete confirmation warning giving the user a choice to delete the entry or cancel.

```
// Confirm Deleting a Journal Entry
Future<bool> _confirmDeleteJournal() async {
  return await showDialog(
    context: context,
    barrierDismissible: false,
    builder: (BuildContext context) {
      return AlertDialog(
        title: Text("Delete Journal"),
        content: Text("Are you sure you would like to Delete?"),
        actions: <Widget>[
          FlatButton(
            child: Text('CANCEL'),
            onPressed: () {
              Navigator.pop(context, false);
            },
          ),
          FlatButton(
            child: Text('DELETE', style: TextStyle(color: Colors.red),),
            onPressed: () {
```

```
                        Navigator.pop(context, true);
                    },
                ),
            ],
        );
      },
    );
}
```

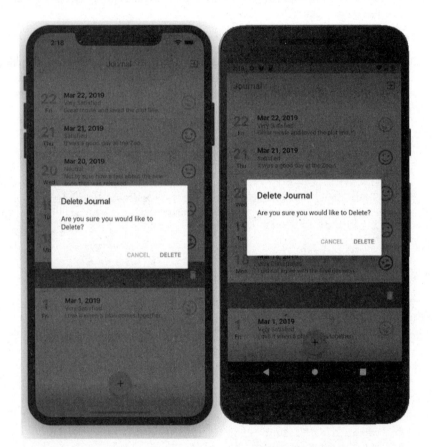

10. Modify the `AppBar` `actions` property and replace the `TODO` comment with the call to the `_authenticationBloc.logoutUser.add(true)` sink. The `AuthenticationBloc` receives the sink value to log out the user, and the main page (containing the app-wide state management) automatically navigates the user to the Login page.

```
actions: <Widget>[
  IconButton(
    icon: Icon(Icons.exit_to_app, color: Colors.lightGreen.shade800,),
    onPressed: () {
      _authenticationBloc.logoutUser.add(true);
    },
  ),
],
```

11. Edit the `body` property and replace the `Container()` widget with the `StreamBuilder` widget, and set the `stream` property to the `_homeBloc.listJournal` stream.

12. Inside the `builder` property, add an `if` statement to check for `ConnectionState.waiting` and return a `Center()` widget with the `child` property set to the `CircularProgressIndicator()` widget.

13. Add an `else if` statement that checks for `snapshot.hasData`, and return the call to the `_build-ListViewSeparated(snapshot)` method passing the `snapshot` variable. You'll create the `_buildListViewSeparated()` method in step 17.

14. Add an `else` statement and return a `Center()` widget with the `child` property set to a `Container()` widget.

15. Add a `Text` widget to the `Container()` child property with the message `'Add Journals.'`

```
body: StreamBuilder(
  stream: _homeBloc.listJournal,
  builder: ((BuildContext context, AsyncSnapshot snapshot) {
    if (snapshot.connectionState == ConnectionState.waiting) {
      return Center(
        child: CircularProgressIndicator(),
      );
    } else if (snapshot.hasData) {
      return _buildListViewSeparated(snapshot);
    } else {
      return Center(
        child: Container(
          child: Text('Add Journals.'),
        ),
      );
    }
  }),
),
```

16. Modify the `FloatingActionButton` onPressed property and replace the TODO comment with the call to the `_addOrEditJournal(add: true, journal: Journal(uid: _uid))` method.

```
floatingActionButton: FloatingActionButton(
  //...
  onPressed: () async {
    _addOrEditJournal(add: true, journal: Journal(uid: _uid));
  },
),
```

17. After the `Widget build(BuildContext context)` method, add the `_buildListViewSeparated(AsyncSnapshot snapshot)` method.

18. Return and call the `ListView.separated()` constructor with the `itemCount` property set to the `snapshot.data.length`, meaning the journal's item count.

19. For the `itemBuilder` property, add the `_titleData` variable and set the value by calling the `_formatDates.dateFormatShortMonthDayYear` method by passing the `snapshot` date value.

20. Add the _subtitle variable and set the value by concatenating the snapshot mood and note values.

21. Add the separatorBuilder property and return a Divider() widget with the color property set to Colors.grey.

```
        Widget _buildListViewSeparated(AsyncSnapshot snapshot) {
          return ListView.separated(
            itemCount: snapshot.data.length,
            itemBuilder: (BuildContext context, int index) {
              String _titleDate = _formatDates.dateFormatShortMonthDayYear(snapshot
  .data[index].date);
              String _subtitle = snapshot.data[index].mood + "\n" + snapshot
  .data[index].note;
              return Dismissible();
            },
            separatorBuilder: (BuildContext context, int index) {
              return Divider(
                color: Colors.grey,
              );
            },
          );
        }
```

22. Add to the Dismissible() widget the key property set to the snapshot documentID by using the Key() class. The Key() class creates a unique identifier for a widget to make sure the correct journal entry is deleted.

```
        return Dismissible(
          key: Key(snapshot.data[index].documentID),
```

23. Set the background property to a Container() widget with the icon set to Icons.delete. Follow the same steps for the secondaryBackground property. When the user swipes on a row to delete the entry, the red background is shown with the delete icons notifying the user that they are about to delete a journal entry.

```
        background: Container(
          color: Colors.red,
          alignment: Alignment.centerLeft,
          padding: EdgeInsets.only(left: 16.0),
          child: Icon(
            Icons.delete,
            color: Colors.white,
          ),
        ),
        secondaryBackground: Container(
          color: Colors.red,
          alignment: Alignment.centerRight,
          padding: EdgeInsets.only(right: 16.0),
          child: Icon(
            Icons.delete,
            color: Colors.white,
          ),
        ),
```

24. Set the `child` property to the `ListTile()` widget with the `leading` property set to the `Column()` widget. Add to the `children` property two `Text` widgets that call the `_formatDates` class. The `leading` property shows the day and day of the week of the journal entry.

```
child: ListTile(
  leading: Column(
    children: <Widget>[
      Text(_formatDates.dateFormatDayNumber(snapshot.data[index].date),
        style: TextStyle(
            fontWeight: FontWeight.bold,
            fontSize: 32.0,
            color: Colors.lightGreen),
      ),
      Text(_formatDates.dateFormatShortDayName(snapshot.data[index].date)),
    ],
  ),
```

25. Set the `trailing` property to the `Transform()` widget with the `Matrix4 rotateZ()` method.

26. Pass the mood icon rotation to the `rotateZ()` method by calling the `MoodIcons` class's `_moodIcons.getMoodRotation` method. For the happiest mood, the icon is rotated toward the left, and for the saddest mood the icon is rotated toward the right.

```
trailing: Transform(
    transform: Matrix4.identity()..rotateZ(_moodIcons
.getMoodRotation(snapshot.data[index].mood)),
    alignment: Alignment.center,
    child: Icon(_moodIcons.getMoodIcon(snapshot.data[index].mood), color:
_moodIcons.getMoodColor(snapshot.data[index].mood), size: 42.0,),
    ),
```

27. Set the `title` property to the `Text` widget showing the `_titleDate` variable.

28. Set the `subtitle` property to the `Text` widget showing the `_subtitle` variable.

29. For the `onTap` property, call the `_addOrEditJournal` method and pass a `false` value for the `add` property and the `snapshot.data[index]` value for the `journal` property. The `onTap` property handles the user tapping a journal entry and calls the `_addOrEditJournal()` method to edit the entry.

```
title: Text(
  _titleDate,
  style: TextStyle(fontWeight: FontWeight.bold),
),
subtitle: Text(_subtitle),
onTap: () {
  _addOrEditJournal(
    add: false,
    journal: snapshot.data[index],
  );
},
),
```

30. For the `confirmDismiss` property, add a call to the `_confirmDeleteJournal()` method showing a dialog to confirm deleting the journal entry.

31. Add the `if` statement to check that the `confirmDelete` variable value is `true` and call the `_homeBloc.deleteJournal.add(snapshot.data[index])` sink to signal the `HomeBloc` class to delete the journal entry.

```
confirmDismiss: (direction) async {
  bool confirmDelete = await _confirmDeleteJournal();
  if (confirmDelete) {
    _homeBloc.deleteJournal.add(snapshot.data[index]);
  }
},
);
```

HOW IT WORKS

You edited the `home.dart` file to contain the `Home` class that extends a `StatefulWidget` to handle showing a list of journal entries with the ability to add, modify, and delete individual records. You accessed the `AuthenticationBlocProvider` and `HomeBlocProvider` classes by using the provider's `of()` method from the `didChangeDependencies` method to receive the state from the main page. You implemented the `AuthenticationBloc` and the `HomeBloc` classes by using the `StreamBuilder` widget to monitor authentication and entry changes. You implemented the `StreamBuilder` widget to monitor the `_homeBloc.listJournal` stream, and the `builder` rebuilds every time a journal entry changes.

The `_addOrEditJournal()` method handles adding or modifying a journal entry. The constructor takes the `add` and `journal` named parameters to aid if you are adding or modifying an entry. To show the edit entry page, you call the `Navigator.push()` method by passing the `JournalEditBlocProvider` and inject the received parameters to the `JournalEditBloc` class.

The `_buildListViewSeparated(snapshot)` method uses the `ListView.separated()` constructor to build the list of journal entries. The `itemBuilder` returns a `Dismissible()` widget that handles deleting journal entries by swiping left or right on the entry. The `Dismissible()` child property uses the `ListTile()` to format each journal entry in the `ListView`. The `separatorBuilder` returns the `Divider()` widget to show a gray divider line between journal entries.

ADDING THE EDIT JOURNAL PAGE

The edit journal page is responsible for adding and editing a journal entry. In this section, you'll learn how to create the journal edit page that implements the `JournalEditBlocProvider` as the provider for the `JournalEditBloc` class. You'll learn to use the `StreamBuilder` widget with the date, mood, note, and Cancel and Save buttons. You'll implement the `showTimePicker()` function to present the user with a calendar to choose a date. You'll learn how to use the `DropdownButton()` widget to present the user with a list of selectable moods with the icon, color, description, and mood icon rotation. You'll use the `Matrix4 rotateZ()` method to implement the mood icon rotation. You'll use the `TextEditingController()` constructor with the note `TextField()` widget. You'll learn how to call the `MoodIcons` class to color and rotate icons in the `DropdownButton DropdownMenuItem` selection list. You'll learn how to call the `FormatDates` class to format the selected date. See Figure 16.4 for the look of the final edit journal page.

FIGURE 16.4: Final edit journal page

TRY IT OUT Creating the Edit Journal Page

In this section, you'll continue to edit the `journal` project. You'll be adding the `JournalEditBloc` class to create or modify and save an existing entry.

1. Create a new Dart file in the `pages` folder. Right-click the `pages` folder, select New ⇨ Dart File, enter `edit_entry.dart`, and click the OK button to save.

2. Import the `material.dart`, `journal_edit_bloc.dart`, `journal_edit_bloc_provider.dart`, `format_dates.dart`, and `mood_icons.dart` classes. Add a new line and create the `EditEntry` class that extends a `StatefulWidget`.

```
import 'package:flutter/material.dart';
import 'package:journal/blocs/journal_edit_bloc.dart';
import 'package:journal/blocs/journal_edit_bloc_provider.dart';
import 'package:journal/classes/format_dates.dart';
import 'package:journal/classes/mood_icons.dart';
```

```
class EditEntry extends StatefulWidget {
  @override
  _EditEntryState createState() => _EditEntryState();
}

class _EditEntryState extends State<EditEntry> {
  @override
  Widget build(BuildContext context) {
    return Container();
  }
}
```

3. Modify the _EditEntryState class and add the JournalEditBloc _journalEditBloc, FormatDates _formatDates, MoodIcons _moodIcons, and TextEditingController _noteController private variables.

The note field uses the TextField widget, which requires the _noteController to access and modify the values.

```
class _EditEntryState extends State<EditEntry> {
  JournalEditBloc _journalEditBloc;
  FormatDates _formatDates;
  MoodIcons _moodIcons;
  TextEditingController _noteController;

  @override
  Widget build(BuildContext context) {
    return Container();
  }
}
```

4. Override the initState(), and let's initialize the variables _formatDates, _moodIcons, and _noteController. Make sure you add the super.initState().

```
@override
void initState() {
  super.initState();
  _formatDates = FormatDates();
  _moodIcons = MoodIcons();
  _noteController = TextEditingController();
  _noteController.text = '';
}
```

5. Override the didChangeDependencies() method and initialize the _journalEditBloc variable from the JournalEditBlocProvider class. Note that the InheritedWidget classes need to be accessed from the didChangeDependencies() method and not the initState() method.

```
@override
void didChangeDependencies() {
  super.didChangeDependencies();
  _journalEditBloc = JournalEditBlocProvider.of(context).journalEditBloc;
}
```

6. Override the `dispose()` method and dispose of the `_noteController` and `_journalEditBloc` variables. The `JournalEditBloc` class's `dispose()` method is called and closes all of the `StreamControllers`.

```
@override
dispose() {
  _noteController.dispose();
  _journalEditBloc.dispose();
  super.dispose();
}
```

7. Add the `_selectDate(DateTime selectedDate)` async method that returns a `Future<DateTime>`. This method is responsible for calling the Flutter built-in `showDatePicker()` that presents the user with a pop-up dialog displaying a Material Design calendar to choose dates.

8. Add the `DateTime _initialDate` variable and initialize it with the `selectedDate` variable passed in the constructor.

9. Add a final `DateTime _pickedDate` (date user picks from the calendar) variable and initialize it by calling the `await showDatePicker()` constructor. Pass the `context`, `initialDate`, `firstDate`, and `lastDate` properties. Note that for the `firstDate`, you use today's date and subtract 365 days, and for the `lastDate`, you add 365 days, which tells the calendar selectable date ranges.

10. Add an `if` statement that checks that the `_pickedDate` variable (the date user picked from the calendar) does not equal `null`, meaning the user tapped the calendar Cancel button. If the user did pick a date, then modify the `selectedDate` variable by using the `DateTime()` constructor and pass the `_pickedDate` year, month, and day.

11. For the time, pass the `_initialDate` hour, minute, second, millisecond, and microsecond. Note that since you are changing only the date and not the time, you use the original's created date time.

12. Add a `return` statement to send back the `selectedDate`.

```
// Date Picker
Future<String> _selectDate(String selectedDate) async {
  DateTime _initialDate = DateTime.parse(selectedDate);

  final DateTime _pickedDate = await showDatePicker(
    context: context,
    initialDate: _initialDate,
    firstDate: DateTime.now().subtract(Duration(days: 365)),
    lastDate: DateTime.now().add(Duration(days: 365)),
  );
  if (_pickedDate != null) {
    selectedDate = DateTime(
        _pickedDate.year,
        _pickedDate.month,
        _pickedDate.day,
        _initialDate.hour,
        _initialDate.minute,
```

```
            _initialDate.second,
            initialDate.millisecond,
            _initialDate.microsecond).toString();
    }
    return selectedDate;
}
```

13. Add the `_addOrUpdateJournal()` method that calls the `_journalEditBloc.saveJournal-Changed.add('Save')` sink to save journal entry. The `JournalEditBloc` receives this request and calls the Cloud Firestore database API.

```
void _addOrUpdateJournal() {
    _journalEditBloc.saveJournalChanged.add('Save');
    Navigator.pop(context);
}
```

14. In the `Widget build()` method, replace the `Container()` with the UI widgets `Scaffold` and `AppBar`, and for the `body` property add a `SafeArea()` and `SingleChildScrollView()` with the `child` property as a `Column()`.

15. Set the `Column` `crossAxisAlignment` property to `start`.

16. Modify the `AppBar` `title` property's `Text` widget to `Entry`, and set the `TextStyle` color property to `Colors.lightGreen.shade800`.

17. Set the `automaticallyImplyLeading` property to a `false` value to remove the default navigation icon to navigate back to the previous page. You want the user to only dismiss this page by tapping the Cancel or Save button.

18. To customize the `AppBar` background color with a gradient, remove the `AppBar` widget shadow by setting the `elevation` property to `0.0`.

19. To increase the `AppBar`'s height, set the bottom property to a `PreferredSize` widget with the `child` property as a `Container` widget and the `preferredSize` property to `Size.from-Height(32.0)`.

20. Set the `flexibleSpace` property to a `Container` widget with the `decoration` property to a `BoxDecoration` widget.

21. Set the `BoxDecoration` `gradient` property to a `LinearGradient` with the `colors` property set to a list of `[Colors.lightGreen, Colors.lightGreen.shade50]`.

22. Set the `begin` property to `Alignment.topCenter` and the `end` property to `Alignment.bottom-Center`. The `LinearGradient` effect draws the `AppBar` color from a `lightGreen` and gradually fades to a `lightGreen.shade50` color.

```
@override
Widget build(BuildContext context) {
  return Scaffold(
    appBar: AppBar(
      title: Text('Entry', style: TextStyle(color: Colors.lightGreen
.shade800),),
      automaticallyImplyLeading: false,
      elevation: 0.0,
      flexibleSpace: Container(
        decoration: BoxDecoration(
          gradient: LinearGradient(
            colors: [Colors.lightGreen, Colors.lightGreen.shade50],
            begin: Alignment.topCenter,
            end: Alignment.bottomCenter,
          ),
        ),
      ),
    ),
    body: SafeArea(
      minimum: EdgeInsets.all(16.0),
      child: SingleChildScrollView(
        child: Column(
          crossAxisAlignment: CrossAxisAlignment.start,
          children: <Widget>[

          ],
        ),
      ),
    ),
  );
}
```

HOW IT WORKS

You created the `edit_entry.dart` file that contains the `EditEntry` class that extends a `Stateful-Widget` to add or edit a journal entry. You implemented the `JournalEditBlocProvider` to receive state from the home page by using the provider's `of()` method from the `didChangeDependencies` method. The `JournalEditBloc` class is responsible for adding, editing, and saving journal entries. You used dependency injection by passing `add`, `journal`, and the `DbFirestoreService()` service to the `JournalEditBloc` class. You implemented the `showDatePicker()` to select dates with a calendar and implemented the `DropdownButton()` widget to select a list of moods and used the `Matrix4 rotateZ()` method to rotate mood icons. You used the `MoodIcons` utility class with the `DropdownButton Drop-downMenuItem` selection list. The `FormatDates` utility class formats the selected date. To give the `AppBar` a color gradient effect, you used the `BoxDecoration` widget to customize the `gradient` property with the `LinearGradient` class.

The following exercise continues to edit the entry page to add individual `StreamBuilder` widgets to handle each entry field and actions.

TRY IT OUT **Adding the StreamBuilders to the Edit Journal Page**

In this section, you'll continue to edit the `edit_entry.dart` file. You'll be adding the `StreamBuilder` widgets to handle the date, mood, note, and Cancel and Save buttons.

1. Continue editing the `Column` created in step 13 from the previous exercise. Add to the `Column` children the `StreamBuilder()` widget with the `stream` property set to `_journalEditBloc.dateEdit` stream. This `StreamBuilder()` widget is responsible for handling the date field.

2. Add to the `builder` property the `if` statement to check whether the `snapshot` does not have data by using the `!snapshot.hasData` expression. Inside the `if` statement, return a `Container()`, meaning an empty space since the data has not arrived yet.

```
if (!snapshot.hasData) {
    return Container();
}
```

3. Add a new line and return the `FlatButton` widget that is used to show the formatted selected date, and when the user taps the button, it presents the calendar.

4. Set the `FlatButton` padding property to `EdgeInsets.all(0.0)` to remove padding for better aesthetics and add to the `child` property a `Row()` widget.

5. Add to the Row children property the Icons.calendar_day Icon with a size of 22.0 and color property to Colors.black54.

6. Add a SizedBox with the width property set to 16.0 to add a spacer.

7. Add a Text widget and format the _selectedDate with the DateFormat.yMMMEd() constructor. Add the Icons.arrow_drop_down Icon with the color property set to Colors.black54.

8. Add the onPressed() callback and mark it async since calling the calendar is a Future event.

9. Add to the onPressed() the FocusScope.of().requestFocus() method call to dismiss the keyboard if any of the TextField widgets have focus. This step is optional, but I wanted to show you how it's accomplished.

```
FocusScope.of(context).requestFocus(FocusNode());
```

10. Add a DateTime _pickerDate variable initialized by calling the await _selectDate(_selectedDate) Future method, which is why you add the await keyword. You added this method in step 7 in the "Creating the Edit Journal Page" exercise.

11. Add the call to the _journalEditBloc.dateEditChanged.add(_pickerDate) sink that passes to the JournalEditBloc the selected _pickerDate variable.

```
String _pickerDate = await _selectDate(snapshot.data);
_journalEditBloc.dateEditChanged.add(_pickerDate);
```

The following is the full FlatButton widget code:

```
StreamBuilder(
  stream: _journalEditBloc.dateEdit,
  builder: (BuildContext context, AsyncSnapshot snapshot) {
    if (!snapshot.hasData) {
      return Container();
    }
    return FlatButton(
      padding: EdgeInsets.all(0.0),
      child: Row(
        children: <Widget>[
          Icon(
            Icons.calendar_today,
            size: 22.0,
            color: Colors.black54,
          ),
          SizedBox(width: 16.0,),
          Text(_formatDates.dateFormatShortMonthDayYear(snapshot.data),
            style: TextStyle(
                color: Colors.black54,
                fontWeight: FontWeight.bold),
          ),
          Icon(
            Icons.arrow_drop_down,
            color: Colors.black54,
          ),
        ],
      ),
    ),
```

```
          onPressed: () async {
            FocusScope.of(context).requestFocus(FocusNode());
            String _pickerDate = await _selectDate(snapshot.data);
            _journalEditBloc.dateEditChanged.add(_pickerDate);
          },
        );
      },
    ),
```

12. Add a new line and add the `StreamBuilder()` widget with the `stream` property set to `_journal-EditBloc.moodEdit` stream. This `StreamBuilder()` widget is responsible for handling the mood field.

```
      StreamBuilder(
        stream: _journalEditBloc.moodEdit,
```

13. Add to the `builder` property the `if` statement to check whether the `snapshot` does not have data by using the `!snapshot.hasData` expression. Inside the `if` statement return a `Container()`.

```
        builder: (BuildContext context, AsyncSnapshot snapshot) {
          if (!snapshot.hasData) {
            return Container();
          }
```

14. Add a new line and return the `DropdownButtonHideUnderline` widget with the `child` property set to the `DropdownButton<MoodIcons>` widget declaring the type as the `MoodIcons` class.

```
          return DropdownButtonHideUnderline(
            child: DropdownButton<MoodIcons>(
```

15. Add the `value` property and call the `_moodIcons.getMoodIconsList()` method by using the `indexWhere` method to search by the `icon.title` value. The value returned is the mood icon's index position in the list.

```
            value: _moodIcons.getMoodIconsList()[
              _moodIcons
              .getMoodIconsList()
              .indexWhere((icon) => icon.title == snapshot.data)
            ],
```

16. Add the `onChanged` property and call the `_journalEditBloc.moodEditChanged.add(selected.title)` sink by passing the `selected.title` value. This event occurs when the user selects a mood from the `DropdownButton` widget.

```
        onChanged: (selected) {
          _journalEditBloc.moodEditChanged.add(selected.title);
        },
```

17. This section creates the pop-up list to choose a mood. Add the `items` property by calling the `_moodIcons.getMoodIconsList()`, and by using the dot operator, call the `map()` method that receives the `selected` mood icon.

18. Add a new line, return the `DropdownMenuItem<MoodIcons>` widget, and set the `value` property to the `selected` variable.

19. For the `child` property, add a `Row` with the `children` property set to the `Transform()` widget, `SizedBox`, and the `Text` widget.

20. Follow the steps from the home page's step 22 to set up the `Matrix4 rotateZ()` method.

21. At the end of this method, make sure you add the call to the `toList()` by using the dot operator.

```
        items: _moodIcons.getMoodIconsList().map((MoodIcons selected) {
          return DropdownMenuItem<MoodIcons>(
            value: selected,
            child: Row(
              children: <Widget>[
                Transform(
                  transform: Matrix4.identity()..rotateZ(
                      _moodIcons.getMoodRotation(selected.title)),
                  alignment: Alignment.center,
                  child: Icon(
                    _moodIcons.getMoodIcon(selected.title),
                    color: _moodIcons.getMoodColor(selected.title)),
                ),
                SizedBox(width: 16.0,),
                Text(selected.title)
              ],
            ),
          );
        }).toList(),
      ),
    );
  }
),
```

The following is the full `DropdownButton` widget code:

```
StreamBuilder(
  stream: _journalEditBloc.moodEdit,
  builder: (BuildContext context, AsyncSnapshot snapshot) {
    if (!snapshot.hasData) {
      return Container();
    }
    return DropdownButtonHideUnderline(
      child: DropdownButton<MoodIcons>(
        value: _moodIcons.getMoodIconsList()[
          _moodIcons
          .getMoodIconsList()
```

```
            .indexWhere((icon) => icon.title == snapshot.data)
        ],
        onChanged: (selected) {
          _journalEditBloc.moodEditChanged.add(selected.title);
        },
        items: _moodIcons.getMoodIconsList().map((MoodIcons selected) {
          return DropdownMenuItem<MoodIcons>(
            value: selected,
            child: Row(
              children: <Widget>[
                Transform(
                  transform: Matrix4.identity()..rotateZ(
                      _moodIcons.getMoodRotation(selected.title)),
                  alignment: Alignment.center,
                  child: Icon(
                    _moodIcons.getMoodIcon(selected.title),
                    color: _moodIcons.getMoodColor(selected.title)),
                ),
                SizedBox(width: 16.0,),
                Text(selected.title)
              ],
            ),
          );
        }).toList(),
      ),
    );
  }
),
```

22. Add a new line and add the `StreamBuilder()` widget with the `stream` property set to `_journalEditBloc.noteEdit` stream. This `StreamBuilder()` widget is responsible for handling the note field.

23. Add to the `builder` property the `if` statement to check whether the `snapshot` does not have data by using the `!snapshot.hasData` expression.

24. Inside the `if` statement, return a `Container()`.

```
if (!snapshot.hasData) {
  return Container();
}
```

25. When you use a `TextField` and the `StreamBuilder` as the user types their note, the cursor keeps bouncing to the beginning of the `TextField`. To fix this, add the `_noteController.value` to be equal to the `_noteController.value.copyWith(text: snapshot.data)` method. The bouncing cursor happens because every time a character is typed the `sink` updates the `stream` and the `StreamBuilder` retrieves the new value and repopulates the `TextField`.

26. Add a new line, return the `TextField` widget, and set the controller property to the `_noteController`.

27. Add the `maxLines` property and set it to the `null` value, making the `TextField` auto-expand to multiple lines as needed, making it a great UX feature.

28. Add the `onChanged` property and call the `_journalEditBloc.noteEditChanged.add(note)` sink by passing the `note` value. This event occurs when the user types in the `TextField` widget.

```
StreamBuilder(
  stream: _journalEditBloc.noteEdit,
  builder: (BuildContext context, AsyncSnapshot snapshot) {
    if (!snapshot.hasData) {
      return Container();
    }
    // Use the copyWith to make sure when you edit TextField the cursor does
not bounce to the first character
    _noteController.value = _noteController.value.copyWith(text:
snapshot.data);
    return TextField(
      controller: _noteController,
      textInputAction: TextInputAction.newline,
      textCapitalization: TextCapitalization.sentences,
      decoration: InputDecoration(
        labelText: 'Note',
        icon: Icon(Icons.subject),
      ),
      maxLines: null,
      onChanged: (note) => _journalEditBloc.noteEditChanged.add(note),
    );
  },
),
```

29. Add a new line, add a `Row()` widget, and set the `mainAxisAlignment` property to `MainAxisAlignment.end`. This `Row()` is responsible for right-aligning the Cancel and Save buttons on the form.

30. Add to the `children` property the `FlatButton` widget and set the `child` to the `Text` widget with the `'Cancel'` value. For the `onPressed` property, call the `Navigator.pop(context)` method to close the page without saving.

31. Add a `SizedBox(width: 8.0)` to separate the next `FlatButton` widget.

32. Add a second `FlatButton` widget and set the `child` to the `Text` widget with the `'Save'` value.

33. For the `onPressed` property, call the `_addOrUpdateJournal()` method to save the journal entry.

```
Row(
  mainAxisAlignment: MainAxisAlignment.end,
  children: <Widget>[
    FlatButton(
      child: Text('Cancel'),
      color: Colors.grey.shade100,
      onPressed: () {
        Navigator.pop(context);
      },
    ),
    SizedBox(width: 8.0),
    FlatButton(
      child: Text('Save'),
      color: Colors.lightGreen.shade100,
```

```
            onPressed: () {
              _addOrUpdateJournal();
            },
          ),
        ],
      ),
    ),
```

HOW IT WORKS

You created the `edit_entry.dart` file that contains the `EditEntry` class that extends a `Stateful-Widget` to handle adding and editing journal entries. The `JournalEditBlocProvider` is used to receive state from the home page. You implemented the `JournalEditBloc` class without using a provider to add or edit and save journal entries. The `StreamBuilder` widget monitors the `_journalEditBloc.dateEdit` stream, `_journalEditBloc.moodEdit` stream, `_journalEditBloc.noteEdit` stream, and each `builder` rebuild every time a value changes.

The `showTimePicker()` function presents the user with a calendar, and the `DropdownButton()` widget presents the user with a list of selectable moods. The `Matrix4 rotateZ()` method is used to implement the mood icon rotation. The `TextEditingController()` constructor handles the note `TextField()` widget. The `MoodIcons` class is responsible for coloring and rotating icons in the `DropdownButton` `DropdownMenuItem` selection list. The `FormatDates` class formats the selected date. You created a custom color gradient effect for the `AppBar` widget by using the `LinearGradient` class.

SUMMARY

In this chapter, you completed the journal app that you started in Chapter 14. You applied the BLoC pattern to separate the UI widgets from the business logic. You implemented BLoC classes, BLoC providers, service classes, utility classes, model classes, and app-wide and local-state management. You passed app-wide state management between pages and local-state management in the widget tree by using providers (`InheritedWidget`) and BLoCs. You used dependency injection to inject service classes into the BLoC classes. You learned that the benefit of using dependency injection keeps the BLoC classes platform-agnostic, giving the ability to share BLoC classes between different platforms like Flutter, AngularDart, or others.

You applied app-wide state management by implementing the `AuthenticationBlocProvider` and `AuthenticationBloc` classes to the app's main page. You used the `StreamBuilder` widget to monitor the `_authenticationBloc.user` stream for user credential changes. When the user credential changes, the `StreamBuilder` builder rebuilds and appropriately navigates the user to the login or home page.

You applied the `LoginBloc` class to validate the user's credentials and email and password requirements. You overrode the `initState()` method to initialize the `_loginBloc` variable with the `LoginBloc` class by injecting the `AuthenticationService()` class without using a provider. Note that the reason you initialized the `_loginBloc` variable from the `initState()` and not the `didChangeDependencies()` is because the `LoginBloc` does not need a provider (`InheritedWidget`).

You used the `StreamBuilder` widget with the `TextField` widget to validate email and password values. The `TextField` widget's `onChanged` property calls the `_loginBloc.emailChanged.add` sink and the `_loginBloc.passwordChanged.add` sink to send the values to the `LoginBloc` `Validators` class. You used the `StreamBuilder` widget to listen to the `_loginBloc.loginOrCreateButton` stream to toggle Login or Create Account as the default button.

You applied the `HomeBloc` class to build a list of journal entries filtered by the user `uid` with the ability to add, modify, and delete entries. You accessed the `AuthenticationBlocProvider` and `HomeBlocProvider` classes by using the provider's `of()` method from the `didChangeDependencies` method. You used the `StreamBuilder` widget by calling the `ListView.separated` constructor to build the journal entries list. You used the `Dismissible` widget's `confirmDismiss` property to prompt the user with the delete confirmation dialog. You called the `MoodIcons` utility class to format mood icons and the `FormatDates` class to format dates.

You accessed the `JournalEditBlocProvider` class by using the provider's `of()` method from the `didChangeDependencies` method. You applied the `JournalEditBloc` class to add, edit, and save journal entries. You used the `StreamBuilder` widget to handle the date, mood, note, and Cancel and Save buttons. You implemented the `showTimePicker()` function to show a calendar and to use the `DropdownButton()` widget to present the user with a list of selectable moods. You used the `Matrix4` `rotateZ()` method to rotate the mood icon according to mood. You used the `MoodIcons` class with the `DropdownButton` `DropdownMenuItem` to present the mood selection list. You used the `FormatDates` class to format the selected date.

▶ **WHAT YOU LEARNED IN THIS CHAPTER**

TOPIC	KEY CONCEPTS
`LoginBloc` class	You learned how to implement the `LoginBloc` class without a provider to handle the authentication credentials and to validate email and password requirements.
`AuthenticationBloc` class	You learned how to implement the `AuthenticationBloc` class with the `AuthenticationBlocProvider` class to handle app-wide state management in the main page.
`HomeBloc` class	You learned how to implement the `HomeBloc` class with the `HomeBlocProvider` class to populate the `ListView` with journal entries by using the `separated()` constructor. You learned to use the `HomeBloc` class to add, modify, or delete existing journal entries.
`JournalEditBloc` class	You learned how to implement the `JournalEditBloc` class without a provider to add or edit and save journal entries.
`InheritedWidget` class	The `AuthenticationBlocProvider`, `HomeBlocProvider`, and `JournalEditBlocProvider` classes extend from the `InheritedWidget` class, and you learned how to access them from the `didChangeDependencies()` method and not the `initState()` method.
`AuthenticationBlocProvider` class	You learned how to implement the `AuthenticationBlocProvider` as the provider for the `AuthenticationBloc` class for app-wide authentication state management.
`HomeBlocProvider` class	You learned how to implement the `HomeBlocProvider` class as the provider for the `HomeBloc` class.
Dependency injection	You learned how to use dependency injection by injecting service classes to the BLoC classes. You learned that by injecting services, the BLoC classes remain platform-agnostic.
`StreamBuilder` widget	You learned how to implement the `StreamBuilder` widget to monitor a `stream`, and when a change occurs, the `builder` rebuilds the widget with the latest data.

TOPIC	KEY CONCEPTS
`ListView.separated` constructor and `Divider()` widget	You learned how to implement the `ListView.separated` constructor to build a list of journal entries separated by a `Divider()` widget.
`Dismissible` widget and `confirmDismiss` property	You learned how to implement the `Dismissible` widget to swipe and delete a journal entry. You learned how to implement the `Dismissible` widget's `confirmDismiss` property to prompt a dialog to confirm deleting a journal entry.
`DropdownButton()` widget	You learned how to implement the `DropdownButton()` widget to present a list of moods with the title, color, and icon rotation.
`MoodIcons` class	You learned how to implement the `MoodIcons` class to retrieve the mood's properties like the `title`, `color`, `rotation`, and `icon`.
`showTimePicker()` function	You learned how to implement the `showTimePicker()` function to present a calendar to choose a date.
`Matrix4 rotateZ()` method	You learned how to implement the `Matrix4 rotateZ()` method to rotate an icon according to the selected mood.
`FormatDates` class	You learned how to implement the `FormatDates` class to format dates.

INDEX

X